THE PUZZLE OF TWENTY-FIRST-CENTURY GLOBALIZATION

The Puzzle of Twenty-First-Century Globalization

An International Economics Primer

Patrice Franko
Colby College

Stephen C. Stamos Jr.
Bucknell University

ROWMAN & LITTLEFIELD
Lanham • Boulder • New York • London

Executive Editor: Susan McEachern
Associate Editor: Rebeccah Shumaker
Senior Marketing Manager: Deborah Hudson
Cover Designer: Neil Cotterill

Credits and acknowledgments for material borrowed from other sources, and reproduced with permission, appear on the appropriate page within the text.

Published by Rowman & Littlefield
A wholly owned subsidiary of The Rowman & Littlefield Publishing Group, Inc.
4501 Forbes Boulevard, Suite 200, Lanham, Maryland 20706
www.rowman.com

Unit A, Whitacre Mews, 26-34 Stannary Street, London SE11 4AB, United Kingdom

World map by Mapping Specialists, Ltd.

British Library Cataloguing in Publication Information Available

Library of Congress Cataloging-in-Publication Data Available

ISBN: 978-0-7425-5691-1 (cloth : alk. paper)
ISBN: 978-0-7425-5692-8 (paper : alk. paper)
ISBN: 978-1-5381-0026-4 (electronic)

∞™ The paper used in this publication meets the minimum requirements of American National Standard for Information Sciences—Permanence of Paper for Printed Library Materials, ANSI/NISO Z39.48-1992.

Printed in the United States of America

CONTENTS

PREFACE

This text was written to address a puzzle and solve a problem. The puzzle is the global economy. What are the key elements a student must understand to explore issues in economic globalization? The problem is that our understanding of international economics is usually presented in silos: trade, finance, and multinational production. An understanding of the changes in our geo-strategic landscape also involves an appreciation of the role of developing economies and the imprint on the environment. This text breaks these silos down to give the student of globalization the economic tools to grapple with our changing global system. We envision this text as the anchor to a course on the economics of globalization or as a guide to the student in an international relations course with minimal grounding in economics.

We began this book before the global financial crisis broke. Of the many lessons of the crisis, we can point to the uncertainty created by the tight interconnections of markets for trade, finance, and production. Although we can't claim to have answers as to where our globalized economy is headed, we hope that the reader of this book will acquire conceptual guideposts to understand the dimensions of our global problems and frameworks to evaluate policies to minimize the pain and maximize the gain of being bound together.

We want to thank our editor, Susan McEachern, for the initial idea for this book and for her patience in seeing it through. We are grateful to our institutions, Bucknell University and Colby College, and to our many colleagues who supported us in our work. We are grateful to our students who have challenged us to think deeply about the economics of globalization. We are especially appreciative of the students who worked on this book including Tara Brian, Jacqueline Boekelman, Alexa Busser, Kelly Chernin, Ellie Franko, Laura Maloney, Becky Newman, Grace Schlesinger, and Alden Southworth as well as the able and cheerful help of our secretary Dianne Labreck. As always we owe an enormous debt of gratitude to our spouses Lucy Stamos and Sandy Maisel for their love and partnership—and fun times when we got together to write. We dedicate this book to our grandchildren—Beau, Nico, Conrad, Weber, Gus, Tyler, and Leo in the hope that their globalized world is more equitable and sustainable.

August 2016

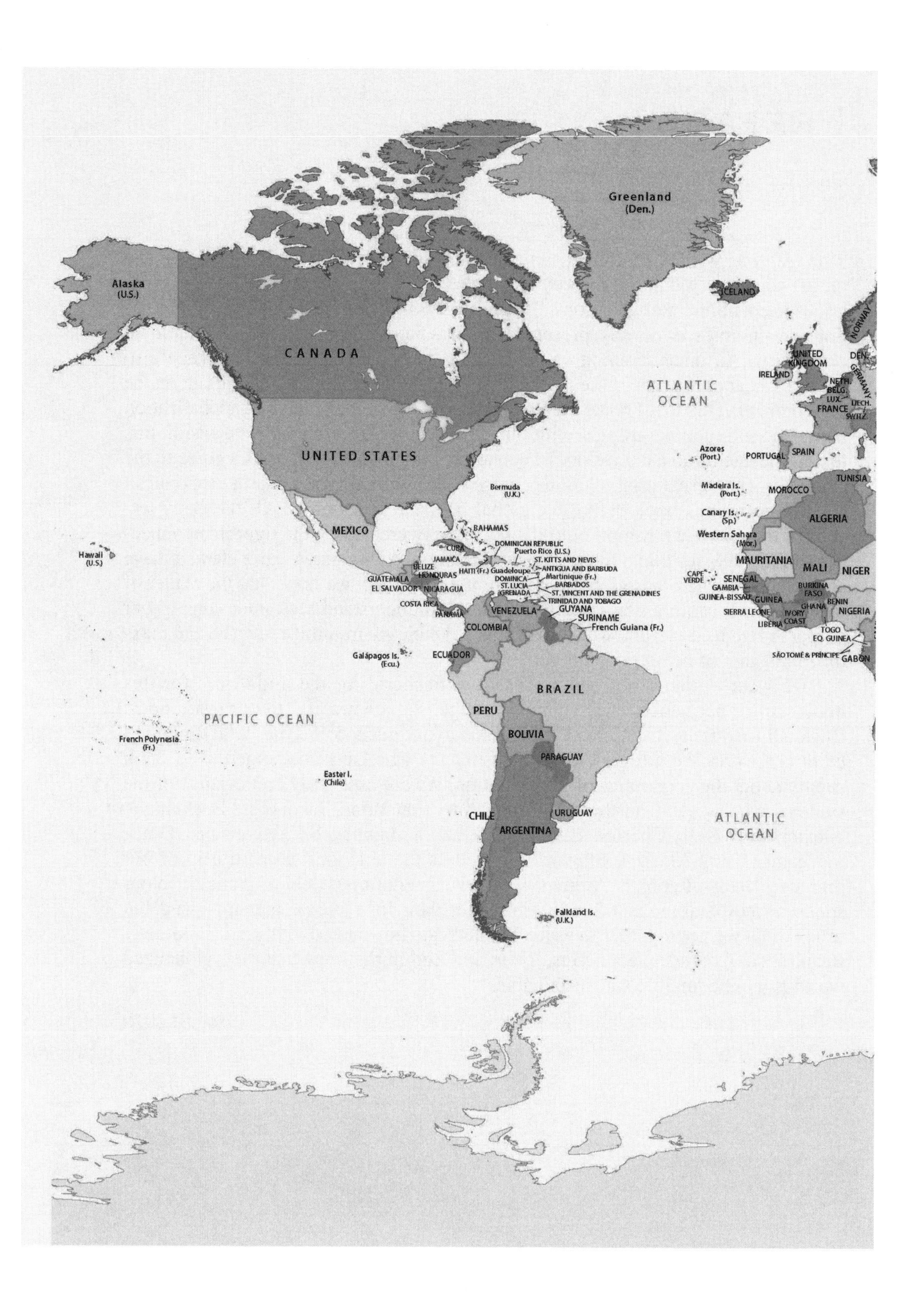

Greenland
(Den.)
Alaska
(U.S.)
ICELAND
NORWAY
CANADA
UNITED KINGDOM
DEN.
IRELAND
GERMANY
ATLANTIC OCEAN
NETH.
BELG.
LUX.
LIECH.
FRANCE
SWITZ.
UNITED STATES
Azores
(Port.)
PORTUGAL
SPAIN
TUNISIA
Bermuda
(U.K.)
Madeira Is.
(Port.)
MOROCCO
Canary Is.
(Sp.)
ALGERIA
MEXICO
BAHAMAS
Western Sahara
(Mor.)
DOMINICAN REPUBLIC
Puerto Rico (U.S.)
CUBA
Hawaii
(U.S.)
JAMAICA
ST. KITTS AND NEVIS
BELIZE
HAITI
(Fr.) Guadeloupe
ANTIGUA AND BARBUDA
MAURITANIA
HONDURAS
DOMINICA
Martinique (Fr.)
MALI
NIGER
GUATEMALA
ST. LUCIA
BARBADOS
CAPE VERDE
SENEGAL
EL SALVADOR
NICARAGUA
GRENADA
ST. VINCENT AND THE GRENADINES
GAMBIA
BURKINA FASO
COSTA RICA
TRINIDAD AND TOBAGO
GUINEA-BISSAU
GUINEA
GHANA
BENIN
VENEZUELA
GUYANA
SIERRA LEONE
IVORY COAST
NIGERIA
PANAMA
SURINAME
LIBERIA
COLOMBIA
French Guiana (Fr.)
TOGO
EQ. GUINEA
Galápagos Is.
(Ecu.)
ECUADOR
SÃO TOMÉ & PRÍNCIPE
GABON
BRAZIL
PERU
PACIFIC OCEAN
French Polynesia
(Fr.)
BOLIVIA
PARAGUAY
Easter I.
(Chile)
CHILE
URUGUAY
ATLANTIC OCEAN
ARGENTINA
Falkland Is.
(U.K.)

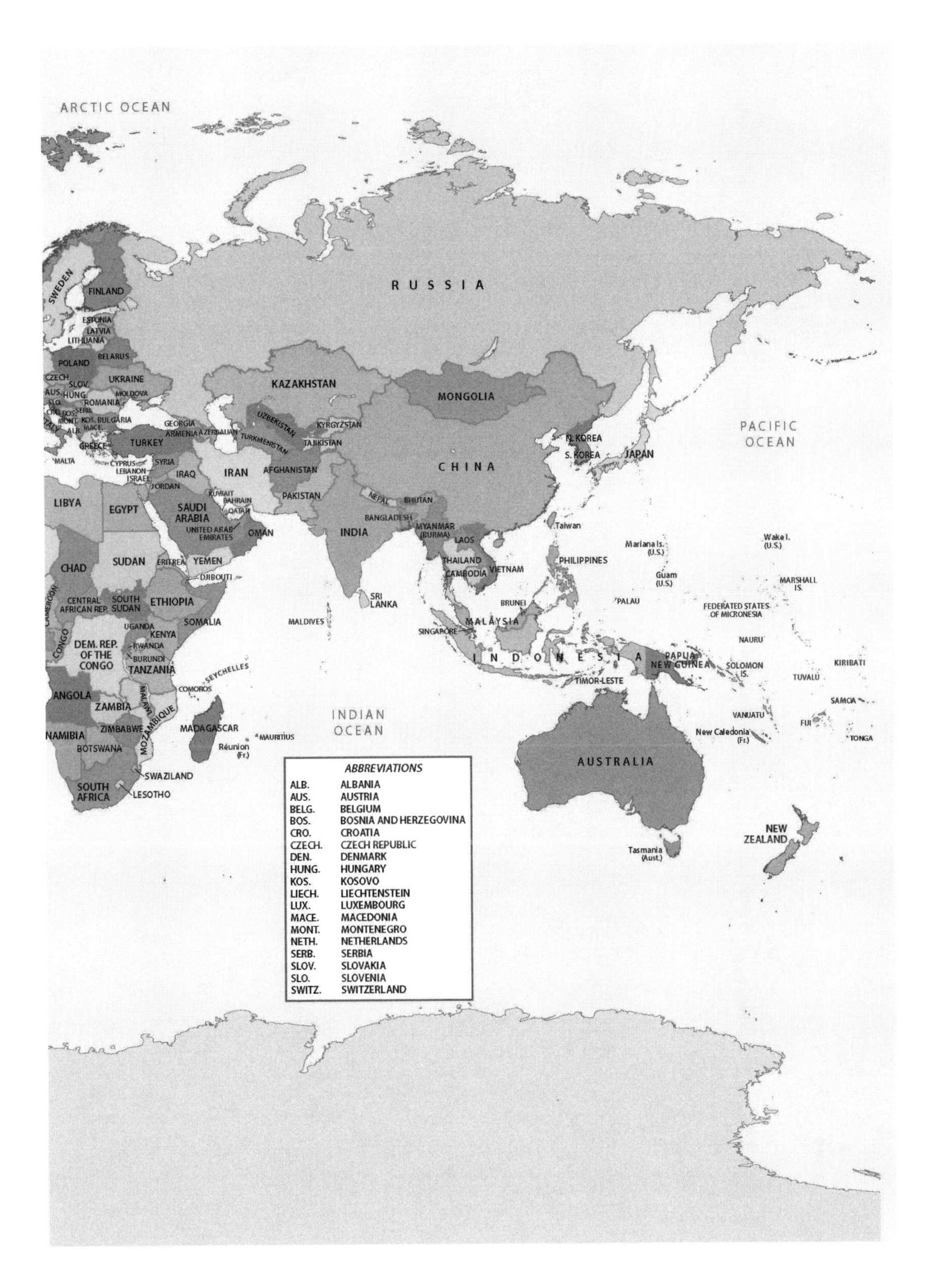
ARCTIC OCEAN
RUSSIA
SWEDEN
FINLAND
ESTONIA
LATVIA
LITHUANIA
BELARUS
POLAND
CZECH.
SLOV.
UKRAINE
AUS.
HUNG.
MOLDOVA
SLO.
ROMANIA
CRO.
BOS.
SERB.
MONT.
KOS.
BULGARIA
ALB.
MACE.
ITALY
GREECE
MALTA
GEORGIA
ARMENIA
AZERBAIJAN
TURKEY
CYPRUS
SYRIA
LEBANON
ISRAEL
JORDAN
IRAQ
IRAN
KUWAIT
BAHRAIN
QATAR
SAUDI ARABIA
UNITED ARAB EMIRATES
OMAN
YEMEN
KAZAKHSTAN
UZBEKISTAN
TURKMENISTAN
KYRGYZSTAN
TAJIKISTAN
AFGHANISTAN
PAKISTAN
MONGOLIA
CHINA
N. KOREA
S. KOREA
JAPAN
PACIFIC OCEAN
NEPAL
BHUTAN
BANGLADESH
INDIA
MYANMAR (BURMA)
LAOS
THAILAND
CAMBODIA
VIETNAM
Taiwan
PHILIPPINES
SRI LANKA
MALDIVES
BRUNEI
MALAYSIA
SINGAPORE
INDONESIA
PALAU
TIMOR-LESTE
PAPUA NEW GUINEA
Mariana Is. (U.S.)
Guam (U.S.)
Wake I. (U.S.)
MARSHALL IS.
FEDERATED STATES OF MICRONESIA
NAURU
SOLOMON IS.
KIRIBATI
TUVALU
SAMOA
VANUATU
FIJI
TONGA
New Caledonia (Fr.)
AUSTRALIA
Tasmania (Aust.)
NEW ZEALAND
LIBYA
EGYPT
SUDAN
ERITREA
DJIBOUTI
CHAD
CENTRAL AFRICAN REP.
SOUTH SUDAN
ETHIOPIA
SOMALIA
CAMEROON
CONGO
DEM. REP. OF THE CONGO
UGANDA
KENYA
RWANDA
BURUNDI
TANZANIA
SEYCHELLES
COMOROS
ANGOLA
ZAMBIA
MALAWI
MOZAMBIQUE
ZIMBABWE
NAMIBIA
BOTSWANA
MADAGASCAR
MAURITIUS
Réunion (Fr.)
SWAZILAND
SOUTH AFRICA
LESOTHO
INDIAN OCEAN
ABBREVIATIONS
ALB. ALBANIA
AUS. AUSTRIA
BELG. BELGIUM
BOS. BOSNIA AND HERZEGOVINA
CRO. CROATIA
CZECH. CZECH REPUBLIC
DEN. DENMARK
HUNG. HUNGARY
KOS. KOSOVO
LIECH. LIECHTENSTEIN
LUX. LUXEMBOURG
MACE. MACEDONIA
MONT. MONTENEGRO
NETH. NETHERLANDS
SERB. SERBIA
SLOV. SLOVAKIA
SLO. SLOVENIA
SWITZ. SWITZERLAND

CHAPTER ONE

Twenty-First-Century Globalization

Globalization is everything and its opposite.

—Thomas Friedman, *The Lexus and the Olive Tree*

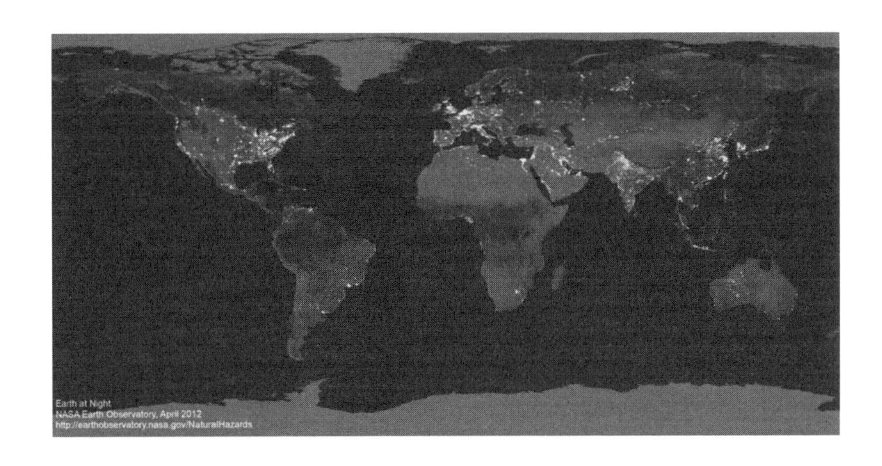

Unprecedented Changes in the Twenty-First Century

Imagine you are an American student of political economy in 1970, writing your final senior essay titled "The Future of the World Economy." You have followed the threats to the Bretton Woods financial system as you picked up your newspaper (of course there were no electronic links or tweets), chronicling the demise of the dollar-based fixed exchange rate system. Your class hotly debated the sustainability of the U.S. trade deficit as threatened by industrial challenges from Japan. You probably would not have studied abroad in your undergraduate years as travel costs were prohibitive; if you were privileged enough to have had an international experience, it is unlikely you paid the $50 phone bill to check back home. Your research consisted of eye-straining hours in the bowels of the library reading microfilm. As you struggled to develop your thesis predicting the effects of Cold War military spending on U.S. power, how could you have imagined that fifty years later a student in your own university might grapple with questions not from the power shift to the East but the global South by Skyping with Brazilian friends from an abroad program while simultaneously searching a database of European working papers and listening to African drumming on a device not much larger than a credit card designed in California but assembled in China with parts from around the globe?

The revolutionary changes in just fifty years in where you go, who you talk to, what you read, and the music you listen to are brought about by the dynamics of globalization and the increased integration of the global economy (Box 1.1). Seen from the vantage point of the twenty-first-century student, the past decades have been a roller-coaster for the global system. Much like the seismic changes since the 1970s, the September 11, 2001, terrorist attacks highlighted a new political and economic reality. Drained by the U.S. wars in Afghanistan and Iraq, the rest of the decade for the United States was defined by a sluggish economic recovery, growing budget deficits, burgeoning trade deficits over 6% of GDP, a housing bubble followed by a financial crisis, and prolonged recession. Excessive public and private American consumption fueled by easy credit was mirrored by the phenomenal growth of Brazil, China, and India. Capital flows followed booming developing country markets demanding not only food and commodities but also cars and

Box 1.1. Thinking about Globalization

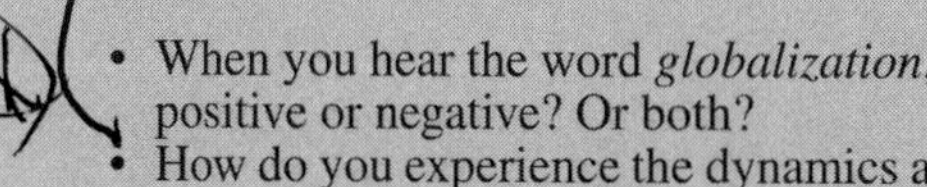

- When you hear the word *globalization*, what comes to mind? Is your first reaction positive or negative? Or both?
- How do you experience the dynamics and realities of contemporary globalization?
- In what ways does globalization impact your life?
- Place yourself in a different life context in another country. Where are you? Who are you? What do you do for a living?
- How would you define *globalization*? Are global capitalism and globalization the same thing?
  - What role does technological change play in the globalization dynamic?
  - What is the difference between international economics and globalization?

electronics. These booms have turned to busts as the global engine of growth has sputtered.

The rapid reshaping of the global economy from your college alum of fifty years ago to the fast-paced economic world where you will work is the puzzle of this book. As a twenty-first-century student of political economy, how do you make sense of changing trade and financial balances, the shifting landscape of production and labor, and the new roles of systemically important emerging market economies? Policymakers today are challenged to build a new architecture for international institutions to navigate the tensions in our dynamic and unpredictable global system. The Bretton Woods institutions formed in 1945 of the International Monetary Fund (IMF) and the World Bank are buckling under the weight of misaligned currencies and globalization's losers. Global trade negotiations remain stymied at the World Trade Organization (WTO), formed in 1995. The International Labor Organization's (ILO) labor mandate from 1919 is poorly equipped to address a globalized work force, and no official worldwide organization exists to address environmental challenges. Revitalized organizations are needed to shepherd sustainable, inclusive growth. More than a billion people have been excluded from the amenities of modernity. Social tensions have risen with growing inequality and widening deficits in education and health. Wrenching changes in the global economy have left many jobless, without the tools to compete with a truly global labor force. The externalities of growth and the pressures on land, seas, and air are not manageable without stronger global environmental institutions.

Global challenges in trade, finance, labor, development, and the environment have forced a rethinking of the best mix of market and state policy to promote sustainable growth. China, India, and Brazil navigate the global economy with both an appreciation for market-led growth and the need for judicious state intervention. We have also seen a new hybrid of public/private policymaking in the United States and Europe; neo-liberal market policies are being complemented by state intervention. New actors in the non-governmental and nonprofit arenas are forging new partnerships with governments and firms. As we explore the changes and challenges in the global system, we'll see when in the twenty-first century the market works best—and when it needs the guiding hand of national and multilateral institutions as mediated by civil sector organizations. Indeed, globalization has made economic policymaking quite tricky; markets for goods, services, finance, and labor are global, but taxpayers footing the policy bills remain quite local. This tension creates political friction in constructing a policy framework for a fair and sustainable globalization.

Globalization: What Is It?

How is the globalized world you live in different from the alumni of fifty years ago? Why is this book titled *The Puzzle of Twenty-First-Century Globalization* and not *International Trade and Finance*? Different people hold very distinct understandings of globalization. We personalize our understanding of global trends based on our own experience of what we have seen, heard, or read. Your focus may be predominately on finance, economics, or politics—or perhaps your orientation is social, cultural, geographic, or environmental. In many ways, quite understandably, contemporary globalization is a misunderstood concept. Box 1.2 highlights only a few of the many definitions ascribed to globalization. Indeed, it may be that the debate about the causes and effects of globalization stems from just how we define and understand this concept.[1]

Box 1.2. Selected Definitions of Globalization

Joseph Stiglitz, *Globalization and Its Discontents* 2002	"The closer integration of the countries and peoples of the world ... brought about by the enormous reduction of costs of transportation and communication, and the breaking down of artificial barriers to the flows of goods, services, capital, knowledge, and people across borders."
BusinessDictionary.com, accessed April 5, 2010	"Worldwide movement toward economic, financial, trade, and communications integration. Globalization implies opening out beyond local and nationalistic perspectives to a broader outlook of an interconnected and inter-dependent world with free transfer of capital, goods, and services across national frontiers. However, it does not include unhindered movement of labor and, as suggested by some economists, may hurt smaller or fragile economies if applied indiscriminately."
R. Robertson, *Globalization*, 1992, p. 8	"The compression of the world and the intensification of consciousness of the world as a whole ... concrete global interdependence and consciousness of the global whole in the twentieth century."
P. McMichael, *Development and Social Change*, 2000, p. xxiii, 149	"Integration on the basis of a project pursuing 'market rule on a global scale.'"
Barry Lynn, "Unmade in America," *Harper's Magazine*, June 2002	"Globalization is many things, and much has been written about it and said. But throw all the tomes and studies and placards into a giant tryworks, and you'll render two simple arguments: globalization is good because it spreads what is good in America, such as a liberal approach to business, and McDonald's. Globalization is bad because it spreads what is worst about America, such as a liberal approach to business, and McDonald's."
Percy Barnevik, President of the ABB Industrial Group, quoted in *Sonali's Subversive Thoughts for the Day*	"[T]he freedom for my group of companies to invest where it wants when it wants, to produce what it wants, to buy and sell where it wants, and support the fewest restrictions possible coming from labor laws and social conventions."

Anthony Giddens, 1990	"Globalization is political, technical and cultural, as well as economic. It is 'new' and 'revolutionary' and is mainly due to the 'massive increase' in financial foreign exchange transactions. This has been facilitated by dramatic improvement in communications technology, especially electronic interchange facilitated by personal computers."
David Held, Anthony G. McGrew, David Goldblatt, and Jonathan Perraton, *Global Transformations: Politics, Economics and Culture* (Stanford, CA: Stanford University Press, 1999), Introduction, pp. 32–86	"Transformation in the spatial organization of social relations and transactions—assessed in terms of their extensity, intensity, velocity and impact—generating transcontinental or interregional flows..."
Marx and Engels, 1848	"In place of the old local and national seclusion and self-sufficiency, we have intercourse in every direction, universal interdependence of nations. And as in material, so also in intellectual production. The intellectual creations of individual nations become common property. National one-sidedness and narrow-mindedness become more and more impossible, and from the numerous national and local literatures, there arises a world literature."
United Nations Poverty and Development Division, *Economic and Social Survey of Asia and the Pacific*, 1999	"While the definition of globalization varies with the context of analysis, it generally refers to an increasing interaction across national boundaries that affect many aspects of life: economic, social, cultural, and political. In the context of this study, in order to keep the analysis within reasonable bounds, the focus is only on the economic aspects, with particular emphasis on the role of ICT [information and communications technologies]. As such, globalization narrowly refers to the growing economic interdependence of countries worldwide. This includes increases in the international division of labor caused by swelling international flows of FBI [foreign-based investment], accompanied by an increasing volume and variety of cross-border transactions in goods and services, international capital flows, international migration and the more rapid and widespread diffusion of technology. This should not be construed to imply that social, cultural and other forms of globalization are unimportant, only that they are less germane to discussions of economic security and development."
International Forum on Globalization, http://www.ifg.org/analysis.htm	"Globalization is the present worldwide drive toward a globalized economic system dominated by supranational corporate trade and banking institutions that are not accountable to democratic processes or national governments."

In the most simple and essential way, globalization is the dynamic process of the integration of markets for goods, services, capital, and labor beyond national borders. The spread of markets and economies is driven by the growth of international trade in goods and services and the cross-border expansion of banking and financial institutions and services. But goods have been traded with accompanying global capital flows for centuries. Globalization fundamentally engages a transformation of the global production system for goods and services driven by changes in transportation technology, as well as information and communications systems. This process of economic change is accompanied by divergent political, social, cultural, environmental, and geographic consequences. That is, more than trade and financial instruments flow across borders, globalization keys our attention on the transnational and transcultural integration of human activity.[2] In a world that is now linked 24/7, globalization is about the speed with which a good, a currency, an image, or an idea circulates across national borders.

THE GLOBALIZATION TIMELINE

Is globalization something new? As our student has morphed from a hippie of the 1970s to an electronic twenty-first-century tweeter, you might wonder whether these transformations are new phenomena or merely a continuation of historical trends. We can characterize the timeline of globalization as a long continuum or as a result of a radical break in how economies operate—or something in between. These views have been categorized as **skeptical**, **hyperglobalist**, and **transformational**.[3]

Globalization skeptics place cultural, economic, political, social, and technological developments on an evolutionary line; they suggest that globalization has existed for many centuries. Skeptics doubt that we are living in a fundamentally different economy and contend that the sum of the developments in the international economy only change the scale and scope of globalization. Hyperglobalists agree with the skeptics regarding continuous history, but insist that there is a historical juncture after which contemporary globalization emerged. In contrast, transformationalists assert that globalization is a fundamentally new force underlying the rapid, widespread social, political, and economic changes reshaping global societies and the world order.[4]

Whether you believe that we are living in a radically different economy or experiencing a historical trend begun centuries ago, most agree that changes in the global economy have five underlying dimensions: *capitalism, technology, politics, society and culture,* and *environment.* Globalization would not be possible without the emergence of capitalism linking market-based economies. Beginning with the fifteenth-century period of European Colonialism continued through the nineteenth-century industrial revolution, the search for profit promoted exploration and innovation—and involved exploitation of resources and peoples. Technology became a driving force of globalization through inventions and innovations in production, transportation, communications, and information systems. As the speed of technological change accelerated, geographers have characterized the compression of time and space as discernable social and cultural consequences of globalization. But economic change generates tensions. The political challenge of governments and international institutions is to facilitate and advance the process while managing the pressures created by globalization. Nation-states are tasked with reconciling the domestic conflicts, costs, and consequences of globalization. At the same time, they must engage the international community to address the environmental externalities that cross borders.

The social and cultural consequences of globalization have been wildly mixed. The increased exposure of people and cultures to each other has transformed the consciousness of the global community. This social and cultural exchange takes place through international business, travel, tourism, study abroad, migration, literature, poetry, film, television, media, and, of course, the Internet. The information age has brought forth a richly multicultural global society. But anthropologists worry about the flattening of diverse cultures and the McMinimizing of cultural difference as multinationals such as McDonalds or Walmart dominate local tastes. Integrated economic systems create negative economic spillovers. As 7.4 billion people on the earth put pressure on the earth's physical resources, we can observe how the growing demand for food, water, raw materials, and energy is progressively undermining the sustainability of the earth's physical and biological systems.

Globalization is more than studying the internationalization of goods, labor, and capital markets. The purpose of this book is instead to puzzle out the ways that the intensification of transnational flows of products, services, money, and people has created new opportunities for growth—and also enormous challenges for policymakers. People in remote Amazonian villages are now connected to Chinese entrepreneurs via the Internet. Workers in the American South directly compete for jobs with laborers in the global South. British investors consider startups in India along with starting companies in London. We can see YouTube streams of videos from factory floors and deforested farms. We can buy a gently used Waterford glass over eBay from a seller in England and recycle our second-hand clothing to markets in Africa. We are a global market—yet our economic policy toolbox is distinctly national. Taking this complex economy into consideration, we define contemporary globalization as:

> An intensification of cross-national cultural, economic, political, social, and technological interactions that lead to the establishment of transnational structures and the global integration of cultural, economic, environmental, political and social processes on global, supranational, national, regional, and local levels.[5]

This synergy between changes in trade, finance, labor, and production invites us to study how these systems interact within the context of twenty-first-century globalization. While you might have the luxury of taking courses in international trade, finance, development, and environmental studies, this book identifies the key concepts in each such that you can piece the puzzle together and analyze contemporary policy options. Policymaking doesn't happen in silos. Changes in the trade arena are squarely affected by finance; how goods are produced in global supply chains determines who sells them. Changes in labor markets draw producers competing for lowest cost advantages. That is, trade, finance, and production need to be studied in relation to one another—something that stand-alone courses in international trade, global finance, or multinational production may miss. Be patient as this book unfolds. Students of international economics have had the time to develop each of the subfields of trade, finance, development, labor, and the environment separately. Our overwhelming task is to bring the essentials together—much as our globalized market does—in one place so that you can puzzle out the ramifications of intense integration.

Globalization's Institutional Challenges

Globalization's challenges to workers, corporations, governments, international institutions such as the IMF or World Bank, and civil society organizations are enormous and at times overwhelming (Box 1.3). Globalization creates winners and losers. Nation-states and international institutions are challenged by the management of a complex global system to minimize the costs and maximize the gains of cross-border transactions. Global markets are strongly integrated, and global governance is frustratingly weak. As we consider the dynamic changes in how goods are traded, money moves, labor markets are permeable, production is globally sliced, and resources are managed, we will grapple with the constraints faced by policymakers in advancing an economically sustainable and equitable globalization. It is important to acknowledge that global capitalism and globalization are generally thought about in economic and financial terms. There is the obvious focus on markets, trade, investment, and employment. Yet, a broader understanding of contemporary globalization requires an understanding of how cultural, ethnic, social, political, geographic, environmental, and security aspects impact global economic systems. But that is beyond the scope of this book.

The Globalization Debate: Competing Perspectives

The debate about globalization and its challenges can be framed (and simplified) in the context of three distinct and competing political economic schools of thought: **Free Market Neo-Liberal**, **Institutionalist–Structuralist**, and **Marxist**. Let's consider these in turn for their varying insights in unpacking just what we mean by globalization and how it might be managed.

At the center of the Free Market Neo-Liberal view is the perspective sketched by the IMF in 2008 in an overview of globalization. The IMF characterizes seven critical principles that underpin the potential prosperity of individual countries: (1) investment, especially foreign investment; (2) the spread of technology; (3) strong institutions; (4) sound macroeconomic policies; (5) an educated workforce; (6) the existence of a market economy; and (7) integration with the global economy.[6] The interplay of these factors in market economies has precipitated

Box 1.3. Snapshots of Change in China

China's opening to the global economy in the new millennium fundamentally transformed the global economic system. The following excerpts give us a brief glimpse of China's global reach. Our student of the 70s would have had a hard time imagining such conflicted change!

For one year, Lu Qingmin did almost nothing but work. She worked on an assembly line at a factory in China's Pearl River Delta, testing hand-held games, digital clocks, and electronic calendars. Her workday stretched 14 hours and ran seven days a week; a rare Saturday afternoon without overtime was the only break, she says. Dinner was rice, a meat or vegetable dish and watery soup. Workers slept 12 to a room, their beds crowded near the toilets. She made $50 to $80 a month, depending on overtime. (Leslie T. Chang, "At 18, Min Finds a Path to Success in Migration Wave," *The Wall Street Journal*, November 8, 2004.)

One of China's lesser-known exports is a dangerous brew of soot, toxic chemicals and climate-changing gases from the smokestacks of coal-burning power plants. In early April, a dense cloud of pollutants over Northern China sailed to nearby Seoul, sweeping dust and desert sand before wafting across the Pacific. (Keith Bardsher and David Barboza, "Pollution from Chinese Coal Casts Shadow around Globe," *The New York Times*, June 11, 2006.)

For several years now the World Bank has ranked Congo as the worst place in the world, bar none, to do business... None of this seems to deter China's state-owned firms, however. In 2007 the Export–Import Bank, through which the Chinese government disburses all of its foreign aid, signed an agreement with the Congolese Government to finance $6.5 billion worth of improvements to the country's infrastructure and $2 billion-worth of construction and refurbishment of mines, using mineral reserves as collateral. The following month a similar deal was signed with China Development Bank. (A Special Report on China's Quest for Resources, *The Economist*, March 15, 2008.)

China has bought more than $1 trillion of American debt, but as the global downturn has intensified, Beijing is starting to keep more of its money at home, a move that could have painful effects for American borrowers. The declining Chinese appetite for United States debt, apparent in a series of hints from Chinese policymakers over the last two weeks ... comes at an inconvenient time. On Tuesday, President-elect Barack Obama predicted the possibility of trillion-dollar deficits "for years to come" even after an $800 billion stimulus package. Normally, China would be the most avid taker of the debt required to pay for those deficits, mainly short-term Treasuries, akin to government i.o.u.'s. In the last five years, China has spent as much as one-seventh of its entire economic output buying foreign debt, mostly American. (Keith Bradsher, "China Losing Taste for Debt from U.S.," *The New York Times*, January 8, 2009.)

In the build-up to the annual summit of G8 countries, which began on July 8th in the Italian city of L'Aquila, officials in China, Russia, and India all called for an end to the dollar's dominance in the international monetary system... The People's Bank of China (PBOC), China's central bank, repeated its call for a new global reserve currency In June and is now taking the first steps towards turning the Yuan into a global currency. ("Yuan Small Step: China and the Dollar," *The Economist*, July 11, 2009.)

Bears have predicted that a Chinese devaluation would send a new wave of deflation round the globe. It would force Asian competitors to respond with their own devaluations, reducing import prices in the developed world. This might lead to job losses in the west or reduced profit margins. Charles Domas of Lombard Street Research, a consultancy, recently wrote that it: "would export the deflationary impact to its trade competitors in the rest of the world. In addition, nations that became notably overvalued, such as the US and UK, could be weakened as cheap imports cut into margins." ("The Curious Case of China's Currency," *The Economist*, August 11, 2015.)

momentous change. Consider some of these ways in which trade, capital, and people have become more globalized:

- The value of trade (goods and services) as a percentage of world GDP increased from 42.1% in 1980 to 62.1% in 2007, but fell to 56% of world GDP in 2010 after the great financial crisis. Foreign direct investment increased from 6.5% of world GDP in 1980 to 31.8% in 2006.
- The stock of international claims (primarily bank loans) as a percentage of world GDP increased from 10% in 1980 to 48% in 2006.
- The number of minutes spent on cross-border telephone calls, on a per capita basis, increased from 7.3 in 1991 to 28.8 in 2006.
- The number of foreign workers has increased from 78 million in 1965 to 191 million in 2005.
- The cost of ocean freight was reduced 70% between 1920 and 1990.
- The cost of air transport fell 84% from 1930 to 1990.
- Expressed in U.S. 2000 dollars, a three-minute phone call from New York to London cost $60.42 in 1960 and 40 cents in 2000.
- In 1960 would have cost $1,869,004 to purchase what $1000 would buy in computer power in 2000.

To the IMF, the obvious benefits from globalization are the increase in the availability of goods and services, lower and more competitive prices, more and better jobs, and an advance in the standard of living. The IMF admits that not all of the potential benefits of globalization are distributed equally, nor do all members of a country have equal access to these benefits. Across the global system, there are distinct regional inequalities; within specific countries there are often dramatic disparities between members of the society in terms of wealth and income distribution. The stark reality is that in a world of seven billion people, over one billion live on less than $1.25 per day and over 2.5 billion live on less than $2.00 per day.[7] But from the IMF's perspective, the best way to improve the lives of those worst off is to continue down the road of market-based globalization.

The IMF understands globalization to be a historic process driven by human innovation and technological progress that overtime has integrated economies through trade and capital flows. These changes in trade and finance have transformed politics, culture, and the environment. While the IMF takes a firm position that the existence of markets is critical to the prospects for economic growth and prosperity, it is soberly aware that often markets fail, producing short-term winners and losers from globalization. Despite these costs, the IMF sees free trade and open capital markets as necessary prerequisites for fostering economic growth. The IMF rejects much of the criticism of the dark side of globalization, labeling a list of negatives "*myths*."[8] It contests the result that globalization puts downward pressure on wages in low-skilled work in developed countries or that there is a "race to the bottom" for low-wage workers creating Southern sweatshops and Northern unemployment. The IMF sees globalization as a reversible process that must be managed to deliver growth.

Thomas L. Friedman, the well-known journalist from the *New York Times*, sketches out the globalized market's momentum for change in *The Lexus and the Olive Tree* (1999) and *The World Is Flat* (2004). As a champion of twenty-first-century globalization, Friedman advocates global free-market capitalism and the unfettered global spread of technology. He does not deny or ignore the uneven and often unfair outcomes that globalization has produced, but concludes that on balance, the globalized economy has been a positive force. In *The Lexus and the Olive Tree*, he provides a new lens to understand the transformational forces of technology. The technological changes of the 1990s, particularly in transportation and communication, brought new opportunities and possibilities to people in countries and cultures still very traditional and resistant to the forces of modernization. The title of his book captured the conflict between global and local tensions. The *Lexus* represented the forces of modernization, whereas the *Olive Tree* represented threats to tradition and cultural practices.

In explaining the source of this change, Friedman identified four democratizations that would forever change the world: (1) the Democratization of Technology, (2) the Democratization of Finance, (3) the Democratization of Information, and (4) the Democratization of Decision-Making.[9] The Democratization of Technology brought rapid and sweeping changes in computerization, telecommunications, miniaturization, and digitization (bandwidth). Democratized finance was propelled by the growth of the corporate bond market, securitization (the packaging and selling of bundles of mortgages, loans, debt, and other financial products), and the expansion of 401 K retirement plans. The Democratization of Information addressed the global expansion of television, satellites, and the Internet. The Internet Revolution in 1995 linked the world forever in a dramatic and fundamental way, allowing instantaneous, interconnected decision-making in financial markets. The Democratization of Decision-Making provided for faster flows of information resulting in the ability of decision-making power to be more and more decentralized. Multiple stakeholders—governments, **non-governmental organizations (NGOs)**, private sector firms, and employees and citizens—had access to information that everyone else shared and could act on any time 24/7. These synergistic democratizations profoundly changed production, trade, and finance; countries and organizations had to adapt to this new reality.

Friedman contended that for a country to be successful, it had to adopt a core set of free-market policies and acquire the technology and infrastructure necessary to compete in the new global economy. Friedman argued that "the golden straitjacket" of free-market capitalism was the necessary formula for success. If countries wanted the benefits of strong capital flows, they needed to assure investors of market-friendly policies. Conservative fiscal and monetary policies, including cutting taxes, reducing government spending, slashing regulations, eliminating subsidies, and shrinking the overall role of the government in the economy, were necessary measures to assure global investors of a country's commitment to neo-liberal politics. The nation-state also needed to pursue free trade initiatives through reducing import quotas, tariffs, and other non-tariff restrictions on trade. With respect to monetary policy, central banks were constrained to reduce inflation by controlling the money supply and manipulating interest rates. To promote trade, exchange rate adjustments were vital to make exports more competitive and imports more expensive through depreciating or devaluing domestic currencies. The elimination of capital controls and other barriers to the free flow of foreign investment would promote economic dynamism. This policy approach, broadly dubbed *The Washington Consensus* by John Williamson in 1991, was seen as the passport to capital flows to fuel growth.

Despite his neo-liberal market focus, Friedman emphasized the importance of the nation-state and other organizations to acquire the proper hardware and software to be able to compete in this new global arena. Government intervention was also necessary to promote transparency, establish standards, eliminate corruption (patronage and nepotism), provide for the freedom of the press and information, and uphold democratic processes and principles. Inherent in his formulation was a belief in the linkage between free-market capitalism and Western-style representative democracy.

By 2004, Friedman extended his characterization of the new global workplace in *The World Is Flat*. He asserted that all countries, organizations, and firms have access to the same technologies to compete with one another. For Friedman, the global playing field has been leveled by ten flattening forces:

1 11/9/89, the fall of the Berlin Wall tipping the balance of power toward democracy;
2 8/9/95, when Netscape went public and brought the World Wide Web alive for the common user;
3 Internet work flow software connecting users to other software programs;
4 Open-source software shared, improved by its users, and made available to anyone;
5 Outsourcing, i.e., any service, call center, or knowledge work digitized and sourced to the most efficient low-cost location;
6 Offshoring or production offshore;
7 Supply-chaining or collaboration horizontally among suppliers, retailers, and customers;
8 Insourcing, synchronizing global supply chains for companies;
9 In-forming, universal access to information in any language;
10 The steroids of globalization, wireless technology, digitization at high speed made possible by computational capability, storage capability, and input/output capability.[10]

Fundamentally, the world of global business has seen the convergence of a set of business practices and skills that allow for unprecedented connection and collaboration. For Friedman, globalized technologies changed the ways we make and exchange goods. This leveling effect creates global competition for workers and companies. Winning in this global supply chain requires investments in skills and innovation.

Challenging the free-market views of Friedman, Joseph Stiglitz, a 2001 Nobel Prize winner in economics and professor of economics at Columbia University, worries about the negative effects of globalization. His 2002 book *Globalization and Its Discontents* derives from his academic work along with his experience in White House as an advisor to Clinton and as the senior economist at the World Bank. Stiglitz focuses on the voices in the antiglobalization movement of the late 1990s, attacking footloose multinational corporations, multilateral financial institutions (the IMF and the World Bank particularly), and government policies for their role in contributing to rising poverty, inequality, and environmental damage. Where Friedman supports IMF and World Bank policies, Stiglitz provides stunning criticism from a policy insider. For Stiglitz, the international system was structured to advance interests of industrial nations over concerns of developing nations. Unequal and uneven outcomes were a natural result of this unfair system. A truly level playing field would require reform of the structure and institutions in the world system. Stiglitz contends that globalization needs to be radically rethought and managed in the interests of the majority of the people on the planet. For this to be possible, Stiglitz argues that governments must have a firmer hand in the economic affairs of nations; states can be seen as complementary to rather than competitive with the market system. Because Stiglitz believes that institutions are necessary market complements and can be reformed, we cast his views here as representative of institutionalist thought.

Stiglitz faults institutions such as the IMF as too ideological and inflexible with free-market perspectives. Paradoxically, the IMF adherence to a free-market approach over more pragmatic interventions may have diminished market efficiency. *Globalization and Its Discontents* takes dead aim at the IMF for its record in the 1980s and 1990s in exacting market-based reforms in exchange for loans to bridge external obligations. The IMF used its ability to make short-term loans to countries experiencing **balance of payments** (BOP) deficits (and in many cases had large external debt obligations with commercial banks) in exchange for a grueling list of neo-liberal disciplines. Stiglitz contested the approach that a basket of strict free-market policies was required for the return of growth. As we will explore in the chapter on global finance, he questioned the presumption that contractionary IMF medicine would promote sustainable economic advancement, especially for the poorest of the world. Stiglitz reminds us that there is not just one market model, but policy mixes appropriate for divergent solutions. Just as Sweden's approach to growth differs from that of the United States, Stiglitz argues for policy space as Asians, Africans, and Latin Americans constructing growth models for their own futures. In *Making Globalization Work* (2006), Stiglitz's understanding of the limitations of markets draws our attention to the ways institutions can be shaped to promote a more just and equitable globalized economy. For Stiglitz, trade should be made fairer, the debt burden should fall on investors as well as the poor, corporations should be pushed to do good in pursuit of profit, and global macroeconomic management should be stabilized through cooperation. Stiglitz sees the benefits of globalization, but only as mediated through institutions promoting a fairer, more just process.

In a 2014 article, Stiglitz continued his critique of globalization by focusing on the trade debate centered on the TPP (Trans-Pacific Partnership), an Obama administration trade agreement to bring twelve nations together (including the United States) in a comprehensive Asian trade pact. Stiglitz pointed out that the conventional theory of free trade was largely focused on reducing tariff barriers between countries. Yet, the TPP is essentially about reducing non-tariff barriers and especially regulations (typically in the area of environmental, health and safety for labor, financial, and legal requirements). His argument is that these non-tariff barrier areas enhance multinational corporate profits and power at the expense of local workers and countries and the interests of workers in the United States. The veil of trying to "harmonize" these non-tariff barriers is for Stiglitz a "race to the bottom" for everyone except the global corporations.[11]

Our third perspective on globalization is a Marxian view, cast in the context of Marx's analysis and critique of capitalism. While there are many variants of this perspective, here we examine the ideas of James Petras and Henry Veltmeyer as expressed in their 2001 book, *Globalization Unmasked: Imperialism in the 21st Century*. Their Marxist approach to globalization takes issue with Stiglitz's optimism for the potential of reforming global capitalism. Petras and Veltmeyer argue that for most people a description of globalization "refers to the widening and deepening of the international flows of trade, capital, technology and information within a single integrated global market."[12] The Marxian critique calls us to analyze the system's unstable and unsustainable long-term effects. While the majority of experts view globalization as an inevitable process to be managed, Petras and Veltmeyer believe that it is neither destined nor necessary. They see contemporary globalization as a form of capitalist development "fraught with contradictions that generate forces of opposition and resistance and that can, and under certain conditions will, undermine the capital accumulation process as well as the system on which it depends." For them, globalization is the new imperialism of the twenty-first century.

The drive for capitalist accumulation has produced powerful monopolies that export capital, divide international markets, and exploit labor and resources. The state, aligning with elites, establishes reforms and a compact with workers and corporations to ease tensions between labor and capital. This serves to enhance the legitimacy of the state and subdue many of the internal contradictions of capitalism. The Marxist anticipates that the state will generally do what is necessary to protect and preserve the interests of the capitalist class. But the imbalances created in promoting the interests of capital accumulation create a systemic proclivity toward crises. In its most recent form, Petras argues in his 2009 book *Global Depression and Regional Wars* that the dominance of financial capital over productive capital led to the 2009 crash.[13] To preserve and advance the capital accumulation process, they argue that global capitalism must continue to restructure itself to address the challenges of the crisis.

In dramatic contrast to the ideas of Thomas Friedman and Joseph Stiglitz, the Marxian school of thought argues that capitalism is prone to systemic crisis. The global economy described by Friedman and Stiglitz is an evolving system that needs the support of the state. Unlike Stiglitz who believes institutions will be reformed, Petras argues that the breakdown of capitalism and the conflicts it creates between workers and elites requires a structural rebalancing of the economic system, wherein the state incentivizes investment to produce goods and services with real value and promotes a social transformation to improve the working conditions of people around the globe. That is, on its own the market will reproduce the values of the capitalist elite—a process that over the course of persistent crises will self-destruct without proactive engagement by the state in the economy.

None of the three schools of thought contests that globalization comes without a price. We must grapple the question of whether government intervention is worth the cost of managing in markets. Has a globalized economy rendered national tools ineffective? Can multilateral institutions be reformed to address global imbalances? What is the future of our globalized economy? Before we can answer these complex questions, we must better understand the distinct parts of our globalized economy. This book will provide a guided tour of the subsystems of trade, finance, labor, and production (Box 1.4). We will analyze the way each interacts with the other and how this is transforming the geo-economic landscape. Just like that bellbottomed student of the 1970s writing his paper at the beginning of this chapter, can you imagine what your economy will be like in fifty years, this economy being shaped by tweets and bytes and cargo boxes connecting labor and capital the world over?

It is to this task that we now turn. The chapters in our book tackle essential aspects of globalization viewed largely from an economic perspective to see what critical insights can be gleaned from this viewpoint—with a full appreciation of its multidisciplinary limitations. With these economic tools in hand, it is our hope that the student of this text will bring a critical eye from the humanities and other social sciences to an understanding of contemporary globalization. And, with the increasing importance of issues related to natural resources, the environment, and energy, there is the need for a full integration and application of the natural sciences and engineering.

Box 1.4. Cell Phones and Globalization

Globalization presents many paradoxes. We love our smart phones, laptops, and digital cameras. Technology does bind us together, making it easier to Skype a friend in the Philippines or subcontract an order in Malaysia. Rafiq Nagar, a Mumbai slum, may have no clean water, garbage pickup, or legal power lines—but nearly each of its 10,000 families has a cell phone.[14] For poor families, a mobile has become a basic need. How else would one get called for a job? E-banking is bringing financial services to those without banks; in Kenya a stunning 43% of its GDP passed through its M-Pesa phone-banking service in 2013, logging over 237 million person-to-person transactions.[15] The cell phone is a tool for education; in Senegal, a program reaching 12,000 people showed those able to write a text message rose from 8% to 62%.[16] That simple flip phone can also be an instrument for democracy, with a camera an ever-present eye toward cleaning corruption through greater transparency. It would surprise many of us to know that these items are built using minerals that are fueling and funding mass slaughter and rape in the Congo.[17] Mineral ore containing tantalum, tungsten, tine, and gold finance warlords in the Congo. More specifically, tantalum from the Congo is used in electrical capacitors (for phones), computers, and gaming devices. These so-called conflict minerals (much like Blood Diamonds) have found their way into global high-tech supply chains. Using cell phones of their own, activists are putting pressure on companies like Apple, Intel, and Research in Motion (maker of the Blackberry) to be sure that their supplies of these raw materials are not coming from the Congo.

Our goal is to develop an understanding of essential economic terms, concepts, theories, and policies critical to grasping contemporary globalization. Then and only then will we be able to apply this knowledge to the rhetorical question at hand—What is the puzzle of twenty-first-century globalization? What are its long-term prospects? It is clear that globalization is being challenged on many fronts. Continued progress is not guaranteed. Will globalization confront challenges addressing economic and social sustainability? Or will a world frustrated and tired of the costs of globalization fail to imagine a future that inclusively embraces all global citizens?

Food for Thought: Solving the Puzzle?

In the following chapters, we attempt to raise and explore many of the questions presented below. At the end of the book, it may be useful to return to this section of Chapter 1 to assess what you have learned and had the opportunity to think about critically.

Chapter 2: Twenty-First-Century Globalization in Historical Context

What is unique about globalization today?
What precisely is globalization?
What is important about the evolution of capitalism and globalization from the fifteenth to the twentieth century?
What is the character of the contemporary debate about globalization?
What is the relationship between contemporary globalization and the emerging global geostrategic landscape?

Chapter 3: International Trade

Why is free trade assumed to be the correct and preferred economic policy?
What is the difference between free trade and protectionism?
What is the difference between free trade and fair trade?
Does trade contribute to economic growth?
What are the economic impacts of trade? Inequality?
Does trade contribute to the growth of employment?
Are free-trade agreements successful?
What is the changing composition and direction of trade?

Chapter 4: International Finance

What is the international BOP?
What determines the value of a country's currency?
What is the impact of the appreciation or depreciation of a currency on trade?
How is a BOP deficit financed?
How important is the free flow of capital between countries?

What is the role of the IMF, the World Bank, and the G-20?
What is the problem with countries that have growing public debt obligations?
What is the character of contemporary global financial imbalances?

Chapter 5: Emerging Market Economies and Developing Nations

Why are many countries poor and underdeveloped?
Does economic growth create economic development?
Is the use of the term and expression "The Third World" relevant today?
What is the new paradigm for development?
What is significant of the BRICS in the global economy?
What is an appropriate strategy for addressing global poverty?
What are the most important and least understood trends in the developing world?
What are the changing demographic realities and projections?
What are the competing perspectives on economic aid?
How effective are microcredit and microfinance programs in developing countries?

Chapter 6: International Labor and Multinational Corporations

What is the character of the international production system?
How does the global value chain change how we understand trade and finance?
What is the role of multinational corporations today?
What can be said about the international labor market?
What are the major issues for labor with regard to contemporary globalization?
How does migration impact globalization?
How important is the movement toward corporate social responsibility?

Chapter 7: Sustainability: Natural Resources, Energy, and the Environment

What are historic trends in terms of natural resource supply and demand?
What is the situation with food, agriculture, and water today?
What is the impact of economic growth on the environment?
What is the relationship between globalization and the environment?
What is meant by the word "sustainability"?
What is it that would constitute sustainable development?
How much energy does the world use, and where does it come from and what cost?
What is the case for and against climate change and global warming?
What is the case for and against a carbon tax? A cap and trade system?

Chapter 8: The Future of Twenty-First-Century Globalization? Solving the Puzzle?

What caused the Global Financial Crisis in 2007–08?
What was the economic and financial impact of the financial crisis and the recession?

What were the policy responses to the crisis and recession?
What are today's global economic growth prospects?
What is the emerging relationship between markets and the state?
What is the nature of the global social deficit?
What is the global energy and environmental challenge?
How can globalization help solve this challenge or make it more difficult?
What are the foreign policy and natural security implications of globalization?
What needs to be done in terms of global financial rebalancing?
What is the future of globalization?

Summary

One Term, Varied Definitions

- Revolutionary changes and unprecedented multilateral integration in the past four decades fundamentally changed our global economy. In particular, evolving trade and financial balances, a shifting landscape of production and labor, and new roles of systemically important emerging market economies provide a novel context for current globalization.
- Contemporary globalization is often misunderstood, with multiple definitions from different perspectives. Globalization is essentially the dynamic process of the integration of markets for goods, services, capital, and labor beyond national borders, driven by the growth of international trade and cross-border expansion of banking and financial institutions. Globalization encompasses a radical change to the global production system for goods and services due to changes in transportation technology and information technology, resulting in a faster speed than ever before to conduct transnational and transcultural transactions.

The Debated History of Globalization

- Skeptics, hyperglobalists, and transformationalists have different views of the history of globalization. Skeptics see globalization as a continuous force, affecting the economy by deepening the scale and scope of international linkages. Hyperglobalists agree with the continuous history globalization outlined by skeptics, but also believe contemporary globalization to be distinct in its form. Transformationalists believe that contemporary globalization is a novel force underlying the widespread social, political, and economic changes restructuring global societies and the world order.
- The emergence of capitalism links market-based economies. As a result, social and cultural exchanges have increased in volume and velocity, but at a cost of growing homogeneity of world culture.

Navigating the Gains and Losses of Globalization with Institutions

- Globalization creates winners and losers. International institutions address complex and interconnected global system to minimize the costs and maximize the gains of globalization—but they are not always effective.
- The political economic schools of thought including Free Market Neo-Liberal, Institutionalist–Structuralist, and Marxist frame the debate over globalization and the role of institutions in promoting the best and reducing the worst aspects of our new global economy.
- Free Market Neo-Liberals believe in the power of institutions, along with market economies, to reach prosperity. These views are often espoused by the IMF. Thomas Friedman's texts asserting that adapted free-market policies led to success also support this view. Institutionalist–Structuralists, represented by economist Joseph Stiglitz, find that institutions are necessary market complements and can be reformed. Stiglitz denounces the market-based reforms used by the IMF, and instead proposes that policies incorporating different kinds of market models are necessary for just and equitable global growth. The Marxian view, championed by James Petras and Henry Veltmeyer, find globalization to be unsustainable due to its negative long-term effects because the state promotes the interests of elites and the capitalist class. The injustices arising from globalization, in the eyes of Petras and Veltmeyer, requires an entire rebalancing of the global financial system.

Notes

1. This point is raised by Nayef Al-Rodhan and Gerard Stoudman, "The literature stemming from the debate on globalization has grown in the last decade beyond any individual's capability of extracting a workable definition of the concept. In a sense, the meaning of the concept is self-evident, in another, it is vague and obscure as its reaches are wide and constantly shifting. Perhaps, more than any other concept, globalization is the debate about it." "Definitions of Globalization: A Comprehensive Overview and a Proposed Definition," Geneva Centre for Security Policy, Program on the Geopolitical Implications of Globalization and Transnational Security, June 19, 2006.
2. This derives from the definition offered by Al-Rodhan and Stoudman, "Globalization is a process that encompasses the causes, course, and consequences of transnational and transcultural integration of human and non-human activities."
3. Ward Rennen and Pim Martens, "The Globalization Timeline." *Integrated Assessment*, 4, no. 3 (2003): 137–144.
4. Ibid., 137.
5. Ibid., 143.
6. "Globalization: A Brief Overview." *International Monetary Fund* (2008).
7. "Poverty at a Glance." *World Bank* (2012).

8. Alassane D. Ouattara, *Deputy Managing Director of the International Monetary Fund,* "The IMF and Developing Countries: From Myths to Realities." *The International Monetary Fund*, November 10, 1998 www.imf.org

9. Thomas Friedman, *The Lexus and the Olive Tree*. New York: Farrar, Straus and Giroux, 1999.

10. Thomas Friedman, *The World Is Flat*. New York: Farrar, Straus and Giroux, 2004.

11. J. Stiglitz, "On the Wrong Side of Globalization," *The New York Times*, March 15, 2014.

12. James Petras and Henry Veltmeyer, *Globalization Unmasked: Imperialism in the 21st Century*. London: Zed Books, 2001.

13. James F. Petras, *Global Depression and Regional Wars*. Atlanta, GA: Clarity Press, 2009.

14. Ravi Nessman, "Lack of Basic Services Limits India's Progress." Associated Press, October 30, 2010.

15. Daniel Runde, "M-Pesa and the Rise of the Global Mobile Money Market," August 12, 2015, Forbes.com.

16. Ibid.

17. Nicholas D. Kristof, "Death by Gadget," *The New York Times*, June 27, 2010; for additional information on the situation in the Congo, see Howard W. French, "Kagame's Hidden War in the Congo," *The New York Review of Books*, 56, no. 14 (September 24, 2009); and Adam Hochschild, "Rape of the Congo," *The New York Review of Books*, 56, no. 13 (August 13, 2009).

CHAPTER TWO

GLOBALIZATION

Historical Perspectives

A young African man on the Internet with his cell phone.

Crisis as Crucible

At the beginning of the second decade of the new millennium, globalization was in crisis. Our global economic and financial system was slowly recovering from the worst crisis since the Great Depression of the 1930s. A prolonged period of low interest rates and easy access to credit concocted a housing and real estate boom and a binge of consumer spending and borrowing with low personal savings. This crisis began in late 2007, precipitated by a U.S. banking crisis involving subprime or risky mortgages being repackaged as investment vehicles with high returns at the height of a real estate bubble. Homeowners were suddenly in trouble; families lost value in homes equity, and retirement accounts were devastated as the stock market tanked. Household net wealth was decimated. With globally integrated capital markets, foreclosures on houses in Florida and Arizona began to impact bank balance sheets in London and Singapore. Risky premiums soared, credit dried up, and the world plunged into a crisis of epic proportions. Banks holding assets with little value (toxic assets) were forced to write down debt and raise capital to allow them to return to solvency. The global financial crisis of 2007–8 called into focus the degree to which markets have become tightly integrated. As investors from across the globe purchased securitized American mortgages, bank balance sheets were infected the world over. Trade contracted in the advanced economies of the North and emerging markets of the South. When crisis flared, it became painfully evident that while capital markets and production lines had globalized, the ability of regulators to deal with global market crises remained at the national level.

The global crisis gave us a peek at the disconnect between globalized markets and nationalized policy instruments. The global financial system has been stabilized by extraordinary programs and policies initiated by governments, central banks, and an array of international financial institutions. But the fear that there was in fact no true global banker capable of calming markets led many to question the desirability of our tightly integrated financial economies. Had our system truly run out of control—or was this just one more spike in a long global financial history of crises spooking markets? To what degree would a financial panic be translated into a deep downturn in production and consumption? Would the profound integration between national markets drown the strong along with the struggling—or would they create a fundamental buoyancy to restore global growth?

The global financial crisis calls us to look backward to examine how our system became so highly integrated and to assess the future stability of our globalized economy. As the transformationalists that we introduced in Chapter 1 suggest, are we living in a fundamentally different economic system than in the past or are we experiencing a sort of hyperconnectivity of markets? The global financial and economic crises emerged with a speed and a force that few anticipated. This crisis challenged the efficacy of global capitalism and its future. Indeed, one could argue that contemporary globalization has been knocked off its prior course. What are we to make of the future direction and impact of globalization as a consequence of the crisis? What needs to be done with respect to global capitalism itself in order for it to provide a future that is peaceful, sustainable, and prosperous? What can we learn from history that will help us answer these questions?

This chapter offers three perspectives on globalization's history, building upon the neo-liberal, institutionalist–structuralist, and Marxist frameworks outlined in the introduction. First, we will look at how new technologies of transportation, communication, and finance propel markets and create opportunities for economic change. We might think about this as a technological market approach. But institutionalist–structuralists, our second group, argue that market-based technological growth will not automatically solve global problems. Instead, structuralists caution that markets need to be intermediated by sound institutions. A third, at times complementary approach, looks at globalization systemically. This explanation pushes beyond technology and institutions to consider why changing economic systems are prone to crisis. Largely drawing from a Marxian perspective, this approach pushes us to understand global capitalism as driven by an irrepressible quest for accumulation of profits that leads to the fundamental instability of the system.

Old and New Technology Drivers of Globalization

The pace and scale of technological change in a market context is a primary characteristic of globalization. New technologies of production, finance, transportation, information, and communication transformed the global production system. As Nayan Chanda of Yale eloquently convinces in his book *Bound Together*, evolving technologies tie markets together.[1] In pursuit of profit, in the name of religion, or in defense of the emerging nation-state, people's search for a better life was facilitated by changing technology. As camels were domesticated between 3,000 and 2,000 BCE and the saddle applied by around 500–200 BCE, trade routes evolved between China, India, and the Eastern Mediterranean. The Silk Road between Europe and the Far East became a transmission belt not only for goods but for religion, art, and ideas. Boats opened long-distance connections; once sailors mastered the monsoon winds, travel time was reduced from thirty months to three to bring goods from the East to Rome. In 1492, Columbus set sail in search of New World spices. Although he didn't find his desired route, government chartered trading companies—the first multinationals—brought New World gold to finance booming European markets. Financial innovation in Venice, including fifteenth-century bills of exchange and other credit instruments, allowed goods to be shipped without countertrade barter deliveries. The messenger posts staffed by homing pigeons on the Silk Road gave way to telegraph as a means of placing orders; by the mid-nineteenth century, a transatlantic cable allowed for real-time ticker tape prices and the ability to execute buy-and-sell orders in a single day. Commerce was forever changed by Bell's telephone in 1876; eighty years later, a transatlantic phone order for goods produced half a world away could be placed. With cell phone penetration quadrupling in Africa from 2001 to 2007, new markets are now emerging as formerly isolated communities have access to credit and price information. By 2010, approximately three-fourths of the world's population had cell phones, linking us electronically.[2] Access to mobile networks currently covers 90% of the world population and 80% of those living in rural areas.[3]

In 1970, delivery modes were transformed; the 186 Fedex packages processed that first day catapulted to today's over eleven million parcels a day in a contemporary holiday season. In addition to air routes, cargo ships propelled by the innovation of the container box deliver electronics and textiles assembled in China for global distribution, with about 15,000 vessels passing through the Panama Canal annually. Global logistics companies provide the parts and parcels demanded by producers and consumers in timeframes that would have seemed like science fiction to your great grandparents.

Invented in 1959, the microchip is responsible for creating the four Vs of globalization: velocity, volume, variety, and visibility.[4] The simple binary system has converted our lives into high-speed multitasking systems with Google as the second part of our brains. Information processed by the microchip has increased both the speed and the volume with which we transmit goods and ideas. We produce our electronics in global supply chains stretching from Cupertino to Shenzhen. Civil society organizations use these electronic icons of modernization to connect factory floors in Ho Chi Minh City to boardrooms of Canary Wharf. YouTube and convergence technologies bring images and sounds from every corner of the globe into your living room in HD color.

Without question, the micro-electronic revolution, the computer revolution, logistics systems, and the emergence of the Internet (1995) were major forces advancing this transformation. The changing character of contemporary globalization has challenged many of our previously held conceptual frameworks, theories, and practices in the fields of economics, finance, and management. Table 2.1 captures the more modern effects of technological revolutions and the ways they redefined our market structure.

From 1995 to the end of the decade, globalization propelled by technological change served the U.S. economy well. The Internet sparked a financial revolution alongside technological change. Many startup firms supported by venture capitalists explored new ways of using the Internet to sell goods, deliver ideas, and connect our lives across borders. Although many of these startups did not even have revenue streams or profits, private investors piled in. Many later went public, listing stocks on exchanges from New York to London. The successful early entrepreneurs experienced a rapid rise to incredible wealth based on the paper value of these firms. Nevertheless, these markets driven by what some had called "irrational exuberance" experienced a dramatic collapse by 2001.

Consolidation following the .com bust left powerful technology players with global platforms. Although some local preferences such as Orkut (owned by Google!) in Brazil and India remain, social media of Facebook and YouTube globally connect homes and workplaces. A bookless schoolchild in the Amazon can study about frogs on Wikipedia—like his Boston second grader email pen pal. The more educated workforce in the global South began to compete with northern workers. Changes in production technology allow Walmarts the world over to rollback prices on jeans and televisions that it sourced from factories in Guatemala and China. Your medical x-rays may be read in Bangalore and your court claim researched in Manila with the outsourcing of services. Technological breakthroughs in medicine, driven in part by the work of mega-NGOs such as the Gates Foundation, make possible the containment of malaria and AIDS. Solar technologies bring sustainable energy to poor rural farmers, and clean-burning stoves make cooking safe for

Table 2.1. The Industries and Infrastructures of Each Technological Revolution

Technological Revolution	*New or Redefined Infrastructures*	*New Technologies and New or Redefined Industries*
First *From 1771* The "Industrial Revolution" Britain	Canals and waterways Turnpike roads Water power (highly improved water wheels) Steam engine	Mechanized cotton industry Wrought iron Machinery
Second *From 1829* Age of steam and railways in Britain and spreading to the Continent and the United States	Railways (use of steam engine) Universal postal service Telegraph (mainly nationally along railway lines) Great ports, great depots, and worldwide sailing ships City gas	Steam engines and machinery (made of iron, fuelled by coal) Iron and coal mining (now playing a central role in growth) Railway construction Rolling stock production Steam power for many industries (including textiles)
Third *From 1875* Age of steel, electricity, and heavy engineering United States and Germany overtaking Britain	Worldwide shipping in rapid steel steamships (use of Suez Canal) Worldwide railways (use of cheap steel rails and bolts in standard sizes) Great bridges and tunnels Worldwide telegraph Telephone (mainly nationally) Electrical networks (for illumination and industrial use)	Cheap steel (especially Bessemer) Full development of steam engine for steel ships Heavy chemicals and civil engineering Electrical equipment industry Copper and cables Canned and bottled food Paper and packaging
Fourth *From 1908* Age of oil, the automobile, and mass production In the United States and spreading to Europe	Networks of roads, highways, ports, and airports Networks of oil ducts Universal electricity (industry and homes) Worldwide analog telecommunications (telephone, telex, and cablegram) wire and wireless Green revolution in agriculture	Mass-produced automobiles Cheap oil and oil fuels Petrochemicals (synthetics) Internal combustion engine for automobiles, transport, tractors, airplanes, war tanks, and electricity Home electrical appliances Refrigerated and frozen foods Expansion of global food supply

continued

Table 2.1. The Industries and Infrastructures of Each Technological Revolution (Continued)

Technological Revolution	*New or Redefined Infrastructures*	*New Technologies and New or Redefined Industries*
Fifth *From early 1970s* Age of information and telecommunications In the United States, spreading to Europe and Asia and then globalized	World digital telecommunications (cable, fiber optics, microchip, radio, and satellite) Internet/electronic mail and other e-services Multiple-source, flexible-use electricity networks High-speed physical transport links (by land, air, and water)	The information revolution Cheap microelectronics Computers, software Telecommunications Control instruments Computer-aided biotechnology and new materials

Source: Based largely on Carlota Perez, *Technological Revolutions and Financial Capital* (Cheltenham, UK: Edward Elgar, 2002), with several additions and adaptations.

low-income households in Africa, Asia, and South America. A focus on technology is an optimistic lens to view globalization. Technological revolutions, summarized in Table 2.1, have transformed economic systems and improved lives. As we saw in Chapter 1, adherents such as Thomas Friedman hold great hope for extraordinary technological breakthroughs advancing the material lives of humans. For a technological purist, the best hope for continued advance is to encourage market-based systems of innovation.

A Structuralist Retrospective on Globalization

If technology has been a driver of globalized change, institutions have been midwives of the conflict that accompanies globalization. Globalization creates tensions as different national rules are called into question; it also creates winners and losers among political constituencies. Diplomatic changes paralleled technological ones; remember that without the commercialization of World War II jet aircraft and transatlantic cables, international diplomacy was conducted via long letters and leisurely five-year residences in Paris enjoyed by the likes Jefferson and Franklin. With the exception of faith-based organizations, early global diplomacy was a monopoly of the state that could afford such stays.

Following the Great Depression and the end of World War II, the post-war international economic and financial system was reconstructed at the famous Bretton Woods Conference in 1944 to stabilize post-war Europe. This system established the U.S. dollar as the key reserve currency (backed by gold) and created the **International Monetary Fund (IMF)** and the **World Bank**. The IMF's primary purpose was to assist member countries with short-term BOP deficit problems through loans and technical assistance. The World Bank's mission was to work with developing countries in their efforts to generate economic growth and alleviate poverty. The system provided the framework for the global economic and financial system from 1944 until the early 1970s. As we will visit in greater detail in Chapter 4, the dollar, the reserve currency that could be exchanged for any other or for gold, was at the center of the Bretton Woods financial system. All countries set their exchange rates in terms of the dollar, and the United States, the country least damaged by World War II, pledged to back dollars with gold to provide an anchor to prices while also offering financial liquidity to the global system. As the United States preferred more autonomy in this role of global banker, the IMF was a far weaker institution than other architects of the agreement, including knighted economist John Maynard Keynes, would have liked. The more coordinated system Keynes advocated would have required surplus countries (then the United States) to adjust along with those experiencing deficits in a symmetrical fashion.

Nonetheless, despite this weaker institutional form, the IMF along with its Bretton Woods twin the International Bank for Reconstruction and Development—later known as the World Bank—worked to help the international economy recover from recession and war. Post-war global policymakers were not able to agree on an international trade organization, but instead pursued a process of multilateral trade talks, named the **General Agreement on Tariffs and Trade (GATT)**, that succeeded in bringing down the prohibitive levels of import protection from its launch in 1947 in Geneva to a relatively open trading system as the Uruguay round closed in 1994.

During the 1950s and 1960s, as the global economic and financial system roared back from the aftermath of World War II, growth accelerated. As world trade grew, U.S. and British banks began to fan out across the international system. The regulatory framework of the IMF and the GATT provided relative stability for this system of Western capitalism that operated in a largely parallel economy to the satellite of centrally planned economies associated with the Soviet Union and China. Both market and state systems delivered strong growth during this period. Internationalization, or increasing interdependence between countries, expanded as multinationals reached into new markets for production and sales.

But the pace, scale, and character of this internationalization produced uneven outcomes that were not mediated by strong institutions. Winners and losers both between and within countries emerged. The 1960s brought fundamental shifts in trade competitiveness. Europe had recovered, and the early formulation of the European Common Market in 1957 provided dynamic economies of scale in production. Japan became an Eastern powerhouse, moving up the value chain from assembly of cheap electronics through automobiles. The United States, struggling to compete while financing the Vietnam War and a war against poverty at home, became a less reliable guarantor of non-inflationary finance. The cumulative structural changes in the 1960s of a rising Europe and ascendant Japan erupted in crisis by the mid-1970s.

The Bretton Woods fixed exchange rate system collapsed under international pressure to manage these rapid changes in relative competitive advantage. Suffering a trade deficit, the United States could no longer guarantee that a dollar was as good as gold; the Bretton Woods system was replaced in 1973 by a floating exchange rate system. Under this regime, major currencies were freely traded while developing country exchange rates were largely pegged to the dominant trading partner as an anchor to stability. The IMF was tasked with surveillance of exchange rate management, a relatively weak institutional role. As the World Bank's mission in European reconstruction was complete, attention turned to the developing world.

But the IMF was soon quite active in managing the effects of the capital flows that began to explode in the 1970s. Private sector bankers pursued large-scale, high-return projects in Latin America and Asia. Much of this lending was to state-owned enterprises under the presumption that the loan was backed by a sovereign guarantee.

Capital flows increased as the **Organization for Petroleum Exporting Countries** (OPEC)'s power on the world stage rose with increasing oil prices and mounting bank deposits that needed to be invested to pay interest. The rising cost of this key commodity caused BOP problems for importers and provoked recessions in the United States in 1973–74. It also paradoxically created a pool of cheap global capital as banks receiving deposits from oil-rich nations needed to recycle these petrodollars in new loans throughout the world to be able to pay interest on OPEC accounts.

This period of high wire global finance over an unstable foundation of debt collapsed when the Mexican finance minister called Washington in 1982, abruptly announcing the country couldn't meet its external obligations. The causes of crisis were both internal and external. The burden of high oil prices produced a global recession for Western countries that lasted from 1979 to 1982. Coupled with cost-push inflation with higher oil costs, the United States adopted contractionary monetary policies to restore price stability. Developing countries that had begun to depend on Western consumption demand were stung as exports plummeted. Loans incurred during the easy finance of the 1970s petrodollar recycling suddenly became unmanageable, and the debt crisis erupted. With the IMF at the center of the storm, countries were cautioned to cut spending to create a surplus for external debt financing. The decade of the 1980s produced recession, growing levels of poverty in the developing world, and a major financial crisis that began in the United States in 1987 with the collapse of the U.S. stock market.

While the crises of the 1980s were largely adjudicated by institutions formed in the 1940s, by the 1990s new actors emerged on the world stage. With the fall of the Berlin wall in 1989 (you might remember this as one of Thomas Friedman's flatteners from Chapter 1), new countries entered the global trading arena. The 1990s produced major challenges to the global financial system. The Mexican Peso Crisis in 1994–95 illustrated the uncontrollable nature of capital mobility, and the Asian Financial Crisis in 1997 demonstrated how economies could crumble by speculation and contagion. Adding countries emerging from long periods of colonization, the number of trading nations increased from the 23 launching the GATT agreement in 1945 to the 135 member states of the WTO in the 1990s.[5] A global trade institution with more force than the GATT became necessary as an arbiter of trading rules and the promotion of free trade.

Equally—if not more—transformational in the 1990s was the mushrooming of NGOs. Although as Table 2.2 shows, NGOs such as the international committee of the Red Cross had been around since 1863, the number and importance of international development, health, environment, and social justice NGOs took off in the 1990s. In part, this emergence of new global actors was supported by new technologies of global communications; as the World Wide Web connected people to people, no longer did the state has a monopoly on transnational dialogue through diplomatic cables. Beyond new technologies, however, globalization created the need for civil society organizations to participate in addressing the tensions between winners and losers under liberalization. As disease and global warming knew no borders and violence spilled from one state to its neighbor, a growing imperative for institutions with reach into communities developed. NGOs operate both independently and as partners to multilateral and bilateral organizations. For example,

Mercy Corps partners with the World Bank and USAID to develop community programs in the developing world. Partnerships also exist between the corporate sector, NGOs, and local and global state institutions to help bridge the perceived sense of unfairness that comes with globalization.[6] Dani Rodrik in *One Economics, Many Recipes: Globalization, Institutions, and Economic Growth* cogently argues that creating national institutions to ameliorate the negatives of globalizations is indeed the key to its sustainability.[7] For the institutionalist, different economic recipes are appropriate for different economic conditions.

Table 2.2. Key Chronological Developments in Global Institutions with a Sampling of NGOs

1863	International Committee of the Red Cross
1919	International Labor Organization (ILO)
1934	League of Nations
1944–47	Bretton Woods Twins: IMF, and the World Bank
	United Nations
	United Nations Food and Agriculture Organization
1947	Establishment of the General Agreements on Trade and Tariffs (GATT)
1948	Universal Declaration of Human Rights
1948	World Health Organization formed
1957	Treaty of Rome establishing the European community based upon the foundation laid by the European Coal and Steel Community (ECSC) in 1952
1960	Foundation of Organization of Petroleum Exporting Countries (OPEC)
1962	Organization for Economic Cooperation and Development (OECD)
1966	Asian Development Bank & African Development Bank
1971	Dissolution of U.S. dollar exchange rate gold standard
1971	Doctors Without Borders
1973	EU is enlarged to nine members
1992	Kyoto framework to cut greenhouse gases
1976	G-7 begins meeting
1994	Bill and Melinda Gates Foundation
1994	Signing of the North American Free Trade Agreement (NAFTA)
1995	Establishment of the World Trade Organization (WTO)
1999	Maastrich Treaty Adoption of the Euro by eleven countries; Euro begins circulating in 2002
	50,000 activists protest WTO Seattle meetings
	Formation of the G-20 to tackle the Asian Financial Crisis
2001	China joins the WTO
2009	Financial Stability Board
2016	Paris Agreement on global climate change

The 2007 global financial crisis, introduced at the beginning of this chapter, stretched formal multilateral organizations beyond capacity. With mature economies at its epicenter, the IMF held little sway in coordinating an emergency response. Instead, with the IMF and the World Bank as associated actors, the G-20, a metamorphosis of the closed group of seven industrial countries to include Brazil, China, India, South Africa, and Russia, among others, took the helm. The G-20 is a flexible mechanism promoting global policy coordination in the international finance system. Flexibility has the advantage of confronting crises in an agile manner—but it remains to be seen whether this ad hoc organization is capable of providing the institutional framework for twenty-first-century globalization. Indeed, when one thinks of the global institutional deficits—effective multilateral institutions to manage tensions in the global labor force (including questions of migration), regulate multinational corporations and global banks, and cope with overwhelming externalities of our globalized economy—it is difficult to imagine what constellation of institutions will handle the next crisis of the twenty-first century.

A Radical Political Economy Analysis: The Search for Profits Leads to Instability

Beyond technological drivers of change and institutional midwives, a Marxian perspective focuses on the inherent contradictions of global capitalism. In its evolution from the late fifteenth-century transition from feudalism to early capital accumulation through industrialization and our information society, contemporary globalization is intricately bound by capitalism. As an economic system, capitalism has been pushed by the interplay of output markets and the supply and demand for the factors of production (land, labor, and capital). It is a system that is propelled by the competitive quest for profits and the accumulation of capital. From its earliest days it has thrived on growth and expansion. As such, it quite naturally expands globally, seeking markets to buy and sell goods, access to natural resources and services, and profitable investment opportunities. But as it surges forward, capitalism is also characterized by periods of cyclical instability and periodic financial crisis. Beyond the technological momentum and attendant problems of inequality, the radical political economy view of globalization pushes us to consider this broader historical picture of economic change driven by a capitalist propulsion to cross geographic and political boundaries.

Writing in *The Communist Manifesto* (1848), Karl Marx and Friedrich Engels argued that due to its inherent need to grow to accumulate capital, capitalism would expand its global reach. They note, "The need of a constantly expanding market for its products chases the bourgeoisie over the globe. It must nestle everywhere, settle everywhere, establish connections everywhere."[8] We can see the momentum for growth and expansion from its earliest days. The medieval period in Europe lasted from the twelfth to the eighteenth century, when feudalism was the dominant mode of production. The distinguishing feature of this system was that land, labor, and capital failed to produce an economic surplus that could be utilized to expand the economy. This period was characterized by stagnation as elites such as manor lords, artisan guilds, and the powerful Catholic Church stifled innovation and growth. But as agricultural changes such as the three-field rotation system and the application of the horse and plow allowed for the production of more food than peasant farmers and their feudal lords required, city spaces began to emerge. Supported by this agricultural surplus, a new class of trading merchants developed to meet the desires of new urbanites delighting in the aromas of coffee and the luxury of wools.

By the late fifteenth century, the newly consolidated European nation-states began the period of global exploration to find new routes to the Orient to secure scarce and valuable commodities, including gold and silver. This nascent period of mercantilism represented a drive on the part of these nation-states to accumulate precious metals as a representation of their power and wealth. The feudal period began to crumble under the pressure of state-led trade and expansionism, the birth of the factory system, the commercialization of agriculture, the emergence of wage labor, the growth of cities and towns, the decline of the guilds, the development of new technologies, religious change, and the use of capital and profits for investment and growth. Feudalism gradually gave way to the new capitalism mode of production. The market system was born in a crucible of global exploration.

Adam Smith, the famous Scottish political economist and philosopher, wrote eloquently about the emergence and dynamics of this system in his 1776 famous book, *The Wealth of Nations*. Smith recognized that the invisible hand of free-market competition propelled by inherently self-interested human nature produced wealth.[9] This emerging capitalist economic system would bring together wage labor, physical resources, technology, and capital; through specialization and division of labor, capitalism produced a greater surplus than the individual worker had occasion for, creating further opportunities for profit and using that profit through trade. For Smith, unfettered self-interest in pursuit of technology, production, and markets would give rise to greater wealth for all. In this framework, the role of the state would be quite limited as this kind of market system would work best if left alone—Smith's legacy of advocating *laissez-faire* approaches. Markets, Smith admonished, should be unfettered to function and to respond to the signals of markets and prices. Trade should also be free and not subject to the regulations of the nation-state. While this evolving capitalist market system had many problems with labor exploitation and violence, Smith felt that they would be ameliorated over time.[10] As capitalism expanded throughout Europe, the constant need for new materials and new markets to avoid stagnation led to a process of imperialism.

The period of European global expansion from 1492 to 1776 was driven by the early discovery and conquest of the New World to meet the voracious desires of growing markets. Writing in *Das Kapital* (1867), Marx detailed the process of the "primitive accumulation of capital" whereby the profits from precious metals, the trade in goods, the access to cheap resources, the exploitation of labor, and the slave trade contributed to the profits (surplus value) that flowed to Europe to advance industrialization and the capital accumulation process.[11] As Marx tells us, "The discovery of gold and silver in America, the extirpation, enslavement and entombment in mines of the aboriginal population, the beginning of the conquest and looting of the East Indies, the turning of Africa into a warren for the commercial hunting of blackskins, signalized the rosy dawn of the era of capitalist production."[12] In its relentless search for profits, capitalism left human destruction in its wake.

Indeed, in contrast to Adam Smith's rather cozy analysis of the internal dynamics of capitalism and the rosy prospects for its future, Marx sketched a more dismal picture. Writing in the middle of the nineteenth century, Marx was able to study Smith and his followers such as the first trade economist David Ricardo. As industrialization and global capitalism both evolved, Marx constructed his critique of capitalism as a system that naturally produced great inequality and poverty. For him, these outcomes were morally objectionable. With a mode of production based on the exploitation of wage labor, the capitalist class (bourgeoisie) owned the means of production (tools and technology) and hired wage labor to produce goods and services. The members of the capitalist class were in ruthless competition with one another. The goal was simple—produce and sell goods and services, pay labor as little as possible, and make as much profit as possible while trying to control and grow markets. For Marx, Adam Smith's invisible hand was irreparably broken.

In counterpoint to Smith's self-regulating system, Marx highlighted the inherent tendencies of capitalism toward cyclical instability and economic crisis. His logic has contemporary resonance. When workers are not paid the fair value of their labor, there will not be enough purchasing power among the members of the working class (proletariat) to buy the goods and services they produced. Underconsumption would result in an overproduction of goods and services and a crash in revenue and profit. In crisis, capitalists would lay off workers. Where possible, capitalists would substitute machines for workers to reduce the labor costs of production and improve earnings. Indeed, Marx may have foreshadowed the U.S. jobless recovery of 2010–15.

While the economy was slowing and workers were being let go, Marx anticipated that the ranks of the unemployed (whom he called the industrial reserve army of the unemployed) would grow and their living in conditions would become progressively worse and worse, a process he called immiseration. Paradoxically, he also surmised that the capitalist logic of replacing capital with labor would not restore profits but in fact result in a declining rate of profit when the sale of goods shrank from immiseration of the working class. Marx also posited that in this process capital and wealth would be more concentrated in the hands of fewer and fewer capitalists. Finally, he argued that the state would always act on behalf of the interests of the capitalist class and against the interests of the working class. Capitalism would repeatedly undergo this kind of cycle of economic crisis until the point when the working class would rise up to topple the capitalist class and the state that protected it. For Marx, his historical materialist methodology places economic forces as the primary determinants of the character of society. As the mode of production was transformed by the technological changes, significant—and sometimes wrenching—social and political changes ensued.

Imperialism represented the response of the capitalist class and the state to resolve the built-in tendencies toward capitalist crisis. The need to find new markets for Europe's surplus production and new ways to reduce the costs of production via cheaper raw material inputs and cheaper labor became an overriding imperative. To postpone crisis, capitalists constantly strove to produce in resource-rich locations with vast supplies of cheap labor. The vehicle to acquire natural and labor resources was the multinational corporation. Not surprisingly, this would require an ideology and philosophy to justify and support these activities. As Marx tells us,

> The bourgeoisie has through its exploitation of the world market given a cosmopolitan character to production and consumption in every country. To the great chagrin of Reactionists, it has drawn from under the feet of industry the national ground on which it stood. All old established national industries have been destroyed or are daily being destroyed. They are dislodged by new industries, whose introduction becomes a life and death question for all civilized nations, by industries that no longer work up indigenous raw material, but raw material drawn from the remotest zones; industries whose products are consumed, not only at home, but in every quarter of the globe. In place of old wants, satisfied by the productions of the country, we find new wants, requiring for their satisfaction the products of distant lands and climes. In place of the old local and national seclusion and self-sufficiency, we have intercourse in every direction, universal inter-dependence of nations. And as in material, so also in intellectual production. The intellectual creations of individual nations become common property. National one-sidedness and narrow mindedness become more and more impossible, and from the numerous national and local literatures, there arises a world literature. The bourgeoisie, by the rapid improvement of all instruments of production, by the immensely facilitated means of communication, draws all, even the most barbarian, nations into civilization. The cheap prices of its commodities are the heavy artillery with which it batters down all Chinese walls, with which it forces the barbarians' intensely obstinate hatred of foreigners to capitulate. It compels all nations, on pain of extinction, to adopt the bourgeoisie mode of production; it compels them to introduce what it call civilization into their midst, i.e. to become bourgeois themselves. In one word, it creates a world after its own image.[13]

The economist John Isbister has argued that in this first phase of European imperialism, the New World was discovered and conquered. Europe's industrialization moved forward in the eighteenth and nineteenth centuries powered by the new technologies of this period. During the second phase of European imperialism from 1776 to 1870, the British Empire grew and expanded—and Americans revolted. The third phase from 1870 to the beginning of World War I in 1914 was characterized by the broad-based European scramble for Africa, Asia, and Latin America.[14]

Between 1870 and 1898, Great Britain added four million square miles and 88 million people to its empire. The countries we now call the developing world became the targets for the European control. Africa (Great Britain, Germany, Belgium, France, and Portugal), Asia (Japan, Russia, and the Netherlands), India (Britain), and China (Japan) were exploited as in the growing quest for political and economic dominance. This "race to partition" the world required a military presence, a political organization, and the imposition of a religious and cultural system to reinforce the process of control and transformation. Characterized by European plunder, territorial expansion, and colonialism, the late nineteenth and twentieth centuries are sometimes called "the age of imperialism."[15]

Expansive European imperialism was halted by World War I. We can raise some interesting questions at this juncture. Did this period of European imperialism set the stage for inter-capitalist rivalries that would result in conflict and war? Is imperialism an exception in human history and society, or is it seemingly a part of the fabric of empires that have existed since for thousands of years and will likely continue to exist albeit in different forms? What can be said of the nature of U.S. imperialism in the twentieth century? How did this shape the character of globalization in the twentieth century? What can we reasonably expect in the early decades of the twenty-first century? Will the new story be about Chinese imperialism and the decline of U.S. hegemony? We will leave these questions for the reader to ponder.

Fast forward from European imperialism to contemporary globalization. As you might recall from our institutionalist section above, the difficult decades of the 1970s and the 1980s made the economic and financial vagaries of global capitalism self-evident. But the parallel communist system did not fare better. By the early years of the 1990s, the Soviet Union collapsed. The Cold War ended, including a cessation of the nuclear arms race between the United States and the Soviet Union. This ushered in a new period where capitalism became the uncontested economic model of choice for much of the world. Even China was on the road toward its own variant of market liberalization.

During the 1990s, the emergence of a new epoch of globalization brought great attention and high hopes to the world stage. This 1990s variant of global capitalism was characterized by the expansion of free markets, international trade, and international finance. As a consequence, the global economic and financial system became more tightly integrated. The need for international institutions and organizations such as the IMF, the World Bank, and the WTO became more acute as guardians against capitalist instability—yet paradoxically their efficacy waned. There was also the simultaneous dramatic growth and expansion of NGOs many of which were addressing the problems created by the new globalization.

Against the backdrop of this new globalization was a set of seemingly intractable global problems: *inequality and poverty*, *environmental degradation*, *global warming and climate change*, *enhanced migration*, *and ethnic genocide.* Despite the optimism of institutionalists, evolving global organizations—both public and private—seemed incapable of managing these crises of capitalism. Taming the volatility of capitalism is made that much more formidable with the "rise of the rest" as characterized by Fareed Zakaria. He argues that what has taken place is not so much the decline of the United States, but that the "rise of the rest" has transformed the global system. The rise of the BRICS—Brazil, Russia, India, China, and South Africa—in the global economy signaled a shift of power in the global system. Growing scarcity of natural resources along with emerging evidence of the frightening long-term consequences of climate change presented challenges to the global system that are beyond the ability of individual nation-states to respond effectively. Despite the need for coordination, nationalist political responses dominated in response to strong internal ethnic, tribal, and religious identification. At times striking xenophobic notes, the rise of the Global south has made many U.S. and European citizens distrustful of the cultures, languages, and traditions of what Zakaria calls "The Rest" (Table 2.3). The effects of the global economic crisis will be deep and prolonged with far-reaching geopolitical consequences. Inward-looking political responses are ascendant. The long movement toward market liberalization has stopped, and a new period of state intervention, reregulation, and creeping protectionism has begun. Indeed, globalization itself may be reversing.[16]

Table 2.3. Globalization Chronology

Time	*Economic*	*Political*	*Technological*
1940s	Establishment of the Bretton Woods System, a new international monetary system (1944–71)	Foundation of the United Nations (1945) Launch of the Marshall Plan (1948–57), a European recovery program	Expansion of plastics and fiber products, e.g., first nylon stockings for women (1940)
	Establishment of GATT (1947) entering into force in January 1948	Founding of the Organization for European Economic Cooperation (1948)	
	Soviet Union establishes the Council for Mutual Economic Assistance (CMEA) for economic cooperation among communist countries (1949–91)	Decolonization starts (1948–62). Independence of India, Indonesia, Egypt, for example China becomes a socialist republic in 1949	Discovery of large oil fields in the Middle East, especially in Saudi Arabia (1948)
1950s	Treaty of Rome establishes the European Community (1957). EC and the European Free Trade Association (1959) favor west European integration	Korean war (1950–53) Suez crisis (1956)	Increased use of oil from the Middle East in Europe and Japan "Just-in-time" production implemented by Toyota
	Major currencies become convertible (1958–64)	Decolonization in Africa (fifteen countries become independent between 1958 and 1962)	Increasing usage of jet engines in air transport (1957–72); sputnik 195
1960s	Foundation of the Organization of the Petroleum Exporting Countries (OPEC) (1960)	Erection of Berlin Wall (1961) and Cuban missile crisis (1962) highlight sharp confrontation between East and West	First person in space (Yuri Gagarin, 1961) and first man on the moon (Neil Armstrong, 1969)
	Development of the Eurodollar Market in London which contributed to petrodollars and international liquidity		Integrated circuits become commercially available (1961)

continued

Table 2.3. Globalization Chronology (Continued)

Time	*Economic*	*Political*	*Technological*
	Kennedy Round, sixth session of the GATT (1964–69)		Offshore oil and gas production developed
	Rapid spread of automobiles and highways in the north accelerates demand and shift in fuels consumption (from coal to oil)		Green Revolution—transforming agricultural production in developing countries (1960s onwards)
	Trade policies of East Asian Countries put more emphasis on export-led development than on import substitution	Soviets invade Czechoslovakia in 1868, ending Prague Spring	First line of Japan's high-speed train system (shinkansen) opened in 1964
			Mont Blanc Road Tunnel (1965)
	Elimination of last customs duties within EC (1968)		Increasing usage of containerization in ocean transport (1968 onwards)
1970s	Departure from U.S. dollar exchange rate gold standard (1971)	Yom Kippur war (1973) helps to trigger oil price hike	First single chip microprocessor (intel 4004) is introduced (1971)
	Tokyo Round of the GATT (1973–79)		
	Oil price "shocks" (1973–74 and 1979) reverse decades of real oil price declines	EU enlargement to nine members (1973)	
	Rise of Asian newly industrialized countries	Soviet invasion of Afghanistan (1979)	
	China's economic reform (1978)		
1980s	Volcker Fed successfully extinguishes U.S. inflation	Gorbachev introduces perestroika (1985)	IBM introduces the first personal computer (1981)
	Developing country debt crisis	Enlargement of the EU to twelve members	
	Mexico starts market reforms and joins the GATT in 1986		Microsoft Windows introduced (1985)
	Louvre Accord promotes stabilization of major exchange rates (1987)	Fall of the Berlin Wall (1989)	

Time	*Economic*	*Political*	*Technological*
1990s	Indian economic reforms launched in 1991	Dissolution of the Soviet Union (1991) leads to the formation of thirteen independent states	Eurotunnel opens in 1994 linking the United Kingdom to continent
	North American Free Trade Agreement (NAFTA 1994); Mexican Peso crisis (1995)		The number of mobile phones increases due to the introduction of second generation (2G) networks using digital technology
	Currency crises: Asian (1997), Russian (1998), and Brazil (1998)	Maastricht Treaty (formally, the Treaty on European Union) signed (1992)	Launch of the first 2G-GSM network by Radiolinja in Finland (1991)
	Establishment of the WTO (1995) following Uruguay Round (1986–94)		Invention of the World Wide Web by Tim Berners-Lee (1989)—first web site put online in 1991. Number of Internet users rise to 300 million by 2000
	Adoption of the Euro by eleven European countries (1999)	Gulf War Desert Storm (1991)	Rio environmental meetings (1992)
2000s	Dotcom crisis (2001)	9/11 attacks 2001	Container ships transport more than 70% of the seaborne trade in value terms
	China joins WTO (2001)	Afghanistan (2001) and Iraq (2003) wars	
	End of the multifiber arrangement (quantitative restrictions on textiles lifted)		
	Global Financial Crisis (2007/8); Greek Financial Crisis	Enlargement of the EU to 27 members	Number of Internet users rises to 800 million in 2005
2010s		Brexit—UK leaves the EU 2015	

Source: World Trade Report 2008, Globalization and Trade with updates by authors.

As the history of globalization unfolds, you can reflect on the relative power of the three schools of thought to explain change. Will technology and markets propel the system forward, can institutions mediate conflicts, or will the fundamental challenges to global capitalism create the conditions for Marxist change? But before we can speculate on where globalization is taking us, we need to dissect the components of globalization to understand its constituent parts. Our next chapters will provide you with the fundamentals to understand international trade theory, global financial flows, new systems for production (and their implications for corporations and labor), the changing role of developing countries, and the impact on the environment. After you understand the fundamentals of international economics, we can return to these big questions of where our globalized twenty-first-century economic system is taking us.

Summary

Technology as the Source of a Unique Twenty-First-Century Globalization

- The pace and scale of technological change is a primary characteristic of globalization; it is an accelerant of twenty-first-century globalization.
- The micro-electronic revolution, computer revolution, development of logistics systems, and emergence of the Internet were major forces in advancing technological transformation. Due to these forces, the speed in which we could trade with one another rapidly increased, intensifying the forces of globalization. Consequently, technology players now work from global platforms, with consumers and producers in every country on the planet.

Institutions within Globalization: An Important and Growing Historical Role

- The Bretton Woods Conference in 1944 marked the creation of the IMF, the World Bank, and established the U.S. dollar as the world's reserve currency. The GATT, launched in 1947, continued the growth of institutionally-sanctioned talks to reduce tariffs and promotion trade as the predecessor to the WTO.
- Partly driven by the negative outcomes of capitalistic globalization, NGOs emerged in the latter half of the twentieth century and particularly in the 1990s. The presence of these organizations helped promote the prioritization of international development, health issues, environmental issues, and social justice on the world stage. Complementing the trends of globalization, new technologies supported the growth of NGOs in addressing these issues.

From a Theoretical Base to a Contemporary, Ever-Changing Application

- Political economist Adam Smith provided the groundwork for capitalism through his landmark 1776 book *The Wealth of Nations* advocating *laissez-faire* policies and the functionality of markets. By 1865, Karl Marx in *Das Kapital* pinpointed the imperialistic logic of capitalism and called attention to the adverse effects for labor and society.
- During the "age of imperialism," Great Britain's empire grew at an extraordinary pace from 1870 to 1898, as colonist-driven territorial expansion took hold. Capitalism subsequently arose as the world's dominant economic force. Crises of capitalism inevitably ensued in the forms of economic downturns and growing social injustices.
- As crises have become more global in scope, some call for stronger mechanisms of coordination; many, however, have turned inward in response to the social and political pressures created by globalization. The presence, role, and efficacy of global institutions within changing geopolitical and economic contexts continue to evolve in the age of twenty-first-century globalization.

Notes

1. Nayan Chanda, *Bound Together: How Traders, Preachers, Adventurers, and Warriors Shaped Globalization*. New Haven, CT: Yale University Press, 2007.
2. "International Telecommunication Union." *United Nations*. Available online at http://www.itu.int/en/about/Pages/default.aspx
3. "The World in 2010." *International Telecommunication Union of the United Nations*. Available online at http://www.itu.int/ITU-D/ict/material/FactsFigures2010.pdf
4. Nayan Chanda focuses on the four Vs in Bound together.
5. World Trade Organization, Wto.org
6. Geoffrey Heal, "Corporate Social Responsibility: An Economic and Financial Framework." *National Bureau of Economic Research* (2005).
7. Dani Rodrik in *One Economics, Many Recipes: Globalization, Institutions, and Economic Growth*. Princeton University Press, 2008.
8. Robert Tucker, "The Communist Manifesto," *The Marx-Engels Reader*. p. 339.
9. Adam Smith, *The Wealth of Nations*. The University of Chicago Press, 1776.
10. Robert Heilbroner, *The Worldly Philosophers*. 7th Edition, Ch. 3 Adam Smith. Touchstone Press, 2004.
11. Karl Marx, *Capital*. NY: International Publishers, 1967.
12. Tucker, *The Marx-Engels Reader*, p. 339.
13. Ibid., 339.
14. John Isbister, *Promises Not Kept*. 5th Edition, Ch. 4 Imperialism, Kumarian Press, 2001.
15. Ibid., Ch. 4.
16. Fareed Zakaria, *The Post-American World*. Norton, 2008; and Parag Khana, *The Second World: Empire and Influence in the New Global Order*. Random House, 2008.

CHAPTER THREE

A New Dynamic of Global Trade

The largest passenger ship to transit the Panama Canal in 1915.

THE PROMISE AND PROBLEMS OF INTERNATIONAL TRADE

International trade and production networks link factories in Shanghai, operators in Mumbai, and financiers in London to consumers in New York. The cotton for your T shirt might be grown in West Texas, stitched in China, imported through Wal-Mart, and wind up re-exported to Africa to a second-hand clothing store.[1] Since the time of the Greeks and the Romans, textiles, gems, and spices have tied our globe together through trade. This impetus to exchange one thing for another of greater value has shaped human history. Those able to meet international appetites for rare goods or produce items at a lower cost gain on the difference between cheaper local prices and demanding global markets.

But trade also creates losers. As production shifts from higher to lower cost areas, jobs can be lost. As trade facilitated by planes, ships, phones, and computers has more tightly woven us together, it has also dislocated workers from traditional employment. Factories have moved to the global South from formerly industrialized economies in the North. Commodity booms turn to busts. Trade is both a force of integration and conflict in the global arena. In this chapter, we analyze these tensions in the global trading system. After unpacking the logic behind trade as a source of wealth, we look at the tensions created by nations wanting to protect jobs and ways of life. We then turn our attention to imbalances in the trading arena and the challenges in creating a more fair and sustainable global system.

CONTEMPORARY TRADE PATTERNS

International trade has grown dramatically in recent years, roughly tripling since the 1950s. We can see in Table 3.1 that the share of exports of goods and services to GDP rose from 12.1% in 1960 to 27.9% in 2010.[2] Why does trade have growing importance in economic systems? Several factors contribute to the rise of trade as a percentage of GDP. Trade is more extensive. Sixty-two countries participated in the Kennedy round of trade negotiations in the mid-1960s.[3] With 162 members of the WTO, more countries participate in the trading system than ever before. Led by industrial country cuts in the 1960s and developing country opening in the 1980s, protectionism has receded with world tariffs falling from 15% to 4%. What is most

Table 3.1. Historical Comparisons of Global Exports

(% of Global GDP)			
World Merchandise Exports[a]		*Exports of Goods and Services[b]*	
1820	1.0	1960	12.1
1870	4.6	1970	13.6
1913	7.9	1980	18.7
1929	9.0	1990	19.0
1950	5.5	2000	24.5
2007	28.9	2010	27.9

a Angus Maddison, *The World Economy: A Millennial Perspective* (Paris: OECD, 2001): 22.
b World Bank, World Development Indicators.

striking over the last decade is the new role developing countries are playing in the global trading arena. Between 1985 and 2006, developing countries' total trade grew at an average annual rate of 9.8%, outpacing the world trade growth of 8.7% over this period.[4] The share of global exports by developing countries reached a stunning 47% in April 2012, the largest proportion ever recorded in the WTO's data series.[5]

In addition to more players, trade is more intensive, driven by the growth of the "global factory." Led by China, emerging markets became more connected through global supply chains. As we will see in Chapter 6, the growth of international production networks was facilitated by improvements in communication and transportation technologies. The Internet instantly connects production lines to consumers; container shipping has dramatically reduced the costs of moving goods from place to place. Our new economic geography of production and trade connects rising middle-class consumers in Latin America to a burgeoning workforce of Asia.

Trade continues to play an increasingly large role in national economies. Of course there is divergence, as shown in Figure 3.1. The United States is one of the countries least dependent on trade; its merchandise trade—a measure of its exposure to the global economy defined as the sum of exports and imports—accounted for 23.2% of GDP in 2014, up from 8% in 1970.[6] China's opening to the world has dramatically changed the importance of trade in its economy; merchandise trade rose from 5% of GDP in 1970 to 41.5% of GDP in 2014. In 2009, China overtook Germany as the world's top merchandise exporter. Focusing on these data for exports alone (rather than merchandise trade), China's exports as a share of GDP amounted to 22.6% in 2014, while in the United States the same figure reached 13.4%.[7,8] With significant intra-European production networks, the European Union (EU) exports accounted for 42% of GDP in 2014. Singapore, a classic *entrepôt*, or big trading economy with a large quantity of re-exports, showed merchandise trade at 251.2% of GDP in 2015. Since Singapore re-exports more than it actually produces, trade exceeds the measure of GDP. Given the importance of trade to

Figure 3.1. World Merchandise Exports by Level of Development

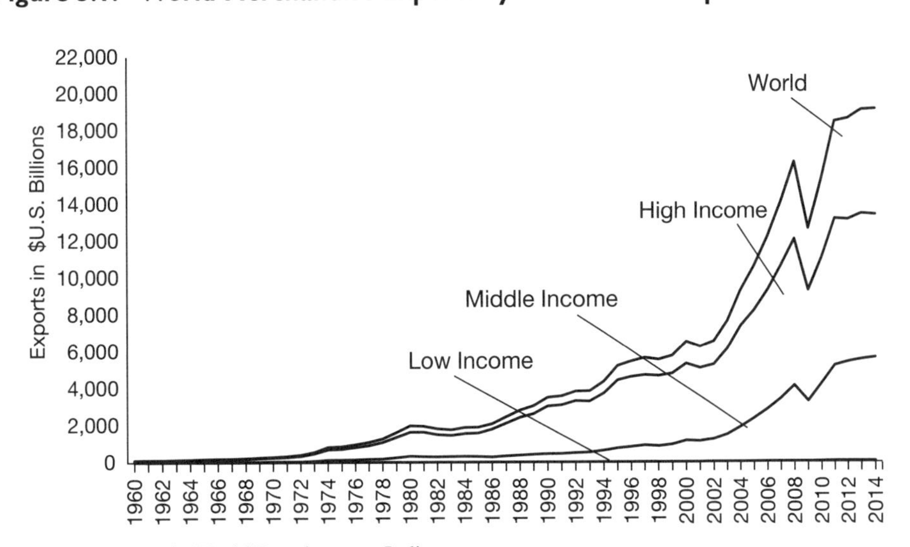

Source: World Bank, World Development Indicators.

countries around the world, understanding trade is critical to our comprehension of what makes economies work. Our puzzle focuses not only on why nations trade but also on why nations are trading more in the globalized economy compared with previous periods in history. After exploring why nations trade, we will then consider situations under which nations choose not to trade but instead to protect against global competition.

The Historical Roots of Trade Theory

International trade has a long and illustrious history. From the beginning of human existence, people have exchanged goods and services. Most civilizations, including the Roman and Chinese empires, the Mayans and Aztecs, and several African kingdoms such as those in modern-day Ghana, have traded.[9] Today, we live in a world where goods cross borders constantly. There are several reasons for this impulse to trade globally. Trade creates gains; otherwise, it simply would not happen. No nation is self-sufficient without great sacrifices. The growth in transnational trade is visible in the products we use every day. An iPod, although branded as an "American product," is actually assembled in China, and truly has a complex story. It contains components manufactured around the world, including a microdrive and flash memory chip from Japan, a controller chip from South Korea, a stereo digital-to-analog converter from Scotland, and Indian software to play your thousands of songs. Your routine cup of morning coffee is likewise globalized, with roots in early trade expeditions. The thirteenth-century discovery of coffee beans in the hills of Ethiopia and their introduction in Yemen evolved into a multibillion dollar industry that today employs millions of growers and processors from Tanzania and Guatemala to the baristas in over ten thousand Starbucks cafés worldwide.[10]

Trade theory developed in tandem with early economic theory. Adam Smith, the father of economics, provided the grounding for trade theory in his 1776 book *The Wealth of Nations*: individuals selfishly specialize in whatever they do best, "truck" the result off, and "barter" or exchange it, generating gains for themselves and society.[11] Smith's student David Ricardo extended this argument of the individual gains from trade to countries in 1817, suggesting that nations focus on what they are relatively best at, trading a lower cost item for a product more dear. The easy case of **absolute advantage** is clear. If France uses fewer workers than Germany to produce wine and Germany uses fewer labor inputs to produce machinery, it is common sense to assume that (holding transportation costs constant) wine should be produced and exported from France and machinery from Germany. Ricardo extended the concept of specialization in accord with **comparative advantage** to argue that even if one country is absolutely better than another in both products, it should produce the one it is **relatively** best at, leaving the other country to the task it is "less bad" at completing. The logic is simple at a personal level. If Kaitlin is better than Conrad at both gardening and writing books, but Conrad is "less bad" at gardening than writing, together the two can make more flowers and prose if Conrad gardens and Kaitlin writes books. Let's follow Ricardo's prescription to increase world output with a numerical example.

Assume that we have two countries, Argentina and Brazil. If Brazil is more efficient than Argentina in producing both cars and beef, we might observe input requirements, or the labor required to produce a unit of each good, as displayed in Table 3.2. Here, we see that in Brazil it takes eight workers to make a car and four to make a shipment of beef. Argentina is worse in both, drawing on twelve workers to make each good. To argue why they should trade, assume the opposite—that we start in **autarky**, or no trade. If Brazil closed its borders and made both cars and beef at home, one car would "cost" two beef. That is, if the goods started circulating (and we assume positive demand), the thirty cars would trade against the sixty beef at a rate of 30–60, or one car would buy a shipment of two beef in Brazil, or one beef would cost "half" a car. In Argentina, one car would trade equally with beef at a 1:1 ratio. This means that in Argentina, one car would only "cost" one beef in this two-good world of domestic trade. Now let the borders open. If you were a Brazilian why not buy your car in Argentina where you could pay with one shipment of beef instead of two? Conversely, Argentines would find it cheaper to buy beef in Brazil where it only costs half a car. If you have only given up half as much beef for your car, you can use the money you have left over to buy more of something else. Indeed, if Brazil were to focus on beef—where it only takes four workers to make a unit shipment—more beef could be delivered to the global market, leaving Argentina to produce cars—the good that it is relatively less bad at.

Figure 3.2 shows the results of trade in accord with comparative advantage by portraying a world **Production Possibilities Frontier** (PPF). A world PPF shows the total possible production of our goods (cars and beef) before and after trade. If we simply sum total possible production in autarky, the combined possible output of cars without trade would be 50; alternatively, if each country's resources were poured totally into beef, together Brazil and Argentina could make eighty beef. The line connecting the points fifty and eighty constitutes the world PPF without specialization in accord with comparative advantage and trade. If instead, Brazil produced beef and Argentina cars, according to the law of comparative advantage, the area labeled G would represent the addition to global output.

Ricardo's theory of focusing on the good in which you have the *relative* advantage—producing your "most best" or "least bad" thing—is based on one factor of production, labor. Classical economists such as Smith, Ricardo, and Marx believed that physical capital or machinery could be reduced to the number of labor hours needed to produce the equipment. Neoclassical economists later expanded on this core concept of comparative advantage in a two-factor model, including capital

Table 3.2. Endowments and Production

240 = Endowment or # of Workers in Each Country	*Input Requirements (Labor Required to Produce One Unit)*		*Output*	
	Car	*Beef*	*Car*	*Beef*
Brazil	8	4	30	60
Argentina	12	12	20	20

Figure 3.2. The Gains from Trading in Accord with Comparative Advantage

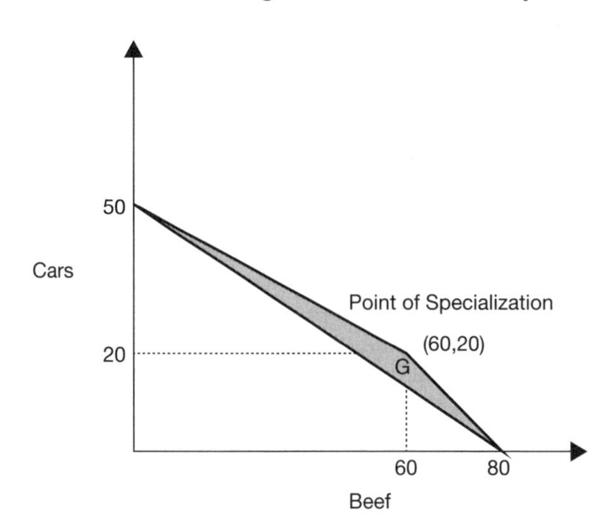

and labor. The central theorem of neoclassical trade was postulated by Heckscher and Ohlin. Their factor proportions model—sometimes called the **H-O model**—says that a country should produce that good that uses relatively intensively its most abundant factor. If we consider two countries, India and the United Kingdom, and India internally has more labor than capital, while the United Kingdom has a higher capital-to-labor ratio, then India should produce and export labor-intensive goods, while Britain should focus on capital-intensive products. The rationale for this again comes from cost. If India is relatively labor abundant, the internal cost of labor will be low. These cheaper wages will allow India an advantage in the global market for labor-intensive goods. Britain's cheaper capital costs will confer it an advantage in machinery products. By trading, both should prosper.

There are two corollaries to the H-O theorem: **Stolper Samuelson** and **factor price equalization**. Stolper Samuelson suggests that trade should increase the welfare of the least well-off in society. If labor is abundant in India, the wage rate will initially be lower than the price of capital. When India's labor-intensive goods are opened to international demand, however, the larger global market should push the price up for Indian products, sending a signal to labor markets in India to raise wages. Labor, therefore, should be made better off by opening up to trade. Factor price equalization tells us that as international trade raises the price of labor in India, falling demand for labor-intensive goods produced in the United Kingdom will draw the world price of labor together.

Here, of course, is where we begin to see the tension between winners and losers in trade. While the workers in India benefit from rising wages, those in Britain begin to feel the pinch of shrinking paychecks. Keeping British workers from labor-intensive sectors such as textiles happy will depend on their ability to find work in capital-intensive sectors such as machinery or aircraft. Of course making a seamstress into an engineer may take a few educational tweaks—or face much political opposition. Labor opposition, supported by the owners of labor-intensive industries, is one of the factors that plays into a nation's demand for protectionism. But before we turn away from the argument for free trade, let's complete our picture of free-trade theory.

The H-O model and its corollaries suggest that a capital-intensive country such as the United States should produce capital-intensive goods. In 1954, Nobel laureate Wassily Leontief tested this proposition and found, to many economists' surprise, that the United States, the world's most capital-abundant country, actually exported labor-intensive goods. This **Leontief paradox** spurred much research. Despite the strong logic of comparative advantage—doing what you are best at—theorists struggled to explain why the capital-intensive United States appeared to be trading labor-intensive products. Trade economists such as Richard Baldwin helped us see alternative explanations, including the fact that many agricultural and natural resource products presumed to be labor intensive actually require complementary heavy machinery such as tractors and cranes. But part of the answer may also have been the evolving global trading system and the stronger role international production lines play in trade. Components of the same product—an iPod—are produced in many places around the world. Rather than simply exporting goods from one country to another, multinationals link our economies in a globally integrated supply chain.

A look at U.S. exports and imports by good reveals some of this interesting pattern in intra-industry trade as the U.S. imports and exports goods in the same industries. For example, we can see in Table 3.3 that vehicles, nuclear reactors, electrical machinery, optics, plastics, iron, and steel are all top categories as both imports and exports. How does comparative advantage square with the data showing the United States importing and exporting the same thing? Two explanations that have gained considerable traction are **economies of scale** and **vertical specialization**. Trade allows companies to take advantage of economies of scale; in some industries costs fall as you produce greater quantities of goods. Consider Japan for a moment. Its 127 million people constitute a market for automobiles. As it opens it borders to trade, it produces even more cars. As it is able to purchase more inputs—seats, tires, and steel—in bulk, costs fall as scale expands. A company—think perhaps Toyota—becomes especially adept at engineering a line of cars.

In industries where economies of scale are important, by trading with another economy companies also open the window to more consumer choice. Nobel laureate Paul Krugman pointed this out in 1979, focusing trade theorists' attention on the tension between variety and cost. If the national market size is limited, the lowest cost production method might be dominated by a single firm and product. This would not be a good outcome for someone who values product choice. Trade creates new possibilities to choose among product varieties. Perhaps someone in Japan prefers a German BMW to a Toyota. Indeed, with this global experience Toyota engages in learning by doing, and becomes an even better producer of cars as feedback from consumers is engineered behind the wheel. Its large size comes to confer advantage—and makes it difficult for new global competitors to enter. In addition, by specializing in select product lines, let's say compact cars, and exchanging them with other countries that produce different goods, such as luxury cars, more types of goods are available to Japanese consumers. In a world without international trade,

Table 3.3. Composition of U.S. Exports and Imports ($U.S. billions)

Top U.S. Exports to World 2013		*Top U.S. Imports from World 2013*	
Nuclear reactors, boilers, machinery, and parts	213.5	Mineral fuels, oils, waxes, and related products; bituminous substances	379.9
Electric machinery, sound and TV equipment, and parts thereof	165.8	Nuclear reactors, boilers, machinery, and parts	304.7
Mineral fuels, oils, waxes, and related products; bituminous substances	149.0	Electric machinery, sound and TV equipment, and parts thereof	298.5
Land vehicles not including railway	134.0	Land vehicles not including railway	249.0
Aircraft, spacecraft, and parts thereof	114.9	Optical, photographic, precision or medical equipment, and parts thereof	71.2
Optical, photographic, precision or medical equipment, and parts thereof	84.4	Precious metals, stones, and pearls; imitations jewelry; coin	66.5
Precious metals, stones, and pearls; imitations jewelry; coin	73.5	Pharmaceutical products	62.9
Plastics and related products	61.0	Iron and steel, and related products	59.7
Organic chemicals	46.6	Manufacturing and Engineering Services	56.8
Manufacturing and Engineering Services	42.1	Organic chemicals	53.5
Iron and steel, and related products	41.7	Furniture	47.7
Pharmaceutical products	39.7	Plastics and related products	44.2
Miscellaneous chemicals	27.0	Knit clothing	43.0
Seeds and legumes	27.0	Clothing, not knit	38.0
Articles of iron and steel	22.1	Aircraft, spacecraft, and parts thereof	29.4
Total	1,579.6	Total	2,268.3

Source: TradeStats Express (Product Profiles of U.S. Merchandise Trade with a Selected Market), at http://tse.export.gov/TSE/TSEOptions.aspx?ReportID=2&Referrer=TSEReports.aspx&DataSource=NTD.

consumers' choices of goods would be limited by the country's economies of scale in production—either luxury or fuel efficient cars but not a choice between the two.

Vertical specialization is also creating new patterns of intra-industry global production. Vertical specialization suggests that a country might have a comparative advantage in parts of more complex goods, such as computer systems in cars, but not in the production of the entire vehicle. Rather than becoming specialized in a particular final good, specialization takes place at different stages in the global supply chain. One country uses an import from another country to produce a good the first country then exports; goods cross many frontiers in the process of production. Production therefore increasingly uses imported content. The foreign content embedded in exports has nearly doubled since 1970, to 33%, with accelerating rates of growth in recent periods.[12] Vertical specialization has been propelled by growing regionalization of trade and production networks, particularly in Asia and Europe.[13] More than one-third of China's exports contain foreign imported components; for Mexico, imported content reaches nearly half (48%) of export value.[14]

As we will discuss in the next chapter, changes in exchange rates will have unexpected effects due to vertical integration. If the Chinese currency were to appreciate, making its exports more expensive, the value of the imported content in its exports will become cheaper, allowing it to dampen the effect of the rising exchange rate on its exports. It is all one big (not always so happy) interconnected world out there! Indeed, the product may largely be made outside the country where the company is incorporated; often the so-called national products are really just *branded* at home. Ironically, Honda—a Japanese company—produces the Odyssey minivan in Alabama with 75% American parts; the U.S. Ford Escape only uses 65% American sourced components.[15] As measured by the vehicle's parts and overall sales, the Japanese Toyota Camry was listed as the top "American made" car.[16] Mexican auto production reached nearly 1.7 million vehicles in 2008—with the "domestic" market divided 23% for each of American GM and German Volkswagen, 17% Japanese Nissan, 16% American Ford, and 15% Chrysler.[17] In 2006, top carmakers in China included Shanghai GM, Shanghai Volkswagen, and Toyota. Given this intricate cross-border production and trade, what indeed is an American car?

Cross-border production is not limited to automobiles. Remember your iPod; different countries specialize in different parts. In fact, one study found that only 3% of the value of a "Chinese-made" iPod actually reflects China's contribution, with the majority of value being added by workers in Japan, the United States, and other countries.[18] What is more American than Campbell's soup? Perhaps the 3,500 shipments of ingredients crossing from Canada into the United States each day may make you think differently about this American icon. Vegetables can even cross the border twice when ingredients from processing plants in both countries are mixed, packaged, and distributed to retailers across the globe.[19] With this "slicing up" of international production, companies produce goods with intermediate inputs that can come from several parts of the globe. Manufactured exports are no longer made in one country and exported to another; instead the global economy is linked through an intricate supply chain.[20] Countries acquire expertise not in final products but in stages of production.

This outsourcing of steps of the production process is facilitated through the decrease in transportation costs, as well as the overall fall in tariff rates between countries.[21] Foreign value added in gross exports—a measure of vertical specialization—doubled worldwide between 1970 and 2005 to reach 33% of exports. More than a tenth of U.S. overall exports (12.9%) and nearly a fifth of high-tech exports (17.4%) from the United States rely on imported parts or components.[22] China is especially reliant on imported components; it is estimated that approximately 26.3% of all exports and 48.5% of China's high-tech exports are attributable to the import of intermediate goods that are then used to make final products.[23] As the exports of rubber from Indonesia show up again as an export of tires from Japan and cars from Mexico, we can see how vertical specialization has fueled approximately one-third of the growth of world trade.[24] Traditional measures of exports attribute all value to the final exporter, underplaying its participation in global supply chains. In this way, the iPod enters China's export with its total value, while only a fraction of the product is assembled in the country.

It is important to note that vertical specialization does not contradict the concept of comparative advantage. It simply suggests that countries may have different advantages at various levels of the production process. We will revisit the importance of this in our later chapter on multinational production. Furthermore, vertical specialization accounts for why a good with high labor content—electronics assembly—may be misperceived as "made in America." Countries are still specializing according to the H-O theory of comparative advantage—they are just doing so at stages of production rather than in final products. Vertical specialization helps explain why a capital-intensive country such as the United States is exporting labor-intensive final products: it is using a global labor pool for the assembly stages, while relying on technology and market sophistication to enhance the value of capital. Some economists, such as the former director of the WTO Pascal Lamy, suggest that conventional trade statistics may be distorted because they fail to capture the extent of vertical specialization that takes place in today's integrated global economy. When we think of China as an export powerhouse, it is important to also remember that between a quarter and a half of Chinese exports rely on imports from other nations. It will also not be surprising, given this vertically integrated production structure, that shocks in one part of the world may be more quickly transmitted that in the past.[25]

Patterns of man-made comparative advantage can and do change over time. The economist Jagdish Bhagwati has labeled this phenomenon "**kaleidoscopic comparative advantage**,"[26] otherwise known as knife-edge specialization that shifts with small changes in cost advantage. Bhagwati argues that "thick" margins of comparative advantage have eroded as globalization permits rapid change. Instead, countries compete in narrow niches. This increases the volatility of comparative advantage and leaves producers to face intense competition from around the world.[27]

Geography also affects trade. Because the northern and southern hemispheres have opposite growing seasons, agricultural trade keeps products like avocados and tomatoes on grocery store shelves year-round and can help to explain why two countries may trade the same products. Overlaying our explanations of comparative advantage and vertical specialization are **gravity models** of trade. Gravity studies incorporate distance between trading partners, whether or not countries have access to the sea, infrastructure quality, and trade facilitation measures. Bilateral distance is highly significant; nearby or neighboring countries trade more as transportation costs are lower. Access to the sea also has a great impact on a country's tendency to trade, with landlocked countries trading between 30% and 60% less than their coastal counterparts.[28] Improvements to physical infrastructure can boost trade volumes by about 25% and enhancements in a country's "soft" infrastructure, such as port facilities, customs procedures, and import–export regulations, can increase trade volumes by over 40%.[29] Policies to accelerate investment in roads and ports or to cut bureaucratic red tape can therefore enhance trade performance. As trade has globalized and vertically integrated supply chains bind global production, the importance of infrastructure as a cost advantage has grown.

As we can see, trade holds many potential benefits. Trade provides consumers with access to more varied goods and services, giving people in Massachusetts access to avocados from Mexico, steel from Brazil, and furniture from China. Imported goods can embody new technology, creating "R and D spillovers" by bringing new research and development across borders and accelerating the flow of technological know-how. Openness may promote growth in productivity by exposing industries to technology from abroad.[30] Domestic firms can access technology, new products, and production processes. The OECD sees trade as a framework condition to strengthen business innovation. Through the import channel, domestic firms can access technology, new products, and production processes.[31] Moreover, increased competition from trade may enhance innovation as companies try to make their products better and cheaper to win over consumers. Inefficient companies are often out-competed, leaving only the most productive. On the downside, this also means that small producers are put out of business by large companies that can afford to sell for less. As we will see later, trade policy must therefore address this political question of winners and losers in globalization.

The Historical Rationale for Protectionism

The concept of comparative advantage, therefore, helps us understand why nations trade. Even in today's more complex and integrated world, a country should produce that thing (or intermediate input to a thing!) that allows it to take advantage of its lowest cost production and geographical characteristics. Despite its apparent benefits, free trade has not always guided policy. Adam Smith railed against the anti-trade logic of his time, the mercantilist philosophy of amassing gold rather than purchasing goods. This strategy was based on the belief that accumulating gold (wealth) provided security for countries to raise large armies in war; furthermore, the stock of gold at home was thought to encourage economic activity.[32] For the mercantilists, the goal of trade was to sell the largest quantity of goods while importing little from abroad, banking the difference in bullion or gold. It is easy to see, however, that if all countries pursue this policy, international trade would come to a halt. For one country to export, another must import.

Like contemporary globalization, earlier periods of increased trade and financial integration created winners as well as losers. At the turn of the nineteenth century, greater openness was driven by the desire for new products and the ability to move goods around the globe. The railway and the steam engine shortened distances dramatically, so that the price gap for wheat between Liverpool and Chicago fell from 60.3% in 1870 to 14.9% in 1912.[33] At the same time that the grain invasion from the New World spread across Europe, England exported its textiles around the world. But afraid of losing their livelihoods, traditional producers attempted to protect local industry from market changes. From 1820 to 1914, the second industrial revolution powered by technological changes such as the internal combustion engine and chemical industries not only decimated many artisan crafts but also made products more available to an emerging middle class. Those replaced by mechanization clamored for help. Global trade was disrupted by the two World Wars and the Great Depression, which provoked a return to very limited trade not as rising economic nationalism prompted countries to protect their domestic markets. The Protectionist Wave was symbolized by the 1930 U.S. Smoot-Hawley Tariff Act that taxed imports of 20,000 products and raised average tariffs to 60%; further retaliation by foreign governments significantly curbed world trade and intensified the Great Depression.[34] Although a multilateral trading organization to parallel the IMF and World Bank was too contentious in the postwar period, progressive opening of trade began through multilateral negotiations under the GATT. As described in Box 3.1, the WTO is working through the Doha round to incorporate a larger number of countries into the global trading system.

Vestiges of mercantilism remain today as some politicians, industrialists, and union leaders view trade and its associated flows of capital as a zero sum game of victory or loss. Today, protectionism is most clearly manifested in three distinct forms: tariffs, export subsidies, and quotas. The simple average tariff rate on goods entering the United States has fallen to 4%. The question remains, however, as the global economy enters a period of uncertain growth whether the long shadow of mercantilism will return to slow the wheels of opening trade. Let's take a look at the tools of trade protectionism before considering opportunities to manage the balance between winners and losers from trade.

Box 3.1. The WTO

The WTO both promotes globalization and enhances trade around the world while also managing and overseeing the complicated global trade environment that has emerged as national economies become increasingly intertwined. Founded in 1995, the WTO replaced the GATT that was adopted by 23 signatories following World War II. Today, the WTO has 162 member countries, representing over 97% of total world trade, as well as thirty observers, most seeking membership.[35] Intending to "help trade flow smoothly, freely, fairly, and predictably,"[36] the WTO has several functions, including administering trade agreements, acting as a forum for trade negotiations, settling disputes between trading partners, reviewing national trade policies, assisting developing countries in trade policy issues through technical assistance and training programs, and working in cooperation with other international organizations. WTO agreements address the following areas:

- Sanitary and Phytosanitary measures (SPS)—Basically these are measures taken by importing countries to protect the health of consumers and plant and animal life. The WTO stipulates that such measures can only be taken based on scientific evidence, that they should not discriminate between countries, and that SPS measures should not act as disguised restriction to trade.
- **TRIPS**—These measures cover copyright and related rights, trademarks, industrial designs, patents, layout design, and trade secrets. Controversy surrounds the areas of health and biodiversity. For instance, should poor countries be allowed to develop and distribute cheap generic drugs to fight diseases like HIV/AIDS? Is

indigenous knowledge of medicinal plants free for the taking by biomedical companies or should it be protected in some way? Is it ethical for traditional knowledge and diverse plant life to be privatized through patents?

- **Environment**—Under the auspices of the Committee on Trade and the Environment (CTE), the WTO claims to foster a constructive relationship between trade and environmental concerns. Yet, the WTO is limited to addressing only the trade-related aspects of environmental policy and cannot act as an international environmental agency. Many criticize the WTO for promoting trade growth without regard for the environmental costs.
- **Labor**—Labor has emerged as a very contentious issue, principally because the WTO does deal with this issue, citing that labor standards are the mandate of the ILO. Advocates argue for WTO oversight over issues such as the right to collective bargaining, freedom of association, workplace abuse, and child labor. However, some see this as thinly veiled protectionism that will harm what they consider the comparative advantage of developing countries. Sanctions for poor labor standards, they claim, would only perpetuate poverty.
- **Trade in agriculture, textiles and clothing, industrial goods, and services**—The WTO seeks to promote free trade by reducing barriers to trade such as import quotas, tariffs, and discriminatory treatment.[37]

While the WTO addresses numerous issues related to trade, in all areas it follows several key principles, most notably the concepts of MFN and national treatment (NT). MFN basically means that countries must not discriminate between trading partners. If one trade partner is granted a special favor, for example a lower customs duty rate for a certain product, this must be extended to all WTO members. Exceptions are granted for FTAs, in certain circumstances with developing countries, or when products are considered to be traded unfairly from specific countries. NT stipulates that foreign goods and services should be given the same treatment as domestic ones—at least once the imports are inside a country's border. This principle extends to foreign and domestic trademarks, copyrights, and patents.

SUCCESSES OF THE WTO

In today's complicated international economic arena, an organization such as the WTO is important to ensure the smooth functioning of the system. While the organization has received its fair share of criticism (as discussed below) it is worth noting some of its successes:

- The WTO's dispute settlement system has been well utilized by both developed and developing countries. Of over 370 disputes only 84 of the rulings have been appealed, pointing to the effectiveness of the system.
- Membership has expanded to include over 160 nations. Recent additions include China in 2001, Saudi Arabia and Vietnam in 2007, Ukraine in 2008, and the Seychelles in 2015.[38]
- The Aid for Trade initiative, which includes trade-related technical assistance to the poorest countries, has become established as a significant vehicle in several development agencies.[39]
- A study by Arvind Subramanian and Shang-Jin Wei found that the WTO has had a strong positive impact on trade, amounting to about 120% of additional world trade. However, the study concludes that this increase has been uneven, favoring industrialized countries that liberalized more fully over developing countries that have been more hesitant to open borders.[40]

continued

continued

THE DOHA DEVELOPMENT ROUND, EXPOSING WEAKNESS, AND RAISING QUESTIONS ABOUT THE FUTURE

In 2001, members of the WTO met in Doha, Qatar, to begin the fourth round of the WTO trade talks. Today, nearly ten years later, negotiations remain stalled and fruitless. Of principal concern are issues involving the liberalization of agricultural trade and the role and treatment of developing countries. The faltering Doha Round has exposed many of the weaknesses of the WTO, raising questions about its limitations and highlighting the need for the organization to be reformed if it is to be effective and relevant into the twenty-first century. The recent global financial crisis has also exposed the inadequacy of WTO disciplines in areas ranging from government procurement, and antidumping practices to industrial tariffs in developing countries.[41] Discontent with the WTO is not new. In 1999, massive protests disrupted WTO meetings in Seattle as demonstrators accused the organization of being undemocratic, calling out the way in which the rules of global trade were decided behind closed doors by a few elites, and criticizing the WTO for not taking into account the diverse interests of civil society. Furthermore, many argued that the WTO facilitated the commercialization of globalization, favoring corporate interest over governments and common people.

While others are not as critical of the WTO, most can agree that the organization must undergo reform. Critics cite several main areas of concern:

- The difficulty of making consensus decisions with such a large number of members.
- The WTO has failed to work effectively with RTAs, often viewing them as impediments to free trade rather than vehicles to advance trade. Currently, the WTO is increasingly bypassed by unilateral, bilateral, and regional processes, and some suggest that failure of the Doha Round will not bring an end to greater liberalization but simply that liberalization will be done through RTAs.[42]
- While trade policies may be negotiated at the multilateral level, they must be complemented by domestic reform to be effective.
- The WTO does not provide sufficient attention to or oversight of the negative externalities of production and trade, namely, the environmental and social consequences.
- The WTO does not effectively address issues of scarcity in food, energy, and natural resources. Nor does it deal with currency manipulation.
- Some argue that while the world has changed dramatically since the GATT's creation sixty years ago, the WTO has failed to adapt itself to these changes.[43]

WHAT CAN BE DONE?

Critics of the WTO range from those who disagree with the basic principles of free trade on which the WTO is based, to those who propose dramatic reforms, to those who see the need for only minor changes. Some suggest that for the WTO to be effective it must adopt a more flexible approach to trade negotiations, tailored to the needs of individual countries and groups. They argue that the institution must move beyond multilateral, all-or-nothing negotiations that bare little fruit and find ways to leverage opportunities where liberalization is taking place. Others suggest the need for the WTO to rely less on consensus and instead enact decisions based on the agreement of a critical mass of members regarding certain industries or issues. Would this compromise be better than the immobility that plagues the Doha Round? Many also believe that the WTO must be more involved in areas of crucial concern, including food security, international financial regulation in the wake of the global financial crisis, climate change, and labor standards.[44]

Barriers to Trade: Tools of Protectionism

To consider the implications of barriers to trade, let's begin by looking at the effect of trade on a market. The key concept illustrated in the supply and demand curves in Figure 3.3 is that trade allows a market to move beyond the domestic equilibrium, marked as P_{d1} and P_{d2}. With trade, two possibilities emerge. A country may export excess domestic production as in the case of dairy products, or import to meet internal demand as illustrated by a car market. In the first panel, the world price (P_w) for dairy is higher than the domestic equilibrium P_{d1}. At a world price higher than domestic equilibrium price, domestic producers are able to meet domestic demand (marked as Q_1) and supply the international market with exports (Q_2 - Q_1). Producers will only want to sell at the higher world price—reducing the domestic quantity demanded from the initial equilibrium to Q_1. Why sell at home for less, they reason, when they can make more money abroad? The second panel shows the case where the international price (P_w) of small cars is lower than the domestic price (P_{d2}). At this lower price, only the most efficient domestic suppliers can compete, providing Q_3 of small cars; consumer demand is met by imports of Q_4 - Q_3. Note, however, that the consumer wins in that the price of the car is lower than the domestic price due to international competition; we call the additional gain to the buyer the consumer surplus.

With these basic models of supply and demand, let's now explore some of the policy tools at a country's disposal to restrain free trade. Let's continue our investigation of panel 2, when the world price of cars is lower than the domestic price. While consumers have benefitted from the lower price, domestic producers—who would have sold more small cars at P_{d2}—are unhappy at being undercut by global competition. If they are able to lobby politicians for a **tariff**, or a tax on imports, we see that they can retake some of the surplus from the consumer. In Figure 3.4, we impose the tariff to increase the world price to P_{w+t} (we do not go as high as domestic equilibrium). With this higher price, we see that fewer consumers want to

Figure 3.3. Identifying Exporters versus Importers: A Look at the World Price versus the Domestic Price

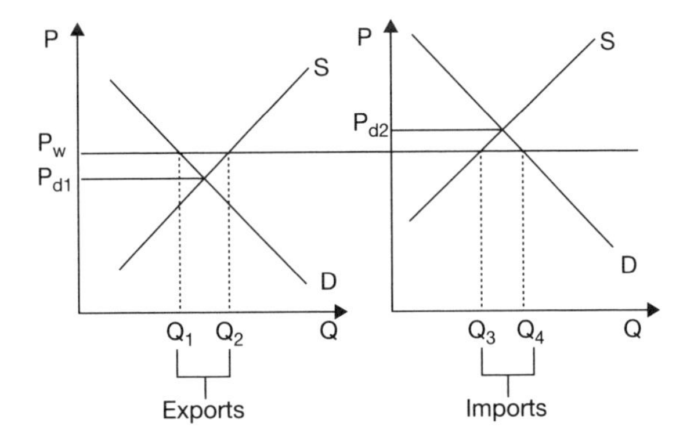

buy small cars, therefore Q_4 falls to Q_5. More domestic suppliers can provide small cars at this higher price, so Q_3 increases to Q_6, decreasing the quantity of imports to the distance Q_6·Q_5. Since the government collects the tariff on these imports, the area labeled G represents the tariff revenue. Note that this comes from the consumer surplus—the extra goods that the consumer could have purchased if the price of small cars were at the lower world price. A tariff transfers value from the consumer to the producer. We can see that the domestic supplier also gets a cut of this surplus—area S on the graph. The two triangles labeled L represent deadweight loss. That is, this area corresponds to the value of the goods the consumer had been able to purchase pre-tariff in addition to the small car when the car sold at the lower world price. This deadweight loss is a key reason why economists tend to be free traders. The value of these goods evaporates as less efficient domestic producers use resources that could be better allocated under free trade. The weight of tariffs in the world economy is one reason for the concerted commitment of governments to open international trade through multilateral talks. But more on that story in a minute. Let's turn now to the tool of protectionism that trade economists find even more damaging to global welfare: the **export subsidy**.

While a domestic tariff hurts national consumers by raising prices, an **export subsidy or a payment to a producer to export** is seen as particularly damaging to producers in other countries. Let's see why. Return to Figure 3.3 and refresh your focus on the first panel of the dairy case where a country is an exporter and the world price is above the initial domestic equilibrium price. Now suppose that these domestic suppliers are able to garner an export subsidy for their good—dairy in our example. This means that the producers are paid a premium—an extra bonus—for exporting. Subsidizing an efficient export may not appear intuitive—why grant a subsidy to a firm already at an advantage price compared to the international market? Wouldn't a subsidy make better sense when your price at home is higher than the world price? Indeed, a subsidy to temporarily support infant industries struggling to achieve international standards was an important policy pursued under import substitution industrialization. But what we want to consider here is the economically illogical case of a lower cost domestic producer gaining privilege largely due to the power of lobbying groups.

Figure 3.4. The Effects of a Tariff on Imported Small Cars

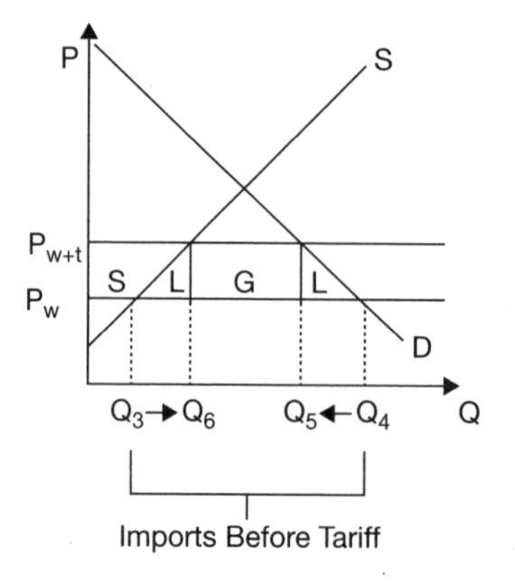

The producer will only sell the good in the home market for what would be received in the international market—the world price plus the subsidy. The logic is simple—why offer something in the domestic market if you can get the same price plus a markup (the subsidy) by selling abroad? This has the unintended effect of pushing domestic prices higher. The price rises in the home market as the firm releases more dairy for export, increasing the domestic price for dairy, as shown in Figure 3.5 panel A and incurring G, government subsidies. As a result, consumers lose areas marked as A and B. Producer surplus increases by A + B + C + D + E. The subsidy costs the government areas B + C + D + E + F. Overall, we see is a net national loss equal to areas B + F.

Now, an especially damaging thing happens. If this is a large country that can influence market prices, the extra dairy exports actually depress global prices. We can see this in panel B of Figure 3.5. As the additional exports from the first frame in this figure enter the world market, represented by the shift in the supply curve, the world price falls. In some cases, subsidies aren't limited to exports—but rather promote production across the board and likewise contribute to the excess supply represented as well in panel B.

If you are a dairy producer in a country that cannot afford export or across the board subsidies, you are driven out of business. The tragedy here is that subsidized rich country producers who may be less efficient are driving poor country producers out of business. This is why the GATT and its later incarnation the WTO have outlawed export subsidies except in special cases. Unfortunately for the developing country producer, these so-called special cases still dominate in many agricultural markets, making it difficult to compete. Politicians see these subsidies as income support for commercial farmers—and their all-important votes. Although policymakers understand the negative global effects, the politics of offending special interests reinforces these illogical trade preferences.

A third type of trade barrier is a **quota** or a limit on the quantity of imports of a given item by requiring a license to import a good or service. As in the case of tariffs, quotas tend to raise the price of the product consumers face; domestic suppliers

Figure 3.5. The Effects of a Subsidy on Exported Dairy Products

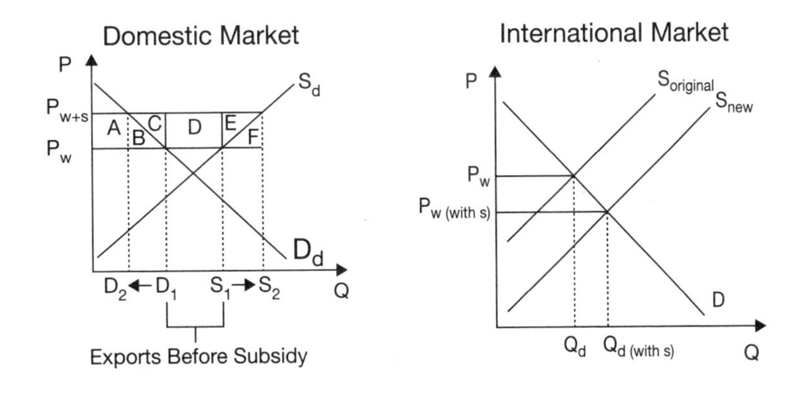

again have more leeway in production to meet the higher price. Figure 3.6 shows the effect of the quota. As an importer, the world price is less than the domestic price, and domestic suppliers provide Q_1. At this low world price, however, domestic buyers want Q_2, with the difference between Q_2 and Q_1 again representing imports. If the government limits the imported quantity in the market to the horizontal distance $Q_3 - Q_4$, this has the effect of raising the price to Pq. At this higher price, domestic firms can supply Q_3 but domestic consumption falls to Q4. As with the tariff, consumers lose L and L', the deadweight loss. In this case, the seller is gaining surplus S through the higher price over the quantitative limit. If the government has auctioned the import permits, it gains G. As you may have noticed, this is the same graph as the tariff. The only difference is the policy instrument: the tariff works by raising the price (which decreases quantity) while the quota restricts quantity (and prices increases to adjust). This is why a tariff and a quota can be seen as equivalent. Economists see quotas as very blunt tools. Since the quota is firmly fixed, even if demand is strong and inelastic, the product cannot be imported. This is in contrast to a tariff; if consumers really want a product, they can have it, albeit with an import tax levied on the consumer.

To decide which companies get to bring in quota-controlled goods, governments may choose to auction **import licenses**. That is, domestic companies that want to purchase a certain good have to pay the government for the right to import. If the quota license is not auctioned, the increase in the price of the import then would accrue to the exporter. This would have the unintended effect of raising revenue for a foreign competitor while trying to protect a domestic producer. Not surprisingly, this revenue could then be reinvested, making the foreign industry even

Figure 3.6. The Effects of Imposing of a Quota

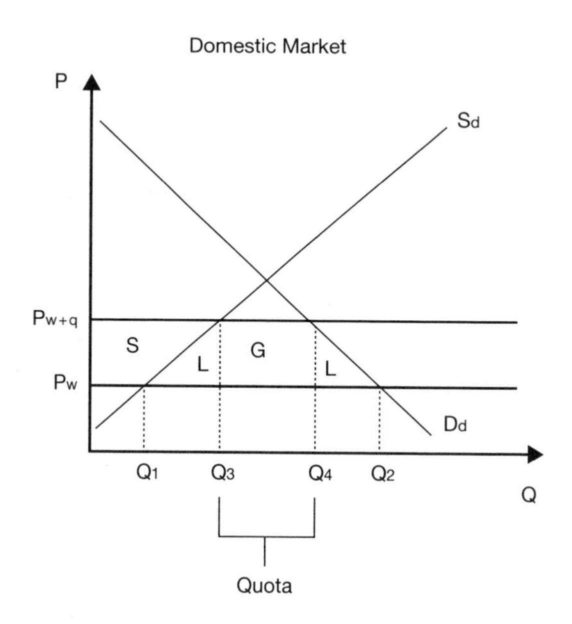

more competitive over time. With some exceptions, quotas are not seen as legal under GATT/WTO rules. Therefore, if a country wants to limit the import of a foreign product, it might ask a trading partner to voluntarily limit exports. Called **voluntary export restraints**, these can give temporary protection to the domestic producer—but the supply shortage will drive the price up with excess profits going to the foreign exporter. This was the case, for example, when back in the 1980s President Reagan wanted to slow the export of small, fuel-efficient cars to the United States. Japanese producers happily complied; as the price of Toyotas and Hondas increased due to the cars' scarcity in the United States, so did the profits of foreign car companies. In a more recent example, Mexico has agreed to restrict exports of automobiles to the Brazilian market; the result may be the same.[45]

Other Trade Barriers: Environment, Health, and Geography

The last type of direct trade interventions falls into the category of "other trade barriers." A government may want to control the import of goods or services that do not comply with national environmental, health or labor standards. It falls within WTO rules, for example, to restrict the import of shrimp that use trawling devices that endanger sea turtles.[46] Due to fears over bovine spongiform encephalopathy (BSE) or "mad cow disease," almost thirty countries impose import restrictions against U.S. live cattle and beef products, restrictions which the Office of the U.S. Trade Representative calls "unwarranted."[47] Sanitary and phytosanitary restrictions such as food safety standards applied to imports are not intrinsically trade measures but can easily be turned into them. These measures are often abused, and are increasingly being used with the deliberate purpose of shielding domestic producers from international competition. It is common that nations introduce such restrictions not to prevent health hazards on the basis of scientific evidence, but in response to public activism from interested parties. It is in recognition of this that sanitary and phytosanitary restrictions are high on the agenda of trade negotiations.

A current debate in trade policy is the use of protectionist tools as a mechanism to counteract poor environmental and labor practices. Some argue that retaliatory measures should be lodged against countries with lax environmental standards or weak labor protection as this unfairly lowers the cost of production. If a manufacturer of toys in the United States, for example, must meet more stringent pollution standards and provide safer working conditions than a Chinese producer, this will reflect a higher cost unrelated to comparative advantage. To counteract advantages obtained through lower environmental standards, the U.S. Congress is considering carbon tariffs against Chinese imports. Arguments for environmental and labor protectionism are, however, complicated by questions of sovereignty. A developing country may decide its scarce resources are better targeted toward providing education for children than meeting pollution standards. Others contend that jobs—even unsafe ones—in developing countries are more important in providing livelihoods than regulations that might decrease employment. We will return to some of these dilemmas regarding workers in our chapter on the globalization of labor and capital.

Protectionism versus Free Trade in Practice: Why Implement Protectionist Measures?

We can see that there are important economic costs to our three direct tools of protectionism: tariffs, quotas, and subsidies. Tariffs and quotas hurt domestic consumers and subsidies can be especially detrimental to small producers in poor countries. Why, then, employ protectionism tools? Trade, as we noted earlier, creates losers as well as winners. The winners are most often the consumers enjoying lower-priced goods, while the losers tend to be displaced workers or industries losing market share to foreign competition. The losers—most often in a concentrated location such as a steel factory in Pittsburgh or an auto company in Detroit—are better equipped to petition for protection from the government as compared to the many geographically dispersed users of steel or buyers of autos.

It makes political sense for a government to protect its workers against market changes. Although there is logic to importing the least cost product, it takes time to retrain and often relocate workers. Imagine, for example, the effect of rapid changes in aquaculture when six new shrimp producers, including Vietnam and India, made it difficult for U.S. shrimp farmers to quickly adjust. The United States alleged that international producers were selling shrimp in the U.S. market below national prices, and slapped a countervailing duty of approximately 10% on certain imported shrimp in 2004. Upon review five years later, the levy was reduced to just 0.8%.[48] In response to its rapidly appreciating currency, Brazil is assessing a 30% tariff on imported cars.[49] Indeed, the WTO allows for such temporary protection against documented import surges to permit adjustment in local markets.

Another reason for protectionism goes to the core of the free-trade model. Perhaps you were somewhat frustrated with the static nature of comparative advantage as a theory. That is, the model takes as its starting point relative efficiencies based upon endowments and costs without explaining *how* these efficiencies came to be. Students of international political economy might quickly question just how England came to be a better producer of machinery compared to most of its colonies. Powerful countries have both exploited resources and prevented poorer nations from acquiring key technologies to grow. In response, many developing countries imposed tariffs on key or "bedrock" industries deemed central to growth. For example, Brazil levied significant tariffs across a variety of industries in the 1960s through 1980s to promote the development of infant industries. One successful case was the protection offered to its domestic aircraft industry, giving rise to the highly competitive Embraer, producer of regional jets. A tariff of 100% was placed on imports of planes; Piper, a U.S. company was exempted as it agreed to work with Brazilians to build aircraft there. However, import substitution can be an expensive strategy. While tariffs are levied on imports to allow the domestic development of the sector, lack of international competition means that local prices are then likely high or domestic quality low. For instance, the Brazilian computer sector did not share the success of the aircraft industry, instead raising the cost of electronic information systems to businesses and making these user sectors less competitive. Smaller countries such as neighboring Argentina experienced even greater difficulties as their small internal markets limited economies of scale. Multinationals were less willing to set up production lines if the output was small. Import substitution industrialization was widely adopted from the 1950s through the late 1970s in the developing world. Ironically, in most cases import substitution called at first for an import surge. Firms needed intermediate capital—machines—to produce planes or computers. This initial increase in imports was expensive, leading in many countries to increase external debt, a topic we'll consider in our chapter on international finance.

Beyond promoting domestic industries, countries may also choose protectionist measures as retaliation against another nation's unfair trade practices. These practices might involve the direct subsidization of exports or perhaps a currency manipulation that makes the price of exports artificially cheap. In March 2010, Brazil threatened to impose WTO authorized trade sanctions after it won a 2002 case against Washington over cotton subsidies. The case was settled in 2014 with the United States agreeing to make a onetime final payment of $300 million to the Brazil Cotton Institute (BCI). In 2009, Mexico took similar actions after the United States failed to allow Mexican trucks to operate in the United States in compliance with the North American Free Trade Agreement (NAFTA).[50] The granddaddy of all trading disputes continues between the United States and Canada over lumber entering the United States from its northern neighbor. At the root of this complex dispute is the U.S. claim that Canadian wood exports are being unfairly subsidized by the government.[51] In each case, protectionism was the result of the perception of an unfair playing field.

If a company exports a product at a price lower than the price it normally charges on its own home market, it is said to be "**dumping**" the product. Is dumping unfair competition? The WTO does not pass judgment. Its focus is on how governments can or cannot react to dumping—it disciplines anti-dumping actions, through the "Anti-dumping Agreement." China and the United States were on the brink of a trade war over alleged dumping of tires, with each country retaliating against the other by imposing import tariffs. In response to union petitions over the loss of more than 8,000 jobs allegedly due to dumping, the U.S. International Trade Commission (USITC) launched an investigation into tire pricing. To prove dumping, it has to be shown that companies are selling below the exporter's home market price. But how should goods be valued in China when market prices aren't operative? The USITC ruled in favor of the workers, pointing to the 215% increase in the volume of tire imports and the 295% rise in the value from 2004 to 2008.[52] In September of 2009, President Obama announced a 35% tariff on all tire imports from China after the United Steelworkers claimed a surge in cheap Chinese imports was costing thousands of Americans their jobs.[53]

In response, China imposed anti-dumping tariffs of between 43.1% and 80.5% on U.S. imports of chicken parts, particularly feet, after a February investigation found chicken products were being sold in China for an unfairly reduced price.[54] While in the United States chicken feet tend to be ground into animal feed, in China they are considered a delicacy. U.S. exporters have no trouble selling cheap in China as feet typically go for $0.60–0.80 on the Chinese market, but are worth pennies in the United States.[55] What is the value of chicken feet in the United States when there really is not a domestic market for them? Clearly U.S. chicken feet sold in China are being purchased at below the U.S. market price—a conflicted case of dumping. While the new tariffs will not have much effect on the flow of goods between China and the United States, the dispute is symbolic of tense trade relations between the two economic powers. Many of the recent trade disputes between the United States and China stem from the fact that the United States believes the renminbi is undervalued, allowing the Chinese economy to benefit from cheap exports. We'll return back to this question of currency valuations and currency wars in our next chapter.

National security is often invoked as another reason to protect domestic industry. Certain sectors may be deemed critical to national security and protected in the event of war. This argument has been applied, for example, to protecting aircraft producers to maintain capacity. Clearly the experience of World War II reminds strategists of the need for autonomous production of aircraft and transport vehicles. The problem of course is that today's strategic environment is far different from that period of total engagement; it is also more likely that an alternate supplier could be located. The World War I argument that shoe makers should be protected to avoid trench foot in war appears absurd in an age of drone warfare.

Murky Protectionism

The global financial crisis highlighted new tensions between the efficiencies of free trade and the desire to protect national industry and workers. Not surprisingly voters like to see stimulus tax dollars spent at home—even if it means consumer prices go up. In 2009, as part of his $787 billion stimulus package, President Obama unleashed a "Buy American" campaign to help keep stimulus dollars circulating and rebuilding the suffering economy. The crisis has also changed the role of government in the market. As nation-states play a more active role in the economy, supporting national enterprises began to trump promoting free trade. The government was later pressured to water down the proposal after key trading partners accused the United States of implementing protectionist policies by preferencing national over imported goods; they argued this would further damage economies around the world. But other governments also introduced stimulus measures with preferences for national firms. Although not a tariff, quota, or subsidy, these political preferences for national firms constitute a kind of "murky" protectionism.

But global supply chains complicate the problem. Consider Duferco Corporation, a Swiss Russian partnership that took over a bankrupt steel plant near Pittsburgh back in the 1990s. It employs 600 American workers to make coils using imported steel slabs not sold commercially in the United States. As a non-American company using imported parts, Duferco Corporation did not meet the criteria under the U.S. Economic Recovery public works projects. Duferco had to furlough 80% of its workforce—600 United States steel workers.[56] The policy was intended to protect steel slab workers; but this rendered U.S. coil workers employer by a foreign company uncompetitive and therefore unemployed. Evaluating whether job protection is in the best interest of workers should include an assessment of not only the direct jobs protected but also the indirect jobs that might be lost due to higher prices for imported components. It should also include the possibility of retaliation by trading partners.[57] Trade retaliation could hurt President Obama's ambitious trade objectives for the United States. His "National Export Initiative" has a goal of doubling American exports over the next four years, to create jobs and reduce the U.S. trade deficit.[58] Retaliation by trading partners could severely limit this ambitious expansion into the global marketplace.

Persistent trade imbalances also prompt protectionist policies. The WTO has addressed over 400 trade disputes since its inception in 1995, while its predecessor, the GATT, handled 100 during its fifty years of oversight.[59] With the growing scale of trade, intra-country imbalances are at unprecedented levels. Although falling since 2011, the much-maligned deficit in exports of goods between the United States and China still hovered at billion USD as of April 2012.[60] Other countries such as Brazil, Argentina, and Russia have sought to protect hard fought gains in industrialization from rapidly changing price advantages by new emerging markets entering the global ladder of production. In contrast, other countries including Chile and Mexico have unilaterally embraced tariff-free movement of goods.[61] In response to slow growth in export markets following the global financial crisis, there was a 36% increase in protectionist measures in 2010 and 2011.[62] The bulk of these measures were implemented by industrial countries and dodged constraining WTO rules with forms of murky protectionism.[63] Discriminatory measures not subject to WTO sanctions included preferential bailouts, state aid, and nontariff barriers. Trade policy activists—countries such as Brazil, India, and Russia—combined protectionist tools with other liberalizing measures.[64] Countries that are members of free-trade agreements (FTAs)—including Mexico (the NAFTA) and Turkey (a customs union with the EU) refrained from trade restricting measures.[65] Countries integrally woven into value chains also showed moderation in trade restrictions while those more distant from supply chain production such as Brazil and Argentina evidenced more activity.

Costs of Protection: Consumers and Intermediate Producers Pay

Whether applied in the interest of labor, industry, environment or national security, protectionism has a price. Consider the example of how sweet governmental sugar subsidies create sour outcomes. Americans pay between two and four times the world price of sugar largely due to quota restrictions.[66] Prior to quotas, sugar imports made up nearly half the U.S. market; today less than 15% is imported, costing the consumer approximately $1.9 billion dollars annually. U.S. sugar is also subsidized. One might feel better about this outlay if it were helping struggling small farmers, but 42% of U.S. subsidies go to just 1% of the growers. Because sugar is an input into candy and cookies, on a net basis, more jobs have been lost than saved through these sweet restrictions. Some food processing companies have been forced to move production out of the United States. For example, Kraft relocated its candy lifesaver factory from Holland, Michigan to Montreal, Canada to take advantage of sugar at half the price. For each growing and harvesting job saved through agricultural protection, three confectionary jobs were lost.

Europe addresses competition from cheaper sugar on the global market by subsidizing it domestically to the tune of €1.25 billion a year. Sugar is most efficiently produced in warm, sunny climates; yet European subsidies so distort incentives that Finland—not exactly replete with the natural comparative advantage of long hot growing seasons—produces sugar.[67] Sugar producers on both sides of the Atlantic don't want to part with preferences for fear of being at a disadvantage. Consumers pay not only for the subsidization of domestic industries but also for the taxation of imports through higher prices for their cakes and candies. Canadians pay roughly $3.4 billion (CAD) in customs tariffs each year. For example, a Toronto resident who buys $187 worth of clothing from L.L. Bean through a catalog order will end up paying a final bill of $233, once customs duties and additional taxes are added. All in all, Canadians give up hundreds of millions of dollars each year in protective tariffs on clothing, agricultural imports, shoes, certain metal products, and anti-dumping fees on steel imports.

Downstream losses due to protecting upstream sectors are also apparent in steel. The importance of steel-using industries in the United States is greater than that of steel producing industries. One estimate suggests that downstream or user industries pay about 2.7 billion more in higher steel costs due to limited supply and lack of competition—or it forks out $450,000 per upstream job saved.[68] Subsidies provided by the United States, China, Greece, and Spain to their cotton farmers in 2002 reached six billion dollars—an amount equal to the world exports in cotton that year.[69] When the U.S. imposed tariffs on Chinese tires in 2009, U.S. consumers bore the cost as many retailers increased tire prices by 3–8%.[70] Policymakers must also worry about the costs of retaliation. If restrictive trade instruments are used, it is likely that trading partners will respond in kind. One in five American jobs is tied to exports; retaliation will affect the export sector. The fear of free traders is that protectionism begets more protectionism—meaning costs will rise and efficiencies will fall for all.

Reversing Protectionism and Leveling the Playing Field: The Road to Doha

Although protective measures may preserve jobs and stem industrial loss in key sectors, protectionism can generate overall losses, including higher consumer prices, hampered access to inputs for production, less dynamic supply chains, inferior technology, decreasing competition in markets, and the slower transfer of knowledge tied to trade. In contrast, free trade returns a surplus to the consumer. Combined with lowered costs of transportation and telecommunications, economists Hufbauer and Grieco calculate that the average American household enjoys an income gain of roughly $10,000 a year from commercial liberalization.[71] They estimate that further liberalization could yield an additional $5,000 per household for a total increase in U.S. income of $500 billion. Table 3.4 shows estimates by various economists for the gains from trade. Although the Hufbauer Grieco calculation is at the upper end of positive impacts of trade liberalization, it does suggest that opening brings with it potential gains. What, then, are the viable steps to capture this gain while minimizing losses?

Table 3.4. Impacts of Trade Liberalization on World GDP

Study	*Scenario*	*Gains ($U.S. billions)*
Shakur, Rae, and Chatterjee (2002)	100% liberalization of Agriculture and Manufacturing tariffs plus elimination of all subsidies (Static)	82
OECD (2003)	100% reduction by OECD, and reduction by non-OECD to 5% max (Static)	98 (LDC[a] 27)
Lippoldt and Kowalski (2003)	100% reduction in Agriculture and Manufacturing plus trade facilitation (Static)	173 (LDC 80)
Hertel et al. (2000)	40% cut on protection of goods and services (Static)	130 (LDC 85)
Anderson et al. (2002)	Full pre Uruguay Round liberalization of goods (Static)	254 (LDC 108)
Francois (2001)	50% cut in pre Uruguay Round trade barriers and 1% decrease in trade costs (Static)	(LDC 138–191)
World Bank (2004)	Elimination of trade barriers (Static)	291 (LDC 59)
World Bank (2002)	Elimination of all trade barriers by 2015 (Static)	355 (LDC 184)
Dee and Hanslow (2000)	100% reduction in Agriculture and Manufacturing (Static)	133
Francois, van Meijl, and van Tongeren (2003)	Full liberalization of goods and services (Static)	367 (LDC 113)
Brown et al. (2002)	33% cut in tariffs on goods (Static)	163 (LDC 50)
World Bank (2004)	Agriculture and Manufacturing cut (Dynamic)	518 (LDC 349)
World Bank (2002)	Full liberalization of goods trade (Dynamic)	832 (LDC 539)
OECD (2003)	100% reduction by OECD, and reduction by non-OECD to 5% max (Dynamic)	1,212 (LDC 459)
OEF (2005)	100% decrease in restrictions on global goods trade	1,200

Source: Julian Morris, "Just Trade: The Moral Imperative of Eliminating Barriers to Trade." *International Policy Network*, 2005.
a Less developed country.

Multilateral Mechanisms

Trade liberalization is ideally negotiated in a multilateral setting. Of course a country could unilaterally choose to reduce trade barriers—but in doing so a nation may open itself to domestic opposition. Recall that American sugar producers don't want to concede subsidies unless Europeans also forfeit domestic support—but joint implementation may be amenable to all. The history of multilateral negotiations has been one of garnering mutual concessions. This reciprocal process, originally centered in the GATT, promoted the reduction of U.S. tariffs from 40% in 1947 to 3% by 2008.[72] Successive rounds of the GATT—the Kennedy Round, the Tokyo Round, and the Uruguay Round—addressed tariffs, quotas, trade in services, and other non-tariff barriers. Two key principles embodied in the GATT and now the WTO are the **most favored nation (MFN)** concept as well as **national treatment**. MFN sets the standard that, with the exception of specifically negotiated trade agreements, treatment given to one member must be extended to all. If France and Canada lower tariffs on perfumes, this increased access must be given to all member countries. National treatment restricts governments from treating foreign goods within a country differently from national products.[73] The GATT also established the standard that quotas were especially trade distorting, although exceptions were granted for agriculture and textiles.

The WTO, founded in 1995 upon the GATT codes, institutionalized the trade negotiation process and provided a mechanism for redress from violations of international trade law. As was explained earlier in Box 3.1, the WTO, unlike the GATT, provides a dispute settlement mechanism and appeal procedure that allow less powerful developing countries an avenue to contest policies in the industrial center. Prior to the dispute mechanism, smaller countries had a harder time making concerns heard. Important advances have been made in trade in services, which now comprise 20% of all trade, through the General Agreement on Trade in Services (GATS). Contentious issues remain, however, as developed countries want to restrain the movement of human capital, and developing countries hope to protect their latitude to use intellectual capital at a low cost. The 1994 TRIPS agreement—the **Trade-Related Aspects of Intellectual Property**—sets the framework for the protection of copyrights, trademarks, geographical indications (think Champagne versus sparkling wine), industrial designs, patents, and layout designs of integrated circuits. Especially contentious within TRIPS is the question of pharmaceutical patents. Tradeoffs between the ethics of universal access to best medicines confront the need to promote incentives to continue investment in costly drug research, prompting particularly thorny debates. Another controversial area is trade and the environment. As no international body exists to sanction poor environmental stewardship, some advocate turning to WTO trade sanctions for violations involving international commerce. Others, however, worry that the WTO already stretches its institutional capacity in addressing trade conflicts, and should steer away from taking up questions such as global warming or rainforest destruction.

Doha, the current round now institutionally lodged in the WTO, is tackling some of the toughest residual problems—historical preferences maintained in agriculture and non-agricultural market access (NAMA) that frame the tensions between the rich and poor world. Dubbed the **Doha Development Agenda (DDA) or the Doha Development Round**, the negotiations focus on bringing developing nations more fully into the trading arena by allowing them to exercise comparative advantage in areas such as food and textiles that the richer world has securely protected. An analysis by the Peterson Institute for International Economics claims that concluding the Doha Round could boost global exports by as much as $180 billion to $520 billion annually, and increase world GDP by $300 billion to $700 billion each year.[74] However, now the longest running round, negotiations are stymied by the large number of participating countries with diverse interests. Earlier rounds were reciprocal bargains between a limited numbers of relatively wealthy countries. Doha, in contrast, engages the divergent agendas of the 155 members of the WTO. The framing document specifically creates the principle of "special and differential treatment" for least developed economies. Emerging economies such as Brazil, India, and China have gained enormous clout—but even their interests differ. The United States and the EU remain deadlocked over agricultural policy, neither wanting to budge until the other reduces farmer support. Despite an agreement in principle that export subsidies are critically harmful, the transatlantic tussle remains over the magnitude of reductions, how certain products might be exempt from formula cuts, and the defining baseline year.[75] In September of 2009, G-20 members pledged to "seek an ambitious and balanced conclusion" to the Doha Round by 2010.[76] Yet, pledges to cut protectionist measures have been largely hollow as countries still recovering from the recent global crisis seek to reduce high unemployment rates and save flailing domestic industries.[77] Furthermore, while estimates of liberalization forecast significant gains, the distribution of these gains is skewed toward a few big countries, provoking further disagreement among G-20 members.[78] As of 2015, trade talks remain at an impasse; many analysts refer to the quiet death of Doha. Critics suggest that the global trading system is in need of greater overhaul than Doha offers.[79] It was launched when China, Brazil, and India were just opening; critics contend it is a negotiation for a past era. Issues such as the effect of trade on labor practices, food supply, and the environment are largely outside this round of negotiations. Weak international institutions to promote standards in labor, food, and the environment make their trade nexus an important entry point for debate. Detractors contend that Doha falls short because it lacks effective means of binding countries to agree upon trade policies.[80]

The Role of RTAs: Road or Detour from Doha?

With formidable roadblocks in the road to Doha, nations have been engaging in **preferential trading agreements (PTAs)**. PTAs, sometimes called regional trade agreements (RTAs) or FTAs, provide a framework for trade opening negotiated on a limited scale. With fewer parties at the table, national interests are more easily navigated. PTAs are the least restrictive of the trade agreements; in this form countries reduce but do not eliminate restrictions. A free-trade area eliminates restrictions on trade between the partners, but does not adopt a **common external tariff (CET)**. The existence of a CET defines a customs union, the stage before a common market that also allows the free movement of labor and capital among members. In reality, the categories may blur; Mercosur, a RTA initially formed by Brazil, Argentina, Paraguay, and Uruguay has attracted other associate partners such as Chile. It aspires to a CET and regional investment strategies, as seen in the EU, but weak financing for the institutions to accompany trade deepening has prevented the organization from achieving its full potential. As of 2015, the WTO records 619 notifications of RTAs; 413

were in approved by the signatories and in force.[81] Table 3.5 provides detailed examples of preferential agreements, highlighting both potential gains and current challenges. Box 3.2 explores the purpose, promises, and performance of the NAFTA in greater depth.

Do RTAs promote or divert from free trade? In part, the answer to this question depends on the implementation of **rules of origin** and a country's trade profile. Rules of origin stipulate a percent of value added by a country to qualify for tariff benefits. Under NAFTA, for example, strict rules of origin prevent a Korean company from setting up a shell business across the Texas border to gain preferential access to the United States. However, strict rules of origin can be trade diverting. If a U.S. firm should, according to the standard of comparative advantage, buy from a Korean firm but instead purchases a lower tariffed Mexican export, this diverts from the principle of efficient trade. RTAs can also impose significant administrative costs. For example, there are more than forty trade agreements involving Central and South America. The burden of knowing the trade law in each instance falls especially hard on small- and medium-sized enterprises without large legal departments to navigate the restrictions. Jagdish Bhagwati has dubbed this the "spaghetti bowl" of RTAs—the entanglements of trade that are just plain messy. Others, however, argue that RTAs are a sound step toward greater openness. Without roadblocks in the Doha process, RTAs can provide important access to markets and technology. Certainly, the experience of the EU stands as an example of the benefits of economies of scale and open market access to growth.

Opening Alone Won't Do It: TAA and Aid for Trade

Although trade may make a country richer, theory doesn't predict that it will always be good for every citizen; Ricardo suggested that the gains from trade exceeded the losses, not that trade didn't have costs. Indeed, as we noted when discussing factor price equalization, in a capital rich country, workers lose, creating demand for protection. Trade with low-wage countries may decrease the wages in a rich country for those without a college degree by 4%.[82] Rather than compound the worker's loss with the consumer's loss of surplus, a country might consider an alternative policy: help the workers move from a sector where advantage is declining to one where it is rising. But moving labor from a dying to a rising sector is tricky. Programs such as **trade adjustment assistance** (TAA) in the United States help move displaced workers from low-end competition to higher value-added jobs when the layoff can be documented to be caused by a surge in imports or shift in production to another country. The U.S. TAA program is targeted first at income and health care support, providing 78 weeks of income maintenance plus 26 weeks of unemployment if the displaced worker is involved in training, a health coverage tax credit covering 65% of the cost of maintaining health care while in transition, and wage insurance for those over fifty to cover the gap between old and new wages subject to a cap of $10,000 over a two-year period. Beyond temporary support, the program also provides incentives to reenter the workforce by covering retraining expenses, 90% of job search expenses (up to $1,250), and 90% of the cost of job relocation (up to the limit of $1,500). To qualify for TAA, recipients must enroll in school.

Table 3.5. Examples of Regional Integration

Agreement	*What Is It?*	*Benefits*	*Challenges of Integration*
South Korea-U.S. Free Trade Agreement (KORUS)	Approved by both the U.S. and South Korea in 2011, KORUS is the U.S.'s second largest free-trade agreement after NAFTA and is Korea's largest. The deal eliminates tariffs on 95% of trade between the two countries within three years of implementation, with virtually all the remaining tariffs being removed within 10 years. The FTA also contains chapters that address non-tariff measures in investment, intellectual property, services, competition policy, and other areas.	The U.S. International Trade Commission estimates that the agreement could boost U.S. exports to South Korea by $10 billion, while Korean exports to the U.S. would increase by around $6 billion. The agreement is expected to increase South Korea's GDP by between 0.4% and 2.4%.[83] In the U.S. annual GDP, gains are expected to be around a more modest $11 billion.	Beef producers in the United States are unhappy with Korean restrictions on imports due to safety concerns.[84] Koreans worry that the FTA adversely affects Korean agriculture and aquaculture and increases prices on pharmaceuticals due to stricter enforcement of intellectual property rights. Both countries fear inadequate transparency, deficient environmental and labor standards, and domestic job loss. U.S. opponents of the agreement allege the deal will cost tens of thousands of jobs in the auto industry. The Korea Rural Economic Institute predicts that increases in U.S. agricultural exports could cost up to 130,000 South Korean jobs.[85] In 2006 and 2007 protests were held in Korea against the agreement, including a nation-wide protest in November 2006 drawing 65,000 to 80,000 people.

continued

Table 3.5 Examples of Regional Integration (Continued)

Agreement	*What Is It?*	*Benefits*	*Challenges of Integration*
African Free Trade Zone (AFTZ)	Implemented in 2008, The Africa Free Trade Zone brings together three regional trade blocs (The Southern African Development Community—SADC, the East African Community—EAC, and the Common Market for Eastern and Southern Africa—COMESA), making a total of 26 members. The AFTZ consists of almost half of African countries (26 out of 54), more than half of the production, trade, population, land mass, and resources of the continent. The AFTZ is seen as a preliminary step to further integrate Africa by eventually establishing a common market, a single currency, full mobility of the factors of production, as well as free movement of goods and services among African countries.	As Ugandan President Yoweri Museveni stated in 2008, "The greatest enemy of Africa, the greatest source of weakness has been disunity and a low level of political and economic integration."[86] Leaders in member countries hope the AFTZ will address these separations through unifying multiple regional groups, increasing intra-regional trade, and bestowing them a stronger voice internationally in favor of a more equitable global trade regime sensitive to concerns of developing countries.	The AFTZ faces the difficult challenge of integrating the economies of member countries plagued by war, pervasive corruption, and refugee crises, such as in the Sudan, the Congo, and Zimbabwe.

European Union (EU)	Beginning formally in 1992, the EU is the most tightly united regional entity in the world, integrating 27 nations. Member states have implemented a standardized system of laws, maintain common trade policies with non-member countries, and ensure the free movement of goods, services, capital and people, even eliminating passport controls between member countries. A CET applies to all goods and services entering the EU and countries are prohibited from applying further quotas or customs duties on goods once they are circulating internally. Created in 1999 with circulation beginning in 2002, sixteen member states have since adopted the euro as their common currency. With a GDP of over $16 trillion, the EU accounts for roughly 21% of global PPP GDP.[87]	The EU allows for the development of economies of scale as well as provides a better regulatory climate for businesses that no longer need to deal with legal systems of different nations. Controlling competition between companies is an area where the EU is particularly powerful. The EU's control over competition policy gives it the power to rule on mergers, takeovers, cartels, and the use of state aid. European consumers benefit from a greater range of products and services and lower prices. Public procurement is enhanced, accounting for 16.3% of the EU's GDP.[88] In addition, higher labor and environmental standards have become the norm across Europe as all members must meet certain criteria in order to join.	Tensions have arisen within the EU over member state sovereignty, including disagreement over economic governance. Members of the Eurozone must abide by the monetary policy set by the traditionally inflation-adverse European Central Bank (ECB). Furthermore, fiscal policies of members are constrained by the Growth and Stability Pact (GSP) which places limits on annual budget deficits and the permitted size of national debt. The GSP has been criticized for being too flexible, too rigid, and inconsistently applied. Tensions have also arisen due to the differences in levels of development of member countries, particularly after recent expansion of the EU into Eastern Europe. Differences also arise over the nature of EU representation in international institutions, as well as a high level of disconnect between the EU Parliament and the European population.

continued

Table 3.5 Examples of Regional Integration (Continued)

Agreement	*What Is It?*	*Benefits*	*Challenges of Integration*
Association of Southeast Asian Nations (ASEAN)	Formed in 1967, ASEAN is both an economic and geo-political organization composed of ten Southeast Asian countries. Economic integration was extended in 1993 with the creation of the ASEAN free trade area (AFTA). Members of AFTA uphold a Common Effective Preferential Tariff (CEPT) which consists of a schedule of preferential tariff reductions on goods originating within the ASEAN. AFTA hopes to achieve zero tariff rates on virtually all goods by 2010 for original signatories and 2015 for newer members. The removal of non-tariff barriers (like quantitative restrictions) is scheduled to be completed by 2015 or 2018 on the path toward an ASEAN Economic Community which would tie members together in a single market.	A study by the World Bank found that the formation of the AFTA has had a positive impact on trade flows among members of ASEAN, without adverse effects for non-member states.[89] The study concludes that an important reason for this positive effect is the unilateral reductions in external tariffs that ASEAN members implemented as a result of their liberalization vis-à-vis each other. In this sense, the authors claim, AFTA has been beneficial for the promotion of free world trade. FDI in the region has increased from US$18 billion in 2002 to over US$61 billion in 2007. The average CEPT rate for trade in goods has decreased in the initial six member states from 13% in 1993 to just 0.79% in 2008.[90] In 2008, ASEAN's GDP reached more than US$1.5 trillion.[91]	ASEAN struggles to address the wide development disparities between (as well as within) its member countries, a condition which impedes the area's future as an integrated region. The GDP per capita and labor productivity of the poorer countries like Cambodia, the Lao People's Democratic Republic, Burma, and Viet Nam is a tenth of Singapore's levels.[92] The ASEAN's policy of non-interference (and the definition of the term itself) in member countries' internal affairs has been criticized for restricting the ability of the Association to combat poor environmental practices and human rights abuses in member countries. Poor infrastructure also limits ASEAN trade. The World Bank estimates that improving port facilities alone could expand trade by up to 7.5% or $22 billion.[93] Other scholars criticize the consensus model of the ASEAN saying it leads to lowest common denominator policies and restricts innovation and efficiency.

Box 3.2. North American Free Trade Agreement (NAFTA) by Tara Brian

You may know that Canada and Mexico are the largest trading partners of the United States, following China.[94] All in all, the two U.S. neighbors account for roughly 30% of total U.S. trade in goods.[95] In part, the enormous volume of goods and services that circulates within North America's borders is the result of NAFTA, enacted by Canada, Mexico, and the United States in 1994. The signing of NAFTA created one of the world's largest free-trade areas, which today links over 477 million people has a combined GDP of roughly $20 trillion.[96] In addition to being the largest of its kind, the agreement was the first major free-trade accord between advanced industrialized countries and a large developing country, with Mexico's gross national income per capita less than one-fifth that of the United States in 2015.[97] NAFTA countries agreed to eliminate traffic on 99% of internally traded goods within ten years and have pursued measures to liberalize foreign direct investment, services, and intellectual property rules. In January 2008, all final agricultural tariffs and quotas were phased out. Today NAFTA supports over thirty working groups and committees as well as intergovernmental bodies to oversee issues of trade in goods, rules of origin, customs, agricultural trade and subsidies, environmental and labor standards, government procurement, and alternative dispute resolution.[98]

NAFTA began in the midst of controversy about its potential impacts, and today its results remain contested. When NAFTA was enacted, the hope was that reduced trade barriers would promote efficiency and accelerate trade and investment in the region. This surge in trade and investment was to generate employment and growth and, in the long run, facilitate wage and regulatory convergence among the three parties.[99] Yet, while official government sources of all three countries proclaim NAFTA's benefits, 22 years after its creation many policy makers, scholars, and citizens groups accuse the agreement of failing to meet promises of equitable growth and contend that instead of promoting a convergence of incomes, wages, and standards, NAFTA has tended to accentuate pre-existing economic and regulatory asymmetries between member countries.[100]

Most can agree that NAFTA has succeeded in increasing flows of trade and investment. U.S. imports from Mexico increased by over 630% from 1993 to 2014, merchandise trade between Canada and Mexico increased eight-fold from 1993 to 2015,[101] and trade between the United States and its NAFTA partners has more than tripled.[102] Cross-border investment has surged in the region as well, with changes particularly evident in Mexico which saw the stock of U.S. foreign direct investment (FDI) in the country increase by 564% between 1993 and 2013.[103]

Despite these promising trends, critics of the agreement argue that investment and trade alone are not enough to promote meaningful economic development that will benefit the entire population of the region. They propose revising NAFTA to deal effectively with the vast asymmetries between participating countries and better address issues of environment, labor, services, investment, agriculture, and migration.[104]

Several areas have raised particular concern. For one, critics argue that governments need more authority to regulate trade effectively in areas concerning the protection of human, animal and plant health, and in the conservation of natural resources. While trade in goods can be restricted for reasons such as harm to exhaustible resources or human and animal health, service trade can only be restricted if such an action is necessary to comply with measures consistent with NAFTA. For instance, in order to stimulate the development of renewable resources, twenty-eight U.S. states have signed on the meet Renewable Portfolio Standards (RPS), which excludes hydroelectric energy from dams greater than 30 megawatts, one of Canada's primary exports to the United States. The Canadian trade ministry claims that RPS laws violate national treatment, the principle that

continued

continued

Canadian hydroelectric energy is not given the same treatment as hydroelectric energy generated in the United States. While the United States could produce several arguments to show how energy from large dams is more harmful to ecosystems than is energy from small dams (for example, large dams stop salmon migration, and concentrate toxins), the government cannot invoke an exception to limit imports of Canadian energy because RPS programs do not enforce another NAFTA-consistent measure, as the exception requires. Some policy makers recommend that services and goods should be given parallel exceptions for legitimate policy objectives.

On a similar note, citizen groups in all three-member countries have expressed great concern over Chapter 11 of NAFTA which grants foreign investors the right to sue governments for actions and policies deemed to be discriminatory, or "tantamount to expropriation," by impeding their profits. This has resulted in threats and actual suits against governments for implementing policies intended to protect the environment or consumer and employee health. One case concerning *Ethyl* is particularly illustrative. Faced by a NAFTA claim, the Canadian government withdrew its restrictions on a gasoline additive called MMT after studies had shown that burning MMT posed an unacceptable risk of nerve and brain damage to humans. The restrictions on MMT were withdrawn after a NAFTA tribunal allowed the manufacturer of the additive to bring its claim under Chapter 11. Besides withdrawing its regulation, the Canadian government also agreed to issue a statement that MMT did not pose a health threat and consented to paying millions in compensation to the manufacturer.[105] Chapter 11 also places limits on the use of capital controls which restricts governments' freedom to manage financial crises and performance requirements. Critics of NAFTA also raise questions of labor and environmental standards and some are concerned about falling competitiveness of North America's manufacturing sector in comparison with China.

Agricultural trade has increased in the region, with exports from the U.S. tripling to Canada and quadrupling to Mexico by NAFTA's 20-year anniversary.[106] However, small farmers in all three countries have suffered and critics argue that NAFTA has altered the relative size and power of the players, helping agri-business such as Cargill and Monsanto, while hurting family farms. According to the National Farmers Union, over 16% of Canadian farmers have been forced off their land,[107] and research suggests almost two million small-scale Mexican farmers were put out of work between 1991 and 2007.[108] Also impacted by the Farm Bill of 1996 and additional factors, a similar story exists in the United States, where farm production has continued to shift to larger scale operations while small commercials farms have seen their share of sales decline.[109] Comparative advantage has altered the structure of agricultural trade, with Mexican exports of fruits and vegetables risings and U.S. exports of grains and animal products growing. Mexico has also begun to import more processed food from the United States, aided by the rapid expansion of Mexico's supermarket distribution system.[110]

Now over 20 years old, NAFTA remains a contentious issue, and was a major point of division and debate in 2016 U.S. presidential election.

Critics, however, contend, that this trade safety net is too porous; the health care benefits do not cover real costs, training funds have been limited, school-based programs are overenrolled, the service sector is poorly covered (only workers in manufacturing are eligible), and farming and fishing fall through the cracks.[111] Communities are also often devastated by plant closings, social costs that TAA does not squarely address. By international standards, U.S. workers and towns fare poorly in shouldering the costs of globalization. Improved TAA can bring with it a win–win outcome—better jobs and greater efficiency in trade paired with a commitment to fairness to compensate the losers.[112]

Parallel to the case for displaced labor, less developed countries may need time to prepare for more open trading rules. In poorer countries labor markets don't easily adjust as people do not have the resources for mobility, and job training is scarce. Social safety nets for those displaced by import competition are limited. With fragile infrastructure, getting goods to international markets through poorly functioning ports can be problematic. Freight costs amount to 10% of value of imports in Africa versus 3% in other areas; the rates are even higher at 20% for Rwanda and 24% for Mali. Long delays at borders and customs account for 40% of transport time. Inadequate physical infrastructure such as roads and ports causes long and costly delays in supply chains. Only 30% of the region's roads are paved and many are inaccessible during the rainy season.[113] To take advantage of trade, these infrastructure costs that act like a tax on trade must be addressed. In short, developing countries may need more policy space and time to be able to take advantage of opportunities created by trade. Indeed, in the run-up to Doha there has been more development assistance targeted to build capacity in national markets to best take advantage of trade. While it may be true that there is no proven alternative to trade and integration as a path to prosperity and poverty reduction, the road to openness can also be managed to mitigate the short costs and pain to the losers in globalization.[114]

Conclusion: Comparative Advantage in a Globalized World

Trade is a central pillar of the globalization puzzle. The basic tenets of David Ricardo's theory of comparative advantage remain relevant—if each country does what it is best at, we enjoy gains from trade. But trade is more complex than in Ricardo's day. Changes in communications and transportation have tightened the economic ties between nations. Countries specialize in processes and products for the global supply chain. With the tripling of trade volume in the past half century, trade has become more resilient than was feared at the onset of the global financial crisis in 2009. Systemically important new players such as China and Brazil have reshaped the geo-economics of the trading arena. Countries don't sink or swim with changes in the U.S. market; instead, they maintain a portfolio of markets and trade partners.

The success of China in the global arena demonstrates how trade liberalization can be an engine for growth. But China has not become a global player using free-market scripts from Adam Smith's notebooks. Instead, the Chinese case suggests using trade strategically to leverage growth opportunities. New industrial policies and national preferences in regulatory regimes complicate fair and open borders. Where new entrants from the global South have nudged old players from market dominance, losers of jobs in less dynamic sectors have clamored for protectionism. This demand for national job and industry protection was reinforced by the economic pain of the Great Recession. Yet despite the motivations to use trade for a country's benefit, cataclysmic slides into protectionism have been avoided. Although imperfect, the WTO has become institutionalized as a watchdog of international trade rules. With more stakeholders in the trading arena, there is a broader constituency for trade. Consumers—including the emerging middle class in the developing world—are hooked on the access to global hypermarkets. Firms are rarely just exporters or importers—but are linked together in a global supply chain. The political calculus in rewarding winners and redressing losers from trade will continue to shape the opportunities for expansion of global trade.

In our next chapter, we will explore how trade is facilitated by global finance. We will also examine the ways that imbalances in trade—persistent surpluses and deficits—are linked to national policies and global rules. This will help us understand global production and labor networks in the following chapter as we piece together our puzzle of globalization.

Summary

International Trade: Theoretical Groundwork and Present-Day Formation

- Cross-border linkages due to world trade have shaped human history and allowed for integration and specialization of production processes across the globe. Yet the job loss associated with trade causes tensions in both national and international political and economic spheres.
- The Ricardian theory of comparative advantage expanded in the present day to include a globalized production pattern and workforce. Countries do not merely produce the goods they are "best" at producing, but take advantage of economies of scale and vertical specialization to perfect the production of a part of a good that can in turn be shipped and re-shipped all over the world, with a final product containing parts from different continents.
- The scale of world trade in the twenty-first century is unprecedented. Technological advancements have also allowed for an integration of supply chains, and speed of delivery unmatched in decades past. As trade grows, imbalances between countries have as well, providing a new and ever-changing dynamic. Institutions like the WTO have expanded their oversight to address more and more complicated cases regarding international trade disputes.

Protectionism and Its Pitfalls

- As countries specialize, the global work force grows, and the ability to use relatively cheaper labor becomes easier in the production process. Employees in sectors facing overseas competition face downward wage pressures and job loss due to the relocation of their positions overseas. These downsides of trade often spur action by governments to protect domestic sectors, and thus domestic jobs.

- Tariffs, export subsidies, and quotas function as barriers to trade implemented by governments to protect domestic industries. These tools often have the unintended consequences of raising either domestic or global prices, hurting both international consumers and foreign producers.
- Protectionist policies can serve to promote the growth of relatively newer industries to become global competitors. Countries may implement protectionist measures in retaliation for similar behavior from other trading partners. National security and the potential to counter lax foreign environmental and labor standards are also cited as reasons for protectionism.

Responses to Protectionism

- Governments and international institutions are balancing the protectionism caused by the "losses" of trade with promoting greater liberalization to increase surpluses to consumers worldwide. Negotiations for the Doha Round illustrate the complications of conflicting interests between developed and developing countries in creating one worldwide agreement.
- Agreements between groups of countries or regions to promote free trade include RTAs, PTAs, or FTAs. The agreements exhibit some of the benefits of common trade practices between countries, yet their geographical bounds can convolute trade within a worldwide market, and their role in global trade remains contested.

Notes

1. Pietra Rivoli, *Travels of a T-shirt in the Global Economy*. New Jersey: John Wiley and Sons, 2005.
2. "World Development Indicators Data Set." *World Bank* at http://databank.worldbank.org/ddp/home.do?Step=12&id=4&CNO=2
3. "Understanding the WTO." *World Trade Organization at* http://www.wto.org/english/thewto_e/whatis_e/tif_e/fact4_e.htm
4. Nihal Pitigala, "Global Economic Crisis and Vertical Specialization in Developing Countries." *PREM Trade Notes* 133 (2009).
5. "Trade Growth to Slow in 2012 after Strong Deceleration in 2011." *World Trade Organization* (April 2012) at http://www.wto.org/english/news_e/pres12_e/pr658_e.htm
6. "World Development Indicators Data Set" (accessed July 1, 2016).
7. Ibid.
8. Sewell Chan, "Rebound in World Trade Is Seen." *The New York Times*, March 26, 2010.
9. Stephen H. Hymer, "Economic Forms in Pre-Colonial Ghana." *The Journal of Economic History* 30, no. 1 (1970).

10. Nayan Chanda, *Bound Together: How Traders, Preachers, Adventurers, and Warriors Shaped Globalization*. Yale University Press, 2007.

11. Adam Smith, *The Wealth of Nations*. University of Chicago Press, 1776.

12. Nagwa Riad, Luca Errico, Christian Henn, Christian Saborowski, Mika Saito, and Jarkko Turunen, "Changing Patterns of Global Trade." *IMF Publications* (2012).

13. Ibid.

14. Ibid., Table 3: Measures of Vertical Specialization.

15. Kelsey Mays, "The Cars.com American-Made Index." *Cars.com* at http://www.cars.com/go/advice/Story.jsp?section=top&subject=ami&story=amMade0808. Ratings are for 2011.

16. Ibid.

17. "Estadisticas." *Asociación Mexicana de la Industria Automotoríz A.C.* at http://www.amia.com.mx/poremp.php

18. Pascal Lamy, "Comparative Advantage Is Dead? Not at All, Lamy Tells Paris Economists" in speech, Paris: Paris School of Economics, 2010.

19. Alec van Gelder, "Don't Throttle Trade." *The Australian*, July 9, 2009.

20. Richard Baldwin and Simon Evenett, "Introduction and Recommendations for the G20." In *The Collapse of Global Trade, Murky Protectionism, and the Crisis: Recommendations for the G20*, ed. Richard Baldwin and Simon Evenett. London: Center for Economic Policy Research, 2009, pp. 2–3.

21. David Hummels, *Have International Transportation Costs Declined?* University of Chicago, 1999.

22. Hogan Chen, Matthew Kondratowicz, and Kei-mu Yi, "Vertical Specialization and Three Facts about U.S. International Trade." *North American Journal of Economics & Finance* 16, no. 1 (2005): 42.

23. Tamin Bayoumi, "New Patterns of International Trade." *The International Monetary Fund,* June 2011 at http://www.imf.org/external/np/pp/eng/2011/061511.pdf; Robert Koopman, Zhi Wang, and Shang-Jin Wei, "How Much of Chinese Exports Is Really Made in China? Assessing Domestic Value Added When Processing Trade Is Pervasive." *National Bureau of Economic Research Working Paper 14109* (2008).

24. Kei-Mu Yi, "Can Vertical Specialization Explain the Growth of World Trade?" *The Journal of Political Economy* 111, no. 1 (2003).

25. Bayoumi, "New Patterns of International Trade".

26. Jagdish Bhagwati, "Why the World Is Not Flat." *World Affairs Journal Blog* (2010) at http://www.worldaffairsjournal.org/blog/jagdish-bhagwati/why-world-not-flat

27. Ibid.

28. Alberto Behar and Anthony J. Venables, "Transport Costs and International Trade." *University of Oxford Department of Economics Discussion Paper Series 488* (2010), 20.

29. Ibid., 4.

30. Lill Andersen and Ronald Babula, "The Link between Openness and Long-Run Economic Growth." *United States International Trade Commission: Journal of International Commerce and Economics* (2008).

31. Nobuo Kiriyama, "Trade and Innovation: Synthesis Report." *OECD Trade Policy Working Papers 135* (2012).

32. John C. Pool and Stephen Stamos, *International Economic Policy: Beyond the Trade and Debt Crisis.* Lexington, MA: Lexington Books, 1989, p. 2.

33. Kevin O'Rourke and Jeffery G. Williamson, "Late Nineteenth-Century Anglo-American Factor-Price Convergence: Were Heckscher and Ohlin Right?" *The Journal of Economic History* 54, no. 4 (1994): 899.

34. Raymond J. Ahearn, "The Global Economic Downturn and Protectionism." *Congressional Research Service* (2009): 1.

35. "WTO in Brief: Organization." *World Trade Organization.* Online edition available at http://www.wto.org/english/thewto_e/whatis_e/inbrief_e/inbr02_e.htm

36. Ibid.

37. Ibid.

38. "Accessions: Work in the WTO." *World Trade Organization.* Online edition available at http://www.wto.org/english/thewto_e/acc_e/completeacc_e.htm#chn.

39. Uri Dadush, "WTO Reform: The Time to Start Is Now." *Carnegie Endowment for International Peace Policy Brief 80* (September 2009): 2.

40. Arvind Subramanian and Shang-Jin Wei, "The WTO Promotes Trade, Strongly but Unevenly." *Journal of International Economics* 72 (2007): 151.

41. Dadush, "WTO Reform: The Time to Start Is Now," 2.

42. Gary Clyde Hufbauer and Jeffrey J. Schott, "The Doha Round after Hong Kong." *Policy Brief 06-2, Peterson Institute for International Economics* (February 2006).

43. Joost Pauwelyn, "New Trade Politics for the 21st Century." *Journal of International Economic Law* 11, no. 3 (2008): 559.

44. Dadush, "WTO Reform: The Time to Start Is Now."

45. James B. Treece, "Voluntary Export Restraints Are Back; They Didn't Work the Last Time." *Automotive News*, April 23, 2012.

46. Frank Asche and Martin D. Smith, "Trade and Fisheries: Key Issues for the World Trade Organization." *World Trade Organization Staff Working Paper* (2010).

47. "Key Sanitary and Phytosanitary Barriers to American Exports." *Office of the United States Trade Representative.* Online edition available at http://www.ustr.gov/about-us/press-office/fact-sheets/2010/march/key-sanitary-and-phytosanitary-barriers-american-export

48. "(India) Seafood Exporters get US Duty Relief." *Vietnam Chamber of Commerce and Industry* (July 2009) at http://chongbanphagia.vn/beta/en/news/2009-07-21/india-seafood-exporters-get-us-duty-relief

49. "First They Went for the Currency, Now for the Land." *The Economist*, September 24, 2011.

50. Alan Beattie, "Global Insight: Skirmishes Are not All-Out Trade War." *Financial Times*, March 14, 2010.

51. "Lobby Threatens to Thwart Canada in Trade Deal." *The Huffington Post*, April 11, 2012.

52. Ken Zino, "ITC Rules China's Largest Tire Maker Is Illegally Dumping in the U.S. and Killing American Jobs." *The Detroit Bureau*, June 30, 2009.

53. Joe McDonald, "China: U.S. Trade Tariffs Violate WTO Rules," *The Huffington Post*, June 10, 2010.

54. Aaron Back, "China Plans Additional Tariffs on U.S. Chicken," *The Wall Street Journal*, April 28, 2010.

55. Austin Ramzy, "Chicken Feet: A Symbol of US-China Tension," *Time*, February 8, 2010.

56. Anthony Faiola and Lori Montgomery, "Trade Wars Brewing in Economic Malaise," *The Washington Post*, May 15, 2009.

57. Baldwin and Evenett, "Introduction and Recommendations for the G20," 3.

58. Chan, "Rebound in World Trade Is Seen."

59. WTO dispute status.

60. United States Census Bureau, "U.S. Import and Export Statistics." Available at http://www.census.gov/foreign-trade/balance/. Note that this is the current account, not the trade balance. The goods deficit was $295 billion and the deficit in goods and services $282 billion.

61. Simon Evenett (editor), "Debacle: The 11th GTA Report on Protectionism." *Center for Economic Policy Research* (June 2012).

62. Ibid., 6.

63. Ibid.

64. Bernard Hoekman, "Trade Policy: So Far So Good?" *Finance and Development* 49, no. 2 (June 2012).

65. Ibid.

66. Chris Edwards, "Agricultural Regulations and Trade Barriers." *CATO Institute* (2009).

67. "Submission to the DEFRA Consultation on Sugar Reform." *CAFOD, ActionAid, and Oxfam* (January 2004).

68. Joseph F. Francois and Laura M. Baughman, "Estimated Economic Effects of Proposed Import Relief Remedies for Steel." *CITAC* (December 2001).

69. Terence Corcoran, "Mr. Harper, Cut Down These Tariffs." *The Financial Post*, March 6, 2010.

70. "Help Quell Tire Price Sticker Shock," *Tire Business,* April 26, 2010. Price increases in the tire market cannot be attributed solely to tariffs however, as rising raw material costs and a resurging demand within the U.S. and abroad are also leading producers to push up prices. Miles Moore, "Raw and Rising; Materials Costs Keep Going Up; Ditto for Tire Prices," *Tire Business*, April 12, 2010.

71. Gary Hufbauer and Paul Grieco, "The Payoff from Globalization." *The Washington Post*, June 7, 2005.

72. Ibid.

73. Kenneth Reinhart, *Windows on the World Economy: Introduction to International Economics.* Mason, Ohio: Thomson/South-Western, 2005: 83.

74. Claire Brunel, Gary Clyde Hufbauer, and Jeffery J. Schott, "What's on the Table? The Doha Round as of August 2009." *Peterson Institute for International Economics Working Paper Series 09-6* (August 2009): 1.

75. Ibid.

76. Jeffery Schott, "A Trade Agenda for the G-20." *Peterson Institute for International Economics Policy Brief 10-11* (May 2010): 1.

77. Aaditya Mattoo and Arvind Subramanian, "Beyond Doha." *World Bank Research Digest* 3, no. 2 (Winter, 2009): 6.

78. Ibid., 6.

79. Aaditya Mattoo and Arvind Subramanian, "From Doha to the Next Bretton Woods: A New Multilateral Trade Agenda." *Foreign Affairs* (January/February 2009).

80. Mattoo and Subramanian, "Beyond Doha," 6.

81. WTO launches new database of preferential trade arrangements, March 14, 2012. WTO.org

82. Robert E. Scott, "Pennsylvania Stagnation: Is Nafta the Culprit?" *New York Times Topics Blog*, posted April 15, 2008. Online edition available at http://topics.blogs.nytimes.com/2008/04/15/pennsylvania-stagnation-is-nafta-the-culprit/.

83. William H. Cooper and Mark E. Manyin, "The Proposed South Korea-U.S. Free Trade Agreement (KORUS FTA)" *CRS Report for Congress* (July 2007): 31.

84. Jeffery Schott, "Implementing the KORUS FTA: Key Challenges and Policy Proposals," in *Understanding New Political Realities in Seoul: Working toward a Common*

Approach to Strengthen U.S.-Korean Relations, ed. L. Gordon Flake and Park Ro-byug (Washington, DC: The Maureen and Mike Mansfield Foundation, 2008): 84–86.

85. "South Korea/US: FTA Jumps Major Hurdles, Faces Others." *Oxford Analytica*, April 3, 2007.

86. "African Free Trade Zone Is Agreed." *BBC News*, October 22, 2008.

87. IMF, *World Economic Outlook Database* (April 2010). http://www.imf.org/external/pubs/ft/weo/2010/01/weodata/weorept.aspx?sy=2005&ey=2009&scsm=1&ssd=1&sort=country&ds=.&br=1&c=001%2C998&s=NGDP_RPCH%2CNGDPD%2CPPPGDP%2CPPPPC%2CPPPSH&grp=1&a=1&pr.x=36&pr.y=15 (accessed June 28, 2010).

88. "EU Tenders and Contracts." *European Union*. Online edition available at http://europa.eu/publicprocurement/index_en.htm.

89. Hector Calvo-Pardo, Caroline Freund, and Emanuel Ornelas, "The ASEAN Free Trade Agreement: Impact on Trade Flows and External Trade Barriers Policy Research." *The World Bank Development Research Group Trade and Integration Team Working Paper 4960* (June 2009).

90. Lim Chze Cheen, "ASEAN Economic Community and Priority Integration Sectors" (presented in session 3a *Global/Regional Integration: What Are Their Respective Roles in the Context of the Current Economic Environment?* at the Global Dialogue on Turning Crises into Opportunities through Regulatory Reforms, Washington, DC, March 2009).

91. Shayne Heffernan, "China Knowledge Report on China ASEAN Relations." *Ebeling Heffernan*, February 24, 2010.

92. "Ten as One: Challenges and Opportunities for ASEAN Integration." UN ESCAP. (Bangkok: United Nations Economic and Social Commission for Asia and the Pacific, 2007): 1.

93. Ben Shepherd and John Wilson, "Trade Facilitation in ASEAN Member Countries: Measuring Progress and Assessing Priorities." *World Bank Policy Research Working Paper no. WPS 4615* (May 2008).

94. Excluding the European Union.

95. United States Census Bureau, 2016. Top Trading Partners—December 2015. Year-to-date total trade. https://www.census.gov/foreign-trade/statistics/highlights/top/top1512yr.html. Accessed on 08.30.2016.

96. GDP calculation from: Trading Economic, 2016. GDP 1960–2016. http://www.tradingeconomics.com/canada/gdp. Accessed 08.30.2016. Populations Calculated from national statistical office data.

97. World Bank, 2015. Gross national income per capita 2015, Atlas method and PPP. Last updated July 22, 2016. Available from http://data.worldbank.org/data-catalog/GNI-per-capita-Atlas-and-PPP-table. Accessed August 30, 2016.

98. Aleksandar Jotanovic and Brad Gilmour, "NAFTA: Outcomes, Challenges, and Prospects," *Agricultural Policy Issues* 2, no. 2 (2009): 2.

99. Kevin Gallaghar, Enrique Dussel Peters, and Timothy Wise, eds., *The Future of North American Trade Policy: Lessons from NAFTA* (Pardee Center Task Force Report, 2009).

100. Ibid.; Alexander J. Kondonassis, A. G. Malliaris, and Chris Paraskevopoulos, "NAFTA: Past, Present and Future," *The Journal of Economic Asymmetries* 5, no. 1 (2008): 4.

101. Government of Canada, 2015. North American Free Trade Agreement (NAFTA). http://www.international.gc.ca/trade-agreements-accords-commerciaux/agr-acc/nafta-alena/info.aspx?lang=eng.

102. Villarreal, M.A., and I.F. Fergusson, The North American Free Trade Agreement (NAFTA). Congressional Research Service, 2015 at https://www.fas.org/sgp/crs/row/R42965.pdf

103. Ibid.

104. Gallaghar, Peters, and Wise, eds., *The Future of North American Trade Policy.*

105. Gus Van Harten, "Reforming the NAFTA Investment Regime," in *The Future of North American Trade Policy*, eds. Gallaghar, Peters, and Wise (see note 6), 45.

106. United States Chamber of Commerce, 2014. NAFTA triumphant assessing two decades of gains in trade, growth, and jobs.

107. Kondonassis, Malliaris, and Paraskevopoulos, "NAFTA: Past, Present and Future," 18.

108. Weisbrot, M., S. Lefebvre, and J. Sammut, Did NAFTA Help Mexico? An Assessment after 20 Years. Center for Economic and Policy Research, 2014. http://cepr.net/documents/nafta-20-years-2014-02.pdf.

109. Hansen-Kuhn, K., NAFTA and US farmers—20 years later. Institute for Agriculture and Trade Policy, 2013. http://www.iatp.org/blog/201311/nafta-and-us-farmers—20-years-later#_edn1; Hoppe, R.A., J. M. MacDonald, and P. Korb, Small Farmers in the United Sates Persistence under Pressure. United States Department of Agriculture, 2010. Economic Research Service Economic Information Bulletin Number 63. http://www.ers.usda.gov/publications/eib-economic-information-bulletin/eib63.aspx.

110. Timothy Wise, "Reforming NAFTA's Agricultural Provisions," in *The Future of North American Trade Policy*, eds. Gallaghar, Peters, and Wise (see note 6), 36.

111. John J. Topoleski, "Extending Trade Adjustment Assistance (TAA) to Service Workers: How Many Workers Could Potentially Be Covered?" *CRS Report for Congress* (November 2007).

112. Howard Rosen, "Strengthening Trade Adjustment Assistance" (Peterson Institute for international Economics Policy Brief 08-2, January 2008); Ianthe Jeanne Dugan, "Crazy-Quilt Jobless Programs Help Some More than Others," *The Wall Street Journal*, April 20, 2009, A1.

113. Tonia Kandiero, Abdul Kamara, and Leonce Ndikumana, "Commodities, Export Subsidies and African Trade during the Slump," in *The Collapse of Global Trade, Murky Protectionism, and the Crisis* ed. Baldwin and Evenett (see note 20), 61.

114. Luis Alberto Moreno, "Keeping Borders Open: Why Is It Important for Latin America and What Can the Region Do about It?" in *The Collapse of Global Trade, Murky Protectionism, and the Crisis* ed. Baldwin and Evenett (see note 20).

CHAPTER FOUR

International Finance

Global Financial Flows and Crises

A small sampling of the world's 180 currencies.

What Are the Global Financial Puzzles?

Global currency markets are bigger, faster, and more unpredictable than at any other time in history. Capital mobility across borders has accelerated as technology has made it possible to move money with the stroke of a keyboard. More than four trillion dollars' worth of currencies are traded each day.[1] Short-term movements, primarily bank loans, increased fivefold as a percentage of world GDP from roughly 10% in 1980 to 48% in 2006.[2] UNCTAD reports that foreign direct investment, a long-term commitment of capital, increased from 9.7% of world's 1990 GDP to 32.2% of world product in 2012.[3] Net inflows of foreign direct investment doubled worldwide from 1998 to 2010.[4] Total financial resources funded by the private sector to domestic creditors, including bank loans and non-equity securities, rose from 125% of the world's GDP to 134.4% over the same time period.[5] **Financial globalization**, defined by the IMF as the extent to which countries are linked through cross-border financial holdings—binds us together.[6] But it also has the power to wreak havoc. Tightly interwoven financial systems were quickly infected by the 2008–9 crisis that began in the U.S. subprime mortgage market. As investors fled from risk, liquidity dried up in the system. The financial crisis quickly and painfully reversed cross-border flows to a fifth of peak levels.[7] Although financial diversification should encourage risk sharing through portfolio diversification, the deep connections across national markets delivered a wallop in the financial crisis of 2008–9.[8]

Financial globalization facilitates the cross-border production of goods and services fueling our economy. Financial systems have developed in tandem with the movement of goods and services since the days of the early explorers. But the size and speed of trading in currency markets today makes it harder to predict the direction or to correct imbalances before they explode into crises. As shown in Figure 4.1, a defining characteristic of the new financial globalization is the extraordinary flows to developing countries. This new wave of financial globalization began in the 1970s, when deposits were piling up in money center banks from payments to Organization of the Petroleum Exporting Countries (OPEC). Bankers in New York and London became more aggressive in identifying global investment opportunities to make interest payments on the so-called petrodollar deposits. Where banking had been a largely national activity for all but the largest players, increasingly investments were made across borders. Recipient countries began to see the allure of international investors, opening national markets to global capital. But the sudden inflows of capital also brought extended vulnerability to international crises. As we will discuss, in the 1980s when interest rates were tightened in the United States, developing nations were strangled by debt. In the 1990s, the rapid inflow of capital pressured exchange rates to burst with the Asian and Latin American currency crises. In 2009, the weakness of the U.S. subprime mortgage market rapidly infected global banking through its associated packages of complex derivatives widely traded across borders. Finally, in 2010, currency wars have erupted and the European Monetary Union (EMU) has come under strain. With globalized capital markets, strains in one part of the financial system infect another.

What are the keys to understanding these important yet volatile capital flows in our global economy? In this chapter, we introduce the basics of international finance. We provide you with the tools to analyze trends in international financial markets and invite you to consider policy options to promote sustainable balance in the global macro economy. We begin with Balance of Payment (BOP) accounting to help us understand the connection between trade and financial flows. In this exercise, we draw upon the fundamentals of macroeconomics to show that a country's external balance is tied to how much its domestic economy absorbs. The key takeaway is that if a country spends more than it produces, it must borrow the balance. We then introduce the all-important price that values goods from one country in terms of another—the **exchange rate**. As we can see in Figure 4.2, the dollar (adjusted for inflation or shown in real terms) against a basket of currencies has had its ups and downs over

Figure 4.1. Capital Flows to Emerging and Developing Economies

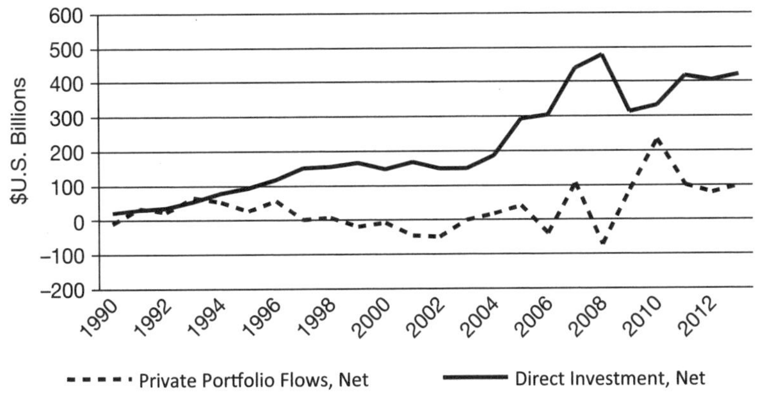

$U.S. Billions

600 500 400 300 200 100 0 −100 −200

1990 1992 1994 1996 1998 2000 2002 2004 2006 2008 2010 2012

Private Portfolio Flows, Net   Direct Investment, Net

As defined by the Balance of Payments Manual published by the International Monetary Fund, direct investment includes the "lasting interest" of a direct investor in one economy in a foreign economy. Private portfolio flows include both debt and equity transactions.

Source: International Monetary Fund, *World Economic Outlook 2012.*

Figure 4.2. Value of the U.S. Dollar Over Time

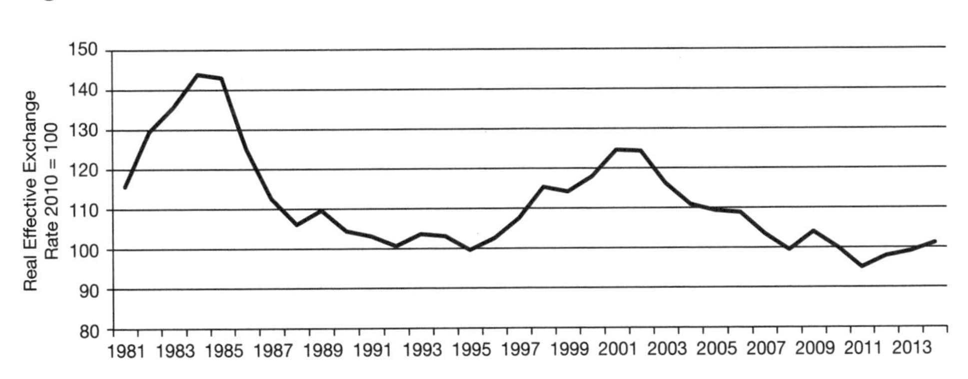

Source: World Bank, World Development Indicators.

the past several decades. What has contributed to this roller-coaster? Finally, we consider the ways that the rules of the game in the global economy have created opportunities but also problems in the global financial system.

IMBALANCES IN THE BOP

Financial flows are tied to the trade of goods and services we studied in the last chapter. Navigation of the global economy in the twenty-first century is challenged by deep structural imbalances between countries. As shown in Figure 4.3, the United States leads the pack of deficit countries, with **current account** deficits over $470 billion in 2010. Spain, the United Kingdom, France, and Italy join Americans as high-consuming nations living off the ability of savers such as China, Germany, and Saudi Arabia to provide the goods and services—and currency—to meet our excess demand for goods and services. Imbalances between surplus and deficit countries strain our global system.

The basics of macro principles provide important insight into our global dilemma. Recall your fundamental components of GDP: Consumption, Investment, Government Expenditures, Exports, and Imports. If a country wants to buy more electronics, beef and oil, or is heavily investing more in business expansion or expensive foreign policy ventures, the sum of spending at home may be greater than what is produced within its borders. Table 4.1 sets up this dilemma. Our international transactions on the right side of Table 4.1 are determined by the national spending or saving on the left side. In this hypothetical country, consumer spending, business investment, and government outlays total $2,950—but our gross domestic product or what we make within our borders—only amounts to $2,800. We export $550, but our imports top out at $700. This deficit of $150 is broadly represented in the current account, seen at the top of the right-hand column. Here, we note that the **balance on our merchandise trade**, the deficit of goods exported compared to those imported, is mitigated by the country's sale of services (perhaps in finance or information systems), the income it is earning on past investments, with a small leakage of unilateral transfers such as remittances that migrant workers send home. Box 4.1 explains BOP accounting in greater detail.

Since this country is consuming more than it is producing, someone must be financing this excess. As other nations won't simply ship goods without payment, financing must flow in an equal amount to cover the deficit. By this logic, the current account (of negative $150) must just equal the **financial account** (of $150). In this case, while domestic companies were setting up productive capabilities abroad, resulting in an outflow of $250 of foreign direct investment, the nation was receiving capital inflows of $390 (**net portfolio investments**) largely perhaps in the form of bonds or stock purchases under 10% of the firm's value. There were some adjustments that needed to be made due to statistical discrepancies ($75), and the country may have needed to sell gold to offset a position in the IMF. For definitions of the different types of capital flows, please see Table 4.2.

Figure 4.3. Top Current Account Surplus and Deficit Countries

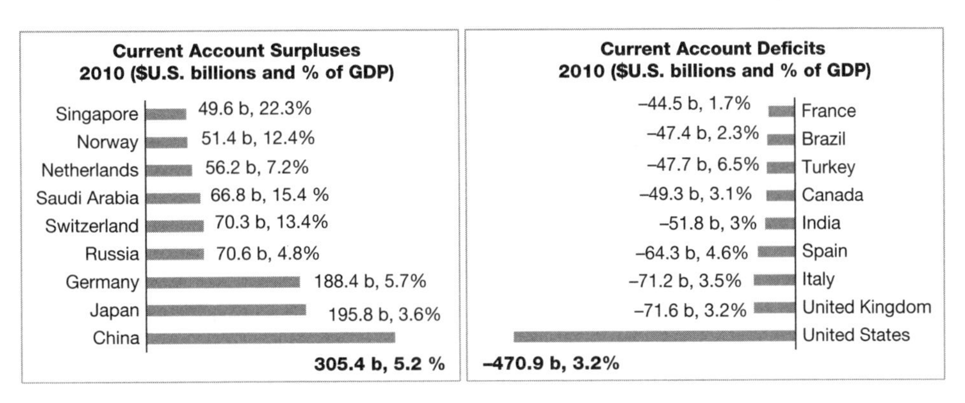

Source: World Bank, World Development Indicators.

Table 4.1. GDP and the Balance of Payments of a Deficit Country

Components of GDP (Y)	*Amounts (in Sample Currency)*	*Balance of Payments*	*Amounts (in Sample Currency)*
Consumption (C)	2,000	**Current Account**	***–150***
Investment (I)	300	*Balance on Merchandise*	–450
Government (G)	650	*Balance on Services*	200
C + I + G	2,950	*Net Investment Income*	150
		Unilateral Transfers	–50
Exports (X)	550		
Imports (M)	700	**Financial Account**	***150***
X - M	-150	*Net Direct Investment*	250
		Net Portfolio Investment	350
GDP	2,800	*Errors and Omissions*	75
		Change in Official Reserves	–25

Source: Adapted from David A. Moss, *A Concise Guide to Macroeconomics: What Managers, Executives, and Students Need to Know* (Boston: Harvard Business School Press, 2007), 14.

Box 4.1. BOP Accounting

The BOP is an accounting of a country's international transactions for a particular time period.

- *A transaction causing money to flow into a country is a credit to its BOP account; an outward flow of money is a debit.*
  - Payments to foreigners → money out → debit
  - Receipts from foreigners → money in → credit
- The BOP statement has three accounts: the current account, the **capital account**, and the financial account. The current account tallies international trade in goods and services and earnings on investments. The capital account adds capital transfers and the acquisition and disposal of non-produced, non-financial assets. The financial account records transfers of financial capital and non-financial capital. The accounts are further divided into sub-accounts.

The Current Account is composed of four sub-accounts:

- **Merchandise trade** consists of all raw materials and manufactured goods bought, sold, or given away.
- **Services** include tourism, transportation, engineering, and business services, such as law, management consulting, and accounting. Fees from patents and copyrights on new technology, software, books, and movies also are recorded in the service category.
- **Income receipts** include income derived from ownership of assets, such as dividends on holdings of stock and interest on securities.
- **Unilateral transfers** represent one-way transfers of assets, such as worker remittances from abroad and direct foreign aid. In the case of aid or gifts, a debit is assigned to the capital account of the donor nation.

The Capital Account transfers include debt forgiveness and migrants' transfers (goods and financial assets accompanying migrants as they leave or enter the country), the transfer of title to fixed assets, and the transfer of funds linked to the sale or acquisition of fixed assets, gift and inheritance taxes, death duties, uninsured damage to fixed assets, and legacies.

The Financial Account records trade in assets such as business firms, bonds, stocks, and real estate, and it has two categories:

- **U.S.-owned assets abroad** are divided into official reserve assets, government assets, and private assets. These assets include gold, foreign currencies, foreign securities, reserve position in the IMF, U.S. credits and other long-term assets, direct foreign investment, and U.S. claims reported by U.S. banks.
- **Foreign-owned assets in the United States** are divided into foreign official assets and other foreign assets in the United States. These assets include U.S. government, agency, corporate securities, direct investment, U.S. currency, and U.S. liabilities reported by U.S. banks.
- **Acquisition and disposal of non-produced, non-financial assets** represent the sales and purchases of non-produced assets, such as the rights to natural resources, and the sales and purchases of intangible assets, such as patents, copyrights, trademarks, franchises, and leases.

Source: World Bank.

Table 4.2. Types of Global Capital Flows

Types of Capital Flows	*Definition*	*Term Structure*	*Impact*
Foreign direct investment	Acquisition of shares by a firm in a foreign entity above 10% or establishment of a production subsidiary	Long-term K flow	+ or –, depending on the bargaining power of the country
Equity portfolio investment	Modest acquisition of stock	Short-term flow; can be traded	Source of funds where risk is shared with the lender (i.e., stock values can decline), but can be unreliable.
Bond finance	Issuing debt in the form of a bond; investors purchase a bond (say for $75) with the promise of a repayment (including principle) in the future (perhaps $100). Various private and institutional investors hold bonds in their portfolios, often in mutual funds.	Relatively short term; can be traded if holder believes performance is deteriorating	Like equity, hot money flows in/out. Risk of non-performance falls on borrower; must pay or default. Hard to negotiate default settlements with large number of bond holders.
Commercial bank lending	A bank loans a company or government a fixed amount to be repaid at a future date with interest	Can be short or long term with fixed or flexible interest rates	Risk is on borrower; if economic conditions deteriorate, must still meet payments. Large banks usually able to act on information about borrower; in default can negotiate repayment more easily.
Official lending	Loans offered through the IMF, WB, regional development banks or on a bilateral country to country basis	Short or long term, can be at discounted rates or be given as aid	Loan may be subject to political manipulation but can be written down in adverse circumstances

BOP Deficit and Surplus Detective Work

In theory, the current account equals the capital and financial accounts. The sum of the BOP statements should be zero. For example, when the United States buys more goods and services than it sells (a current account deficit), it must finance the difference by borrowing, or by selling more capital assets than it buys (a financial account surplus). A country with a persistent current account deficit is, therefore, effectively exchanging capital assets for goods and services. Large trade deficits require that the country borrow from abroad. In the BOP, this appears as an inflow of foreign capital. In reality, the accounts do not exactly offset each other because of statistical discrepancies, accounting conventions, and exchange rate movements that change the recorded value of transactions. We adjust the difference between the current and financial accounts through the statistical discrepancy.

Table 4.3 presents the U.S. BOP through 2011. Comparing lines 2 and 18, we can see that the United States exports less than it imports. The goods deficit is moderated by a surplus on services, seen as the difference between lines 4 and 21 and expressed as a summary balance in line 73. The current account deficit (as a memorandum in line 77) is compounded by government grants and private remittances flowing abroad that make up unilateral transfers (line 35). The current account deficit of 466 billion in 2011 is financed through net positive inflows of assets into the United States (the difference between lines 40 and 55) and adjusted by the statistical discrepancy (line 71) and net financial derivatives.[9] Try it yourself—add U.S.-owned assets abroad (a negative because it is an outflow), foreign-owned assets in the United States (which comes in positive as an inflow), adjust for the statistical discrepancy (negative in 2011), and add the value of financial derivatives. With rounding, this total should equal the current account, illustrating that if a country consumes more goods and services than it produces, it must borrow from the rest of the world to do so. You can go to the Bureau of Economic Analysis (BEA, www.bea.gov) website to analyze the data for the current year. Has the external position of the United States improved?

With double entry balance bookkeeping and taking the statistical discrepancy into account, the BOP is always zero. The key is to read between the lines. A deficit on the current account can be good flows and bad flows just like good cholesterol and bad cholesterol. What factors drive the flows? Are firms investing for future growth or are consumers living beyond their means? Is an economy adjusting to a temporary shock such as a crop failure or is a government spending unsustainably? On the financial account, are investors acting bullish by sending capital into the economy, or is the government forced to manage balance of trade disequilibrium? Are capital flows short-term hot money or do they represent a long-term commitment to the economy? (Table 4.2 describes some of the impacts of different kinds of capital flows.) These are some of the key questions you should ask when analyzing a country's BOP position.

Table 4.3. U.S. International Transactions Accounts Data ($U.S. millions)

Line	(Credits +; debits –)	$U.S. 1960	1970	1980	1990	2000	2011
Current account							
1	**Exports of goods and services and income receipts**	**30556**	**68387**	**344440**	**706975**	**1421515**	**2847988**
2	Exports of goods and services	25940	56640	271834	535233	1070597	2103367
3	Goods, BOP basis	19650	42469	224250	387401	784181	1497406
4	Services	6290	14171	47584	147832	286416	605961
5	Transfers under U.S. military agency sales contracts	2030	4214	9029	9932	6088	17946
6	Travel	919	2331	10588	43007	82400	116115
7	Passenger fares	175	544	2591	15298	20687	36631
8	Other transportation	1607	3125	11618	22042	25318	43064
9	Royalties and license fees	837	2331	7085	16634	43233	120836
10	Other private services	570	1294	6276	40251	107904	270193
11	U.S. government miscellaneous services	153	332	398	668	786	1176
12	Income receipts	4616	11748	72606	171742	350918	744621
13	Income receipts on U.S.–owned assets abroad	4616	11748	72606	170570	348083	738810
14	Direct investment receipts	3621	8169	37146	65973	151839	480238
15	Other private receipts	646	2671	32898	94072	192398	256649
16	U.S. government receipts	349	907	2562	10525	3846	1923
17	Compensation of employees	—	—	—	1172	2835	5811
18	**Imports of goods and services and income payments**	**–23670**	**–59901**	**–333774**	**–759290**	**–1779241**	**–3180861**
19	Imports of goods and services	–22432	–54386	–291241	–616097	–1E+06	–2663247
20	Goods, BOP basis	–14758	–39866	–249750	–498438	–1E+06	–2235819
21	Services	–7674	–14520	–41491	–117659	–218964	–427428

continued

Table 4.3. U.S. International Transactions Accounts Data ($U.S. millions) (Continued)

Line	(Credits +; debits –)	$U.S. 1960	1970	1980	1990	2000	2011
22	Direct defense expenditures	–3087	–4855	–10851	–17531	–12698	–29510
23	Travel	–1750	–3980	–10397	–37349	–64705	–78651
24	Passenger fares	–513	–1215	–3607	–10531	–24274	–31103
25	Other transportation	–1402	–2843	–11790	–24966	–36712	–54711
26	Royalties and license fees	–74	–224	–724	–3135	–16468	–36620
27	Other private services	–593	–827	–2909	–22229	–61223	–191973
28	U.S. government miscellaneous services	–254	–576	–1214	–1919	–2883	–4854
29	Income payments	–1238	–5515	–42532	–143192	–329864	–517614
30	Income payments on foreign–owned assets in the United States	–1238	–5515	–42532	–139728	–322345	–503796
31	Direct investment payments	–394	–875	–8635	–3450	–56910	–158559
32	Other private payments	–511	–3617	–21214	–95508	–180918	–212506
33	U.S. government payments	–332	–1024	–12684	–40770	–84517	–132731
34	Compensation of employees	—	—	—	–3464	–7519	–13817
35	**Unilateral current transfers, net**	**–4062**	**–6156**	**–8349**	**–26654**	**–58645**	**–133053**
36	U.S. government grants	–3367	–4449	–5486	–10359	–16714	–47350
37	U.S. government pensions and other transfers	–273	–611	–1818	–3224	–4705	–8947
38	Private remittances and other transfers	–423	–1096	–1044	–13070	–37226	–76756
Capital account							
39	**Capital account transactions, net**	—	—	—	**–7220**	**–1**	**–1212**
Financial account							
40	**U.S.–owned assets abroad, excluding financial derivatives (increase/financial outflow (–))**	**–4099**	**–9337**	**–86967**	**–81234**	**–560523**	**–483653**

41	U.S. official reserve assets	2145	2481	–8155	–2158	–290	–15877
42	Gold	1703	787	—	—	0	0
43	Special drawing rights	—	–851	–16	–192	–722	–1752
44	Reserve position in the International Monetary Fund	442	389	–1667	731	2308	–18079
45	Foreign currencies	—	2156	–6472	–2697	–1876	450
46	U.S. government assets, other than official reserve assets	–1100	–1589	–5162	2317	–941	–103666
47	U.S. credits and other long–term assets	–1214	–3293	–9860	–8410	–5182	–7307
48	Repayments on U.S. credits and other long–term assets	642	1721	4456	10856	4265	3333
49	U.S. foreign currency holdings and U.S. short–term assets	–528	–16	242	–130	–24	–99692
50	U.S. private assets	–5144	–10229	–73651	–81393	–559292	–364110
51	Direct investment	–2940	–7590	–19222	–37183	–159212	–419332
52	Foreign securities	–663	–1076	–3568	–28765	–127908	–146797
53	U.S. claims on unaffiliated foreigners reported by U.S. nonbanking concerns	–394	–596	–4023	–27824	–138790	–11608
54	U.S. claims reported by U.S. banks and securities brokers	–1148	–967	–46838	12379	–133382	213627
55	**Foreign–owned assets in the United States, excluding financial derivatives (increase/financial inflow (+))**	**2294**	**7226**	**62037**	**139357**	**1038224**	**1000990**
56	Foreign official assets in the United States	1473	7775	16649	33910	42758	211826
57	U.S. government securities	655	9439	11895	30243	35710	158735
58	U.S. Treasury securities	655	9411	9708	29576	–5199	171179
59	Other	—	28	2187	667	40909	–12444
60	Other U.S. government liabilities	215	411	1767	1868	–1825	9063
61	U.S. liabilities reported by U.S. banks and securities brokers	603	–2075	–159	3385	5746	30010
62	Other foreign official assets	—	—	3145	–1586	3127	14018

continued

Table 4.3. U.S. International Transactions Accounts Data ($U.S. millions) (Continued)

		$U.S.					
Line	*(Credits +; debits –)*	*1960*	*1970*	*1980*	*1990*	*2000*	*2011*
63	Other foreign assets in the United States	821	–550	45388	105447	995466	–789164
64	Direct investment	315	1464	16918	48494	321274	233988
65	U.S. Treasury securities	–364	81	/19/2645	–2534	–69983	240878
66	U.S. securities other than U.S. Treasury securities	282	2189	5457	1592	459889	–56442
67	U.S. currency	—	—	2773	16586	–3357	54996
68	U.S. liabilities to unaffiliated foreigners reported by U.S. nonbanking concerns	–90	2014	6852	45133	170672	6567
69	U.S. liabilities reported by U.S. banks and securities brokers	678	–6298	10743	–3824	116971	309177
70	**Financial derivatives, net**	**n.a.**	**n.a.**	**n.a.**	**n.a.**	**n.a.**	**39010**
71	**Statistical discrepancy (sum of above items with sign reversed)**	**–1019**	**–219**	**22613**	**28066**	**–61329**	**–89208**
	Memoranda:						
72	Balance on goods (lines 3 and 20)	4892	2603	–25500	–111037	–446233	–738413
73	Balance on services (lines 4 and 21)	–1385	–349	6093	30173	67453	178533
74	Balance on goods and services (lines 2 and 19)	3508	2254	–19407	–80864	–378780	–559880
75	Balance on income (lines 12 and 29)	3379	6233	30073	28550	21054	227007
76	Unilateral current transfers, net (line 35)	–4062	–6156	–8349	–26654	–58645	–133053
77	Balance on current account (lines 1, 18, and 35 or lines 74, 75, and 76)	2824	2331	2317	–78968	–416371	–465926

Source: Bureau of Economic Analysis News Release: U.S. International Transactions, June 14, 2012.

Box 4.2 Key Dates in International Financial History

1600s coins gain intrinsic value that is not linked with commodity. Banks also begin issuing paper money that is backed by gold held in banks.

1800–15

Napoleonic wars. Austria, France, Russia, the German states all default under the cost of financing armies.

1826

Greece defaults for the first of five times. Its first king, Otto, spends his rule fruitlessly trying to stabilize finances.

1870

The international gold standard is established. This meant that the value of a country's currency was determined by the amount of gold held in its central bank. Countries could also import and export gold without restriction and were permitted free coinage of gold at the mint.

1914

A series of problems lead to the end of the gold standard system. The United States inherits the role of world banker from Great Britain.

1932

Germany, devastated by hyperinflation, war reparations, and Depression, repudiates debt-owed to U.S. investors.

1944

A conference on the international monetary system is held at Bretton Woods in New Hampshire. Two new institutions are created to better manage and monitor international finance: the IMF and the World Bank. Currencies are pegged to the U.S. dollar, which in turn is tied to gold.

1946–52

As Europe reels from the devastation of WWII, U.S. banks enjoy increasing control over the financing of foreign trade and dollar credits.

1953–57

As Western Europe recovers and European currencies regain stability, global financial markets become increasingly liberalized and international lending and foreign exchange trading expand.

1960s

Large outflows of capital from the U.S. contribute to the development of a sizable BOP deficit in the U.S. and may believe the dollar was overvalued, further exacerbating the BOP deficit.

1971

Confidence in the dollar breaks down and many private holders try to convert their holdings into European currencies. This results in the devaluation of the dollar and the permission of a wider band of currency rate fluctuation.

continued

continued

1973

A second currency crisis takes place, leading to further devaluation of the dollar. A floating exchange rate is adopted, allowing currency values to fluctuate.

1974, 1978–79

Oil prices skyrocket in two international oil shocks. This places many oil importers further in debt, forcing them to borrow in order to import. U.S. banks enjoyed unrestricted lending of petrodollar proceeds to countries in debt.

1973–89

In Latin America, debt balloons from $29 billion in 1970 to $327 billion in 1982.[10] Sixteen Latin American countries default on tens of billions of dollars, owed mostly to U.S. banks. Citibank almost goes under.

1994

Mexico suddenly devalues the peso, which had been under mounting pressure. The peso's crash triggers a crisis that requires intervention from the U.S. Treasury.

1997–98

Thailand, Indonesia, and South Korea prove unable to repay dollar-denominated debt as their currencies collapse. IMF boss Michel Camdessus imposes draconian budget cuts in return for aid.

2001–02

Argentina, beset by budget woes, partly defaults on its foreign debt and abandons the peg to the dollar. Bondholders have still not settled.

2007–10

The collapse of the U.S. sub-prime mortgage market sends ripples throughout the world, exposing weaknesses in the global financial system, and plunging the world into a financial crisis that some claim is the worst the world has seen since the Great Depression.

2009–10

Greece, Latvia, Romania, Bulgaria, and Hungary all face a sovereign debt crisis.

2011

Sovereign debt crises intensify in Europe. Fiscal austerity measures supported by Germany and implemented in countries like Greece, Spain, and Italy hurt growth in the short term and incite public unrest, while disputes on how to handle the crisis within Europe intensify.

2012

Conditions in global financial markets improve in the first quarter but yields on debt issued by members of the euro remain above pre-crisis levels.

Source: "Defaults, Near-Defaults, and Other Financial Disasters: A Crisis Timeline," *Bloomberg Businessweek*, April 22, 2010; "Global Economic Prospects," *World Bank*, June 2012.

An Inverted View of International Balances

Another way to think about the relationship between the domestic economy and the international sector is by focusing on the trade balance of exports minus imports, $(X - M)$ as a residual after people consume (C), businesses invest (I), and governments (G) implement programs. Recalling the Keynesian diagram $C + I + G + (X - M)$ as the determinants of national income (Y or GDP) and remembering that all national income is either consumed or saved (let S stand for saving), we can rearrange our formula such that $S - I - G_t = X - M$. In this case, let's consider G_t as net government spending, that is, the fiscal balance between tax (the subscript t), revenues, and outlays.

Here are the steps:

Given:	$Y = C + I + G_t + X - M$
Then by isolating $X - M$ on the right,	$Y - C - I - G_t = X - M$
But $Y = C + S$ so that rearranging	$Y - C = S$.
By substitution of S for $Y - C$,	$S - I - G_t = X - M$

This is an important result, underscoring that what is left over after people consume, businesses invest, and governments spend is our trade balance. It directly connects our domestic fiscal deficit (when G_t is negative) to our external balance. If governments spend national resources, there is less left over for export. Let's look at this key relationship graphically, in Figures 4.4 and 4.5. We remember in a simple Keynesian model that savings increases with income, investment is assumed to be planned in a prior time period, government budgets are set for the year, exports are a function of another country's economy, and imports increase with income.

We can then subtract these lines graphically to reflect our formula $S - I - G_t = X - M$. $S - I - G_t$ is upward sloping as the constants, I and G_t, are subtracted from savings that rises with income. Conversely, $X - M$ is negative because exports, fixed by the other country's income, are overrun by imports rising with the domestic economy.

We can now visualize the effects of a change in domestic spending—say perhaps government outlays—on growth and our trade balance in Figure 4.6. If we increase G, S – I – Gt shifts downward. This should have the positive effect of increasing income from Y_1 to Y_2 as seen on the horizontal axis. However, absorbing more goods and services domestically will also mean that $X - M$, our trade balance, will deteriorate. We can see that the distance between where $S - I - G_{t2}$ crosses with $X - M$ has grown farther from the horizontal axis. Crucially, if we consume, invest or provide more government services at home, we will need to borrow to pay for these goods and services. The vertical distance between the intersection of the external balance $(X - M)$ line with the internal spending (S – I – Gt) line and the zero baseline illustrates the imbalanced financing gap. In consuming more from the rest of the world than we produce at home, the United States must at the same time borrow to pay for these net imports. In other words, we exchange future liabilities on the financial account for current spending at home. Indeed the United States has been consuming more than it produces; foreigners now hold over fourteen trillion dollars of U.S. debt to finance expenditures by consumers, businesses, and government.[11]

Figure 4.4. Basic Keynesian Relationships

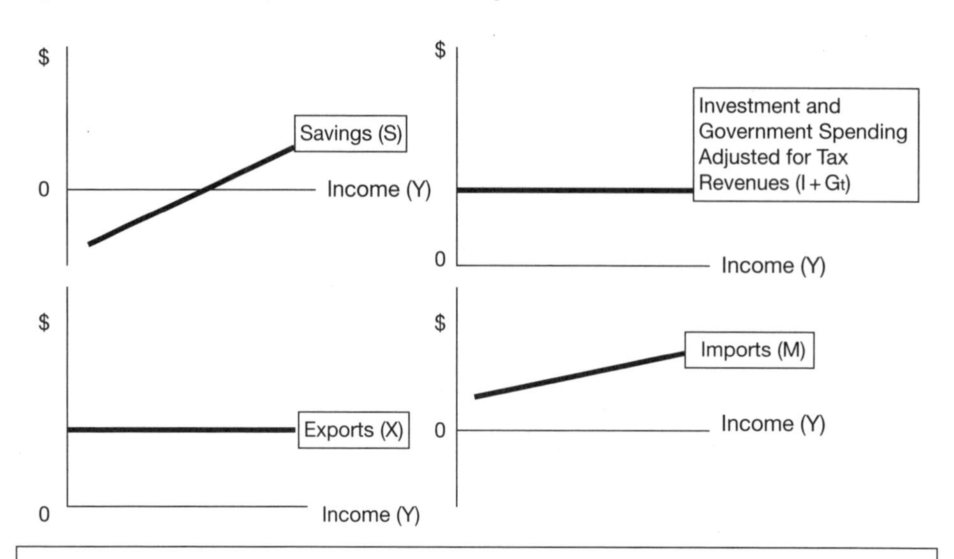

Savings and Imports increase with income and so have positive slopes. You might dissave (borrow) at low income; with aid you may also import at low income. Exports are exogenous, determined by the other country's demand. Business and net government spending are fixed in an earlier period and so don't vary with current income. If income increases, the tax collection should rise in a subsequent year.

Figure 4.5. X – M = S – I – G

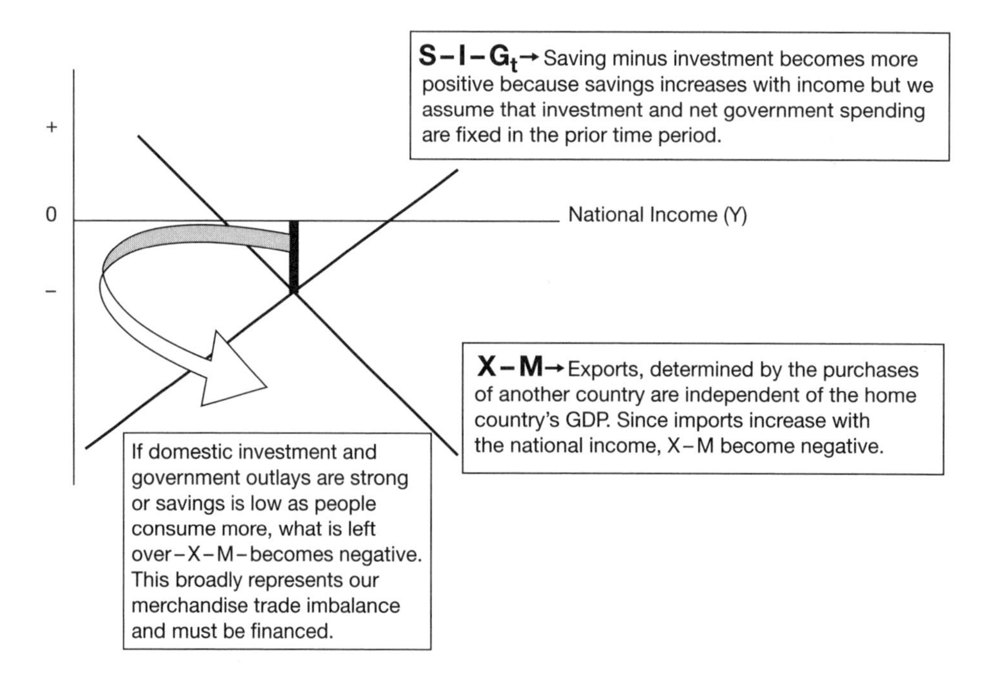

Figure 4.6. Financing Required

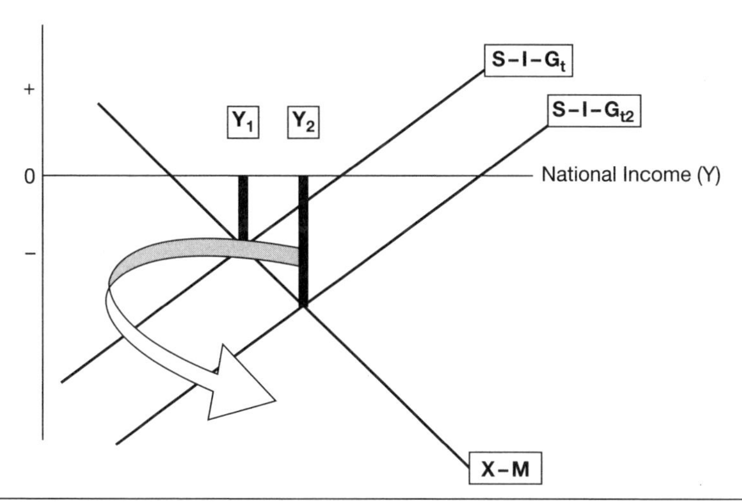

An increase in government spending increases the domestic deficit and shifts the S–I–G$_t$ curve down, increasing income but also adding pressure to the trade deficit.

Is It Bad to Run a Current Account Deficit?

The answer to this question is "it depends." Factors include how big the deficit is relative to the size of the economy, the depth of financial markets to channel the capital flowing in to offset the excess spending, who is doing the spending and what the money is being used for. To understand this more fully, we need to examine just what is happening in the current and the financial accounts. A look at the U.S. BOP can help us parse out dangerous current account deficits from ones that can be sustainably financed into the future; this is the widening divide reflected in Figure 4.6.

The current account deficit for the United States was a gaping -$731 billion in 2007; it fell to -$471.7 billion in 2011.[12] This latter figure is approximately 3.6% of our GDP.[13] Although exports have risen steadily over the past 50 years, imports have increased more dramatically. Indeed, the United States is running the largest industrial country trade deficit on record. Oil has been a significant pressure on U.S. imports; from 2002 to the third quarter of 2008 our oil bill rose by 2% of GDP,[14] and in 2011 oil imports cost the U.S. $327 billion, up from $229 billion in 2005.[15] The government has also been absorbing resources in purchases to support our foreign policy in Iraq, Afghanistan, and the Middle East. In short, U.S. consumers, businesses, and the government have been spending more than we are making.

As shown in Figure 4.7, the current account deficit for 2009 was an improvement over the year before due to the slowing of the U.S. economy as cautious and unemployed consumers imported less as well as a weakening of the U.S. dollar. As we'll talk about below, a cheaper dollar helps U.S. exports and makes imports

Figure 4.7. U.S. Trade in Goods and Services

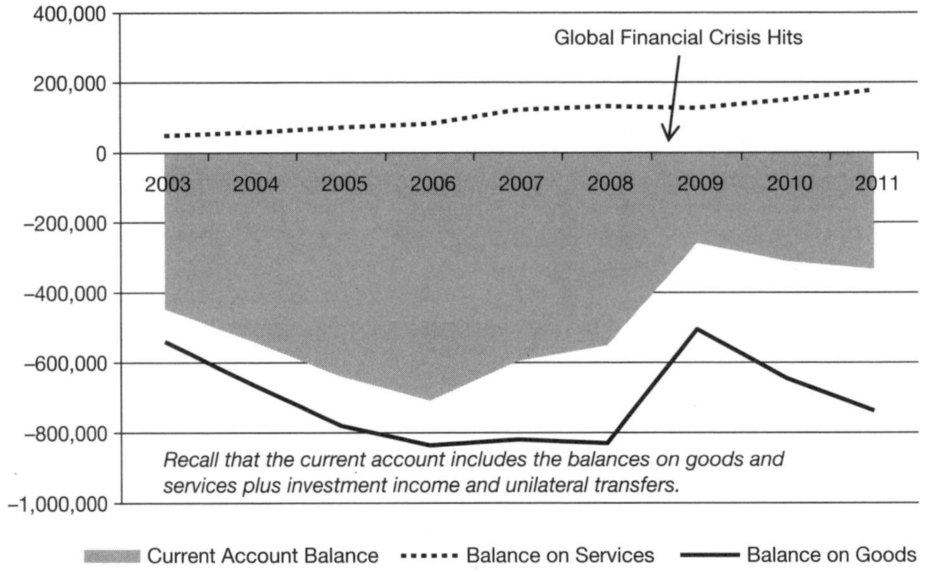

400,000
200,000
0
−200,000
−400,000
−600,000
−800,000
−1,000,000
2003 2004 2005 2006 2007 2008 2009 2010 2011
Global Financial Crisis Hits
Recall that the current account includes the balances on goods and services plus investment income and unilateral transfers.
Current Account Balance
Balance on Services
Balance on Goods

Source: Bureau of Economic Analysis.

more expensive. Nonetheless, unless the American preference to stock up on consumer goods over socking away savings is reversed—and the Chinese and Germans become more comfortable dipping into their nest eggs for current purchases—the fundamental imbalance in the global economy is likely to persist.

Our pattern of spending more on goods and services than we produce must of course logically be matched by other countries saving today and selling us their products. It makes sense as well that other nations aren't going to send us their cars or clothes or oil for free: we must pay for them. Return for a second to our simple determinants of national income $C + I + G + (X - M)$. If another country is producing more than it is consuming, it is saving; this is translated into a current account surplus. Since China and Germany are running a surplus, they can lend their excess savings to us—so we can buy the goods and services they are selling us.

Indeed, that is what is happening in the global economy. As we are buying more at home, foreigners are lending us money to finance this spending boom. We can see this on the BOP accounts: a current account deficit must be matched by a financial account inflow to finance the excess demand. Since the United States has roughly been buying $800 billion more of goods and services per year from the rest of the world than they from us, other countries have been lending us the equivalent to finance these purchases. But foreigners don't just send us IOUs to buy their TVs and cars. Instead, Americans get the cash to send back to foreigners from the money international investors inject into our system when they purchase assets that they believe will have value out into the future. Foreigners bought U.S. stocks and public and private bonds to the tune of $1.9 trillion in 2006. At the same time, Americans invested $1.1 trillion in assets abroad, leaving the $800 billion difference—just about what we needed for our excess spending over savings.[16]

To some clever minds this is starting to sound like a scam—can Americans continue to buy more than we make because foreigners are sending us money? The answer is, again, it depends. If foreigners believe that the U.S. economy is a more promising place to invest capital than other choices, money flows in. The credibility of open U.S. financial markets encourages investment. However, if investors get jittery about getting their money back, foreign capital will begin to dry up. They will want to cash in the dollars we send them and invest in another country. Thus far, unlike crises in Mexico in 1982 or Asia in 1998, investors continue to willingly finance American excess. By the end of 2014, foreign investments in the United States exceeded the value of U.S. investments abroad by $6.9 trillion.[17] Called our **net international investment position** (NIIP), this measures our outstanding liabilities to the rest of the world. Where the financial account picks up the annual flows, the NIIP is the full outstanding bill. For the United States, it is a big one.

What has been surprising to many analysts is that the rest of the world has continued to invest in the United States despite the towering size of this external debt. Imagine for a minute that the United States were a developing country—say Mexico, which found itself in deep debt in 1982. It made no sense to continue to send a debtor country more money. When Mexico began to run persistent current account deficits, funding from the rest of the world evaporated. As capital flowed out of Mexico, its exchange rate came under pressure. Strangely, during the global financial crisis, international imbalances did not unwind, and the value of the currency of the world's biggest debtor, the United States, rose rather than collapsed. Understanding why the United States has not been subject to the same tough medicine as Mexico involves an understanding of currencies and exchange rates—our next topic.

Exchange Rates and the International Financial System

An exchange rate is simply the price of one currency in terms of another. It is a crucial link between the domestic economy and global markets. Figure 4.8 (a + b) shows the impact that an increase in demand for a nation's good on its currency. If the United States increases its demand for oil from Mexico, it will need to buy pesos to pay the Mexican oil producer, Pemex. We call this demand for pesos an **imputed demand**—a demand for the currency driven by the demand for the good. Have a look at the vertical axis on the left figure. As the market demands more pesos to pay for the oil, the price of the peso rises. You should read the vertical axis as what each peso (the denominator in this case) "buys" or its value in dollars. Before the increase in demand, one peso was worth $2, or a ratio of 2:1. (We have chosen "easy math" rather than true exchange rates between the United States and Mexico to illustrate our point. In reality in 2013, each peso only bought $.07.) After the shift in demand, each peso is worth $2.5, or a ratio of 2.5 to 1. We call this an **appreciation** of the peso. The right hand side of the figure is the mirror image in the U.S. market. Now dollars are on the horizontal axis. As the market is demanding fewer dollars relative to pesos, the price expressed in terms of dollars falls. From an initial equilibrium of one dollar buying half a peso, the new intersection would show that the dollar would buy fewer pesos, signifying that the dollar had undergone a **depreciation**.

This presentation underscores that exchange rates are ratios. We can look at the home currency divided by the foreign or take its reciprocal, the foreign currency divided by the home. This allows us to express prices in either currency as shown in Table 4.4. In the first column we are looking at the home ($) divided by the foreign currency (F); in the second the foreign (F) is divided by the home ($). In column 1, you would read that €1 buys $1.24 or $1 buys €.8003. A quick check shows that 1/.8003 equals 1.24. Confused? Go to Google "currency converter" and put a few values in for a currency of interest.

Figure 4.8. Supply and Demand for a Currency

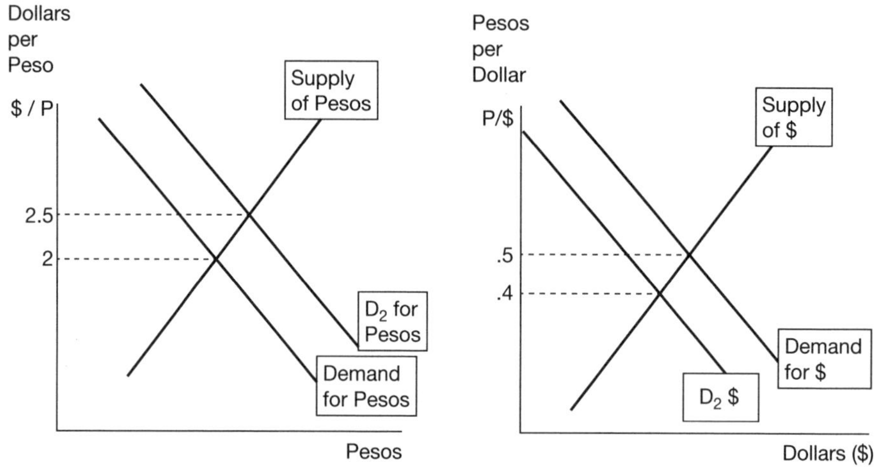

Source: U.S Census Bureau, Foreign Trade Division, 2008.

Table 4.4. Currency Conversions

	How Much One Unit of the Foreign Currency Buys in $; Ratio Is $/F)	*How Much One Dollar Buys in Foreign Currency Units; Ratio Is F/$)*
Euro	1.2496	0.8003
Pound	1.5638	0.6395
Yen	0.0126	79.4700
Yuan	0.1572	6.3626
Peso	0.0728	13.7453
Dollar	0.9766	1.0240

Source: Google Currency Calculator. Calculated on June 26, 2012.

It is convention to express the exchange rate with the dollar as the denominator—with the exception of the pound as historically it was the central currency before the dollar. If you are confused which to use when buying something, write the rate out as a ratio and multiply. You should end up in the home currency. For example, if you were at a shop in Ireland and you saw a knit sweater you'd like to buy priced at €100, how many dollars would it cost given the rates above? The sweater €100 × \$1.2496/€; the € in the numerator cancels with the denominator leaving you with the price in dollars, \$124.96. If you took the same €100 and multiplied it by the €.8003/\$ rate, you would have a nonsensical $€^2/\$$. If you are ever confused while traveling as to which of the \$/€ or €/\$ exchange rates to use, save yourself a negative surprise when the bill comes in by writing out the price in local currency and making sure the currency signs cancel to leave you back in dollars.

Understanding that an exchange rate is a ratio, what, then, determines the price of the currency? A currency only has value if someone wants to hold it. Therefore, the underlying value of the piece of paper we call a dollar is a function of what it can buy. If the rest of the world is less excited about buying American goods than the United States is about importing foreign products, the value of the U.S. dollar should decline relative to other currencies. A country running a current account deficit should show a weakening currency; the demand for a surplus country's goods should drive up the value of its money. That is, with a floating, or market determined, exchange rate, excess demand for your goods should cause your currency to appreciate; when the rest of the world is buying less from you than you want from them, your currency should depreciate or decline. A depreciating currency should help to correct trade imbalances. As the price of your goods in terms of others become cheaper, they should become more attractive to foreign buyers. Unfortunately, at home your consumers—which as we understand with the global value chain include industries that use imported components—must pay higher prices for products such as TVs and machines, decreasing their purchasing power. To understand the results of an appreciation or depreciation on factors ranging from a domestic current account to global reserves, consult the appendix of this chapter.

From a BOP perspective, a deficit should therefore be associated with a depreciation of a currency and a surplus with an appreciation. As we have seen with the United States, however, the data don't always support this logic. A look at Figure 4.9 presents this puzzling evidence. As the current account deficit as a share of GDP was deteriorating throughout the 1990s, the value of the dollar was paradoxically strengthening. Although post-2000 we broadly see a decline in the dollar as the current account tips over 5% of GDP, despite the persistent current account deficit most recently the dollar held its value. The value of the dollar defies logic—at least in the short run. What is going on? Why is the dollar strengthening when conditions in the United States are weakening?

In addition to the **BOP approach** to exchange rate determination, which focuses on trade pressures on deficit or surplus countries, we also need to take into account another market: money. Not only can currencies buy goods, but they are also assets that can transfer value into the future. You can choose to hold dollars as an investment today in anticipation that the dollar will rise over time, and you can buy more goods in the future. But rather than stuffing the dollars under your mattress, you will likely

Figure 4.9. U.S. Current Account and the Dollar

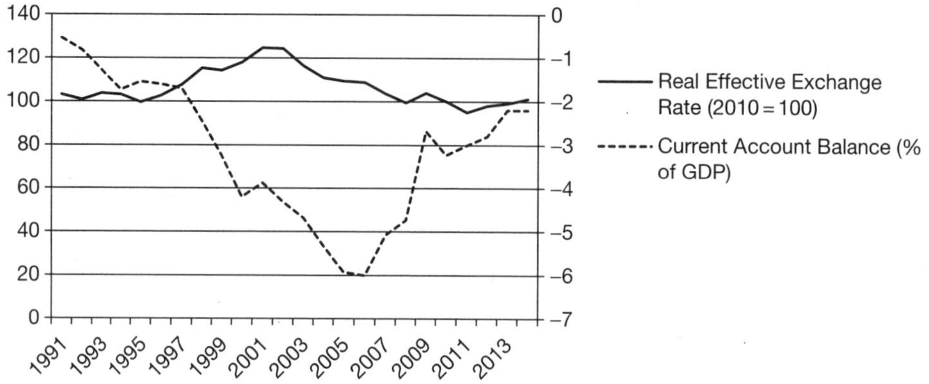

Source: World Bank, World Development Indicators.

put them into dollar denominated stocks or bonds that will earn interest while you are waiting for the value to increase. The **asset approach** to exchange rate determination provides a clue as to why the U.S. dollar was rising while the current account was deteriorating: investors wanted dollars to buy the stocks of U.S. companies or American Treasury bills. If the expected value of American financial assets is higher relative to foreign assets, the dollar will appreciate. Focus on two things in that last sentence: expected and relative. It is what investors *think* will happen *compared* to similar investments in other countries that determine its value. The U.S. economy might be weak, but if its prospects are stronger than the rest of the world, the dollar should strengthen. Our global supply chain also complicates asset markets. If the U.S. market is weak, you might expect that people will not want to buy the stocks of American companies. But as corporations are now global, people may still want to buy GM or Apple stock because the Chinese or Indian markets are booming. This will paradoxically make the current account worse as the stronger dollar buys more imports and deters the purchase of American goods abroad.

Analyzing the price of financial assets—most basically money—also gives us insight into the way financial systems link economies. If you are free to invest in another country's currency—that is, there are no **capital controls** or rules preventing you from purchasing a foreign asset—you will look at the difference between the returns on the home asset (say a U.S. Treasury) versus a foreign asset (perhaps a British T bill). But if you are to invest in a British security, you need to look at a couple of other things. First, to buy a British T bill you will need pounds. What is the price that you can buy pounds today? Second, you will want to estimate what the value of your asset will be worth when it matures. If your British T bill comes due in six months, what do you think the pound will be worth then? How much you will make on your investment in a British T bill will therefore be the sum of the interest rate and the difference between the exchange rate today—sometimes called the **spot rate**—and what the markets expect the pound to be worth six months from now—expressed as the **forward rate**. Now think about how interest rate management may complicate economic policy in an open economy. Let's say that I want to dampen inflation in the

United States; one way to do this is to raise interest rates so that people buy bonds and have less to spend on goods. But not only I am attracting the interest of my citizens, but I am also enticing British citizens to purchase U.S. bonds, whose returns are now higher than those in the United Kingdom. In doing so, British investors would need dollars, selling pounds to obtain them. The price of the dollar would rise or appreciate; the value of the pound may decline. But if the price of the pound becomes cheap today relative to its long-term value, this may induce investors to purchase British notes as they can buy them cheaply today, making money on the appreciation as the pound returns to a long-run equilibrium in the future. Furthermore, an interest rate increase in the United States, as it attracts capital to U.S. markets and appreciates the dollar, will have a dampening effect on exports. Confused? The bottom line here is that an interest rate move on the part of one country (here the United States) affects the currency of both countries and the price of their relative exports.

We can think about this relationship between interest rates and exchange rates by using a more generalized model of the asset demand for a currency in Figure 4.10. Rather than spot and forward rates, let's use $E_{\$/£}$ to represent the spot rates and E^e to approximate the forward rate as a proxy for what the market expects the exchange rate to be in the future. Rh is the return on the home currency (that is, broadly speaking, its interest rate) and R_f is the parallel interest return on the foreign asset. But we know from our discussion above that there is more to the return than just the interest rate since what you would actually receive when you cashed in your foreign asset for dollars would be not only the interest rate on the foreign asset but also the premium from whether the foreign exchange rate strengthened or the discount if it weakened in the time you had your money in the foreign bond. We can represent this earning from the exchange rate as the difference between E^e (that expected future rate) and E expressed as a percent of the spot rate E that you buy today. This is actually a pretty simple lesson. If the foreign currency is expected to strengthen in the future, this will add to your total return; if it weakens when it is

Figure 4.10. Asset Demand for a Currency

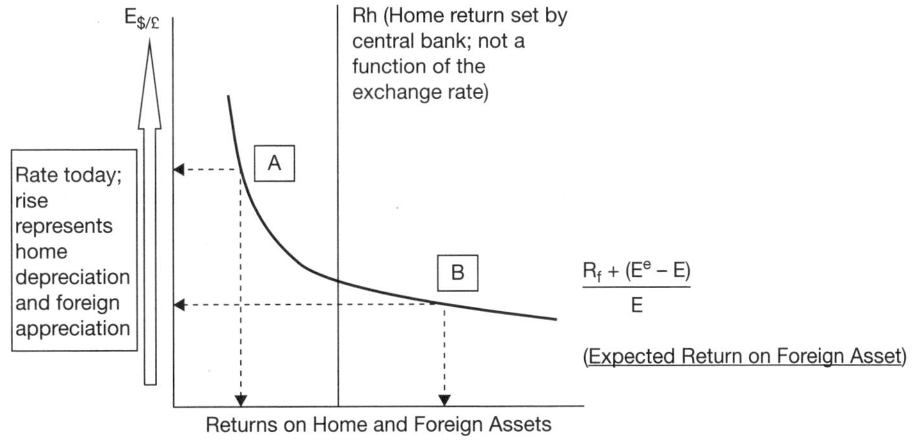

Source: Adapted from Krugman/Obstfeld International Economics.

time to turn your British T bill into dollars, then you get fewer dollars back. Let's see how this plays out on the graph. Notice that as £ rises (goes up on the vertical axis), each pound is buying more dollars or the pound is appreciating and the dollar is depreciating. So if you are at a point such as A above, this means that the current rate of exchange is stronger than the future rate that is expected to prevail. If you are a dollar-based investor, you'd be buying a British T bill with weak dollars, getting fewer pounds for your currency, and cutting into future returns. In contrast, if the dollar is strong today as at point B, it buys more pounds today. When it comes time to exchange your British T bill back into dollars, if the pound has strengthened to that long-term expect rate E^e your return (measured on the horizontal axis) increases. This is the simple rule of buy cheap and sell dear. If the foreign currency is cheap today, use your stronger home units to buy lots of the weaker currency if you anticipate that when the asset matures you will be paid out in then stronger units to use to buy your newly weakened home currency.

Indeed, this in part explains the rise in the U.S. dollar throughout the 1990s. Americans were purchasing more abroad, but the perception of growing American affluence attracted foreigners to invest in our economy. Of course, foreign investors in U.S. markets can choose to take their money out at any point—so their investment is our liability. As our liabilities piled up—that is, as our NIIP soared past the trillion dollar mark, some investors began to get nervous that Americans would not have the money to pay back these loans in the future. We can see in Figure 4.9 that the dollar weakened from 2005 to 2008 reflecting investor uncertainty in the United States relative to other markets. But why, you might ask after examining this figure, did the dollar recover in 2008? The key to understanding this is that the asset value of the dollar is always a relative concept. That is, even as the American economy went into a tailspin, as it was a safer bet than many foreign investments, investors kept their money in the United States. For example, U.S. Treasury bills are seen as a safe haven investment; the demand for dollars to buy these treasuries continued to be a better investment than government bonds offered by the rest of the world.

We can conclude then, that countries spending more than they are producing can continue to pursue these profligate consumption behaviors so long as other nations want to provide them their own savings for investment. But we haven't yet completed the story. It also matters how your currency fits into the global financial system.

Exchange Rate Systems in Historical Perspective

Let's go back to our example of Mexico as it was running a BOP deficit in 1982, the year the developing country debt crisis erupted. One could argue that Mexico was a good place to invest: it had recently discovered ample supplies of oil that could be used in the future to finance the liabilities. In fact, much of the deficit was driven by business investment in the petroleum sector. But investors just weren't sure; there was also negative news of budget deficits and inflation. Given uncertainty as with other developing nations at the time, they didn't want to hold assets denominated in pesos. If something went wrong on the road to oil wealth and the economy imploded, they simply didn't trust that the peso would hold value. International banks and other investors therefore required that Mexico (and other developing nations in the twentieth century) borrow its money in dollars, leaving it with a mountain of dollar-denominated debt.

Now let's say that there is a shock to this system as shown in Figure 4.11. In this case, the result of the 1982 global recession caused the rest of the world to buy less from Mexico. The current account tumbled further into deficit, spooking investors who decline to lend more to Mexico to continue to finance its spending. As the demand for the peso fell, its value tumbled, too. Now this isn't entirely a bad thing. A weaker peso makes Mexican beer, tomatoes, or auto parts cheaper in the United States, and spurs exports. But it also makes the number of pesos needed to service the dollar-denominated debt rise. If before the crisis 245 pesos bought a dollar, and after the crisis it traded at 1,200 pesos to the dollar, Mexico then needed roughly five times as many pesos to service the same $100 million bond.[18]

In this case, Mexico fell into the condition that economists dubbed **original sin**: the inability to issue international instruments in one's own currency. This example tells us a lot about the debt crises of the 1980s and the currency crises of the 1990s: it matters if your money is universally accepted as a store of value into the future.

In addition to currencies such as the Japanese yen and the euro, the dollar has, like the British pound before it, a special position in the international system: that of a reserve currency. A **reserve currency** (or anchor currency) is a currency that is held in significant quantities by many governments and institutions as part of the international financial system. The dollar's role as a reserve

Figure 4.11. Mexican Debt Crisis

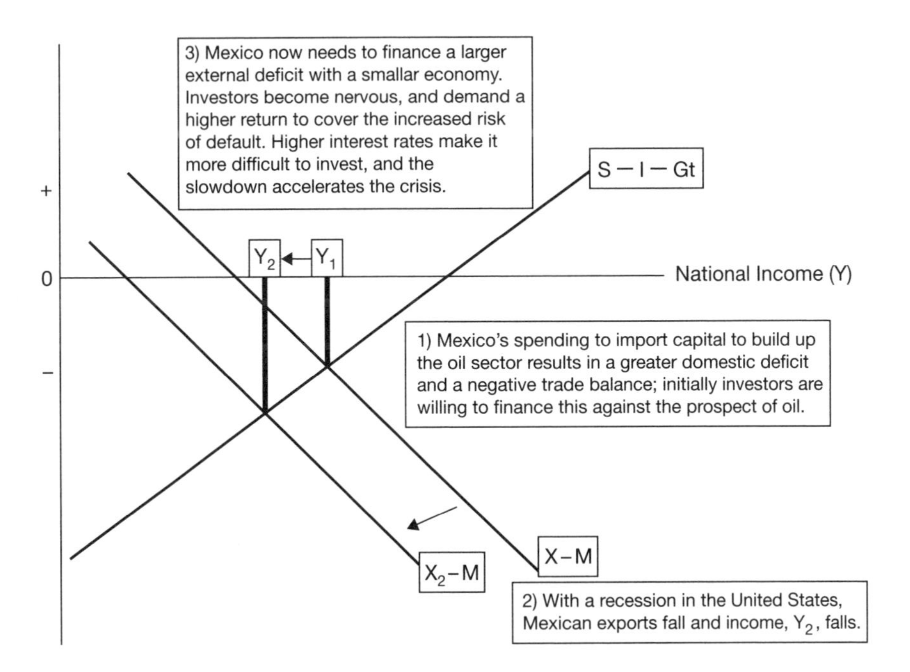

currency dates back to the Bretton Woods system of 1945. Under this system, designed by Ambassador Harry Dexter White of the United States and John Maynard Keynes of the United Kingdom, the United States acted as a guarantor of last resort for the international financial system. (Have a look at Box 4.2 for key dates in international financial history.) It guaranteed the exchange of dollars for gold at $35 an ounce. Since a dollar was as good as gold, people were happy to hold easy-to-use dollars instead of lugging heavy bags of gold. Other

Box 4.3. The IMF: A Contested Institution in Search of a New Mission

The IMF has grown from its 29 founding members in 1945 to an organization promoting financial stability for 186 nations in 2010. Formed as one of the Bretton Woods twins, in counterpart to the World Bank's developmental mission the IMF was designed to promote exchange rate adjustments and short-term BOP lending to promote macroeconomic stability and growth.[19] Unlike the grander vision held by John Maynard Keynes at the Bretton Woods conference for an international clearing union with its own currency and rules for both surplus and deficit nations to adjust, Ambassador Harry Dexter White's more limited scope of a stabilization fund prevailed. Indeed throughout the history of the IMF, the tension between the need for a global banker and the limited instruments at its disposal have shaped its performance.

The immediate post-war tasks of reinstituting exchange arrangements, begun with a loan to France in 1947 during the European Reconstruction, gave way to activities largely centered on developing countries. The IMF was at the forefront of managing the debt crises in the 1980s. Its highly contested conditionalities replaced state centered tools of import substitution employed in the 1940s–70s with market mechanisms. Receipt of credit tranches were contingent upon signing a letter of intent to liberalize the economy by opening it to international trade and investment, privatizing state-owned enterprises, eliminating subsidies, and correcting exchange rate overvaluations. Decreasing the rate of growth of wages and government spending was crucial to its formula of reducing absorption at home in order to release resources for the repayment of debt. Macro targets, particularly for inflation and fiscal policy, had to be achieved for the release of additional funds. A restructuring under an IMF policy signaled a green light to the private sector that indebted countries were worthy of additional lending to help them muddle through debt crises.

But IMF packages were hotly criticized for their social costs and for their standardized cookie cutter approach to different country's debt problems. Others suggested that the IMF "bailouts" were a too generous use of tax money and that countries should be left to sink or swim. The rigidity of the conditionality model was blamed for exacerbating the currency crises that slammed the Asian region in the late 1990s. Similar demand reduction prescriptions were applied to countries that were not suffering from an excess of private or public spending. Asian nations along with other developing countries vowed never to return to IMF medicine, and built reserve war chests to cushion shocks when necessary. IMF defenders alleged that as its funds are derived from assessments of quotas by members, its policies by right had to be highly conservative. Voting power in the institution is distributed by quota shares, with the United States holding the lion's share. As the steward of global money, some see the need for a lean and mean IMF machine.

To its credit, the IMF has adopted more flexible facilities over the years. The oil facility and the compensatory financing facilities, for example, have more generous terms to help nations hit by external shocks adjust without imposing an additional domestic distress. It has also become more attune to the needs of the poorest nations. The IMF provides two primary types of financial assistance to low-income countries: low-interest loans under the Poverty Reduction and Growth Trust (PRGT), debt relief under the Heavily Indebted Poor Countries (HIPC) Initiative, and the Multilateral Debt Relief Initiative (MDRI). These resources come from member contributions and the IMF itself, rather than from the quota subscriptions.[20]

The shifts taking place in global finance as traditional debtor countries such as Brazil have not only repaid their external obligations, but have become creditors with access to sovereign wealth funds caused the IMF to be an institution in search of a mission. The global financial crisis renewed the IMF's relevance as a facilitator of global credit. Creating a flexible credit line, it promoted credibility for countries pursuing sound economic policies, but rocked by global turbulence. It has also assumed a central role in organizing credit for Eastern and Central European economies in distress and in promoting cooperation among the G-20 nations. Debate continues, nevertheless, regarding its ability to provide the surveillance necessary for crisis prevention, the liquid resources for effective crisis response, or the mechanisms to redress the buildup of international reserves and global imbalances. Although the IMF may have gained a new lease on life in response to the financial crisis, proposals abound for institutional reform to enhance effectiveness.[21]

countries pegged their currencies to the dollar and vowed (except under unusual circumstances) to defend the par rate. Under the rules of this system, a country running a BOP deficit was obliged to decrease its money supply; a surplus country was supposed to increase its stock of money.

This process took place automatically. If a country, say France, was running a deficit, it would need more dollars to buy the international goods it wanted. The central bank was obligated to sell dollars to meet this excess demand. But to sell dollars it had to buy francs—thereby decreasing the domestic currency available to buy goods on the shelves in the French stores. As less money is available domestically, prices fall, making these goods more attractive to foreigners—and automatically reversing the current account deficit. The benefit of this system was price stability. Harkening back to the days when money supplies were tied to the slowly rising global stock of gold, in theory this agreement tempered the ability of a country to run the printing presses in order to jump-start the economy. Global financial stability was as good as gold—or the dollar.

This **automatic adjustment mechanism**, as it was called under the fixed exchange system, only worked so long as governments didn't cheat. That is, when a government is facing a contraction precipitated by a fall in the money supply, it is tempting for politicians to **sterilize**, the term used to print money to buy an international currency. Since inflation in small amounts might be less painful than unemployed voters, countries often resorted to this mechanism. As illustrated by the **impossible trinity** in Figure 4.12, under a fixed exchange rate system, a country is bound to give up one of the three points of the triangle. One must concede sovereignty in monetary policy to the automatic adjustment mechanism if you have a fixed exchange rate and freely mobile capital. Capital flows, either in response to trade patterns or asset investments, pressure the exchange rate. According to the

Figure 4.12. Impossible Trinity: The Monetary Trilemma

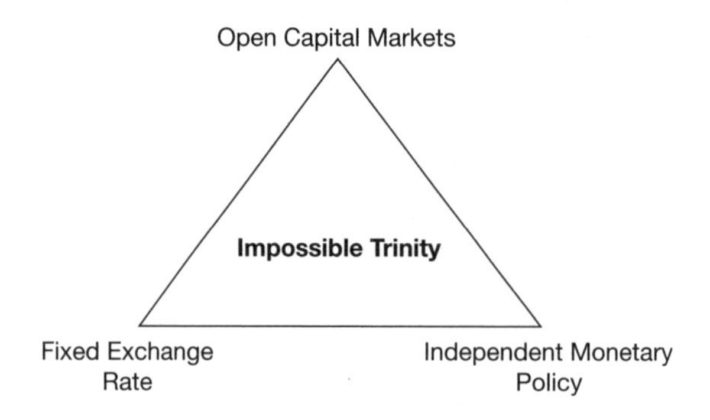

rules of the fixed exchange rate regime, countries must then intervene to buy or sell international reserves to defend the par rate and forego an independent monetary policy. The lesson is that freely mobile capital impedes the discretion of central bankers to set autonomous monetary policy under a fixed exchange rate regime. Any attempt to ease pressure on the economy is thwarted by the need to defend the exchange rate. Since downward economic adjustment is painful, the tendency to sterilize international reserve flows is strong, especially in election years. Of course one ultimately pays the cost in terms of higher inflation—but that is most frequently after the political crisis has passed. We will see later in this chapter that with highly globalized capital markets, even replacing a fixed rate with a floating currency doesn't guarantee monetary autonomy.

But under the fixed Bretton Woods regime, the United States had special status and a reprieve from the impossible trinity. The reserve currency—the U.S. dollar—wasn't obligated to adjust its money supply in response to a deficit or a surplus. Instead, its role was to defend the par rate versus gold. So long as people believed the dollar was as good as gold, the United States could continue to run the printing press in pursuit of an independent monetary policy. Much like today, the key was confidence in the financial system. This fixed exchange rate system, although imperfect, worked best in the post-war period when the United States was strong relative to war torn Europe and Asia. The rest of the world needed American goods and was therefore happy to hold an excess of dollars to purchase them. When global economic power began to shift in the mid to late 1960s and the United States became mired in Vietnam while fighting the war on poverty at home, cracks appeared in the system, and confidence in the United States eroded. In August 1971, President Nixon slammed the window on gold, refusing to back the excess dollars floating around, effectively forcing the international system into a float. Despite attempts to patch the fixed exchange rate system back together, by 1976 the Jamaica agreement formalized reality: countries were to let their currencies float one against the other. A legacy of the Bretton Woods system—at least to date—has been that as long as the rest of the world is content to hold dollars, there is less pressure on the United States to adjust.

Currency Union in Practice: Evaluating the Euro

The euro and the renminbi have aspirations to challenge the role of the dollar as a reserve currency. In the short term, however, the euro is in crisis and the renminbi is not fully convertible for global trade. Let's look at these issues. When the international financial system moved to a float, many European nations found the uncertainty tied to exchange rate fluctuations an impediment to trade. Under a fixed system, readjustments in the par rate were by design rare. Under a float, the currency can move daily—and sometimes for unpredictable reasons. Imagine trade between Germany and France. Before, the French ship cases of *Beaujolais to Germany,* the vintners required a letter of credit from a bank to release the wine. But the importer may not receive the shipment for several weeks. Let's say the value of the Deutschmark weakens in the interim. The German company would now have to come up with more local currency to cover the shipment—cutting into profit. If the importer didn't want to take the risk of a currency change, the company could go to the bank and buy the francs in the forward market—that is, lock in the price today from someone willing to bet that the franc (and not the deutschmark) would fall. But this also comes at a business cost. Simply having to keep track of all these currency positions for trade between increasingly integrated countries led many European countries to adopt the euro.

The road to the single currency wasn't easy. European nations had tried linking their currencies before, through a kind of fixed exchange rate parity grid. Countries were required to intervene when the value of their currency slipped outside a predetermined band of cross rates. In 1989, the Delors report laid out the goals of monetary union: to reduce exchange rate fluctuations and uncertainty, lower inflation, facilitate integration, and improve investment. Because monetary union goes beyond linking exchange rates to sharing one money supply, conditions, called the **Maastricht criteria**, were developed to promote macroeconomic convergence prior to the launch of the new system. Inflation had to be at 1.5% of the average, long-term interest rates within 2% of the average three lowest rates, budget deficits under 3% of GDP and public debt at a maximum of 60% of GDP. Eleven countries qualified and chose to join in 1998. As Eastern European countries have acceded to the Union, four others have qualified; 16 out of 27 total EU countries participated in the single currency in 2009. More may qualify and choose to join in the next few years but some opted to stay out. Notably the United Kingdom, Denmark, and Sweden remain outside the Eurozone, believing their economies to be too unlike the continental countries to share a single monetary policy.

Monetary policy is directed by the European Central Bank (ECB) which maintains a firm commitment to price stability. Under the guidance of the bank, the euro evolved from a unit of account—a kind of "super" fixed exchange rate, established in 1998, to an actual currency note in 2002. Although at its launch the euro was weak, increasing confidence in the ECB led to a strengthening of the currency by 2005. Indeed, during that time some members felt the value of the euro was too strong and was compromising the ability of countries to export. We can see the strengthening of the euro up to 2008 in Figure 4.13. Despite radical differences in labor practices and industrial structures between a country such as Portugal and one such as the Netherlands, the same currency price must clear both markets. Asymmetric

Figure 4.13. U.S. Dollar to Euro Exchange Rate

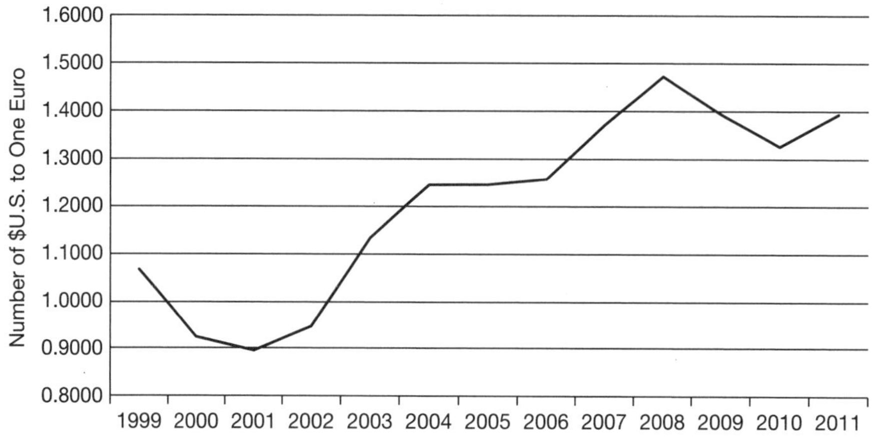

Source: Federal Reserve Bank of St. Louis Economic Data.

shocks—jolts, such as the financial crisis that hit a more labor-intensive country differently from to a more industrialized economy—add enormous stress into the system. By joining the euro, countries have forfeited a key macro tool, independent monetary policy, in favor of price stability and enhanced creditworthiness. Through the European Growth and Stability Pact (GSP), an agreement that governs fiscal expenditures, countries must over time respect the 3% budget deficit as a percent of GDP rule but also allows for extraordinary circumstances. Yet adhering to the GSP means that not only have countries forfeited independent monetary policies, but they have also tied their fiscal arms behind their backs.

As the euro turned ten in 2008, some economies were groaning under these constraints—and indeed fudged compliance. Remember that when monetary policies are fixed, if a country wishes to sell more abroad it must either raise productivity or lower costs, including labor. These actions create tough political problems. The Greek crisis of 2010 was precipitated by expenditures outrunning revenues and a population unwilling to swallow tough austerity measures. Ireland and Italy are struggling to reduce their budget deficits and enhance productivity. But the global financial crisis also underscores the stability and credibility benefits of the euro. Iceland, which is not in the Eurozone, looked longingly for such an anchor as its currency and much of its national wealth melted in a bank panic. Small businesses, such as those in Hungary (not within the Eurozone) were especially exposed to exchange rate changes on debt. Many Hungarians borrowed in Swiss francs and Euros; when the independent Hungarian forint plummeted, they were buried under foreign currency debts. One borrower began with a monthly payment of 110,000 forints on his loan; by 2009, after the currency crash his bill is 230,000 forints a month—more than twice what he had budgeted to come up with.[22] In Romania, one of the EU's poorest members, over 60% of household borrowing is held in foreign currency debt.[23] Smaller European countries that use the euro are able to get access to cheaper credit because of their association with the ECB, lowering borrowing costs at home.

Sharing the creditworthiness of German fiscal and monetary discipline, stable euro-based borrowing can finance investments at a lower cost than debt issued in more volatile currencies.

The price of lost autonomy is a lower cost of capital. Dani Rodrik's reconfiguration of the monetary trilemma as a political conundrum highlights the tradeoffs of economic union. As depicted in Figure 4.14, democratic countries are caught in a bind as their own constituencies will always vote for adjustment policies that will benefit the home nation. Yet deep integration engages tradeoffs that at times requires domestic pain for the union's gain. Autonomy to pursue national strategies is constrained. As Rodrik notes, "If we want more globalization, we must either give up some democracy or some national sovereignty. Pretending that we can have all three simultaneously leaves us in an unstable no-man's land."[24] Indeed the euro crisis is a prism for the dilemma of globalization. The strength of the euro up to 2008 caused some to wonder whether it will challenge the dollar as a reserve currency. In 2007, euro-denominated securities accounted for approximately 32% of outstanding issues; the dollar still beat this at 43.1% but its share has fallen.[25] In the same way that the dominance of the pound sterling waned as the dollar overtook it in the post-World War I era, so, too, we may see a changed role for the euro. Yet this potential shift depends critically on the success of repairing the Eurozone, as Europe is currently in a two-speed zone. Table 4.5 gives a snapshot of the divergence in the Eurozone. Stronger and stable growth in Germany is markedly different than conditions in Spain and Greece, where federal governments need monetary aid from the rest of the Union continue to pay their massive debts to avoid default, hurting already-bleak growth and unemployment prospects within those countries. Further integration of the Eurozone to strengthen the monetary union is an option, but the extent to which this will happen—and the extent to which the current state of the euro will improve—will depend on the commitment of all member governments to such a change.[26] The 2016 exit of the United Kingdom from the European Union, while never a euro currency country, has, however, stalled further unification. Regardless of the developments in the Eurozone, the potential replacement of the dollar as the world's reserve currency also rests heavily on what takes place in a country on the other side of the world: China.

Figure 4.14. Rodrik's Trilemma

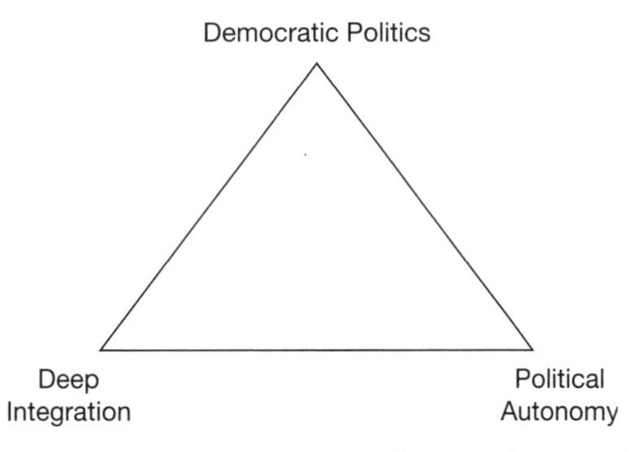

Source: Adapted from Dani Rodrik web blog, http://rodrik.typepad.com/dani_rodriks_weblog/2007/06/the-inescapable.html

Table 4.5. Euro Crisis

Country	*Diagnosis*	*Does the Euro Help or Hurt?*
Germany Largest European economy Historically the guardian of stability	Chancellor Angela Merkel continues to be a dominant presence at Eurozone negotiations. As one of the most fiscally sound members and largest economy in the currency bloc, German-stated conditionality ultimately determines bailouts and aid for others. The two-year note reached record low-interest rates in July of 2012 as demand for German debt remains strong, unlike the debt of its neighbors.[27]	The lowered value of the euro helps boost German exports, which accounts for almost half of Germany's GDP.[28] German taxpayers show discontent for funding fiscally irresponsible neighbors while others contend that the fate of the euro still rests in German hands through providing adequate bailout funds and promoting integration of the Eurozone.
France Second largest European economy Historically promotes an active role for the state	With the transition from right-of-center Nicolas Sarkozy to socialist president François Hollande in 2012, France's position in Eurozone negotiations will change. While Sarkozy was supportive of Germany's austerity-based approach, Hollande campaigned by repeatedly refusing international fiscal compact rules without simultaneously promoting growth.[29]	Although less export-dependent than Germany, the lowered value of the euro also helps make French goods more attractive worldwide. To comply with EU demands, France also needs to reduce its deficit. Measures to balance the budget to meet EU requirements, such as tax increases, are expected to hinder growth.[30]
Ireland Ireland is a small economy with high per capita GDP exceeding Germany and the United Kingdom	Ireland erupted into crisis in 2008 as its real estate bubble was burst by the global financial crisis. The Irish quickly acknowledged their problems and imposed tough IMF style austerity. After much pain, Ireland returned to market borrowing in July of 2012 and is growing again in 2015.	The so-called Celtic Tiger roared on the back of EU investments and Eurozone stability between 1995 and 2007. Finance Minister Michael Noonan credits the bailout and improved sentiments from investors due to Eurozone support in helping resolve the crisis and decrease domestic borrowing rates.[31]

Greece Greece is a small country, about one-tenth the size of Germany It is relatively poor, with per capita GDP at 60% of the German rate	Greece's financial binge crashed into crisis in 2009. One of the most troubled economies in the Eurozone, Greece is downsizing government debt through privatization, reducing the size of the government, and wage and pension cuts to abide by austerity measures agreed upon to receive bailout funds from the European Commission, ECB, and IMF.[32]	Austerity measures imposed as a condition to receive bailout funds by other euro members severely hurt domestic growth prospects and incited social unrest, while the aid itself helps stave off debt default. Borrowing rates, while high, are also probably lower than what they would be outside of the currency. Social and political unrest sparked talks of a Greek exit from the eurozone, a move that most financial analysts fear would devastate global markets. Some, however, point to the benefits of a "Grexit" coming in the form of increased monetary authority.
Italy Third largest European economy	Prime Minister Mario Monti's technocrat government, installed in 2011, is in the process of addressing fiscal deficits through spending cuts and other unpopular measures like reducing pensions and raising the retirement age.	Abiding by EU conditionality is hurting growth and meeting strong internal resistance, and bond yields continue to rise alongside Spain's despite a better overall fiscal position and a banking sector without the same asset crisis.[33]
Spain A middle-sized country in the Eurozone, with per capita GDP on par with Italy.	Prime Minister Mariano Rajoy's is addressing Spain's fiscal issues, which were actually better than those of other troubled neighbors before the crisis. Banks in Spain, with risky assets due to property-value speculations similar to those in the United States, present a more significant problem in regards to a future position for growth.[34] Spain also faces social unrest related to austerity, and youth unemployment is over 50%.[35]	The European Commission supports euro-funded aid to Spain's troubled banking system, but such aid still requires full guarantees by Spain for bailout funds. Despite progress on these agreements to reach solvency for Spanish banks, borrowing rates on 10-year Spanish debt reached almost 7% in July of 2012, near-record highs. High borrowing rates worsen the government's position to address its fiscal battle.[36]
Portugal A relatively small and poor Eurozone member	Portugal is struggling to meet eurozone bailout terms with political strife at home, and is also facing high unemployment and contraction in growth.	Other Eurozone members provided funds to prevent a worsening of the sovereign debt crisis. Similarly to Greece, Italy, and Spain, growth in Portugal is slowing in part due to austerity measures required by acceptance of the bailout.[37]

Chinese Currency Positions

London and New York may be the financial centers of the world, but China holds most of the global money. After years of saving more than it consumes, China has emerged as the world's largest holder of foreign exchange reserves. China's accumulation of currency is a direct parallel to its booming entry into world trade. As can be seen in Figure 4.15, China radically opened its economy to trade in 2000; by 2007, its exports had more than tripled their value.

Payment for Chinese exports has piled up. As of May 2010, China's Treasury securities holdings were $867.7 billion, accounting for 21.8% of total foreign ownership of U.S. Treasury securities and replacing Japan as the largest foreign holder of U.S. Treasuries. As shown in Figure 4.16, the buildup of reserves parallels China's opening to trade. In addition to the underlying preference of the Chinese to save rather than consume (recall that if savings is greater than investment and government spending, the current account as X – M will be positive), some argue that the accumulation of reserves is tied to the manipulation of China's exchange rate. Although a floating exchange rate system is accepted throughout the globe, countries can deviate and choose to fix or manage their exchange rate. From 1994 through 2005, China pegged its currency, the yuan (also called the renminbi, sort of like dollars and bucks), to the U.S. dollar at a rate of 8.25 to the dollar. Since there was more demand for the yuan by Americans buying Chinese goods, if this rate had been floating the yuan would have strengthened—perhaps so that it only took ¥6 to buy one dollar's worth of goods, increasing purchasing power.

However, the Chinese government intervenes in the currency market, effectively taking the dollars coming in to buy yuan (needed to pay for the toys and electronics made in China) and pulling them out of the domestic financial system, putting them

Figure 4.15. Chinese Trade Shares

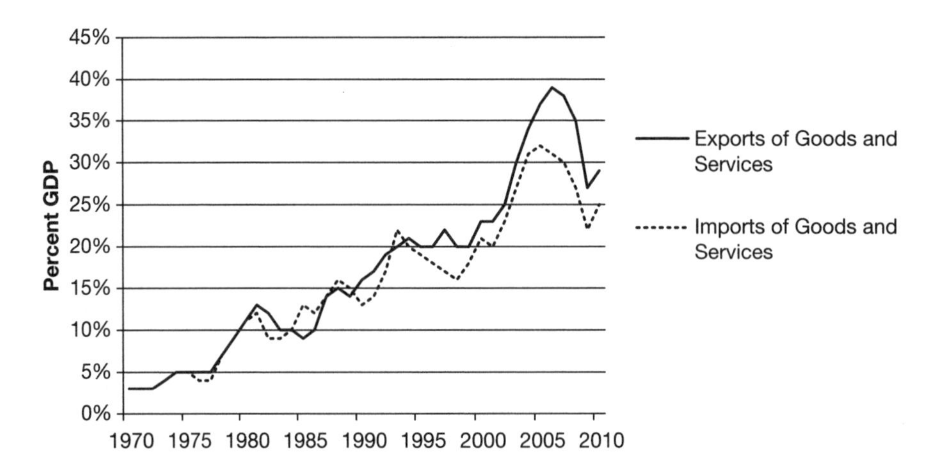

Source: World Bank, World Development Indicators.

Figure 4.16. Chinese Reserve Assets

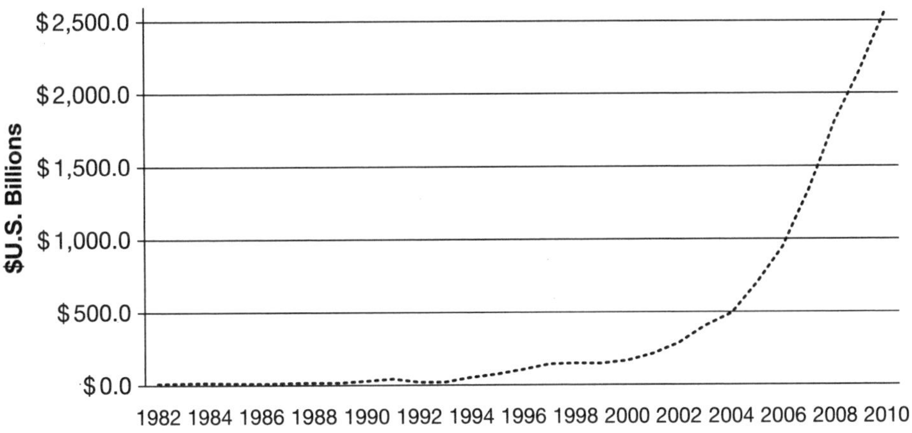

$U.S. Billions
$2,500.0
$2,000.0
$1,500.0
$1,000.0
$500.0
$0.0
1982 1984 1986 1988 1990 1992 1994 1996 1998 2000 2002 2004 2006 2008 2010

Source: World Bank, World Development Indicators.

into international reserves. This preserves the weaker value of the yuan—where US$1 buys more Chinese goods and keeps the Chinese factories humming, sending goods to the American market. Under pressure from the U.S. government, the Chinese allowed a slow appreciation of the pegged yuan in 2005, resulting in an overall 21% appreciation by 2008 of the yuan; they again allowed for gradual change in May 2010 with a one-month appreciation of less than 1%.[38] Many Americans charge this is still too weak, resulting in Chinese trade surpluses. An IMF report in the summer of 2010 concluded that indeed the currency is undervalued, and called for more flexible policies.[39] More recently, in August 2015 the PBOC allowed for the largest one-day fall in the yuan since 1994, triggering fears of a declining Chinese economy and subsequent devaluation from other East Asian countries in order to remain competitive against cheaper Chinese exports.[40] The Chinese counter that the problem isn't the exchange rate but profligate American spending habits. Who is right?

PPP to the Rescue: Hamburger Parity

One way to assess if a country has the "right" exchange rate is to apply the concept of **purchasing power parity** and the tool of the **real exchange rate.** The logic is simple and elegant. Imagine there is only one good in the world—for now, Brazilian shoes. If shoes in Brazil are very cheap, some enterprising person is going to take shoes from Brazil and bring them to London, New York, and Shanghai. The price of shoes will rise in Brazil and fall in other markets until they cost the same in all locations. This is called the **law of one price**: a good should sell for the same price in all markets after transportation costs are factored in. Now let money enter our one good world of shoes. The exchange rate should equal the ratio of the price of shoes in the United States to the price of shoes in Brazil. If the Brazilian government had pumped up the supply of Reais (the "real" is the Brazilian currency) in the system, you would have to give up more Brazilian currency as compared to dollars. Once adjusted for by the exchange rate, the shoes should sell for the same price in all markets. By extension, if this logic of **arbitrage**—buy cheap, sell dear—works for one good, it should work across the sum of all goods in an economy. The exchange rate between two currencies, then, should be equal to the ratio of all prices in one country with all prices in the other.

Another way of thinking about this is that when you take the price effect out of the exchange rate, you are left with what is called the real exchange rate—the rate adjusted for inflation. That is, after adjusting for inflation or changes in prices, this is the real measure of a country's purchasing power. However, if a government intervenes to prevent a currency from floating to its true purchasing power value, it is considered over- or undervalued. Comparing the real exchange rate (the value adjusted for inflation) with the operational exchange rate allows us to measure divergence from the law of one price. Is a country, for example, underpricing its goods in global markets to promote exports? Is a country engaging in exchange market intervention to keep its money too strong, allowing it to import more goods?

About twenty years ago, *the Economist* magazine tested this theory with its now famous Big Mac Index (Table 4.6). It suggested that the price of a hamburger—like shoes—should be the same in each country. If it wasn't, there was something funny going on with the exchange rate. Indeed, when we look at the McParity index, as published in January of 2012 we see that by this measure the Chinese currency is significantly undervalued. The predicted rate of a Big Mac should be around 4.2, yet the actual cost of a burger in U.S. dollars is only 2.44. On the other hand, the Economist found that the Brazilian real was "too strong"—by something on the order of 35%. Keep in mind that this index is imperfect—we certainly aren't transporting burgers across borders the way we might arbitrage a good such as shoes. However, more sophisticated estimates of exchange rates that take into account local prices for a broad range of goods and services also suggest that the Chinese currency is cheaper than the underlying demand for the country's goods might imply.

Beyond the Big Mac index, economists' estimates of the undervaluation of the Chinese yuan range from 15 to 40%. In response to the perception that the Chinese government is manipulating its currency, several bills have been introduced in the U.S. Congress to impose countervailing tariffs on Chinese imports. While the question of retaliation for currency manipulation is on the Obama administration's agenda, it is important to note that our trade deficits would not disappear if the yuan appreciated. China only accounted for 16.3% of all U.S. imports in 2014. Furthermore, China's trade surplus is complicated by the fact that "Chinese" exports are often goods that are only assembled in China. That is, many of these exports as part of the global supply chain are products of foreign companies that use China as a labor platform. (The varying effects of changes of the exchange rate on production are summarized in the appendix to this chapter.) Taxing these imports with a retaliatory tariff to the U.S. would penalize U.S. companies such as Apple, Ford, and Microsoft who assemble in China. There are other dangers to such protectionist legislation. If the United States imposes counter-veiling duties on Chinese products for

Table 4.6. The McCurrency Menu, January 2012

The Hamburger Standard

Country	*Big Mac Prices* *In Local Currency*	*In Dollars*[a]	*Implied PPP*[b] *of the Dollar*	*Actual Exchange Rate (January 11, 2012)*	*Under (–) Over (+) Valuation against the Dollar*
United States[c]	$4.20	4.20	—	—	
Argentina	Peso 20.0	4.64	4.77	4.31	10
Australia	A$4.80	4.94	1.14	0.97	18
Brazil	Real 10.25	5.68	2.44	1.81	35
Britain	£2.49	3.82	1.69[d]	1.54	–9
Canada	C$4.73	4.63	1.13	1.02	10
Chile	Peso 2,050	4.05	488	506	–3
China[e]	Yuan 15.4	2.44	3.67	6.32	–42
Colombia	Peso 8,400	4.54	2,001	1,852	8
Costa Rica	Colones 2,050	4.02	488	510	–4
Czech Republic	Koruna 70.22	3.45	16.73	20.4	–18
Denmark	DK31.5	5.37	7.50	5.86	28
Egypt	Pound 15.5	2.57	3.69	6.04	–39
Euro Area[e]	€3.49	4.43	1.20	1.27[f]	6
Hong Kong	HK$16.5	2.12	3.93	7.77	–49
Hungary	Forint 645	2.63	153.67	246	–37
India	Rupee 84.0	1.62	20.01	51.9	–61
Indonesia	Rupiah 22,534	2.46	5369	9,160	–41
Israel	Shekel 15.9	4.13	3.79	3.85	–2
Japan	Yen 320	4.16	76.24	76.9	–1
Malaysia	Ringgit 7.35	2.34	1.75	3.14	–44
Mexico	Peso 37	2.7	8.82	13.68	–36
New Zealand	NZ$5.10	4.05	1.22	1.26	–4
Norway	Kroner 41	6.79	9.77	6.04	62
Pakistan	Rupee 260	2.89	61.95	90.1	–31
Peru	Sol 10.0	3.71	2.38	2.69	–12
Philippines	Peso 118	2.68	28.11	44.0	–36
Poland	Zloty 9.10	2.58	2.17	3.52	–38
Russia	Ruble 81.0	2.55	19.30	31.8	–39

continued

Table 4.6. The McCurrency Menu, January 2012 (Continued)

Country	*Big Mac Prices* *In Local Currency*	*In Dollars*[a]	*Implied PPP*[b] *of the Dollar*	*Actual Exchange Rate (January 11, 2012)*	*Under (–) Over (+) Valuation against the Dollar*
Saudi Arabia	Riyal 10.0	2.67	2.38	3.75	–36
Singapore	S$4.85	3.75	1.16	1.29	–11
South Africa	Rand 19.95	2.45	4.75	8.13	–42
South Korea	Won 3,700	3.19	882	1,159	–24
Sweden	SKr41	5.91	9.77	6.93	41
Switzerland	SFr6.50	6.81	1.55	0.96	62
Taiwan	NT$75.0	2.50	17.87	30.0	–40
Thailand	Baht 78	2.46	18.58	31.8	–41
Turkey	Lira 6.60	3.54	1.57	1.86	–16
UAE	Dirhams 12	3.27	2.86	3.67	–22

Source: The Economist, January 12, 2012.
a At market exchange rates (January 6, 2016).
b Average of four cities.
c Weighted average of member countries.
d Average of five cities.
e Maharaja Mac McDonald's; *The Economist*.
f SIMADI exchange rate.

exchange rate manipulations, we must consider whether the Chinese government will retaliate. The Chinese economy relies on its export engine to absorb labor and keep social peace. It is unlikely to silently stand by if the United States intervenes against its currency strategy. The biggest threat of course is that China may choose to pull out of its position in the U.S. securities market. Where would the United States be without its major lender? Others contend that the Chinese wouldn't dump our securities, as this would depress their market value. But can we be sure? The exchange rate dilemma that confronts the Obama administration is complicated by tight trade and financial ties in our globalized economy. Geo-economic power is shifting, and not all of the old rules apply.

From Buildup and Blow Up to a Changed Geo-Economic Order

As evidenced by the recent financial crisis, our global system is prone to the building up of imbalances that lead to an international blow up of currencies with huge economic costs. Financial crisis are not a new phenomenon. In 1857, the failure of a New York bank set off a series of events that sparked financial panic throughout the United States and the rest of the world; in the financial crisis of the early 1980s, sixteen Latin American countries were forced to reschedule huge debts.[41] However, as technology and rapid information flows have made the movement of money instantaneous, our global financial fortunes have become more strongly intertwined. As mentioned in the introduction to this chapter, we can mark the beginning of modern financial globalization with the lending of petrodollars to developing countries.[42] The developing world was showing promise as many countries implemented industrialization strategies leading to strong growth. Capital began to flow south to São Paulo, Manila, Lagos, and other developing countries. The financing was attractive to the money center banks as country lending implied a sovereign guarantee. That is, it was assumed that loans made to the Brazilian aircraft company Embraer or to build a road in Manila would implicitly carry the backing of the national banks.

By the 1980s, the developing countries of the Third World experienced what many called The Lost Decade. The global recession that began in the United States in 1979 lasted well into 1983. By the middle of the 1980s, the developing countries that had borrowed excessively from private commercial banks had amassed an external debt (dollar denominated) of over $1.5 trillion that required enormous debt servicing (interest and principal payments). Not only had they exhausted their ability to borrow from the IMF, but they also had to earn and/or borrow foreign exchange to service their debt. This was money leaving their countries at the very time that they needed money for investment and public spending. Box 4.3 summarizes the contested policies of the IMF.

The policy response from the global financial institutions essentially required debtor countries to abandon their development models and strategies that positioned the state as a central player. The new emphasis was on reducing the size and role of the state sector and expanding the role of the private sector (free-market system). This would inevitably induce periods of slow or declining growth and austerity that would generate difficult political and governance issues. The question was—Would economic growth emerge and would it be sustainable? By the end of the 1980s, the development crisis and the challenge of global poverty were as great as ever.

The 1990s brought forward the collapse of the Soviet Union and the end of the old socialist model of development. The global transformation of the 1990s driven by the technology revolution in the areas of microelectronics, information systems, finance, and medicine ushered in a period of rapid change and strong economic growth and prosperity more evenly distributed across the global economy. In this decade, we see the evolution of developing countries as **Emerging Market Economies** (EME); we will take a closer look at these new players in our chapter on Development.

But the success of macroeconomic changes also created new vulnerabilities. Financial markets once again saw promise in the developing world and capital rapidly flowed to these higher returns. As foreign currency investments flooded in, this increased the value of the national currencies in emerging markets. People were hot for stocks from the high-growth emerging markets. Remember that buying emerging market stocks required purchases of emerging market currencies.

The overheated local currencies allowed consumers to import more at cheap prices. The overvaluation also paradoxically began to choke off the export engines that contributed to growth. Most developing countries at this time retained a fixed exchange rate, anchoring national prices to a vehicle currency such as the dollar. As trade balances deteriorated under the weight of rising imports and weak exports, central bankers intervened in exchange markets. They were forced to sell reserves to defend inappropriate exchange rates. As investors then saw the pressures on overheated economies, speculators bet on a crash by selling currencies, driving the value down. Uncertainty was exacerbated by the fact that while adjustment to debt generated significant macro reforms, few economies invested in institutions promoting stable growth. This roller-coaster of good growth becoming flooded by international investment and disequilibrium created currency crises in Latin America, Asia, and Russia. The decade was characterized by episodes of financial crisis with the Mexican Peso Crisis in 1994, the Asian Financial Crisis in 1997, the Ruble Crisis of 1998, the 1998 collapse of Long-Term Capital Management (a U.S. hedge fund), and at the end of the decade .com bust. Tough reforms ensued in many developing countries—reforms that in many economies shored up national bank regulatory systems and decreased the vulnerability to the international financial system.

When the next crisis arrived with its seeds in the U.S. subprime market, EME were less vulnerable. The subprime crisis began with weaknesses in the U.S. mortgage sector. In an effort to extend home ownership, loans were made to more risky borrowers. These mortgages were then sliced into packages to distribute their risk. Called CDOs or **collateralized debt obligations**, they were resold in the market in a way that assumed that poor performance of loans in Atlanta wouldn't also become afflicted by foreclosures in southern California. But the attempt to diversify risk backfired as these instruments became so complex that buyers weren't able to readily assess their underlying value. Traditional mortgage lending had a community banking flavor—a house was a recognizable asset to hold as collateral. As derivatives or assets that represented ownership in a package of mortgages based on "slices" of housing projects from around the country began circulating around the world, global financial systems were made vulnerable to infection. Investors became anxious, and credit markets tightened up. It became more difficult not only for small lenders to borrow but also for colossal corporations such as General Motors to finance operations. As financial giants in New York such as Lehman brothers crumbled with the largest bankruptcy in U.S. history, other banks found it difficult to assess the degree to which trading partner's balance sheets were infected with toxic assets, those indecipherable CDOs. The financial system, the grease to the wheels of production and trade, drew to a near standstill.

International institutions were inadequate to deal with the scope of the global financial crisis. The IMF was not significantly capitalized to take on such a task—nor was its country-based prescriptions appropriate to a systemic crisis. In an odd twist of geo-economic fate, this crisis propelled large emerging markets to the world stage. It became clear that adjustment in the international arena must include the SIEMs—the **systemically important emerging markets** such as China, India, and Brazil. Made up of a balance of nineteen developing and developed countries plus the EU, the ministers from the G-20 countries met to manage coordinated intervention and promote confidence in global financial systems. The crisis significantly cemented a new seat at the global table for large emerging markets; as Josef Ackermann, Chairman of Deutsche Bank notes, "The financial crisis reinforced the relative decline of the West," reflected in seismic shifts in the seats of financial power to places like São Paulo, Shanghai, and Seoul.[43]

In our final chapter we will return to consider the resiliency of the global financial architecture, questioning whether a stronger international financial institution could prevent the eruption of crises. It is important to leave open the possibilities of multiple pathways to stabilization and growth. A quick return to the impossible trinity of Figure 4.9 helps underscore this point. As economies struggle with stabilization and growth, even under a flexible exchange rate they must make choices. Financial globalization has put the strength and speed of capital market on steroids. Capital flows bring resources for investment and create vulnerabilities. As shown in Figure 4.17, the trilemma of international finance forces choices. The United States has chosen to keep its doors open to the flood of international capital while also pursuing an independent monetary policy to attack unemployment and slow growth; it must let the dollar fluctuate. Europe is likewise attracted to the benefits of free capital flows but prioritizes a stable exchange rate over an interventionist monetary policy. This of course reflects that priority of promoting predictability in trade much as one can between California and New York. In China, a stable exchange rate has been construed as one tied to the largest consumer market, the United States. The Chinese are also highly cautious, and like many other emerging economies, have thrown sand in the wheels of global finance to slow movement through capital controls. Capital controls include restrictions on foreign investment, trading, or the time period capital must stay in the country to avoid hot money spurts. By slowing financial flows, countries hope to contain the appreciation of an exchange rate caused by movement of money rather than goods. Although more vulnerable countries sometimes fear spooking markets by appearing anti-capital, the global financial crisis and the divergent roads to recovery demonstrate the need to explore alternative pathways to growth in an era of financial globalization.[44] Where they will take us remains a puzzle.

Figure 4.17. The Monetary Trilemma Revisited

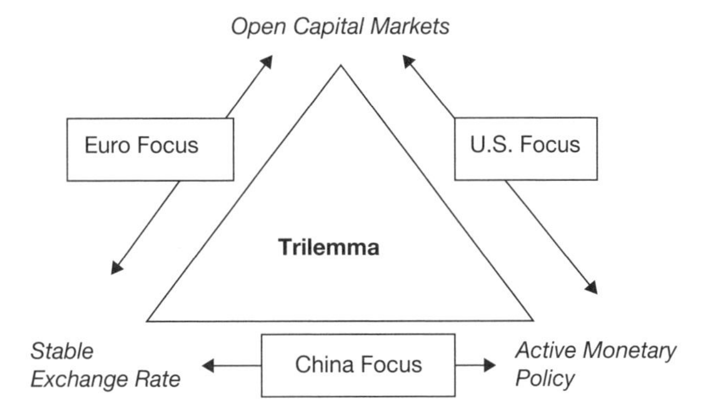

Summary

The Twenty-First-Century Puzzle of International Finance: Finding a Balance

- International links through financial markets have strengthened remarkably over the last few decades, resulting in a systemically connected global financial system largely characterized by cross-border imbalances.
- Based on macroeconomic principles, a country's current account should be equal to the sum of the capital and financial account, and the total BOP should equal zero. Yet this is rarely achieved in practice. A positive or negative BOP most often exhibited around the world is not strictly good or bad. To evaluate the potential risks of unbalanced current and financial accounts, it is essential to look deeper into the demand driving the imbalances.
- If a country imports more than it exports, it must borrow to fund such behavior (such as the U.S. purchasing goods from abroad and selling bonds to fund the purchases); conversely, if a country were exporting more than it were importing, it would essentially be credited by foreigners for their exports. If a country is already running a deficit, an increase in government spending or consumption requires more borrowing from abroad to continue to fund the current account deficit.
- Investors are willing to fund high American consumption and government spending through purchasing U.S.-denominated assets, despite already-high U.S. debt levels because of the strength and depth of U.S. financial markets. This dynamic allows countries spending more than they are producing (negative current account balances) to continue to live beyond their means so long as foreigners are willing to provide the funds for this behavior. Small countries with weak financial markets do not enjoy this privilege.

Exchange Rates and Prices

- An exchange rate is a ratio of two currencies. The underlying value of a currency is a function of what that currency can buy, thus representing demand for the currency itself. Both the demand for a country's goods and services and the demand for assets issued in a country's currency influence the value of that country's currency.
- According to the BOP approach, a country running capital account deficit (or importing more goods and services than it is exporting) should see its domestic currency depreciate since consumers in that country demand relatively more foreign goods and thus foreign currency to import those goods. Current account deficits do not necessarily correspond with depreciation in practice; therefore, we must look at the asset approach to see how investor demand for certain currency-denominated assets influences the value of that currency.
- Utilizing an asset approach to take into account the demand for assets denominated in a certain currency also influences demand for a currency, and thus its value relative to other currencies. Evaluating the BOP method and asset approach separately illustrate different dynamics contributing to an overall imbalance.

- For example, the United States diverges from traditional macroeconomic principles. It exhibits a large current account deficit yet a relatively strong currency. Merely looking at the BOP approach and the current account deficit would indicate the dollar's value should be decreasing due to decreased demand for U.S. goods relative to foreign goods, yet the asset approach explains the relatively steady value of the U.S. dollar: foreign investors still wish to own dollar-denominated assets like bonds thus still demand dollars to purchase these assets.
- According to the law of one price, goods should have the same price in every country that they are present once you factor in the exchange rate and transportation costs. This concept, however, does not always work out. Looking at the differences in price for the same good in different countries, indicators such as the Big Mac Index provide insight into artificial valuations of a currency relative to others. Expanding on this, the concept of purchasing power parity is used to evaluate differentials in values of currencies by measuring the relative prices of goods and services in one currency to another.

Exchange Rate Systems: Past and Present

- Countries cannot simultaneously promote open capital markets, independent monetary policy, and a fixed exchange rate system. Ever since the Bretton Woods fix of the dollar to gold was abolished in 1971, relationships between countries based on exchange rates have been a mix of floating, fixed and managed exchange rate systems.
- Both the growing worldwide presence of the euro and the renminbi present a challenge to the U.S.'s half-century-long dominance as the world's reserve currency. Yet both the euro and the yuan face challenges. Charges of undervaluation and restrictions on capital inflows discredit the yuan, and countries close to debt default within the Eurozone in 2011/2012 are weakening the bonds of the currency union.

An Interconnected Financial System: A New Geo-Economic Order

- With technological and informational flows, sovereign financial systems become intertwined. This interconnectedness gives way to vulnerabilities as oscillations in one country or region (like the Eurozone) can negatively affect consumer and investor confidence in the rest of the world. Traditional flows of capital from developed to developing countries, like traditional BOP accounting, is outdated in the current financial system as capital flows in large quantities across many different borders.
- International institutions such as the IMF are open to different avenues for stabilization and growth of the global financial system. Navigating to promote fair and just policies with conflicting concerns over currency values and barriers to trade will prove difficult, especially considering the ever-changing dynamics not only between developed and developing powers but also among all countries within this integrated global setting.

Appendix

Table 4.7. The Effects of a Currency Change and an Overvalued or Undervalued Currency

	Depreciation/ Devaluation	*Appreciation/Revaluation*	*Overvaluation*	*Undervaluation*
Exports	Exports will become cheaper.	Exports will become more expensive.	Currency is too strong relative to economic fundamentals. Exports are hurt.	Currency is weaker than its fundamentals indicate. Exports get a boost.
Imports	Imports will become more expensive.	Imports will become cheaper.	The "overly strong" currency buys imports; this can help if a country is industrializing via import substitution but may also create LR imbalance.	The weak currency makes it difficult to buy intermediate imports.
Current account	Your CA should improve if your goods are price sensitive—that is if Marshall Lerner conditions hold such that the sum of M + X elasticity is greater than one.	Your CA should deteriorate as your consumers import more and foreigners buy less of your more-expensive good.	A current account deteriorates as imports outrun exports.	A surplus emerges as exports gain advantage.

Companies	A depreciation should help national companies if the bulk of their production and inputs are sourced at home; if the company is integrated into the global supply chain the results are indeterminate.	An appreciation can help national companies if they import significant portions of their components. Don't assume a national company will be hurt by a strengthening currency; one needs to assess the global production chain.	Again, depends on whether you have a high import content in your production. An overvaluation helps you purchase intermediate imports. But you should also check your global markets. If trading partner currencies are weak, this will hurt demand.	If you are exporting a good with little imported content, this should help sales as trading partners stronger currencies fuel demand.
Debt	If your debt is denominated in a foreign currency (original sin), a depreciation means that you must come up with more units of your currency to repay your creditors.	If your debt is in another currency, an appreciation lower the number of units of national currency you owe to service international debt.	If markets perceive that your currency is too strong, this may make it difficult for you to acquire debt as they believe that in the future the value of that currency will decline.	If markets see your currency as undervalued, they may want to purchase your debt to be able to receive higher future payments at a stronger exchange rate.

continued

Table 4.7. The Effects of a Currency Change and an Overvalued or Undervalued Currency (Continued)

	Depreciation/ Devaluation	*Appreciation/Revaluation*	*Overvaluation*	*Undervaluation*
Global reserves ($ gold)	If the value of the dollar decreases, the asset value of dollar-based securities falls when transferred back into the other currency. For example, if the dollar weakens and the Chinese sell Treasury bills, they will receive fewer dollars than before the depreciation for the value of the asset.	As your own currency strengthens, you can purchase more units of another country's assets, and the value of foreign holdings of your assets rise.	If your currency is overvalued, you might purchase global reserves as a hedge against future weakening.	If you are a holder of global reserves (China), a chunk of your wealth is tied to another country's currency (dollar). If your currency strengthens, the trillion dollars of assets you hold in the other country will lose value as its exchange value weakens.
Confidence and expectations	A currency is often seen to represent the performance of an economy. If markets drive a currency down, this may signal weakness and induce others to dump assets based on this currency.	If a currency appreciation is seen to reflect a strengthening economy, people may buy more assets in this currency—overshooting or increasing the value of the currency even further. This may have negative effects on the economy if it relies on exports for growth.	The demand for your assets (and your currency) will be a function of market confidence in your ability to maintain the overvaluation. If you have health reserves to intervene, markets shouldn't be spooked.	If markets believe that you will no longer be able to sterilize foreign inflows and your currency will be forced to rise, they will buy your assets before they rise, putting upward pressure on the undervalued currency when you would like it to retain more downward flexibility.

Notes

1. UNCTAD Annex Table 08: FDI outward stock as percentage of gross domestic products, by region and economy, 1990–2012, June 26, 2013.

2. Tom Laricella and Dave Kansas, "Currency Trading Soars." *The Wall Street Journal*, August 31, 2010.

3. Julian Di Giovanni, Glenn Gottselig, Florence Jaumotte, Luca Antonio Ricci, Stephen Tokarick, and Mary Yang, "Globalization: A Brief Overview, 2008." *International Monetary Fund* (May 2008) http://www.imf.org/external/np/exr/ib/2008/053008.htm#P32_4753 and Claudio Borio et al., eds., "BIS Quarterly Review: International Banking and Financial Market Development." *Bank for International Settlements* (December 2006): 29. Quoted in Di Giovanni and others, "Globalization: A Brief Overview, 2008."

4. Ibid. Expressed in current U.S. dollars. This figure also nearly doubled from 1998 to 2007 but fell during the Global Financial Crisis and recovered to current levels thereafter.

5. "World Development Indicators Data Set." *World Bank* at http://data.worldbank.org/topic/private-sector.

6. Paolo Mauro and Jonathan D. Ostry, "Putting Financial Globalization to Work." *IMF Survey Magazine: IMF Research Development* (August 2007) at http://www.imf.org/external/pubs/ft/survey/so/2007/res0816a.htm.

7. Peter Thal Larsen, "Capital Flows to Developing World at Risk of Collapse." *Financial Times*, January 27, 2009.

8. Simon Johnson (app.), "Reaping the Benefits of Financial Globalization." *IMF Research Department* (June 2007). Online edition available at http://www.imf.org/external/np/res/docs/2007/0607.pdf.

9. Net financial derivatives measures the balance of trade in instruments such as options. As the value of derivatives is highly volatile and changes several times over the accounting period, and the concept is not clearly a financial flow (it could be considered tied to an earlier income flow and enter as an income receipt), the value is now reported separately. Please see The Bureau of Economic Analysis, Concepts and Estimation Methods Transactions in Financial Derivatives, www.bea.gov.

10. "The LDC Debt Crisis." In *History of the Eighties—Lessons for the Future Volume I: An Examination of the Banking Crises of the 1980s and Early 1990s* (Federal Deposit Insurance Corporation, 1997): 193, 199.

11. "United States Gross External Debt Position." *U.S. Department of the Treasury* (September 2010) at http://www.treasury.gov/resource-center/data-chart-center/tic/Documents/debta910.html.

12. "News Release: US International Transactions, 4th Quarter and Year 2011." *Bureau of Economic Analysis* (2012) at http://www.bea.gov/newsreleases/international/transactions/2012/trans411.htm.

13. Edwin M. Truman, "The US Current Account Deficit and the Euro Area." In speech: Frankfurt, Germany, *Peterson Institute for International Economics* (2004).

14. Gian Maria Milesi-Ferretti, "Fundamentals at Odds? The US Current Account Deficit and the Dollar." *VOXeu.org* (2008).

15. Neelesh Nerurkar, "U.S. Oil Imports and Exports." *Congressional Research Service* (April 2012). Online edition available at http://www.fas.org/sgp/crs/misc/R42465.pdf.

16. Diana Farrell and Susan Lund, "Why Debt Hasn't Killed Us Yet." *Newsweek*, January 2, 2008.

17. "U.S. Net International Investment Position at Year End." *Bureau of Economic Analysis* (2015) at http://www.bea.gov/newsreleases/international/intinv/intinvnewsrelease.htm.

18. Alan Heston, Robert Summers and Bettina Aten, Penn World Table Version 6.2, Center for International Comparisons of Production, Income and Prices at the University of Pennsylvania (September 2006).

19. A terrific resource on IMF history and reform is Edwin M. Truman, "Reforming the IMF for the 21st Century." *Institute for International Economics* (April 2006).

20. "Where the IMF Gets Its Money." *International Monetary Fund Factsheet*, April 30, 2010 at http://www.imf.org/external/np/exr/facts/finfac.htm.

21. "The IMF Has a New Lease on Life." *The Financial Times,* October 1, 2009.

22. Gordon Fairclough, "Rate Swings Sting Europe's Borrowers." *The Wall Street Journal*, July 27, 2010.

23. Ibid.

24. Dani Rodrik, "The Inescapable Trilemma of the World Economy," blog post, June 27, 2007. http://rodrik.typepad.com/dani_rodriks_weblog/2007/06/the-inescapable.html.

25. "The International Role of the Euro." *European Central Bank* (July 2008), 74. Online edition available at http://www.ecb.int/pub/pdf/other/euro-international-role200807en.pdf.

26. Gabrielle Steinhauser, "New Plan Sees Closer Euro-Zone Ties." *The Wall Street Journal*, June 26, 2012.

27. Lukanyo Mnyanda and Roxana Zega, "German Bonds Surge as ECB Cuts Rates without Supporting Spain." *Bloomberg*, July 7, 2012.

28. "World Development Indicators Data Set" *World Bank.*

29. Vanessa Mock, "Hollande to Submit Measures to French Parliament." *The Wall Street Journal*, June 29, 2012.

30. Willian Horobin and Gabriele Parussini, "France Set to Raise Taxes on Firms, Rich." *The Wall Street Journal*, July 4, 2012.

31. Eamon Quinn, "Ireland Hails T-Bill Sale as Milestone." *The Wall Street Journal*, July 5, 2012.

32. Alkman Granitsas and Stelios Bouras, "Greece to Quicken Selling Off State Firms." *The Wall Street Journal*, July 6, 2012.

33. Guy Dinmore, "Italy Denies Need for Bailout." *Financial Times*, June 12, 2012.

34. "How to Save Spain." *The Economist*, June 2, 2012.

35. Ciaran Giles, "Spanish, Italian Borrowing Rates Rising Again." *Associated Press*, July 6, 2012.

36. Matina Stevis, "Doubts Emerge in Bloc's Rescue Deal." *The Wall Street Journal*, July 6, 2012.

37. James G. Neuger and Anabela Reis, "Portugal's $111 Billion Bailout Approved as EU Prods Greece to Sell Assets." *Bloomberg,* May 17, 2011.

38. Aaron Back, Andrew Batson, and Bob Davis, "Early View on China's Currency Overhaul: Little Change." *The Wall Street Journal*, July 16, 2010.

39. Bob Davis, "IMF Review Called Yuan Undervalued." *The Wall Street Journal*, July 28, 2010.

40. Lingling Wei, "China Moves to Devalue Yuan." *The Wall Street Journal*, August 11, 2015.

41. "The LDC Debt Crisis," 192.

42. S.L. Schmuckler, "Financial Globalization: Gain and Pain for Developing Countries." *Federal Reserve Bank of Atlanta Economic Review* (2004). Online edition available at http://www.frbatlanta.org/filelegacydocs/erq204_schmukler.pdf.

43. "Crisis Triggered Historic Financial Sector Changes." *International Monetary Fund Survey Magazine*, July 14, 2010 at http://www.imf.org/external/pubs/ft/survey/so/2010/new071410a.htm.

44. The Trilemma was recalled to our attention by W. Gregory Mankiw's article "The Trilemma of International Finance" in *The New York Times*, July 9, 2010.

CHAPTER FIVE

Emerging Market and Developing Economies

As humans, we first become aware of the world the way it is.

We see a snapshot of the world first and the motion picture only much later.[1]

—Michael Spence, *The Next Convergence: The Future of Economic Growth in a Multispeed World*

A construction crane towers over Hong Kong.

Development in the Twenty-First Century

Stronger trade, financial and production ties in a global system with increased frequency of interactions have altered the international division between rich and poor countries. Our alumni friend looking at the post-World War II economy fifty years ago would have found a classification of first, second, and third or developing world countries useful. Today that taxonomy has become a misleading guide to understanding global flows. Countries do not easily break down between rich, powerful nations, and poor marginalized societies. Rich nations are becoming relatively poorer; formerly poor countries have entered the league of the most powerful in the world. This chapter looks at the ways globalization has turned our understanding of development upside down. After analyzing this tectonic shift in economic power, we'll also discuss the new geography of poverty, considering how poverty in a globalized world requires different policy measures than one where poor countries were cordoned off from the world of the rich. While some countries formerly known as poor have become global powers, others remain trapped in poverty. In a tightly integrated world, however, poverty in one corner spills over into disease, environmental degradation, or violence in another. Forces of globalization have not only changed who will be rich and poor but also why we should care about poverty on the other side of the globe.

A Historical Snapshot: From Third World Developing Nations to Emerging Market Economies

The far-reaching rebalancing of global economic activity has had a tumultuous history. Indeed, few would have predicted the radical reordering of the largest economies even fifteen years ago. Since the early 1960s, the nations of what was then called the Third World (Asia, Africa, and Latin America) began a long quest for economic development. Periods of rapid yet unsustainable economic growth followed by painful crashes were the norm. Some countries in Africa were dealing with post-colonial transitions; others in Latin America and Asia struggled with fragile political systems. Uneven economic records were intertwined with political instability. The central challenge of development has been building institutions for sustainable economic growth that create employment and reduce the many social and economic inequalities plaguing poor societies.

The post-World War II era can be characterized as a period of wrenching and volatile change throughout the Third World. Following the global conflict nations in the South observed deteriorating relative standards of living compared to those in the United States. The market-led period of the gold standard brought disappointing stagnation. Rather than catching up with industrial Europe and North America, the South was falling further behind.[2] The takeoff of the Soviet Union in the post-World War II period inspired some nations to pursue a non-market path to development. The Chinese (1949) and Cuban (1958) revolutions provided alternative pathways to economic change. The Cold War conflict between the United States and the Soviet

Union shaped the global context in which developing nations were embarking upon their societal transitions.

Many countries in Africa, Latin America, and Asia rejected pure capitalist (free-market) paths to development, instead constructing mixed political and economic institutions with strong roles for the state sector (government) in the context of private markets. The majority of countries pursued **import substitution industrialization (ISI)** strategies to promote indigenous industries and technological acquisition. The 1960s saw a distrust and often outright hostility toward multinational corporations and their role in developing countries as part of a large and widespread nationalist and at times anti-imperialist movement. In Asia, inward-looking ISI was complemented by state incentivized export promotion to expand markets.

International crises of the 1970s constrained state-led market development. The OPEC used its control over the global supply of oil production and political conflict in the Middle East to push oil prices up in 1973–74 and again in 1979. This produced two periods of global economic recession that resulted in spiraling inflation, rising interest rates, slowing international trade, and increased borrowing on the part of countries with BOP deficits. As discussed in the chapter on global finance, the debt crisis of the 1980s was marked by active involvement of the IMF in the financial crises of developing nations, including painful and controversial policies of conditionality and contraction. A green light after a tough IMF adjustment package reopened the doors to global capital, albeit at a price.

By the 1980s, the mountain of debt accumulated by the Third World and the associated adjustment costs resulted in the so-called Lost Decade for development. The global recession that began in the United States in 1979 lasted well into 1983, depressing the demand for Third World exports. By the middle of the 1980s, the developing countries that had borrowed excessively from private commercial banks had amassed an external debt (dollar denominated) of over $1.5 trillion that required enormous debt servicing (interest and principal payments), austerity measures, and a BOP surplus. As we recall, our current account balance is a residual of what is not consumed at home, so releasing a surplus required an enormously painful adjustment in internal spending.[3] Box 5.1 characterizes key global institutions such as the IMF that engaged in debt servicing; Box 5.2 presents characteristics of development economies.

Opportunities for development were lost as debt servicing drained national treasuries of money needed for investment and public spending in education and health. Conditionality under the IMF required structural adjustment program required debtor countries to abandon state-led development strategies, substituting private markets for public investment. With little space for countercyclical policy, periods of slow or declining growth and austerity were seen as tough but necessary tonic for macroeconomic stabilization. This macro medicine brought adjustment pains. By the end of the 1980s, standards of living in the developing world were largely as they had been at the beginning of the 1960s. Oppressive global poverty was as great as ever.

Alternatives to market-led growth also disappeared as the socialist model of development collapsed with the Soviet Union in 1991. The global transformation of the 1990s driven by the technology revolution in the areas of microelectronics,

Box 5.1. Development Institutions

THE WORLD BANK AND THE IMF

The World Bank since its inception has been involved in the development process by making long-term concessionary loans to developing countries for public projects (infrastructure, education, health, etc.). The expertise of the World Bank staff has been available to the countries granted loans for these kinds of projects. In recent years, the World Bank found itself making structural adjustment loans (like the IMF) to assist with the pressures from growing external debt. Criticism of the World Bank has come from developing countries that would like to see more financial resources made available, a greater sensitivity to local conditions, more expertise applied to the use and evaluation of project resources, and more appreciation of the positive and negative externalities that derive from specific projects. The bank at times has been more inclined to support projects that drive exports and growth than those that more directly address the problems of poverty, health, education, and environmental sustainability.

Likewise, developing countries have critiqued the IMF for its singular focus and mechanistic formula for seeking economic adjustment and stabilization at whatever economic and social cost. The IMF's historic role of making short-term market interest rate loans to address what are perceived to be short-term BOP deficits has been called into question. Indeed, in recent years, even among free-market economists, there has been serious discussion about doing away with the IMF altogether.

Yet, the global financial crisis and recession of 2008–09 placed the IMF back into the center of the global economy and financial system as having an important role to play in providing large-scale assistance to developing countries that have been hit very hard by the crisis. We are seeing the IMF challenged to make itself relevant in the current and future context of the pressing realities of the global community.

NON-GOVERNMENTAL ORGANIZATIONS AND NOT FOR PROFITS

In recent decades, there has been a veritable explosion of non-governmental organizations and nonprofits that deal directly with developing countries. These are institutions and organizations that work alongside of the more multilateral traditional players—the United Nations, the World Bank (and its regional banks, the Inter-American Development Bank, the Asian Development Bank, and the African Development Bank), the IMF, the WTO, The International Red Cross, CARE, etc.

Who are some of these newer players? Doctors without Borders, Oxfam, Greenpeace, The Rainforest Action Network, the Clinton Foundation, and The Bill and Melinda Gates Foundation represent a sample of these newer organizations. NGOs play a critical role in enhancing the work of governmental organizations, multilateral organizations, and private sector activities as partners in corporate social responsibility programs. When working at their best, NGOs connect global institutions with grassroots communities, using their deep social knowledge to promote change. Some, however, question the role of NGOs in development. As NGOs compete for financing, they can become more attuned to the donor needs than the poor. Transparency in terms of fundraising and project effectiveness is critical in assessing the contributions of NGOs in the development arena.

information systems, finance, and medicine ushered in a period of rapid change and strong economic growth and prosperity. Technology enhanced productivity and created new ways of doing business across borders. But again growth was not a smooth ride. As the new fast flow of global capital created overheating in underdeveloped financial markets, the decade was characterized by episodes of financial

Box 5.2. Characteristics of Low-Income Emerging Market Countries

- A low standard of living, a high level of poverty.
- A low level of labor productivity and educational attainment.
- A high rate of population growth.
- A high unemployment rate and high underemployment rate.
- A high dependency on agricultural production.
- A high level of primary product exports.
- A high vulnerability to the global trading system.
- A high vulnerability to the global financial system.
- A high inequality of wealth and income distribution.
- A low level of capital investment.

crisis including the Mexican Peso Crisis in 1994, the Asian Financial Crisis in 1997–98, the Ruble Crisis of 1998, and the Brazilian crisis of 1998. "Contagion" was the buzzword for flu-like financial epidemics jumping from one country to the next. For many emerging market economies, their vulnerability to the international financial system created economic and financial dislocations as portfolio money (hot money) moved easily and quickly in-and-out of countries.

By the end of the 1990s, globalization and global capitalism were being questioned and challenged by survivors of painful IMF adjustment. This brought forward a surge of populism, particularly the "pink tide" in Latin America (Mexico, Nicaragua, Venezuela, Bolivia, Ecuador, Uruguay, Paraguay, Brazil, Argentina, and Chile), as many citizens began to elect leaders who promised to replace the market-driven neo-liberal strategy with a more government-directed structuralist approach. However, a strong role for the state requires financing for infrastructure and distribution programs. Nations pursuing social goals through a strong state hand can largely only afford to do so when financed by resource rents. For example, in Venezuela, the socialist government could only afford generous investments in health or food subsidies as long as the price of oil remained high. Yet, despite these daunting challenges of exchange-rate crises and tough adjustment in the 1980s and 1990s, by 2000 some developing economies emerged from crisis as formidable global players including the big emerging market countries of Brazil, Russia, India, China and South Africa, the so-called BRICS. Indeed, as shown in Figure 5.1, dynamic growth in the developing world through 2015 significantly outperformed advanced countries. Growth of the global economy and the spread of globalization produced very strong and positive results for emerging market economies from 2000 to 2015 compared to the decades of the 1970s, 1980s, and the 1990s.

Of particular interest were the large current account surpluses and deficits that were concentrated in a few developing economies during the 2005–07 period. Between 2005 and 2007, the five largest surplus countries accounted for 71% of the total current account surpluses and the five largest deficit countries accounted for 79% of total current account deficits. As the United States represented 57% of the total deficit and China represented 26% of the total surplus, these global imbalances reflect a changing international economic order.

Figure 5.1. Real GDP Growth, 1970–2020

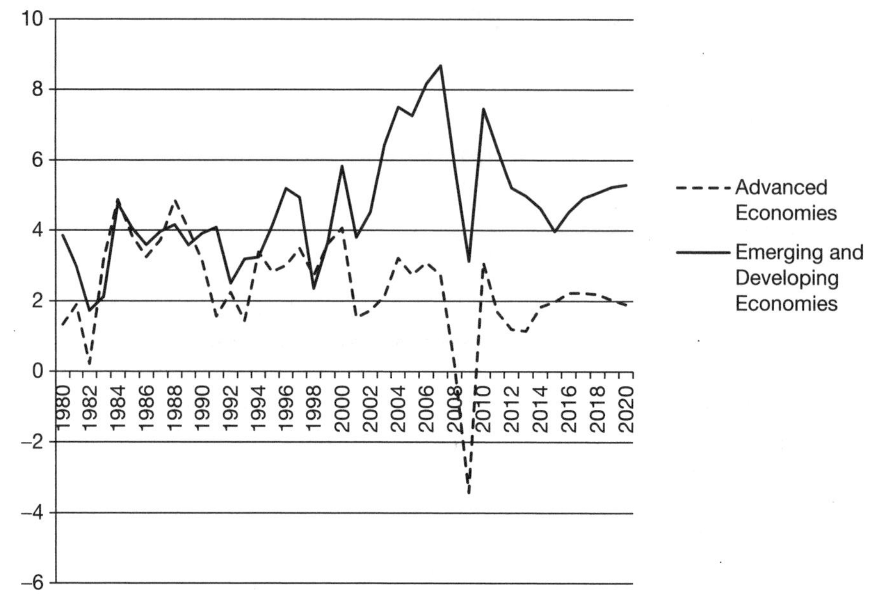

Source: IMF, *World Economic Outlook Database.*

The period from 2010 to 2012 was also very significant. The global recession and weak recovery over these three years indicated that the developing/emerging countries had real GDP growth rates of 7.4% in 2010, 6.1% in 2011, and 5.3% in 2012 compared to the anemic real GDP growth rates of the advanced countries of 3% in 2010, 1.6% in 2011, and 1.4% in 2012.[4] Mid-decade, reflecting a slowing of the Chinese growth engine, emerging market growth stalled, falling to 4.6% in 2014, and 4.2% in 2015.[5]

Rethinking the Third World

The geo-economic landscape has changed radically in the past fifty years. Following World War II, nations described as the First World were the market-oriented and typically democratic countries of Europe, North America, and Japan. In the Cold War era, the Second World was comprised of the former Soviet Union and other Eastern Bloc countries included in the Soviet sphere of influence; they followed a system of centralized planning and communist party rule. The Third World was a residual, represented as the poor and underdeveloped countries of the world system. These countries adopted varieties of economic and political systems; over time they became known as developing countries.

As we recall from Chapter 2, with the fall of the Berlin Wall, Tom Friedman notes that the old categories have dissolved. Today, there is virtually no reference to the Second World as the Soviet Union became the Commonwealth of Independent States (with Russia being the largest), and the Eastern Bloc countries have independently pursued variations of political systems and economies. Russia has become a market economy without strong institutions to reign in cronyism and excesses of capitalism. The Third World has morphed into a mosaic of countries with different development patterns. It is diverse and daunting to understand, ranging from destitute hovels in Harare to hyper-luxury shopping in São Paulo. More dynamic economies are often called emerging market economies, an expression coined in 1981 by Antoine Van Agtmael, a Dutch financial consultant. He argued that many of the countries previously included in the Third World or Developing category were on their way to becoming market-oriented economies more inclined to build genuine political democracies. Although emerging markets continue to struggle with social deficits in health and education, they became increasingly attractive platforms for trade and finance.[6] They were, in a word, hot.

Van Agtmael was indeed prescient in calling our attention to the largest shift in the global economy since the industrial revolution, dubbing it the emerging market century. As we can see in Figure 5.2, emerging and developing countries share of GDP now exceeds that of advanced economies. Measured in terms of purchasing power parity, or the ability to buy a basket of goods in a given currency, we can see how the rankings of the largest countries will further change by 2050 when the Chinese economy is forecast to surpass that of the United States, and India, Brazil, and Mexico will be larger than that of Japan, the UK, or Germany.[7] The economic world as we have known it in the post-World War II era has ended. Advanced economies can no longer assume economic and political dominance; a new global economic period has indeed begun.

Our new global economy may feel a bit like Alice through the Looking Glass. As demonstrated in Table 5.1, those who were big may become small; the formerly

Figure 5.2. Share of World GDP Held by Advanced versus Emerging and Developing Economies

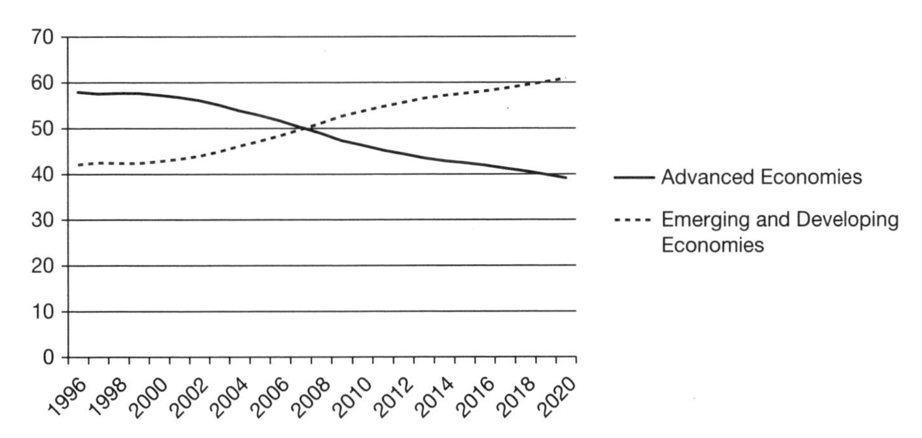

Source: IMF, *World Economic Outlook Database.*

Table 5.1. Present and Future Estimates of Percentage Share of G20's GDP

	2010		*2050 (Estimated)*	
Rank	*Country*	*% of G20 GDP, PPP$*	*Country*	*% of G20 GDP, PPP$*
1	United States	26.4	China	33.2
2	China	18.2	United States	17.5
3	Japan	7.8	India	15.4
4	India	7.2	Brazil	4.3
5	Germany	5.3	Mexico	3.4
6	Russia	4	Russia	3.3
7	Brazil	3.9	Indonesia	2.7
8	United Kingdom	3.9	Japan	2.7
9	France	3.9	United Kingdom	2.1
10	Italy	3.2	Germany	2.1

Source: Dadush and Shaw, *Juggernaut*, p. 3.

rich world has become indebted to the poor. Van Agtmael makes the case that this change isn't one driven by traditional factor proportions. That is, growth in emerging markets isn't taking place due primarily to cheap labor or abundant resources but to the ability of actors in emerging economies to innovate and dominate niches in high value-added production. Although global demand for commodities such as soya and oil have made some countries wealthier, there has been a fundamental change in where goods are designed and made in global value chains. We fly on Brazilian aircraft, talk on phones made in China, and drive Korean cars.[8] Globalized access to technology, intermediate products, capital, and labor has broken traditional first and third world categories. Much like the fall of the Berlin Wall, there's no going back.

Emerging market corporations provide a formidable challenge to advanced countries and their firms. These countries are developing new and successful innovations in the areas of business models, product and service development, production and service technologies, marketing strategies, financial practices, and market-state relations. They are becoming competitive in their own countries and in global markets as well. There are over 21,000 multinational corporations based in the emerging world. The number of companies from Brazil, India, China, or Russia on the Financial Times 500 list increased six-fold between 2006 and 2014, from 15 to 95. In 2006, Brazil's top-20 multinationals more than doubled their foreign assets. Western multinationals expect 70% of the world's growth over the next few years to come from emerging markets, with 40% coming from China and India.[9] Even with a slowing of emerging markets in 2015, growth rates remain roughly double those of the advanced economies.[10] Companies in the Fortune 500 list have 98 R&D facilities in China and 63 in India. Companies like GE, Microsoft, Cisco, and Accenture are becoming more and more deeply entrenched in these countries.

The opportunities in big emerging markets are based on a firm's ability to capture market share from the entire population, not just those at the upper end of the income scale or even the emerging middle classes. Companies understand offering products and services to peasant farmers, workers, and to the rising white-collar middle class living in the global south. In the first decade of the twenty-first century, BRICs added $8,000 billion to the world's GDP; in the next decade they are likely to add another $12,000 billion, more than double the United States and the Eurozone combined.[11] As Northern markets contract with aging populations, profitability lies in the growing affluence of the South.

Developing world multinationals have become globally competitive by adapting to conditions in less-advanced economies. Cemex, the Mexican cement producer, was challenged to innovate by adapting GPS technology to avoid hardening blocks while navigating Mexico City's traffic gridlock. India's Tata offers new drivers a stripped-down car for under $3,000, affordable to first-time car owners in the middle class. No air conditioning, CD players, or air bags help cut costs. Operating in the developing world requires what has been baptized "Frugal Innovation," the process of taking expensive advanced technologies and adapting them to an emerging market. General Electric in Bangalore, India, has created a hand-held electrocardiogram (ECG) called the Mac 400. This miracle of compression sells for $800 instead of $2,000 for a conventional ECG, and has reduced the cost of an ECG to just $1.00 per patient. Companies are taking the needs of the poor consumers as a starting point and working backward. Such reverse or constraint-based innovation is changing global production.[12]

Global managers must understand the new business models that are emerging in the developing world. C.K. Prahalad's book, *The Fortune at the Bottom of the Pyramid*, provided seminal guidance in identifying markets among the poor. The lower classes in the developing world have new buying power—but they buy things differently than middle-class America. One cannot roll a SUV laden with oversized boxes from Wal-Mart or Sam's club down the winding alleys of a Brazilian favela. Supersized savings on personal care items may need to be repackaged into smaller units that fit the buying habits of the poor. Anthropologists are being sent to live in China to listen to consumer demands, handing out free products as test marketers. The sheer size of emerging market populations connected to globalized value chains for production makes the bottom of pyramid marketing profitable. Simplicity and volume are the watchwords. Markets for managers have themselves become global, with talent at the top easily crossing borders to provide genuinely international perspectives. The internationalization of production has brought with it access to new sources of equity capital and the consolidation of operations across borders. International business simply cannot ignore the sheer size of emerging markets, creating opportunities for volume and economies of scale when combined with rapid transfer of information and goods across borders.[13]

Changing patterns of demand and production also affect resource allocation. Emerging and developing counties account for 85% of the world's population. As incomes rise, the global grocery basket is filling with more and higher value-added products. The demand for better housing—including electricity and heating—is putting pressure on non-renewable energy resources such as oil. As of 2011, the emerging world accounts for one-half of global oil production—up from one-third ten years ago.[14] Citizens in the advanced world consume 32 times the resources and produce 32 times more waste than those in the emerging world. But as emerging economies race on to global dominance by 2050, low-impact societies will become high-impact economies. Unless we can magically multiply the Earth's assets, a new way of managing global resources will have to be achieved.[15]

The global financial crisis has accentuated the trend of the emerging world as drivers of growth. Aid dependency for many has diminished as flows of direct private foreign investment and exports earnings (especially commodity exports) increased. Trade has increased dramatically with both the advanced countries but importantly with other emerging market economies (especially China, India, Brazil, and Russia). It is time to see the world differently. Some used to believe that globalization driven by the West would be imposed on the rest. This way of thinking is now mistaken. Westerners must adopt a new worldview. Those who hold the money—big emerging markets—will increasingly make the rules.

Given the changed geo-economic reality for the advanced countries, a new strategy for creating dynamic sustainable economic growth must be created. This will require not only adapting to a new period of fiscal responsibility and austerity but also a more successful strategy for the private sector in this new global context. It remains to be seen if the West can make this transition. If it does not, the West may find twenty-first-century globalization as something to be feared and resented. Populist pressures in Europe and the United States indicate that this is already happening; we will return to this possibility in our last chapter.

Powerful but not Entirely Rich

Despite being powerful in the global economy, not all in development countries experience a standard of living meeting basic human needs. Rising to the top of the list of largest economies doesn't automatically place you on a list of richest nations as measured by per-capita income. Nearly three-fourths of the world's poor live in middle-income countries. Although growth in middle-income countries such as China and India has propelled them to middle-income status, their large populations leave almost a billion people behind.[16] Table 5.2 shows that three of the largest countries in 2050 will also be home to masses of the poor. The remaining quarter of the world's poor largely live in forty low-income countries, including many fragile states operating under conditions of conflict. This juxtaposition of wealth and poverty in a more tightly integrated world economy is the central challenge of development in an era of globalization. Let's take a closer look at these new dimensions of development: sustaining rising standards of living in middle-income countries and providing new opportunities to those trapped in poverty in the poorest countries.

Table 5.2. Countries Most Populated by Poor People

Where Do the Poor Live?

Rank	*Country*	*Number of Poor People ($U.S. millions 1 .25, 2007–08)*	*LIC or MIC Status (Based on 2008 Data)*
1	India	456	MIC
2	China	208	MIC
3	Nigeria	89	MIC
4	Bangladesh	76	LIC
5	Indonesia	66	MIC
6	Democratic Republic of Congo	36	LIC
7	Pakistan	35	MIC
8	Tanzania	30	LIC
9	Ethiopia	29	LIC
10	Philippines	20	MIC

Source: Kanbur and Sumner, "Poor Countries or Poor People?" p. 4.
LIC low income country, *MIC* medium income country.

The World Turned Upside Down: The Changing Geo-Economic Role of Emerging Powers

What does it mean to be among the world's poorest billion? How can we understand underdevelopment? According to Dennis Goulet,

> Underdevelopment is shocking: the squalor, disease unnecessary deaths, and hopelessness of it all! No man understands if underdevelopment remains for him a mere statistic reflecting low income, poor housing, premature mortality, or underemployment. The most empathetic observer can speak objectively about underdevelopment only after undergoing, personally or vicariously, the "shock of underdevelopment." This unique cultural shock comes to one as he is initiated to the emotions which prevail in the "culture of poverty." The reverse shock is felt by those living in destitution when a new self-understanding reveals to them that their sense of personal and societal impotence in the face of disease and death, of confusion and ignorance as one gropes to understand change, of servility toward men whose decisions govern the course of events, of hopelessness before hunger and natural catastrophe. Chronic poverty is a cruel kind of hell, and one cannot understand how cruel that hell is merely by gazing upon poverty as an object.[17]

The cruel hell of underdevelopment portrayed by Professor Goulet is almost impossible for those of us who live in a modern advanced economy to appreciate. Even those of us with great emotional sensibilities combined with some exposure to underdevelopment and chronic poverty can barely get past Goulet's claim that "merely gazing upon poverty as an object" will not allow us to truly know and understand the reality. His perspective powerfully asserts that underdevelopment is an economic condition; yet, at the same time, it is a human and social state. The cruel realities of underdevelopment are at once more present and distant in our tightly integrated, globalized world. Images of famine in Somalia or outbreaks of cholera in Haiti flash across our electronic devices. Troops of volunteers, quite likely many of the readers of these pages, donate time and resources to those marginalized from the basic human rights of access to reliable food sources and clean water. But we can push our off switches or get back to comfort in hours. Despite ample global assets, the hellish tragedy is that the bottom billion of the world's citizens cannot satisfy basic human needs.

Global assets are unequally divided. The World Bank indicates that in terms of the share of world's private consumption in 2005, the world's poorest 20% consume only 1.5%, the world's middle 60% consume 21.9%, and the world's richest 20% consume 76.6% of the world's private consumption, representing a dramatic inequality of consumption. In our twenty-first-century globalized economy you may be shocked by some of these facts:

- *At least 80% of humanity lives on $10 per day.*
- *More than 80% of the world's population lives in countries where income differentials are widening.*
- *According to UNICEF, 25,000 children die each day due to poverty.*
- *Nearly a billion people entered the twenty-first century unable to read a book or sign their names.*
- *Infectious diseases continue to blight the lives of the poor. An estimated forty million people are living with HIV/AIDS, with three million deaths in 2004; every year there are 350–500 million cases of malaria, with one million deaths: Africa accounts for 90% of malarial deaths and African children account for over 80% of malaria victims worldwide.*
- *Over 1.1 billion people in developing countries have inadequate access to water, and 2.6 billion lack basic sanitation.*
- *Around 1.8 million child deaths each year are a result of diarrhea.*
- *In the years prior to the global recession of 2008–09 global poverty began to decline but that decline came almost exclusively from the decline in China.*
- *Of the 2.2 billion children in the world, one billion live in poverty.*[18]

One indicator that presents a snapshot of poverty and lack of opportunity is the **Human Development Index (HDI)**. It broadens our focus from poverty defined as living on $1.25 a day to the opportunities created by investments in health, education, and infrastructure to create new opportunities for the bottom billion. Figure 5.3 provides a visual on how it is calculated, underscoring the incorporation of indicators in the social sector. As shown in Table 5.3, dismally low data in Zimbabwe or Afghanistan reflect not only meager income but also lack of access to health care or schooling.

Figure 5.3. Human Development Index

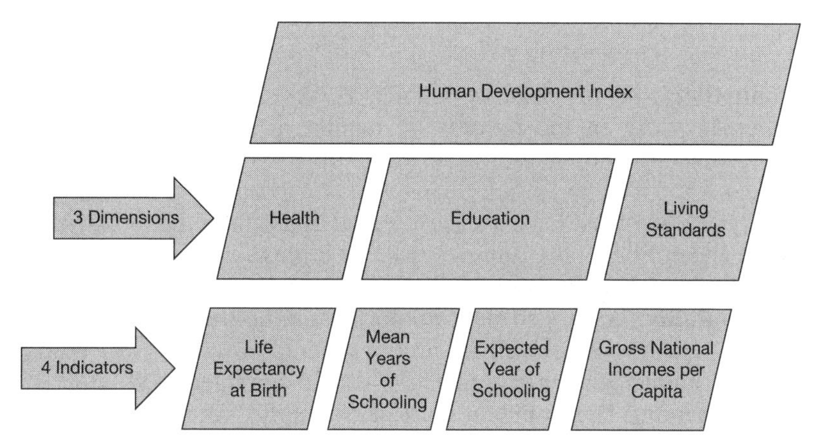

Source: United Nations Human Development Report.

Table 5.3. The Human Development Index in Selected Countries

Country	*1980*	*2000*	*2005*	*2010*
Norway	0.788	0.906	0.932	0.938
United States	0.810	0.893	0.895	0.902
Ireland	0.720	0.855	0.886	0.895
Japan	0.768	0.855	0.873	0.884
Korea (Rep of)	0.616	0.815	0.851	0.877
Spain	0.680	0.828	0.848	0.863
Italy	0.703	0.825	0.838	0.854
UK	0.737	0.823	0.845	0.849
Mexico	0.581	0.698	0.727	0.750
Russian Fed		0.662	0.693	0.719
Brazil		0.649	0.678	0.699
China	0.368	0.567	0.616	0.663
Sri Lanka	0.513		0.635	0.658
Indonesia	0.390	0.500	0.561	0.600
South Africa			0.587	0.597
India	0.320	0.440	0.482	0.519
Pakistan	0.311	0.416	0.468	0.490
Sudan	0.250	0.336	0.360	0.379
Afghanistan			0.307	0.349
Zimbabwe	0.241	0.232	0.159	0.140

Source: United Nations, HDI.

The United Nations identifies the four key components of the Human Development Paradigm, which address many of the aspects of underdevelopment that Goulet details:

- **Productivity:** People must be enabled to increase their productivity and to participate fully in the process of income generation and remunerative employment. Economic growth is, therefore, a subset of human development models.
- **Equity:** People must have access to equal opportunities. All barriers to economic and political opportunities must be eliminated so that people can participate in, and benefit from these opportunities.
- **Sustainability:** Access to opportunities must be ensured not only for the present generations as well as future generations. All forms of capital—physical, human, and environmental—should be replenished.
- **Empowerment:** Development must be by people, not only for them. People must participate fully in the decisions and processes that shape their lives.[19]

Despite these aspirations for human development, roughly 12% of humanity lives in societies that prevent the opportunity of choice and fulfillment in life. These sad facts provide the contours to understand dimensions of global poverty, consumption, and income distribution. They stand in contrast to the goals of the human development paradigm espoused by the United Nations. Why, however, does such poverty persist?

Underdevelopment and Poverty: What and Why?

Two basic processes propel growth: the accumulation of capital and improvements in productivity. In *The End of Poverty*, Jeffrey Sachs explores the self-perpetuating nature of poverty. He calls our attention to what he characterizes as the "Basic Mechanics of Capital Accumulation." For economic growth to be possible, household income must cover consumption spending, taxes to the government, and generate savings that can contribute to increasing the ratio of capital per person. That is, a society needs to generate a surplus and transform it into capital that carries value into the future. Growth demands public and private investment. The tax payments allow the government to support public infrastructure and education, enhancing the amount of capital per person be used.[20] When the basics of consumption, taxes, and savings can't be covered, nations languish in the poverty trap.

For Sachs, the "Poverty Trap" perpetuates a vicious cycle. An impoverished household cannot meet its basic needs, nor make tax payments or save. Poor families often self-insure by having many children to work and take care of them in their old age. The result is that there is a decline in the amount of capital per person and the growing population undermines growth. Growth is prevented by declining capital per person.

In addition to more capital per person, growth can be incubated by making capital and labor more productive. Called total factor productivity, these improvements in output while holding capital and labor constant are largely the result of

Figure 5.4. Comparative Labor Productivity

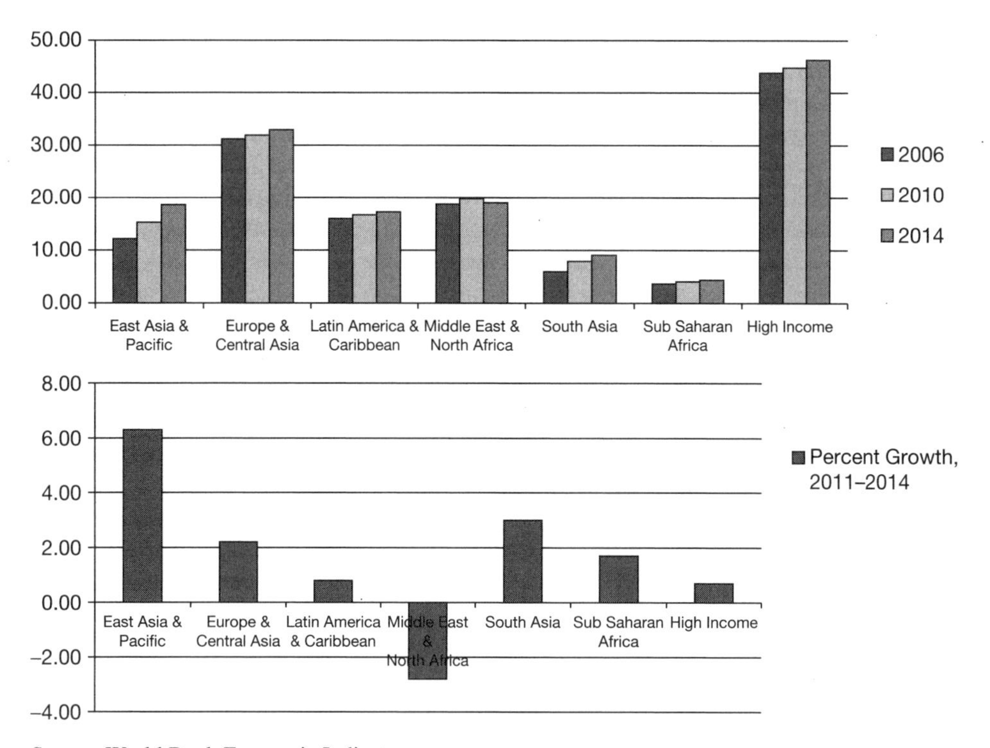

Source: World Bank Economic Indicators.

changes in technology adopted by a society. Technological change can create more output with fewer inputs—the key to rising living standards in a poor society the gains from rising output are fairly distributed. As we can see in Figure 5.4, while labor productivity is growing in the developing world, it remains a fraction of that in high-income countries.

Underdevelopment and the poverty that accompanies it generate higher rates of unemployment and underemployment. Productivity is undermined by poverty because the poor do not have the ability to invest in adequate levels of health and nutrition, or education. Weak human capital fares poorly in a global economy rewarding high productivity and low cost. This is the cycle that needs to be broken. What should be done?

Competing Schools of Thought

The holy grail of development theory is increasing capital and technology as drivers of growth. How can this best be done? Since the 1950s, the development literature has been filled with competing theories about what is responsible for underdevelopment and what should be done to address it. We again return to three basic schools of thought: (1) the Neo-Liberal school, (2) the Institutionalist–Structuralist school, and (3) the Marxist school. To get started, it is necessary to review the core assumptions of each school as they relate to development.[21]

The **Neo-Liberal school** (its early version in the 1950s and 1960s as well as its variant in the 1980s and 1990s) views underdevelopment as a natural and original condition born out of backward and traditional beliefs, values, and institutions. Overcoming underdevelopment requires modern progress and modernization characterized by industrialization, the mechanization of agriculture, urbanization, the adoption of secular (modern) values, and political stability (democracy eventually). Widespread underdevelopment can be a consequence of geography and culture but always reflects the lack of capital and technology. Without the ability to invest in assets, people suffer from low productivity and poverty. So, what is the way out? The neo-liberal solution, embedded in the **Washington Consensus**, is for the country to adopt and implement a strategy that is based on free and open markets in land, labor, and capital. This strategy requires a country to pursue conservative fiscal and monetary policies and gives the government a limited role in the economy. The domestic savings gap can be filled foreign capital; the transfer of modern technology will stimulate economic growth. The neo-liberal model positions multinational corporations and international financial institutions (private and multilateral) as key players in the strategy to reduce the level of underdevelopment and to generate sustainable economic growth.

The **Structuralist–Institutionalist** (or Growth with Equity) school was born out of the experience of Latin America during the 1960s and 1970s. This school was led by Raúl Prebisch, an Argentine economist who worked for the United Nations Economic Commission on Latin America. He and others argued that underdevelopment needed to be examined in its unique historical context with attention to how a colonial relationship transformed the domestic economy and society. The structuralists focused attention on the distribution of income and wealth, the concentration of land ownership, the historic dependence on primary export products, declining terms of trade, investment by foreign capital, the relationship between local and foreign elites, and the irrelevance of orthodox macroeconomics and microeconomics for a country with large-scale underdevelopment. For structuralists, markets in the developing world failed to approximate the assumptions made by neo-liberal economists.

To redress market failure, structuralists advocated active state involvement in development policy. Given the failure of private markets to deliver necessary inputs locally, public investment in bedrock industries would take place through state-owned enterprises. Structuralists believed that foreign capital was a necessary partner since global corporations controlled technological frontiers, but they cautioned that the state would need to regulate foreign activity in the domestic economy. Although the structuralists believed that markets, properly leverage and supervised, could deliver on development, in the context of unequal power and market failure, a partnership with the state was required.

The **Marxist school** saw underdevelopment and dependency as the direct consequence of capitalist development and the manner in which developing countries were integrated into the global capitalist system. Hence, this 1960s and 1970s analysis argued that the character and structure of a country's economic and political system as well as its class and social stratification system have been shaped by its historic experience with imperialist colonialism and the on-going expansion of global capitalism. This school argued that the reason poor countries were poor and underdeveloped was that their economic surplus was being appropriated by domestic and international capitalist elites, or the process of capital accumulation that Marx discussed. The notion of dependency suggested that the current and future reality for a poor country was determined by its relationship to the global capitalist system and that its future was not in its own hands.

Dependency theorists admit that capitalist development would bring progress and modernization, but that it will be uneven and dependent development. They argued that institutions fundamentally served the interests of the domestic and international capitalist class and could not be counted on to pursue policies that would threaten the process of capital accumulation driving underdevelopment. For dependency theorists, capitalism was the root problem and had to be done away with by creating a responsive and democratic socialism through either violent or peaceful revolution.

History has not delivered a successful socialist revolution. The historical experience of the former Soviet Union (1917), The People's Republic of China (1949), and the Cuban Revolution (1959) collapsed as socialist models. The 1970 peaceful democratic (electoral) socialist revolution of Salvador Allende's in Chile and the Sandinista revolution in Nicaragua in 1979 were thwarted by American Cold War opposition. Bolivarian socialism introduced by President Chávez in Venezuela is imploding under weak oil prices. Although the Marxian dependency analysis provides a useful lens to critique global capitalism, the model has not been successful in delivering sustainable growth. But the neo-liberal model has also failed, marred by volatility crisis and a low growth poverty trap. The fundamental question comes down to what should be the appropriate role for the State and the Market in the development process? To generalize, the experience since the 1980s witnessed the widespread promotion and adoption of the Neo-liberal model with very mixed results. The 1990s brought forward a newer version of this model wrapped in the excitement and optimism of the new globalization that was rapidly integrating the global economic and financial system. Yet, the results for developing countries continue to be uneven and disappointing.

The first decade of the twenty-first century produced mixed results. While some economies have demonstrated high growth rates, others have lagged abysmally. Populist regimes self-financed by national resource wealth have been able to improve social spending, but the sustainability of this depends critically on high commodity prices. Designing and implementing a successful and sustainable development strategy has proved to be extremely difficult if not elusive. There are clear winners in the cases of the big emerging markets but also dismal losers within more fragile states. Globalization appears to have heightened volatility in the developing world.

Sustainability and Development

Growth in the Global South is further constrained by climate change and resource scarcity. Since the publication of Our Common Future (the U. N. Brundtland Commission Report) in 1987, the concept of sustainability has framed conversations about natural resources, the physical environment, and energy. Sustainable growth balances the use of both renewable and non-renewable resources. The availability of non-renewable resources limits economic growth; how renewable resources are grown, extracted, transformed, used, and disposed of creates global tensions. We will explore the issue of sustainability in greater detail in Chapter 7; here we call attention to challenges in the world's least well-off economies.

Typically, for a developing country, the *availability* of vital natural resources (arable land, access to clean potable water for drinking and cooking, water for irrigation, materials for agricultural production, building, manufacturing, and energy/fuel resources for cooking, the operation of machinery, various modes of transportation, and electricity) is of critical importance. The quality of the physical environment—land, air, and water—must be protected to promote health, vitality, and sustainability of the society. But poor societies may have other priorities. Investments to reduce global warming decades in the future may feel less pressing than channeling money toward the malnourished and poorly educated today.

Increasing production to meet needs in a poor society also increases externalities. Pressures in the agricultural sector such as soil erosion, deforestation, overgrazing, overfishing, overharvesting compound with industrial emission of pollutants (carbon dioxide, nitrogen dioxide, sulfur dioxide, and other dangerous chemicals) into the atmosphere along with the improper disposal of toxic wastes undermine the local environment's capacity to produce over time. On a global scale, the addition of carbon dioxide and methane hasten climate change—the costs of which are disproportionately borne by the Global south. The imperative of sustainable development requires that the mode of production in developing countries takes into account all of these paradoxes: growth today can weaken future prosperity. Very poor people are often forced to seek their daily subsistence and survival by doing things that actually undermine their own sustainability and physical health, thereby contributing to their on-going condition of living in poverty and being unhealthy. Sustainable development must find ways to resolve this contradiction by resolving the poverty trap that has perpetuated the cycle and culture of underdevelopment.

Challenges of climate change are at the heart of tensions between the global North and South. Industrialized countries became wealthy in a process that recklessly exploited the environment and warmed the earth. Now aware of these environmental costs, wealthy nations are asking poorer countries to slow their growth and divert money toward adaptation and mitigation. The long-term challenge of sustainability is to address this global-macro problem at the local level everywhere. Yet, in the context of the vast inequalities between advanced industrial countries and developing countries, the ability of developing countries to respond to this challenge is constrained by the availability of financial and technological resources as well as the necessity of economic growth to address the pressing challenges of underdevelopment.

Since 1997, the UN Kyoto Agreement began a global process for addressing climate change, developing countries have indicated their understanding and support for actions to reduce carbon emissions to meet agreed upon targets for reductions. The 2015 Paris Agreement on climate change, while flawed, is an enormous step in addressing the North–South tensions in climate change (more on this in Chapter 7).

A Strategy for Sustainable Economic Development

Any individual country's effort to design and implement a strategy for sustainable economic development will take place in a larger international context that will either facilitate this effort or hinder it. Those who are optimistic about the prospects for sustainable economic development in the early decades of the twenty-first century envision a century of convergence. Jeffrey Sachs characterizes a global context in which there will be a narrowing of the income gap, political stability, more open societies, and a decrease in conflict related to class and ethnic lines. He also anticipates that developing countries will be able to more successfully tap into advanced technology. This will require domestic savings that will find their way into investments in people, capital, and infrastructure. The ability to export remains necessary to purchase vital capital imports. And, most importantly, the technology being utilized must be appropriate and adapted to the specific needs and circumstances of a developing country. Geography will be a determining factor that will either accelerate the development effort or present difficult challenges that must be overcome. Geography will challenge the development process with regard to agricultural productivity, the availability of natural resources, transportation logistics, disease ecology, and natural hazards.

Successful development strategies of the large emerging markets that are converging with the advanced world reveal a mix of market and state-private stakeholders working with the government to frame and guide the development strategy. Planning is an inherent part of designing a development strategy. For there to be success, the public and private sectors must play complementary roles. Sachs argues that the public sector should help those who are destitute, provide vital infrastructure, create a stable and attractive business environment, promote science and technology, and provide stewardship of the environment. In order to do this, the public sector must address the challenge of governance and build the capacity to perform all of these functions.[22]

While Sachs points to this policy mix for sustainable growth, he calls the global community to start by addressing the poverty trap. As extreme poverty in the least well-off countries leads to low savings and marginalization from global capital flows, a big push from international donors is key to promote changes in underlying productivity.[23] Market dynamics alone fail, relegating poor countries, especially in Africa, to a low-growth equilibrium. The poverty trap is the starting point because without resolving the ability to save, countries can't invest in people or the environment.

From a Damaged Brand to a Hybrid Model?

The global financial crisis created an unexpected turning point in development policy. As advanced and emerging countries alike turned to counter-cyclical state tools of investment during the global financial crisis, the legitimacy of pure neo-liberal recommendations was undermined. The IMF could no longer point to the beauty of a pure market model that has so obviously failed to avoid a devastating crisis. A hybrid set of tools appeared, relying on a partnership between the public and the private sectors. We now observe a strong state hand guiding global capitalism in the BRIC success stories. An eclectic consensus of what works—and what to avoid in development policy—appears to be emerging. Let's turn to this set of practices.

The failure of the neo-liberal package of development prescriptions—as well as the Neo Marxian critique—to deliver on growth leaves us with what we might characterize as a hybrid model for economic development. One size fits all models have crumbled to a pragmatism of diagnosing the key constraints on growth. Ricardo Hausmann, for example, suggests that a growth diagnostic be applied to identify the constraints on growth in a given period. Learning from mistakes in the Asian crisis in 1998 and the global financial crisis of 2007–08, policymakers have taken due note of the need to design policies appropriate to national conditions. Table 5.4 contrasts some of the neo-liberal prescriptions embedded in the Washington Consensus with emerging, hybrid practice in the developing world.

The strongest residuals from the neo-liberal model are a commitment to fiscal discipline and stable monetary policy. The developing world learned painful lessons of adjustment through the debt and currency crises of the 1980s and 1990s. A commitment to fiscal and monetary discipline evolved not because it was imposed by the IMF, but because macro stability is a prerequisite to accessing capital at reasonable rates in global markets. As the United States and Europe are now appreciating, profligacy results in a downgrade of a country's credit rating; this increases the cost of capital and slows growth. As countries like Brazil and China have become net global creditors, it is not the threat of an IMF visit that keeps macro management in line but rather a return to high risk and higher cost credit. This is the golden straight jacket of capital markets.

Emerging markets have also developed a new pragmatism with respect to foreign direct investment. Driven in part by their own multinationals operating abroad, borders are more open to foreign investment. Nonetheless, certain sectors are reserved for national capital. In most countries, for example, resources such as oil or copper are managed by state-owned enterprises. Conventional wisdom with respect to exchange-rate policy has radically changed since the packaging of the Washington Consensus in the early 1990s. Where fixed exchange rates were the instrument of that time, floating exchange rates have become the preferred policy for many. There is, however, great divergence as China, for example, continues to maintain a fixed rate, while Brazil employs capital controls to counteract the so-called super real, its overvalued currency.

State spending has become more selective. Broad interventions in support of the poor such as subsidies for staples such as corn or rice have been replaced in many countries by targeted policies. One strategy that has been widely adopted—even by

Table 5.4. Competing Development Strategies

Pillar of the Washington Consensus	*Neo-Liberal Goal*	*Hybrid State/Market Policies*
Fiscal discipline	Small budget deficits not requiring an inflation tax	Healthy respect for capital markets via the golden straight jacket—but deficits can be tolerated to combat crisis
Positive real interest rates	Market determined rates	Inflation targeting replaced interest rate determinants
Foreign direct investment	Open to multinational investment	Open but unequal treatment
Privatization	Sell private enterprises	Nationalized sectors remain
Competitive exchange rates	Unified, competitive exchange rate	Managed floats with capital controls
Public expenditure re-prioritization	Move away from populist policies to targeted interventions in education and health with high returns	Results-based interventions; CCTs, scaling up, partnerships
Trade liberalization	Eliminate quotas, reduce tariffs	Derailed Doha; regional integration promoted
Property rights	Secure property rights	Formalization of dead capital to address incomplete property rights
Tax reform	Broad base, low rates	Varies with state capacity to collect; informal markets untaxed
Deregulation	Limit the hand of the state	Competition/antitrust policy are weak and need reinforcement

Source: United Nations, HDI.

New York City's mayor Bloomberg—has been conditional cash transfers or CCTs. If students post suitable attendance records in school and meet health requirements of vaccinations and visits, the family (usually the mother) receives a cash transfer. Ideally these programs encourage investment in human capital and don't inadvertently subsidize the rich and middle class with below market subsidized prices at the grocery store. The private sector has also been brought into partnership with public entities. For example, given the enormous need for infrastructure investment, in a constrained fiscal environment firms are licensed to build private roads or operate ports for profit. Growth requires a mix of market and state.

There is greater attention to what is actually working in the development arena. In the past, money was often spent without scientific follow up to understand what works and what does not in the conditions of extreme poverty. Randomized trials where some receive a treatment or transfer and others don't, despite raising ethical questions of who decides who gets what, give practitioners a better sense of good policy. This can tell us how poor families in Africa respond to bed nets as a means of reducing malaria. Comparing midwives given training focused on reviving a baby to those who did not receive training was able to indicate the usefulness of relatively cheap training programs to save infant lives. In a world of interconnected computers, this information can be widely shared to scale up successes.[24]

Other pillars of the Washington Consensus show the eclecticism of hybrid approaches leading to policy confusion. As we discussed in our chapter on trade, the Doha development round is interminably stalled. The advanced economies buckling under their own debt crises see little promise in making concessions to the developing world. As adjustment pain bites in Europe and the United States, politicians find it hard to explain why special considerations should be offered to the poor of the world. With global trade negotiations deadlocked, developing countries have increasingly pursued regional integration agreements. South–South trade tripled between 1996 and 2006; nearly half of imports to low- and middle-income countries now come from other countries like them.[25] Some, however, contend that regional agreements are trade diverting, reducing global gains from specialization.

Although there is strong recognition in large part due to the work of Hernando de Soto of the need to bring the "dead capital" of the informal sector into the formal economy through strengthened property rights, this is easier said than done. In India, for example, extensive state regulations, referred to as the "bureaucratic raj," make it difficult to incorporate new private firms. Indeed, in the developing world informal sector rates of 50% of GDP remain common. This is a huge loss to productivity; informal sector workers have less capital available to them than formal sector counterparts. This is also a big tax drain as informal sector activity is most often not taxable. Returning to Sachs's development trap, the incapacity to fund public or private investment prevents the capital accumulation crucial for growth. Overall, reform of the tax code in the South has dogged policymakers as it has in the North. Southern politicians also find it difficult to regulate huge private monopolies such as Carlos Slim's Mexican empire. This richest man in the world accrues wealth through monopoly power—a position that results in higher prices for telecommunications customers in Mexico. Concentrated markets without strong anti-trust regimes steal rents from poor consumers' pockets with higher prices than would be the case with more competitive markets. Overall, a new pragmatism appears to guide development policy. The market isn't magic and the underfunded state lacks all the answers. Nonetheless, with a broad acceptance that macro stabilization is a prerequisite to growth and poverty reduction, countries are working through combinations of state and market to promote economic change.[26]

Contemporary Issues and Topics in the Development Debate

The changes in the geo-economic landscape create additional pressures on poorer developing countries. As advanced countries struggle with policies of fiscal adjustment and debt repayment, political sentiment turns inward, making the justification for foreign aid more difficult. Experience with the hybrid policy approach in a globalized economy is mixed. We are witnessing a radical shift in global economic power from North to South, but not all Southern countries have become powerful. As some systemically important emerging markets gain voice and economic heft, what of those left behind? Are they further ignored by northern economies straining under debt and southern powerhouses with residual poverty problems of their own? Yet our integrated international economy makes investment in global public goods all the more important. Disease bred in the humidity of the tropics is quickly carried to Northern communities. Violence born of poverty spills over borders. Curtailing outlays to reduce global warming in poor countries has catastrophic effects in both North and South. Our institutions, including the World Bank and the IMF, hardly seem up to the task of managing the global commons in time of conflict. NGOs, particularly in partnership with the state and the corporate sector, hold some promise but are hardly a panacea. Let's briefly explore each of these tough development challenges made that much more acute by globalized markets.

The Role of Foreign Aid and Assistance

The role of foreign aid and assistance is one of the most controversial topics in the development debate. The structuralist view has supported the position that the advanced countries should contribute a minimum of 0.7% of their GDP to developing nations in the form of aid and assistance. This level of aid and assistance can offset the absence of sufficient domestic saving and public resources. As seen in Figure 5.5, only the Nordic countries and the United Kingdom hit the 7% mark. Although in absolute terms, the United States is the largest donor at $33.5 billion in 2014, as a percent of GNI it doesn't even come halfway to the global goal.

Figure 5.5. Net Official Development Assistance as a Percentage of GNI

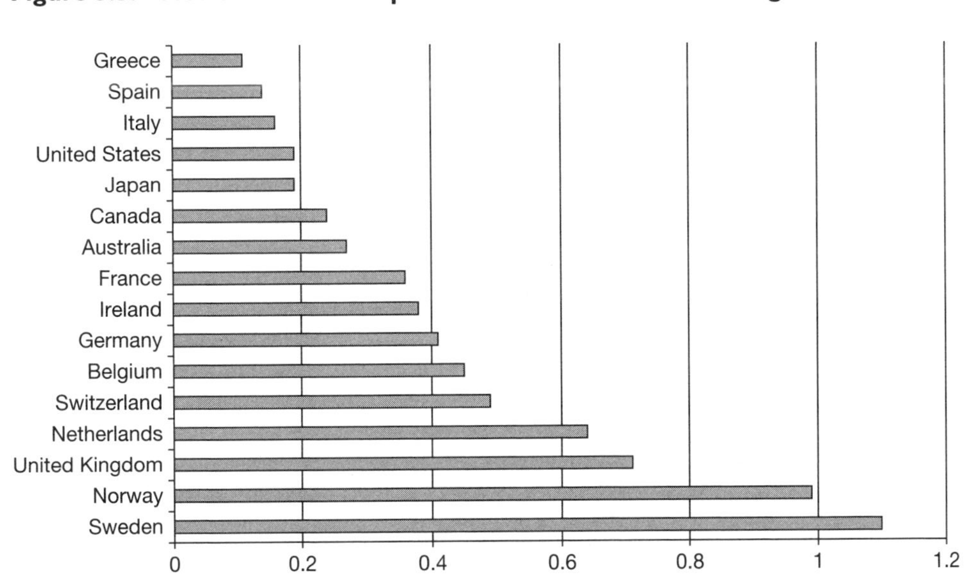

Source: OECD, 2015.

The adoption of the Millennium Development Goals (MDGs) toward eradicating poverty in the first decade of the twenty-first century began to galvanize the debate on the best way to support global poverty reduction. As presented in Box 5.3, the MDGs reaffirm the commitment to provide .7% of GNI for global assistance.

The MDGs tasked us to direct development assistance to the neediest countries. Development assistance is comprised of grants or loans to developing countries and territories undertaken by the official sector with promotion of economic development and welfare as the main objective at concessional financial terms. In addition to financial flows, technical cooperation is included; grants, loans, and credits for military purposes are not. Post-Cold War, a new category of assistance was inaugurated, "official aid," delivered to countries and territories in transition. Official development assistance (ODA) and official aid (OA) are combined in comparing assistance flows. Instead of sending the bulk of its money to the world's neediest, in the United States and European Union, ODA and OA have focused on a basket of countries including those with geostrategic importance. Figure 5.6 shows the disbursements of ODA for the United States in a snapshot of the past thirty years. The least-developed countries are squeezed by those with strategic importance.

Box 5.3. The Millennium Development Goals

- Halve the proportion of people living on less than a dollar a day.
- Ensure all children complete primary school.
- Educate boys and girls equally.
- Reduce the mortality rate among children under five by two-thirds.
- Reduce the maternal mortality rate by three-quarters.
- Halt and begin to reverse the spread of HIV/AIDS, malaria, and other diseases.
- Halve the proportion of people without access to safe water and sanitation.
- Increase aid and improve governance.

Figure 5.6. Disbursements of ODA

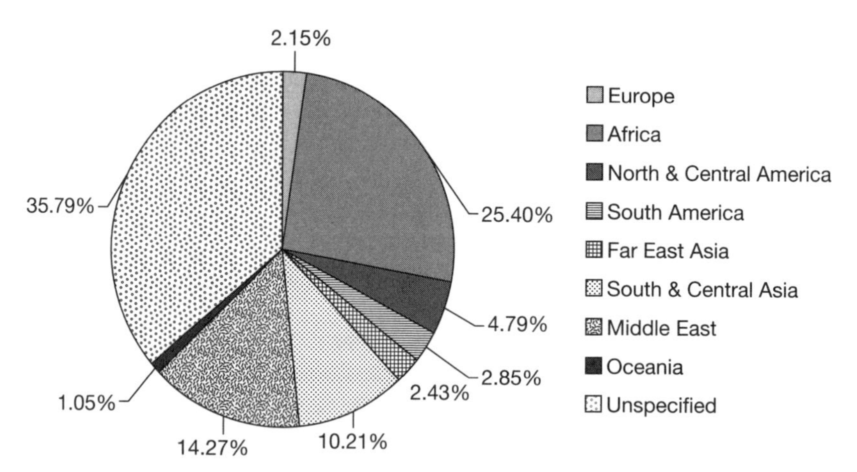

Source: OECD Database.

The goal of .7% GDP was adopted in the 1970s as part of the UN Second Decade of Development. Currently at approximately fifty billion USD a year, ODA has been declining in real and nominal terms since its peak in 1990–91. Bilateral aid accounts for approximately half of all OA flows. Private aid flows are not inconsequential—USAID estimates that the United States provides nearly 33.6 billion, six times the official assistance—through foundations, corporations, private and voluntary organizations, college and universities, religious organizations, and individuals.[27] This might make us feel better in raising U.S. assistance to the .25% level—but it is still far from .7%. And of course if we raise ours, comparatively the Danes reach 1.39% and the Brits .5%. Countries reaffirmed the thirty-year commitment to .7% at the International Conference on Financing for Development held in Monterrey, Mexico in March 2002—but despite good feeling summitry rhetoric, there is a profound reluctance on both sides of the Atlantic to ramp up international assistance.

Much like post-war reconstruction in Europe, the need for a new Marshall Plan—which at its height reached 5% (not .5% in case you missed the decimal before) and averaged 1% of GDP—is seen in the tragic misery of 1.3 billion people living in extreme poverty, defined by less than $1.25 a day. Three billion people, nearly half the world's population, have it a bit better and live on less than $2.50 a day—about the same, as a tragic aside, as daily subsidies to each European cow. The benefit of making the world's poorest better off has important spillovers. Reducing poverty will slow the spread of disease, reduce population growth, stem refugee flows, and enhance environmental sustainability. Economic stability facilitates political stability. Since 1980, more than fifty countries have experience conflict, including fifteen of the poorest twenty. The United States spends $1 billion per month on the war on terrorism; some of this might be better directed at the poverty breeding discontent. Indeed, improving the lives of the world's destitute can be seen as an international public good as the benefits are not excludable nor does consumption by some groups decrease the good for others.

At the Rio +20 meeting in 2012—plus twenty reflecting the meeting twenty years earlier that introduced the MGOs—nations articulated a new set of global objectives. Although non-binding, the Sustainable Development Goals (SDGs) build on the achievement of basic human needs to embrace standards of environmental and social sustainability. The 2030 agenda for development take aim at the causes of poverty, inequality, and destructive growth cycles.

The Aid Record

Sachs has argued that free markets alone will not solve the problem of underdevelopment, and that only a planned set of interventions can extricate the poorest one-sixth of humanity out of poverty. But, many decades of tracking development assistance and aid has given neo-liberal adherents cause to question the value and efficacy of this aid. What has the impact actually been? William Easterly, an economist from The University of Maryland, has challenged the structuralist view.[28] For Easterly, the primary problem is that bad and corrupt government makes it almost impossible for foreign aid and assistance to have a positive impact. Aid also often ignores the institutional context that creates incentives for saving, investment, and innovation. Poverty as such is not a technical problem that can be fixed with administrative interventions. Indeed, for Easterly, the Sachs position tends to ignore or de-emphasize the importance of the social causes of poverty linked to bad institutions, corrupt politics, misguided policies, trading networks that exclude the poor, high transaction costs in markets, and ineffectual aid donors.[29] Although the market doesn't offer a grand solution for dilemmas of poverty, for Easterly it also doesn't offer false and costly promises of development through aid.

Beyond good intentions gone awry, others point to the growth debilitating effects of aid. Dambisa Moyo, a former economist at Goldman Sachs, is the author of *Dead Aid: Why Aid Is Not Working and How There Is a Better Way for Africa.*[30] She argues that aid is part of the problem, not the solution. Contending that aid to Africa has made the poor poorer, slowing growth, increasing indebtedness, and crowding out private investment. Moyo calls aid "an unmitigated political, economic, and humanitarian disaster."[31] This is a debate in which both sides have many salient and defensible positions and perspectives. A more balanced and eclectic view would suggest that developing countries could use foreign aid and assistance if administered properly with transparency by global donor institutions and responsible (honest) host governments, while at the same time using market-based solutions effectively.

Despite these potential gains, the world's wealthy countries have under-invested in the public good of poverty reduction. Much of the reluctance can be tied to a perception that aid dollars are ineffectively used. Suffering from 'aid fatigue,' many policymakers viewed aid as pouring public funds down foreign rat holes—as characterized by *The Economist*.[32] This widespread pessimism was challenged by a major research effort into aid effectiveness in the late 1990s. The facts contested the perception that aid was largely inefficient. The seminal work of Craig Burnside, Paul Collier, and David Dollar demonstrated that foreign aid *could* work.[33] But—they argue—aid doesn't work *everywhere*. Instead, their cross-country regressions show that foreign aid leads to growth in countries with good policy environments. Holding political stability constant, Burnside, Collier, and Dollar show that the quality of institutions, the depth of financial markets, and sensible macroeconomic policies make aid effective. The policy recommendation was therefore straightforward: allocate aid to those low-income countries with sound economic management.

Political conservatives—and analysts in the aid community—responded well to this upbeat report. The MDGs morally obligated the U.S. government to increasing development assistance. But Congressional opposition was stubborn. "Why throw more good money after bad?" cynics argued. The Burnside, Collier, and Dollar evidence, however, provided those charged with delivering on our international commitment a positive spin consistent with "compassionate conservative" American values—reward success.

You may find the support for the Burnside, Collier, and Dollar research by the development assistance community—broadly writ to include NGOs and think tanks—surprising. Development assistance analysts have long criticized aid conditionality. Humanitarian concerns, they argued, should drive the agenda. Nonetheless, support for the recommendation of **policy-based selectivity**—choosing recipients in proportion to successful record of good governance—was widespread. This is despite the fact that many studies critiqued the Burnside, Collier, and Dollar policy selectivity results. Tarp and Hanson surveyed 131 empirical studies, finding that the majority showed positive links between aid and growth without the good policy qualification.[34] Questions arose regarding the robustness of the empirical support underlying the policy selectivity recommendations. Policy selectivity results, argue critics, are fragile and extremely data dependent. Indeed Burnside, Collier, and Dollar's exclusion of five observations—in Gambia (1986–89 and 1990–93), Nigeria (1970–73 and 1990–93), and Nicaragua (1978–81)—critically influenced the main parameter.[35] One may show, on an equally valid statistical basis, that aid spurs growth unconditionally. Tarp and Hanson find with a public domain dataset and the Burnside, Collier, and Dollar dataset a positive, robust, and significant correlation between aid and growth, not conditional on the policy variable.

Microcredit and Microfinance

The lack of external finance through aid increases the need to develop sources of capital at home. In 2006, Muhammad Yunus of Bangladesh and founder of the Grameen Bank (in 1976) was awarded the Nobel Peace Prize. He is the author of *Creating a World without Poverty: Social Business and the Future of Capitalism.*[36]

His book tells the story of the creation of the Grameen Bank that is based on the concept of small loans—microcredit—without collateral being made to groups of poor people, especially women, so that they could invest in income-generating activities. Yunus was attempting to tap the productive power of the poor who have been hurt by the market's failure to deliver credit. While creating income-earning opportunities, the concept was designed to bring about increased access to social services for the members of the bank. Indeed microcredit can be seen as a new way of doing business, requiring a change in organizational and cultural operations toward sensitivity to the needs and capacities of the poor.[37] In the years since the creation of this bank, there has been a veritable explosion of similar institutions and organization throughout the developing world particularly in India, Latin America, and Africa. In India, loans outstanding from Indian microfinance institutions went from $0.1 billion for 53 institutions reporting in 2004 to $2.4 billion for 233 institutions in 2009.[38] The microfinance industry is a patchwork of more than 10,000 institutions, about 25% of which are NGOs, 29% self-help groups, and 17% commercial entities with the balance in the public sector.[39] While many of the microcredit and microfinance organizations are non-profits, there are many for-profit entities as well.

Mohammad Yunus himself was outraged by what he termed unconscionable extraction of profit by a commercial microlender Compartamos for charging interest rates above 90%. But others defend such practices in that the expansion of microcredit has provided capital to the poor. Commercial microcredit can be expensive to deliver with high managerial costs of monitoring a large number of small loans. Donor-based microfinance seek to be sustainable rather than profitable, turning donor funds into viable projects. Nonetheless, as donor-based microfinance tends to make grants in small amounts, the more successful micro businesses are creamed off into the commercial sector. Microcredit arms of international banks also have advantage in bring remittances from migrants working in North America or Europe back to local communities, a growing business worth nearly $400 billion a year.[40] Whether commercial or not, success is a function of understanding the financial lives of the poor, developing niche products that meet the needs of the unbanked, and lowering the cost of delivery. One successful organization is Root Capital, targeting the rural sector and agricultural entrepreneurs to allow future sales as collateral for larger loans. Root also helps to make the crucial connection to global markets, bringing coffee from micro entrepreneurs to your Starbucks cup.[41] The biggest hope in making microcredit work is the technology in your hands: mobile phones. Where branches of microcredit institutions for deposits or payments are expensive to maintain in remote locations, cell phones can be used to identify markets and undertake financial transactions.

Jacqueline Novogratz, author of *The Blue Sweater,* used her experiences working for Chase Manhattan Bank, the African Development Bank, and the Rockefeller Foundation to set up the Acumen Fund in 2001.[42] The Acumen Fund was conceived as a social venture capital organization to promote patient capitalism. It is an odd mix of charity and a traditional for profit investment fund. Those who borrow from the fund must be creating for profit private ventures that serve the poor by bringing social benefits that can be measured. The approach is focused on the role of market forces and accountability. Another recent account of the impact of microcredit appears in Nicholas D. Kristof and Sheryl WuDunn's book, *Half the Sky: Turning Oppression into Opportunity for Women Worldwide*.[43] Many development experts would argue that these diverse institutions have been enormously successful at creating small-scale local businesses and employment opportunities for women, and the potential has hardly been tapped to date.

But there are those who are skeptical about the efficacy of microcredit. Central to the debate is the scarcity of empirical evidence. Although accounts abound of lives changed, some economists question whether microcredit alone is the answer. Perhaps, they argue, it only works for the most ambitious and not the poorest of the poor. Dean Karlan of Yale and Innovations for Poverty Action set out to test this. He studied the outcomes of borrowers who were initially rejected by a microcredit agency. In this randomized controlled study where half of the formerly rejected are now given microcredit and the other half remained without additional resources, he found that borrowers showed increased employment, reduced hunger, and reduced poverty.[44] Despite more than fifty years of experience in development economics, we know frustratingly little about what really works. Better reporting—not just the brandishing of successes—but scientific, balanced studies of investments should shed more light on where success is limited to certain political or geographic circumstances or where we might truly scale up to change the lives of the least advantage.

Emerging Market Economics: The Near Term Future?

The future of emerging market countries is inextricably tied to the prospect of a strong and sustainable global economic recovery. It will also require a global rebalancing of the global trade and financial system. It remains unknown, however, whether the cooperation and coordination necessary to build a new international architecture and institutional framework for rebalancing will take place. The Group of 20 has the heft to create and coordinate policies and programs to provide a stable and prosperous global economic and financial system. Nevertheless, the success of the G-20 will be critical for economic recovery and sustainable economic development. The jury is out on this question.

Summary

Historical Roots to Current Growth

- Since the early 1960s, nations referred to then as the third world have been on a long path of economic development. The central challenge since is building institutions capable of supporting sustained economic growth.
- Many developing countries in the mid-twentieth century rejected purely market-based models and turned to an increased presence of the state within private markets in the 1960s, particularly characterized by ISI. In the 1970s, international crises constrained market-led development and promoted higher borrowing in countries with BOP deficits. Debt led to a troubled decade in the 1980s, with painful internal adjustments. Many developing countries struggled under the burden of repaying foreign, dollar-denominated debts. In the 1990s, fortunes improved due to technology-led development, although debt and currency crises still plagued some countries in Latin America, Asia, and Europe.
- The end of the decade marked the ascendance of major emerging economies, including the BRICs, as foreign direct investment and exports increased (evidenced by thrilling growth rates) throughout the aughts. Growth rates in developing countries outpaced those in developed counterparts throughout the global financial crisis.
- The current picture of this development replaces the old categories of first, second, and third world as developing economies now include disparate levels of development and incomes within their own borders. Emerging market economies, now with market-based orientations, display strong growth rates and represent the geopolitical and economic dynamics of the twenty-first century.

Poverty and Development: Stopping the Cycle

- While emerging economies are some of the largest in the world, they are not necessarily the richest. Underdevelopment and chronic poverty define the lives of billions of people within developing economies. The majority of the world's poor live within these countries. Because of this dynamic, a unique challenge to current development is sustaining rising standards of living for the middle class while simultaneously providing new opportunities and stopping the cycle of poverty for the poor.

- The accumulation of capital and improvements in productivity propel growth. This growth requires public and private investment. Poverty is a vicious cycle; poor families cannot accumulate savings to convert to capital and produce growth. The poorest economies are caught in what Sachs calls a low-equilibrium poverty trap.
- Neo-liberalism, Structuralism, and Marxism provide valuable lenses through which to evaluate the problems and potential solutions to underdevelopment. Neo-liberals find underdevelopment to be born out of backward and traditional beliefs, values, and institutions, and find the solution to underdevelopment embedded in free and open markets in land, labor, and capital. Structuralists accredit underdevelopment to unique historical contexts, particularly in regards to unequal colonial relationships. Active state involvement to counter market failures are the structuralists' preferred methods to address underdevelopment. Marxist/dependent schools of thought see underdevelopment as a result of capitalism. The continuation of capitalism in the current day with colonial legacies, according to Marxists, results in dependent development on surplus-rich elites. Revolutions and calls for socialism are the alternatives for Marxists, yet in practice such economic systems have not promoted equal development either.
- The neo-liberal priorities of fiscal discipline and stable monetary policy avoid a repetition of the currency and debt crises faced by emerging markets in the 1980s and 1990s. Increased foreign direct investment receipts also point to a neo-liberal opening. Yet the activist national governments in currency markets, including fixed or pegged interest rates and capital controls, divert from neo-liberal policies and create a hybrid model to promote internal development.

Domestic and Foreign Aid: Addressing Problems Sustainably

- The role of foreign aid and assistance is widely disputed in development literature. While developed countries do provide aid, some argue it is not enough, while others believe the aid should not be distributed in the first place due to its inefficacy. Some find that aid is only effective so long as sound institutions and governments receive the aid, whereas others find aid categorically yields growth.
- One interesting and innovative form of assistance to the extremely poor in developing countries is the growing use of microfinance. Microfinance aims to promote viable projects and sustainably increase capital amongst the poorest members of society. The effects of microfinance have unambiguously changed lives, but the empirical evidence supporting this practice is questioned by some in the academic literature.
- Due to constraints on natural resources, the environment, and energy sources, sustainability is a major and absolutely crucial focus in the field of development. The ability to reconcile economic growth and environmental concerns will play a major role in determining the future course of development in emerging economies.

Notes

1. Michael Spence, *The Next Convergence: The Future of Economic Growth in a Multispeed World*. 2011, p. 16.
2. "World Bank World Development Indicators." *World Bank.*
3. Ibid.
4. International Monetary Fund, *World Economic Outlook*, April 2012, Ch. 1.
5. Ibid. July 2015.
6. "An Emerging Challenge." *The Economist*, April 17, 2010.
7. Uri Dadush and William Shaw, *Juggernaut: How Emerging Powers Are Reshaping Globalization*. Carnegie Endowment for International Peace, 2011, p. 3.
8. Min Zhu, "Emerging Challenges." *Finance and Development*, 48, no 2. (June 2011).
9. "The World Turned Upside Down: A Special Report on Innovations in Emerging Markets." *The Economist*, April 17, 2010.
10. IMF, *World Economic Outlook*, 2015.
11. Jim O'Neill, "Panic Measures Will Ruin the BRIC Recovery." *Financial Times*, August 9, 2011.
12. "The Charms of Frugal Innovation." *The Economist*, April 15, 2010.
13. *The Economist*, April 15, 2010.
14. Min Zhu, "Emerging Challenges."
15. Paul B. Farrell, "Population Bomb: 9 Billion March to WWII." *The Wall Street Journal*, June 28, 2011.
16. Ravi Kanbur and Andy Summer, "Poor Countries or Poor People? Development Assistance and the New Geography of Global Poverty." Working Paper Charles H. Dyson School of Applied Economics and Management, Cornell University (2011), p. 2. They argue that 960 million people are poor in middle income economies.
17. Denis Goulet, *The Cruel Choice*. Atheneum, 1975.
18. www.globalissues.org/article/26/poverty-facts-and-stats./
19. UN Human Development Report, 1995.
20. Jeffrey D. Sachs, *The End of Poverty*. Penguin Press, 2005.
21. Tom Riddell et al., *Economics: A Tool for Understanding Society.* Boston, MA: Addison-Wesley, 2011, Ch. 21.
22. Jeffrey Sachs, *Common Wealth: Economics for a Crowded Planet.* Penguin Books, 2009, Ch. 9.
23. Jeffrey Sachs, "Ending Africa's Poverty Trap." Brookings Papers on Economic Activity, 1: 2004.
24. Dean Karlan and Jacob Appel, *More Than Good Intentions: How a New Economics Is Helping to Solve Global Poverty.* New York: Penguin, 2011.
25. Otaviano Canuto, "South-South Trade Is the Answer." *World Bank* May 11, 2011. Available at http://blogs.worldbank.org/growth/south-south-trade-answer.
26. Nancy Birdsall, Augusto de la Torre, and Felipe Valencia Caiocedo. Policy Research Working Paper 5316, "The Washington Consensus Assessing a Damaged Brand," *The World Bank Office of the Chief Economist, Latin America and the Caribbean Region and Center for Global Development* (2010) 23.
27. Andrew Natsios, "Foreign Aid in the National Interest: Promoting Freedom, Security, and Opportunity." *United States Agency for International Development* (2002).
28. William Easterly, "The Big Push: DejaVu." *The Journal of Economic Literature* 44, no. 1 (2006).
29. Ibid.

30. Dambisa Moyo, *Dead Aid: Why Aid Is Not Working and How There Is a Better Way for Africa*. Farrar, Straus and Giroux, 2009.

31. Dambisa Moyo, "Why Foreign Aid Is Hurting Africa." *The Wall Street Journal*, March 21, 2009.

32. *Economist* December 10, 1994.

33. Paul Collier, Craig Burnside, and David Dollar, "Aid, Policies, and Growth." *American Economic Review, American Economic Association*, 90, no. 4 (2000): 847–68, September.

34. Henrik Hansen and Finn Tarp, "*Aid* effectiveness disputed." *Journal of International Development*, 12, no. 3 (2000): 375–98.

35. Carl-Johan Dalgaard and Henrik Hanson, "On Aid, Growth and Good Policies." *The Journal of Development Studies* 37, no. 6 (2001): 17.

36. Muhammad Yunus. *Creating a World Without Poverty: Social Business and the Future of Capitalism*. New York: Public Affairs, 2007.

37. Strahan Spencer and Adrian Wood. "Marking the Financial Sector Work for the Poor." *The Journal of Development Studies* 41, no. 4 (2005): 658. Quoting Rutherford (2000).

38. Ketaki Gokhale,"A Global Surge in Tiny Loans Spurs Credit Bubble in a Slum." *The Wall Street Journal*, August 13, 2009.

39. Dean Karlan and Jonathan Morduch, "Access to Finance: Credit Markets, Insurance, and Saving." *Handbook of Development Economics* 5, Ch. 2.

40. Officially recorded remittance flows to developing countries recovered quickly to $325 billion in 2010 after the global financial crisis. The World Bank forecasts remittance flows growth at lower but more sustainable rates of 7–8% annually during 2011–13 to reach $404 billion by 2013. Sanket Mohapatra, Dilip Ratha, and Ani Silwal, "Outlook for Remittance Flows 2011–13." *Migration and Development Brief* 16 (2011).

41. Suzie Boss, "Root Solutions." *Stanford Social Innovation Review* (2009).

42. "The Patient Capitalist." *The Economist*, May 23, 2009.

43. Nicholas D. Kristof and Sheryl WuDunn, *Half the Sky: Turning Oppression into Opportunity for Women Worldwide*. New York: Knopf, 2009. See Chapter 11, Microcredit: The Financial Revolution.

44. Dean Karlan and Jonathan Zinman, "Expanding Credit Access: Using Randomized Supply Decision to Estimate the Impacts." *Center for Global Development* (2007).

CHAPTER SIX

Globalized Production and Labor Markets

Workers at a garment factory in Southeast Asia.

Working across Borders

Globalization has changed the productive structure of the global economy. More than tighter trade and financial ties, the modern period of globalization has created a complex new geography of production and distribution that engages the global North and South.[1] Firms now do much more than produce through internally controlled vertical supply chains. Instead, evaluating relative advantage at each stage of production, they network with business partners at all levels of international commerce. In response to this evolving global production structure, the market for labor has also been transformed from national labor pools to a global workforce. As the factory has gone global, wealthier countries have experienced this change in international production differently from poorer countries, accentuating the inequality between countries. Within countries, deeper global markets have also created winners and losers. Different modes of combining capital and labor across national boundaries have created new opportunities and challenges for stable growth and the wellbeing of workers worldwide.

This chapter investigates these far-reaching changes in global production. We begin by characterizing how the new multinational firm is different from its transnational forerunner. Equipped with a better understanding of the drivers of contemporary global production, we puzzle out why and in what ways workers in the Global North are differently affected by global production than workers in the Global South. How has globalization influenced wages and how has the off shoring of production changed employment opportunities and job security in the North? As globalization has fueled increasing flows of migration, how are workers in industrialized economies affected by the competition of workers from poorer countries?

After looking at the challenges, a globalized workforce presents to workers in industrialized countries, we will then invert our lens to look at the ways corporations, mostly from the North, affect labor markets in the South. Does the globalization of production create a race to the bottom in a search for low labor costs? Are certain groups, such as women or ethnic minorities, affected differently? Have transnational production networks upheld core labor practices with respect to human rights and child labor? As we work in a global factory and shop in a global marketplace, how have national and international institutions, corporations, and consumers responded to the needs of those hurt by these sweeping changes in our international economy? What responsibilities do we all have to promote markets that fairly reward work and innovation? This chapter takes up some of these puzzles raised by globalized production and integrated labor markets.

The Global Nature of Production

Why produce multinationally? In the contemporary economy where size and power matter, this may seem obvious. Firms have extended their global reach since the Middle Ages. It is important to remember, however, that going global has its costs. Global companies must deal with the complications of managing across languages and cultures, paying and invoicing in multiple exchange rates, coping with the environmental and labor regulations of several countries, and complying with a suite of government actors. Unless motivated by a compelling advantage, it would be far easier to keep core business activities close to home and take advantage of international markets through trade rather than production. Why produce things globally rather than just trade in the international market place? When companies set up production abroad, known as foreign direct investment (FDI), this involves a long-term commitment of assets, such as factories or machinery, in a host country. Why tie your business down on foreign soil?

Theorists of international business explain that different companies may have different motivations for going global. In his book on multinational corporations, Ted Moran notes that understanding FDI in Nigerian oil is distinctly different from providing Argentine electricity, investing in Kenyan cut flowers, running a sweatshop in Honduras, making disk drives in Malaysia, or operating retail chains in Mexico.[2] The purpose of the investment matters. ECLAC, the Economic Commission for Latin America and the Caribbean, suggests four drivers of multinational activity: resources, efficiency, markets, and technology. Multinationals may be seeking raw materials, expanding production in search of oil, minerals or food. Other global firms may seek greater efficiency through lower labor costs abroad. The cost of sewing a shirt is much less expensive in San Salvador than in San Francisco, which might explain why very little of your wardrobe is made in the United States. Still others rely on international production to gain entry to new markets. This was particularly important when many developing countries implemented import substitution industrialization, tightening their borders against foreign imports and severely limiting the option to trade. Producing abroad is also of special significance for heavy products that may be difficult to transport. For example, since beer and soda are heavy and expensive to ship relative to their price, beverage companies have integrated global production facilities to attend to local thirst. Finally, other firms invest in local production to acquire host country technology; this usually involves investment in industrial countries. Whether multinational production benefits the host country is likely to be influenced by the motivation behind FDI: resources, labor, markets or technology.

International production that takes advantage of market proximity is called **horizontal FDI**. These multinationals locate production closer to customers, avoiding trade costs. **Vertical production**, on the other hand, takes into account factor differences between countries.[3] Lower labor costs in Guatemala or China deliver more affordable clothing for Wal-Mart customers worldwide. Traditionally these advantages have been conferred by cheaper labor, but increasingly factors such as access to fuel, raw materials, and water will drive efficiency calculations, according to Bob Hormats of the investment firm Goldman Sachs.[4] Minimizing transactions costs at each level of business while retaining tacit knowledge, the "how-to" in production within the firm, can add to global competitiveness.[5] Firms also find that internalizing specific knowledge such as patents or production processes within firm subsidiaries is important to maintain competitive advantage. In automobiles or electronics, firms want to protect production secrets through closely held foreign subsidiaries.

But the **global factory**, a term coined by Peter Buckley, moves beyond these horizontal or vertical elements.[6] The global factory initiates with the original equipment manufacturers (OEMs) that develop and design the product and control the brand, perhaps in concert with specialized R&D subsystem developers. Contract manufacturers (CMs) perform manufacturing services, minimizing cost by matching cheap labor to mass production processes. A given product may rely on multiple parts, suppliers, and subcontractors from around the world. Warehousing, distribution, and adaptation is the third part of the chain, using local firms with on the ground marketing intelligence.[7] The global factory is best seen as a network of companies delivering different services in a consolidated value chain. Both vertical and horizontal, this network attempts to maintain control over information flows while also attending to increasing the need for flexibility to source from the lowest cost producer in the global economy.[8] Logistics, product development, and other functions are sliced and compared to the potential cost savings and information generating capabilities of outsourcing partners at each level of production. As the information age has transformed business, companies now integrate with local partners at multiple levels of the business line. When producers enter into contract services rather than internalize production through subsidiaries or FDI, this is called the **non-equity mode (NEM) of production**. The United Nations Conference on Trade and Development (UNCTAD) estimates that NEM production as value at about $2 trillion in 2010.[9]

A key feature of the global factory is increased resilience; strikes in one plant or lower sales in another market can be offset by activity in a partner country. In the production of the Pentium chip, for example, Intel Costa Rica draws on component producers from around the world, hires local providers of back office services such as accounting, and relies on UPS facilities set up inside its San Jose plant to ship its processor to customers in a hub and spoke design geared to reduce the risks of shutdown from similar chip factories in Asia. If a monsoon or strikes prevent shipping chips from Southeast Asia, the chips can be overnighted from Central America.

The need to create and control knowledge in the global economy has led to the clustering of operations that rely on the development of markets for skilled labor and innovative ideas. **Clusters** are geographic concentrations of interconnected companies, specialized suppliers, universities, trade associations that facilitate important linkages, create spillovers of technology, and circulate information on production techniques and customer needs.[10] Michael Porter of Harvard argues that these clusters are incubators of information flows between companies, universities, and labor. Drawing again on the Costa Rican case, the Intel plant, while not directly attracting additional computer suppliers, has fostered the development of a medical cluster that relies on similar high-tech workforce characteristics. Clusters can create pools of knowledge that attract global investment from the global value chain.

Although multinational corporations move abroad to reach customers and reduce costs, global value chains may also contribute to global instability. The contraction in international trade from the global financial crisis is likely to have been affected by global value chains. As ever-finer specialization of production processes are tied together by global networks, the sharp reduction of demand in the North was immediately spread "upstream" to subcontractors in developing countries.[11] The global factory slowed when the industrialized countries sputtered.

The Magnitude of the Transnational Production Network

Transnational production is big business. Transnationals are an increasingly diverse set of firms with global reach. The U.N.'s World Investment Report counts some 82,000 transnational companies with 810,000 foreign affiliates. Transnational production is estimated to account for a quarter of world GDP.[12] Roughly one-third of global exports are accounted for by affiliates shipping among transnational networks.[13] Calculated by the UNCTAD, The Transnationality Index (TNI) measures the degree to which a firm relies on a global production network by averaging the ratios of foreign assets to total assets, foreign sales to total sales and foreign employment to total employment. Table 6.1A shows the top-15 non-financial transnational firms, with General Electric and Royal Dutch Shell leading the pack. Top financial organizations shown in Table 6.1B include the German Allianz and the U.S. Citigroup. You may, however, be surprised by the third set in Table 6.1C—emerging market multinationals. You may own Korean Samsung, or drive a Hyundai. Petrobras of Brazil has become a global (albeit troubled) oil giant. The Mexican telecommunications empire has made Carlos Slim the richest man in the world, and various holding companies in China and Hong Kong control diverse

Table 6.1A. The World's Top-15 Non-Financial TNCs, Ranked by Foreign Assets, 2013 ($U.S. millions)

Ranking by				*Assets*	
Foreign Assets	*TNI*	*Corporation*	*Home Economy*	*Foreign*	*Total*
1	81	General Electric Co	US	331 160	656 560
2	34	Royal Dutch Shell plc	UK	301 898	357 512
3	67	Toyota Motor Corporation	Japan	274 380	403 088
4	56	Exxon Mobil Corporation	US	231 033	346 808
5	21	Total SA	France	226 717	238 870
6	38	BP plc	UK	202 899	305 690
7	9	Vodafone Group Plc	UK	182 837	202 763
8	68	Volkswagen Group	Germany	176 656	446 555
9	66	Chevron Corporation	US	175 736	253 753
10	36	Eni SpA	Italy	141 021	190 125
11	73	Enel SpA	Italy	140 396	226 006
12	17	Glencore Xstrata PLC	Switzerland	135 080	154 932
13	3	Anheuser-Busch InBev NV	Belgium	134 549	141 666
14	97	EDF SA	France	130 161	353 574
15	1	Nestlé SA	Switzerland	124 730	129 969

Table 6.1B. The Top-15 Financial TNCs Ranked by Geographical Spread Index (GSI), 2012 ($U.S. millions)

Rank 2012	*GSI*	*Rank 2011*	*GSI*	*Financial TNCs*	*Home Economy*	*Assets* *Total*
1	72.8	1	75.0	Allianz SE	Germany	915 788
2	72.4	2	73.7	Citigroup Inc.	United States	1 864 660
3	71.2	3	72.4	BNP Paribas	France	2 514 570
4	68.5	6	67.2	Assicurazioni Generali SpA	Italy	582 398
5	68.3	5	68.1	HSBC Holdings PLC	United Kingdom	2 692 538
6	65.9	8	65.6	Deutsche Bank AG	Germany	2 653 053
7	65.0	7	65.6	Societe Generale	France	1 648 917
8	64.1	9	61.1	Unicredit SpA	Italy	1 221 929
9	58.3	10	59.5	AXA S.A.	France	1 004 421
10	57.4	13	53.0	Standard Chartered PLC	United Kingdom	636 518
11	56.4	12	56.2	Credit Suisse Group Ltd.	Switzerland	1 009 756
12	54.8	11	56.6	Zurich Insurance Group AG	Switzerland	409 270
13	53.1	4	69.2	UBS AG	Switzerland	1 375 684
14	52.9	14	51.2	Munich Reinsurance Company	Germany	340 622
15	49.6	17	50.3	ING Groep NV	Netherlands	1 540 724

Note: The GSI takes into account both total assets, geographic presence and the number of foreign affiliates as a percentage of all affiliates. In contrast to ranking by solely assets, a Chinese bank with largely domestic assets is not ranked highly—although by size alone it may be one of the biggest in the world. GSI, the "Geographical Spread Index," is calculated as the square root of the Internationalization Index multiplied by the number of host countries.

infrastructure and real estate projects. As the power of emerging markets expands in the twenty-first century, so has the number and size of its transnational corporations. Some suggest that the incubation of these transnationals under the adverse conditions of incomplete markets in developing countries has indeed made them stronger global competitors. Knowledge of production challenges and consumer needs in low-income markets give emerging multinationals an edge. India's Tata corporation has, for example, brought the "people's car" to market; priced at $2,500, it attends to first time, low-income car owners.

FDI also operates on a large scale. In Figure 6.1, we see the aggregate investment of these large corporations with the overall rise in FDI inflows and the growing importance of investing in the developing world. After steeply rising from 2003 through 2007, global FDI flows were significantly affected by

Table 6.1C. The Top-15 Non-Financial TNCs from Developing and Transition Economies, Ranked by Foreign Assets, 2012 ($U.S. millions)

Ranking by				*Assets*	
Foreign Assets	*TNI*	*Corporation*	*Home Economy*	*Foreign*	*Total*
1	19	Hutchison Whampoa Limited	Hong Kong, China	85,721	103,715
2	93	CITIC Group	China	78,602	565,884
3	16	Hon Hai Precision Industries	Taiwan Province of China	65,471	70,448
4	70	Petronas—Petroliam Nasional Bhd	Malaysia	49,072	163,275
5	63	Vale SA	Brazil	45,721	131,478
6	59	China Ocean Shipping (Group) Company	China	43,452	56,126
7	91	China National Offshore Oil Corp.	China	34,276	129,834
8	58	América Móvil SAB de CV	Mexico	32,008	75,697
9	67	Lukoil OAO	Russian Federation	31,174	98,961
10	20	Cemex S.A.B. de C.V.	Mexico	30,730	36,808
11	92	Petróleos de Venezuela SA	Venezuela, Bolivarian Republic	27,462	218,424
12	80	Samsung Electronics Co., Ltd.	Korea, Republic of	26,077	169,702
13	39	Singapore Telecommunications Ltd.	Singapore	25,768	32,242
14	83	Hyundai Motor Company	Korea, Republic of	25,443	113,906
15	44	Jardine Matheson Holdings Ltd.	Hong Kong, China	24,284	63,460

Source: UNCTAD World Investment Report 2014: Annex Tables.

the global economic and financial crisis, falling to under $1.2 trillion in 2009 from a high of $1.7 trillion in 2007. The United States is the largest recipient country of multinational investment and the EU is the largest host region, but developing and transition country markets continue to attract the attention of global producers. As incomes rise in the developing world and its labor pools become increasingly educated, companies are drawn to these large, untapped markets. To the degree that the potential for attracting new consumers is more distinctly embedded in developing country networks, emerging markets may have an increasing advantage in attracting new business.

Figure 6.1. FDI Inflows, Global and by Groups of Economies, 1980–2011 ($U.S. billions)

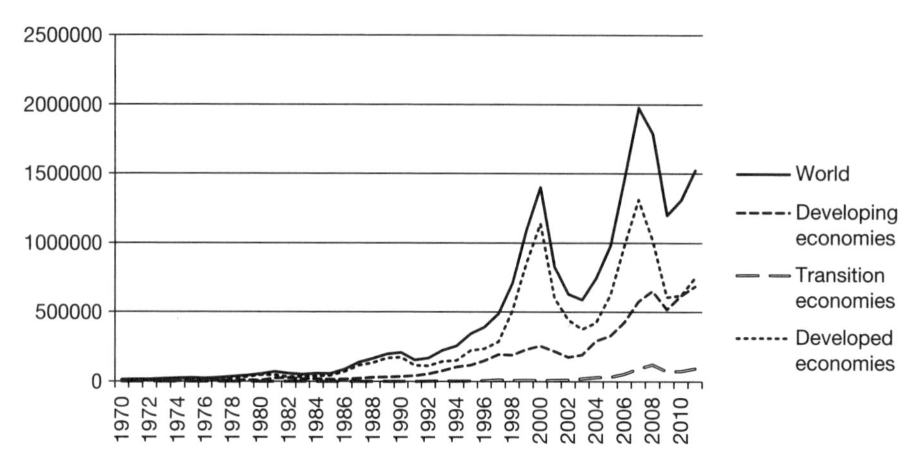

Source: UNCTAD Foreign Direct Investment Database, http://unctadstat.unctad.org/TableViewer/tableView.aspx?ReportId=88.

Exploitation or Productive Energy?

Given the enormous reach and impact of global corporations, does FDI help developing countries? Two contending theoretical perspectives arrive at different answers to this question. **Modernization theorists** believe that the capital investment and superior technology of transnational companies are especially important to developing country growth. In the modernization literature, multinationals also play a prominent role in providing organizational and managerial skills, marketing know-how, and increasing factor productivity.[14] **Dependency theorists** contest this conclusion, arguing that dependence on foreign investment stifles national growth and contributes to income inequality. Control by foreigners crowds out local entrepreneurship and creates barriers to entry for national firms.[15] The lower absorptive capacity of the developing country weakens the opportunities for technological spillover. For dependency theorists, a modern foreign sector propels imbalanced growth.

Although the behavior of policymakers who try to attract international production through generous tax incentives or other subsidies might suggest that multinational activity has positive externalities, the empirical evidence does not support this belief.[16] Ideally, a developing economy should benefit from the forward and backward linkages provided by the multinational company. That is, one might anticipate that automobile production would call for an increase in parts supplied and garages to service the cars. Proponents hoped that the higher international quality standards employed by multinationals would contribute to improved overall production processes and that technology would spillover to local firms. Instead, several studies find that skill enhancement and technology sharing do not take place over time as foreign companies operate in less-developed markets.[17] One explanation for the lack of spillover is the global value chain; multinationals keep the high technology activities in industrial countries while using cheaper labor of global factories to achieve cost advantages.

Measuring the effects of FDI is also problematic. Firms tend to be attracted to stable growing markets, creating a problem of causality in understanding whether international production is a cause or consequence of growth. For example, was China's success in attracting FDI because its economy was already growing, or did FDI give growth a dramatic boost? The answer is probably both. Recent research that is better able to control for these intervening factors indicates that for countries to benefit from multinational production, complementary conditions need to be in place. These include a minimum level of human capital, functioning capital markets to promote backward linkages, and openness to trade.[18] There is also evidence that firms vertically integrated into multinational production benefit more strongly than horizontal spillovers to other firms in the same industry. For example, a Sony plant in Reynosa, Mexico, may help its sister plan in Mexicali or Tijuana, but will do little for other companies in the electronics cluster in Mexico. FDI, particularly without complementary policies of the state to manage flows of people, capital and technology, promotes an **enclave economy** with low linkages.[19] This makes sense in that knowledge is at the center of the global production game; multinationals therefore work to promote barriers to entry in global supplier networks and to keep information about better processes and products secure within the firm.[20]

FDI may have different outcomes in industrialized countries compared to the developing world. In the industrialized world, foreign investment tends to create quality new jobs. In the United States, affiliates of foreign companies employ approximately 5.3 million Americans, accounting for just under 5% of the overall workforce and 12% of manufacturing jobs. On average, affiliates of foreign firms pay 32% more than U.S.-based companies. The McKinsey Global Institute finds that in developed economies, exposure to global best practices promotes the adoption of productivity-enhancing measures.[21] FDI largely comes to industrialized countries when seeking skilled labor; in developing areas, it seeks a cheap wage alternative.

In addition to well-articulated labor and capital markets, policy may make the difference in outcomes between the North and South. Industrial countries often require a fixed percentage of local content in production to promote linkages and minimum requirements for reinvestment of profits into research and development. Of course, the bargaining power of a developing country to extract these concessions from multinationals will be a function of the domestic appeal of the market. China or India may be able to negotiate better terms for foreign capital than a small country market such as Vietnam or El Salvador. As we will see later in this chapter, it may also be the case that partnerships with NGOs can enhance the gains to multinational production while minimizing the negative effects.[22] The success of negotiations for better terms brings us to our question of why the multinational firm is producing abroad. Cheap labor can be found in many countries, weakening the bargaining power of workers worldwide. Countries with resources or markets have a better chance of extracting a fair bargain. But before we assess the potential for policy reform, let's now look at the effects of multinational production networks on the global labor market.

Globalization and Labor Markets

Globalization, propelled by the increased mobility of transnational capital, has greatly increased the abundance of the labor supply available to firms. The integration of large emerging markets such as China, India, and Brazil into the global economy has, in conjunction with population growth, led to an approximately fourfold increase in the effective global labor force. Indeed, this could double again by 2050, transforming the labor supply to the world's corporations.[23] How has this dramatic shift in the global labor supply affected workers in the North and in the South?

Global wages, based on 83 reporting countries, grew an average of 1.9% each year from 2001 through 2007, 2.15% year over year from 2006 to 2009 and 1.85% a year between 2010 and 2013.[24] Excluding China, the annual wage growth worldwide for 2010–13 was only 0.97%.[25] Inflation-adjusted wages, however, grew slower than overall growth rates. Although opening an economy to trade may initially result in a loss in employment in industrialized countries, after a time lag of about four years the impact becomes positive as growth creates jobs in open economies.[26] Furthermore, FDI-intensive industries and export sectors pay significantly above mean wages; this may be due to the fact that in opening to trade the most productive firms are drawn to the potential of larger markets in the export sector. Workers in export-led industries gain relative to those in uncompetitive sectors; those left behind tend to fend in informal markets.[27]

As with trade, the globalization of production creates winners and losers. It has fostered a labor market dualism where skilled workers benefit while those unable to invest in human capital lose out. **Dualistic labor markets** have developed where those in low skilled, often informal markets are especially vulnerable to shifts in the global economy. Social safety nets, however, have not been universally strengthened to compensate those workers losing out to a globalized workforce. As firms scour the global market for cheap labor, the bargaining power of workers is eroded and individuals tend to report a greater degree of insecurity.[28] Although consumers benefit from cheaper products assembled abroad, workers and communities losing jobs suffer.

The loss for workers out-competed by foreign labor is compounded by the effects of technology, which increases firm productivity without leading to similar pay raises for employees at the bottom of the pay scale. Consider, for a moment, a minimum wage-earning employee at a Worcester, Massachusetts plastic maker; she hasn't received an increase in her minimum wage for years. Yet she feels lucky to have her job as mechanization has replaced twelve of her former colleagues. As technology and globalization have combined to create alternatives to manual labor, those on the bottom fifth of the income scale have seen an erosion of real wages of 1–3% while those in the top fifth—the creators and innovators of technology—saw earnings rise between 16% and 56% in the 1990s.[29] Globalization can also call for certain skills within nations, favoring one income class over another and exacerbating domestic income inequality. The ILO documents that more than two-thirds of countries saw an increase in wage inequality, driven by either rising top wages or a weakening bottom. Moreover, despite educational gains for women, the gender wage gap widened as well.[30] Openness to trade and finance may increase the growth of GDP, but without complementary policies in the social sector, it is likely to also add to inequality.

Globalization and Inequality

The degree to which globalization shapes inequality is a hotly contested topic. Data tell multiple stories depending upon how globalization is measured, the time period chosen, and the countries in the dataset. To measure globalization, some studies look only at trade openness, while others include financial globalization as well. The time period chosen is important because economic policies also change during periods examined, making it hard to separate out the effects of globalization from policy choices. Technological changes also tangle outcomes. Technology that is labor saving tends to hurt unskilled workers, yet a similar innovation can favor the highly educated. As an innovation spreads around the globe, it is difficult to identify the effects of technology as a separate variable from greater international integration. Finally, as we compare incomes between countries, the choice of when to measure the exchange rate and the local buying power of currency matters. A dollar in New York doesn't go as far as a buck in Mumbai. For this reason, purchasing power parity exchange rates that account for local prices and buying power are used.

We also have to separate out increasing inequality between countries from inequality within countries. As poorer countries such as India and China have made great strides, the average gap between the rich and poor world has shrunk. This may not, however, change the fates of those in Sub-Saharan Africa marginalized from access to the global economy.

Let's look as some measures of inequality. We measure income inequality with the **Gini coefficient.** To understand the Gini, imagine we are able to line a population up from poorest to richest. We then plot this perfectly ordered population on the horizontal axis. On the vertical axis, we measure the percent of income held. In a perfectly equal world, the bottom 20% of the population would hold 20% of income. If we plot these coordinates of each quintile, holding an equal share of income, we have the line of perfect equality shown in Figure 6.2. Yet, perfect equality is never the case in reality; the **Lorenz curve** gives us the actual picture. If the bottom 20% of society holds 3% of income, that will give us the first point on the Lorenz curve. The Gini is a ratio of the area between the line of perfect equality and the Lorenz curve, marked A on the graph, and the full triangle formed by capturing 100% of the population, an area labeled as A + B. A low Gini—something around 0.25, as in the case of Slovakia—indicates that the area A is small and the country is relatively equal. A high Gini—for example, 0.55 in the case of Brazil—shows a comparatively larger area A as the poor hold a lower percentage of income than the very rich.[31] Keep in mind that income data for the poor is difficult to gather; measuring changes over time is even tougher. Remember that in the developing world, the poor often don't have official addresses but live in informal settlements that are not exactly amenable to a knock on the door by a census worker. Inequality is therefore a tricky thing to measure across countries.

Figure 6.2. Global Income Distribution

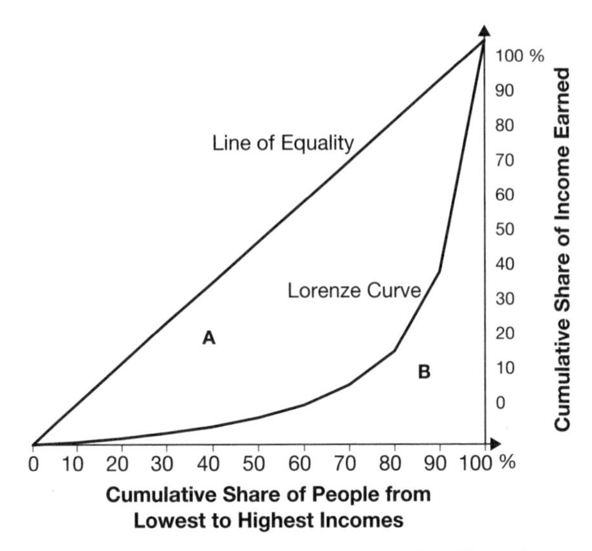

Source: Branko Milanovic, "Global Inequality Recalculated: The Effect of New 2005 PPP Estimates on Global Inequality" (World Bank Policy Research Working Paper 5061, 2009).

In addition to looking at inequality within a country we can analyze international income differences. Global inequality is stunning. A mere 10% of the world population holds more than 57% of global income; the richest 5% control over one-third of global income.[32] Average income in the United States was about $45,000 in 2007; in Sierra Leone, on average people make less than a dollar a day or $284 per year. If the data in the world Lorenz curve were used to calculate a Global Gini coefficient, it would be about 0.70—an extraordinarily high number.[33] We live in a globally connected world marked by extraordinary inequality. While there have historically always been large income differences among global citizens, as we have become more closely connected through YouTube videos and Facebook images, differences become more glaring. Not only are people experiencing unequal outcomes in a globalizing economy but also images of how others live different lives can be deeply unsettling.

We need to be careful, however, to disentangle the multiple causes of inequality from whether global inequality has increased or decreased with greater international integration. Despite stronger perceptions of inequality, data suggest that income inequality weighted by population size fell in the last twenty years of the twentieth century and the first seven of the next, largely driven by the inclusion of China and India into the global economy. Inequality not weighted by the Chinese growth locomotive showed an increase until 2001, but has fallen since then due to stronger growth in Latin America and Africa.

Despite these modest improvements, some suggest that the problem of globalization is that it hasn't gone far enough as an equalizing force. As many countries rapidly integrate their economies, others are left out and find themselves falling behind. Indeed, the *Economist* says that Sub-Saharan Africa plainly suffers not from globalization but from the lack of it.[34] Martin Wolf of the *Financial Times* notes that, "the poorest regions of the world were not hurt by globalization; they just failed to be a part of it." But others contest this view. Mark Levinson, a labor union official, blames the nearly unlimited labor supply in China for the downward pressure on wages and increased inequality within countries. For some, globalization has gone too far in propelling inequality.

Income inequality can rise due to either a growing top or a falling bottom; a 2008 study by the ILO found that between 1990 and 2005, approximately two-thirds of countries experienced an increase in income inequality due to a rise in the incomes of richer households.[35] However, with poverty rates falling in developing countries, the Gini coefficient actually fell in three-quarters of the developing economies included in the same survey after the Great Financial Crisis.[36] The income gap, a ratio of the top 10% and the bottom 10% of earners, increased in 70% of the countries for which data are available. This may change in the coming years as much of this increased in-country inequality was driven by extraordinary increases in financial sector and executive pay—bubbles that have since deflated with the global financial crisis. As advanced industrial economies adjusted to austerity cuts due to the financial crisis we saw changes in a downward pressure on wages—one that hasn't revived with recovery.

The degree of inequality both within countries and between countries is critically affected by a number of variables, including technology, worker bargaining power and the stability of labor markets, the quality of government institutions to redistribute income, the transmission of knowledge through supply chains, the enforcement of labor standards, and the leverage exercised by consumers and stockholders.[37] Technology is an especially important factor, creating more jobs for those with higher skills and reducing the demand for low-skilled labor. Export industries in developing countries tend to draw on better-trained labor; perhaps paradoxically, within some labor rich developing countries globalization has not favored the average laborer.[38] The spread of technology and globalization are not independent; improved technology has helped deepen trade and financial ties, and is thus integrally important to facilitating globalization.[39]

In developing countries, a digital divide has emerged that separates workers between the technologically literate and those without access to technological skills.[40] Imports of intermediate goods for production that accompanied liberalization have made skilled labor complementary.[41] Those with skills receive a higher return, increasing the gap with the unskilled. According to Paul Krugman, a similar bias in the technological mix toward highly skilled labor also favors the better-educated worker in the developed world. In the United States, for example, the earnings gap between skilled and unskilled sectors has widened by 25% over the past two decades.[42] In Continental Europe, wages of unskilled workers haven't fallen as drastically as their skilled counterparts—but the numbers of unskilled workers employed has declined. As Mark Malloch Brown, head of the UN Development Programme warns us, failing to address this information gap risks widening income gulfs that increase inequality and leave the poor behind.[43] Inclusive policies for the least advantaged in society, discussed later in this chapter, may help address the marginalization some confont in a globalized economy.

Offshoring: Productivity Enhancer or Job Thief?

Multinationals have long moved in search of cheap, unskilled manufacturing labor either through subcontracting or setting up subsidiaries abroad. But today, globally integrated companies tap skilled services as well. As technological change in information technologies has brought offices in Bangalore as close as Boston, companies evaluate the cost of completing business processes at home and abroad. Beyond wage differences between skilled and unskilled workers in their own country, many workers in the global North feel threatened by the lower salaries of professionals in the South. Some agree with Greg Mankiw, President Bush's former chairman of the Council of Economic Advisors, who famously wrote in the Economic Report of the President that offshoring was just another form of trade. Suggesting that, "More things are tradable than were tradable in the past, and that's a good thing," Mankiw angered both Republicans and Democrats in his characterization of offshoring as international business as usual.[44] Was Mankiw right? Is offshoring a natural extension of the theory of comparative advantage from goods that can be packed in boxes and shipped overseas to services that can be compressed into bytes and sent over the Internet?

To some, the answer is no. They suggest that offshoring is more than moving jobs; rather, is it is changing the structure of global business. Jobs are no longer tied to particular places and industries. Instead, as Gary Gereffi points out, the global labor market is integrated by the demand for jobs that cut across industries in the global services value chain.[45] This unprecedented delivery of the service of labor allows not only low-skilled manufacturing jobs to move from Indiana to Shenzhen but also high-technology jobs to be completed in Seoul rather than Silicon Valley. As the global workforce has become more educated, simple service provision has moved from basic tasks of data entry or application support to customer interaction via call centers, product development and design, medication and engineering services, as well as strategic partnerships in the design, integration, and research of new products. Technology and transportation connects labor markets, effectively quadrupling of the global labor pool; the key distinction is in identifying those services that can be delivered electronically and those that cannot.[46] If you could have your tax return completed at half the cost, would you? Healthcare providers recognize the economic benefits of outsourcing certain services.[47] For instance, roughly half of U.S. hospitals have outsourced some of their radiology services, some using trained specialists in India to look at films for 6.3% of what it would cost to employ a domestic radiologist to complete the same task. Is it unethical for a hospital not to use these lower cost services to release something on the order of $195 million to purchase other forms of health care? Clients are now demanding that law firms use less expensive legal services from India or the Philippines, containing legal costs to as much as one-tenth the fees for routine document reviews and due diligence. [48] While big clients such as General Electric will readily pay top dollars for the big legal guns, they no longer want to foot the $500 an hour bill for the associates surrounding them. Table 6.2 summarizes some of the effects of offshoring for developed and developing economies.

Table 6.2. Effects of Offshoring

	Developed Economies	*Developing Economies*
Employment Level	22–29% of the U.S. Workforce is cited as *potentially offshorable* over the next two decades. Its forecasted that 15–20 million jobs are at risk of being off shored to labor-abundant countries. Many predict that by 2015, 3.3 million U.S. business-process jobs well have moved abroad. By July 2003, 400,000 jobs already had. However, in the last decade 35 million new jobs have been created. According to the OECD, job growth was fastest in high-wage occupations.	The McKinsey estimates that in India, Outsourcing IT and business processes generates more than $10 billion a year for the country and employs at least half a million workers. Suppliers to the companies that provide outsourced services employ another half million people.
Unskilled Employment	–: Companies are likely to move low skill jobs abroad to take advantage of lower cost labor. 40% of the jobs in the manufacturing sector are likely to be offshored. +: For every dollar of spending moved abroad, U.S. companies save 58 cents mostly in wages.	+: In India, the textile and apparel industry employs 88 million. Jobs created in the manufacturing sector abroad have given millions new opportunities and lowered the poverty rates in many developing countries.
Skilled Employment	+: High-skilled capital and technology intensive jobs coincide with the United States' comparative advantage are not likely to experience as much volatility.	+: Investment in FDI towards technology indicates that there will be a higher demand for skilled labor abroad. For example, The McKinsey Global Institute estimates 134,000 software-related jobs were created in India to serve firms in the United States. Overall, tech companies in India employ two million workers.

continued

Table 6.2. Effects of Offshoring (Continued)

	Developed Economies	*Developing Economies*
Wage Gap Between Skilled and Unskilled Labor	+: When low-skilled workers lost jobs to markets abroad, they found replacement jobs that paid 20–40% less than previous salaries. –: In the United States, the earnings gap between skilled and unskilled sectors has widened by 25%.	+: Investment in technology and increased FDI leads to the gains from globalization increasing incomes of higher skilled works. Although, the poor are no worse off, and usually made better off with creation of new jobs. In India, wages in the IT sector are 50–100%s higher on average than wages for other white-collar occupations, creating a new middle class of educated workers.
Productivity Effect	+: The Institute of International Economics estimated that outsourcing boosted productivity growth from 2.5% to 2.8% a year from 1995 to 2002. This gain tallied at least $230 billion to the country's total output of goods and services.	+: Companies operating overseas helped boost the productivity of the local industries by injecting new capital, technology, and management skills. In addition, by increasing the level of competition, they force less-efficient domestic companies to improve or go out of business.
	+: For every dollar of spending on business services that go abroad, U.S. companies save upwards of 58 cents, mostly from wages. Firms can gain access to new markets abroad, better serve clients and customers that were moving abroad themselves, and access new talent abroad. Ultimately offshoring creates net value for the U.S. economy, about $1.12 to $1.14 for each dollar that is shipped abroad.	+: For every dollar spent in India by United States businesses in outsource, India earns a net benefit of at least 33 cents through government taxes, wages paid by U.S. companies, and revenues earned by Indian vendors.
	+: A survey by the Ventoro Institute found that 36% of executives claimed their offshoring strategies had failed. The Institute found that offshoring increased costs in 28% of cases and had no cost savings in 25%. Firms also have to worry about quality control, information security, and political stability in the country of operation.	–: Local companies are in danger of being forced out of business by larger multinational companies, or risk losing substantial market share. In addition, countries face the risk of their currency appreciating and businesses moving to lower cost countries. In 2008 in India, the rupee appreciated 11% against the dollar costing 500,000 textile workers to lose their jobs in six months.

Source: McKinsey Quarterly, Peterson Institute, Business Week.

Outsourcing of services is most frequent in those activities with an impersonal nature. For instance, services such as customer support or software development are easily delivered via electronic commerce. By contrast, some services require face-to-face contact, such as childcare or the touch of a nurse, while others rely on high levels of personal trust, such as psychotherapy, or depend on location specific attributes, such as lobbying. As information technology improves, more personal services will become impersonal. We see this, for example, in the case of distance learning; some of you may be reading this book with your instructor in another city, connected by online chats.[49]

Is offshoring therefore likely to grow? Some estimate that 3.3 million U.S. jobs are potentially offshorable; others suggest a number as high as forty million.[50] Offshoring of finance and accounting is moving beyond India to Latin America; Mexico, Brazil, and Argentina are new hotspots for invoice processing, travel and expense processing, and accounts receivable work.[51] But one also needs to filter estimates by asking which workers are genuinely multinational ready, a number that is the fraction of the workers available. Roughly one-third of offshoring attempts fail and eventually return to the home country, evidence that simply having workers available doesn't mean they will successfully complete the job. Clearly those people losing jobs to offshoring are worse off in the short run. Is the pain of their dislocation worth the gain to the firm and the nation? Firms benefit from the lower costs of services. A study by Deloitte Touche Tohmatsu found that in 2006, over 75% of major financial institutions had operations offshore and that more than half of the financial institutions that participated in the study saved over 40% against their onshore costs.[52] Those in financial services in the United States might make $35 an hour while comparably trained specialists in India are paid about $10. This reduces the firm's labor costs for that activity by more than 60%. At the country level, lower costs translate into a lower rate of inflation and a higher rate of productivity. Perhaps paradoxically, offshoring allows a firm to concentrate on core competencies and contributes to a more competitive export sector.

Changes may not occur as quickly as some anticipate. The momentum toward offshoring has also been challenged by changes in the labor market in the developing world and the costs of running a globally integrated company. The trend toward moving more processes offshore is slowed by rising labor costs abroad. Some companies are reverse offshoring or "onshoring" as they find operating at a distance introduces inefficiencies. The strong demand for Indian engineers and software specialists not surprisingly has narrowed the wage gap between India and the United States. The average worker in China makes more than twice today what was paid ten years ago. For processes that also move in boxes and not bytes, higher freight costs slowed down overseas expansion.[53] Offshoring clearly features in business strategies, but it is likely that its rate will temper.

The Movement of Labor

Companies can move overseas or people move to where jobs are. Although capital is the more mobile factor to take advantage of lower wages in other countries, labor, facilitated by more accessible transportation and communication networks with family living abroad, is also transnational. Immigrants to the United States have been arriving at a rate of 1.3 million per year over the last decade; in 2012, over 13% of our residents were foreign born.[54] Of the forty million foreign-born residents, roughly a quarter entered without documentation. As of 2011, there were some 11.5 million undocumented migrants living in the United States.[55] These undocumented workers account for just 5.1% of the U.S. civilian labor force in the United States.[56] Why are people willing to leave families to live in far-off places?

Migration has multiple motives. As shown in Table 6.3, people migrating are either pushed to leave by domestic factors or pulled to emigrate by the prospect of a better life. The drive to migrate is largely economic; significant wage differentials between countries cause people to move from low wage, high unemployment regions to higher wage, low unemployment areas.[57] An educated Nigerian male will make eight times as much working in New York as in Abuja, the Nigerian capital.[58] A Mexican man with nine years of schooling raises his salary from $2.30 an hour in Mexico City to $8.50 an hour in Chicago—even with wages adjusted for the relative costs of living. These ambitious workers want more for themselves and their families; no wonder, given salary differentials, they are willing to take extraordinary risks to move. Paralleling the movement of capital, logically the factor of labor should indeed move to places with the highest returns. The fact that only 3% of the global population is foreign born is perhaps of greater surprise than the millions that move each year.

Typically, the influx of foreign labor confronts significant resistance from national workers. Not surprisingly, domestic workers fear they may lose their jobs to foreign nationals. To what degree is this fear valid? Overall, does immigrant labor hurt or help an economy? In part the answer to these questions relies on

Table 6.3. Motivations for Migration

	Push Factors	*Pull Factors*
Economic and Demographic	Poverty Unemployment Low wages High fertility rates Lack of basic health and education	Prospect of higher wages Potential for improved standard of living Personal or professional development
Political	Conflict, insecurity, violence Poor governance Corruption Human rights abuses	Safety and security Political freedom
Social/Cultural	Discrimination based on ethnicity, gender religion, and others	Family reunification Ethnic (diaspora migration) homeland Freedom from discrimination

Source: Ali Mansoor and Bryce Quillin, *Migration and Remittances: Eastern Europe and the Former Soviet Union* (Washington, DC: World Bank, 2007), 78.

understanding where immigrant workers are employed. Foreign-born workers gravitate to sectors where American-born workers are scarce. Labor scarcity in the manual sectors in the United States is a natural result of a better-educated domestic workforce; only 10.8% of native-born working-age Americans drop out of high school. In 2013, over 32% of American adults over the age of 25 reported having at least a bachelor's degree, representing more than a five-fold increase in college attainment since 1940.[59] Many native-born workers, particularly those with a secondary education, are not especially excited by the prospects of roofing, packing fish, or picking broccoli. Indeed, the United Farm Workers organization, at the website www.takeourjobs.org, has launched a campaign promising to find employment for Americans eager to work under condition that include using hand tools such as knives, shovels to weed, thin and cut, stoop and bend under all weather conditions.[60] Not surprisingly, there are few takers for this backbreaking work. In general, immigrants are clustered at the lowest levels of education with another cluster at the top end of education, while natives are clustered in the center.[61] However, trends vary depending on the country of origin; immigrants from Mexico and Central America (the largest source of those emigrating) tend to be very poorly educated, while those from India and the Philippines are often better educated than the average U.S. citizen.[62] Foreign-born workers are found in construction, food preparation, meat and fish processing, cleaning services, building and grounds crews, and farming.

The availability of immigrants in the low-skilled labor market depresses wages among the American working poor. Empirical evidence suggests that immigrant labor decreases the wages of the least-skilled workers on the order of 5% in the United States.[63] George Borjas estimates that a 10% rise in immigration of any kind lowers wages for native-born workers by approximately 3–4%.[64] In Europe, where wages are less flexible, increased immigration is associated with higher unemployment among unskilled native-born workers.

Yet, the net impact of immigration on most native-born workers is slight; indeed, there may be a complementary effect where lower-priced unskilled workers makes higher-skilled workers more productive.[65] Furthermore, immigrant labor may aid consumers and increase the efficiency of local economies; cities with larger immigrant flows are able to access services in housekeeping, gardening, childcare, and other labor-intensive fields, leaving more skilled citizens time for other work. Firms benefit as lower-priced workers increase productivity. Look, for example, in the kitchen in a restaurant in the United States. Doubling the wages of the dishwasher and prep cook will increase the price of the dinner on your menu. Immigrants provide a cushion in recession; typically the first to lose their jobs, domestic unemployment might have been higher without the invisible labor of migrant workers.[66] Overall, a 1% increase in immigrant labor may improve GDP per worker (productivity) by 0.63% within a seven-year period.[67] According to the World Bank, an increase in migration from developing countries to boost the labor force by 3% in industrial countries would general welfare gains on the order of $356 billion or 0.6% of world GDP, gains greater than full liberalization of the trade in goods.[68] Nonetheless, studies on the impact of immigration on wages have contradictory results.

Brain Drain and Empty Homes

Just as immigrants have a profound effect on the countries in which they arrive, so too do they change the ones they leave. U.S. Census data counts more than 2.5 million highly educated immigrants from developing countries over the age of 25.[69] Some studies claim that immigration has a substantial impact on wages in labor-sending countries.[70] Lives lost in illegal border crossings are an avoidable and heartbreaking tragedy. Increased militarization of the U.S.-Mexico border has led to more risky and remote crossings and has contributed to a rise in the number of deaths, which total around 5,600 since 1994, mainly from heat exhaustion, drowning, and vehicle accidents.[71] Beyond lives lost in transit, more than half the university-educated citizens from Central America and the Caribbean were living abroad in 2000,[72] and nearly 20% of skilled workers have left Sub-Saharan Africa.[73]

This **brain drain** of human capital creates burdens at home. Another negative effect is that many communities are left without their most productive young minds and local industries die. Women are left to raise children alone and take on tasks their husbands typically did. Also, traditional governance structures change in communities as men are not there to take on their positions. Domestic governments lose the higher tax revenue from these well-remunerated workers. The lack of skilled workers such as managers, teachers, and engineers in the home country may decrease the productivity of remaining workers. Without a dynamic pool of skilled labor it is also more difficult to attract foreign investment.[74] Sadly for the sending country, rates of return migration are low, and those that return are seldom among the most talented.[75]

Capital Flowing South: The Importance of Remittances

Economists continue to examine whether or not the negative consequences of the brain drain and low-skilled emigration can be sufficiently offset by gains to the sending country such as increased FDI, technology adoption, and greater investment in human capital.[76] Perhaps the most obvious gain to home countries in the developing world is the flow of **remittance money** sent back home by those working abroad.

Globally, remittances amounted to $431 billion in 2015,[77] about two-thirds of the flow of FDI, equal to private debt and equity flows and roughly three times development assistance to the developing world.[78] For many developing countries, remittances are an important source of income; in Nepal remittances reach 29% and in Liberia they account for 21% of GDP (Figure 6.3). Remittances have been shown to reduce poverty, act as counter-cyclical buffers, meet humanitarian needs during natural disasters, and provide hard currency directly to families in the developing world. They balance trade deficits and cover import bills. To take advantage of this capital flow, some countries, such as Haiti, are considering issuing Diaspora bonds to further encourage expatriates to invest back in the home country. This type of debt instrument denominated at say $1,000 and purchased by the 200 million

Figure 6.3. Remittances as a Percentage of GDP, 2010

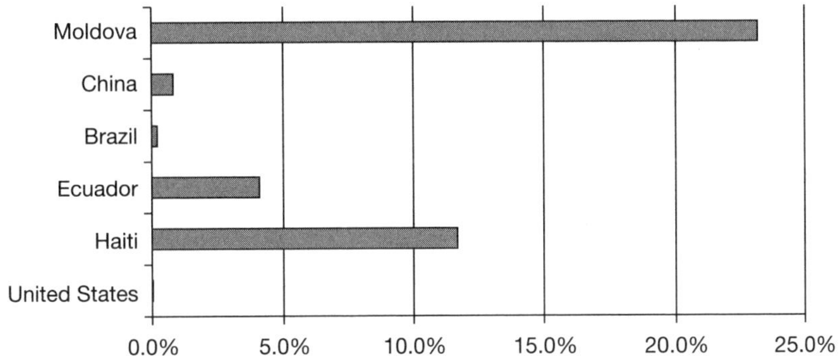

Source: World Bank Remittances Data.

Haitians living abroad has the potential to raise $200 million for development at home.[79] Remittances can act to decrease economic insecurity among the poor. In Sri Lanka, children in remittance receiving households have a higher birth weight as compared to those without relatives abroad.[80]

The benefits of remittances are conditioned by the way in which the money is used. Unfortunately, remittances are most frequently channeled to consumption: food, rent, and other non-durable expenses. While these are typically necessary, they do not have the same long-term impact that focused investment might offer. Development agencies and NGOs have been working to channel this enormous cash flow away from present consumption to investments in a stronger asset base for the future. Technological innovations in banking have helped the poor use their money more wisely. Foreign-born workers in Long Island, NY, for example, can set up an account that can be drawn on by family members building a home in Oaxaca, Mexico. Pilot programs in microfinance are allowing a steady remittance history to act as collateral in lending.[81] Remittances from Mexicans working in California are now also tied to car loans in Puebla; added mobility can certainly help those at home acquire better jobs. Policy questions remain centered on how to transform consumption-based remittance spending into productive investment that will sufficiently offset the brain drain. Other policy questions regard how to encourage the positive effects of human capital development in home countries, network building, and technological transfer such that the brain drain becomes a brain gain.

Human Trafficking

Some people seek to work away from home; others are forced. Beyond the global trade in illegal narcotics, the second largest sector in international organized crime is trafficking in people. The UN Palermo Protocol defines **human trafficking** as recruiting, transportation, harboring or receiving persons by use of force or coercion or deception for the purpose of exploitation, which includes prostitution, forced labor, slavery, or servitude.[82] A 2010 UN Study estimates that the illegal smuggling of economic migrants is worth about $6.6 billion a year to those who run the trade.[83] The trade in women for sexual exploitation is now worth about $3 billion a year. Beyond the transfer of those who want to move for economic reasons, it is estimated that 2.5 million children, women and men are forced across international borders every year, put to work against their will or held under threat.[84] Others are taken from or tricked into leaving their local communities by the promise of jobs that in reality bring nothing but debt. The World Bank estimates that at least 12.5 million people are subject to nonconsensual exploitation or forced labor, including both those in their home countries and abroad.[85] **Bonded labor**, where workers are enticed to jobs but incur unsustainable personal debt for food, transportation or lodging in acquiring these positions is particularly important in South Asia but also present in other regions. In Brazil, work in remote logging locations leaves vulnerable workers there dependent on the company for survival. In total, at least 25,000 Brazilian men are subjected to slave labor within the country, typically on cattle ranches, logging and mining camps, sugar-cane plantations, and large farms as their transportation to arrive from urban centers combined with accommodations at the work site mount to an unmanageable debt.[86] In India, debt bondage is precipitated by jobbers or contractors who organize the migration to divest the company from risk. Usually by someone from the village, workers are enticed by bonds of trust to work in abject conditions for low wages that rarely meet the initial advance.[87] Women and girls are the main targets of commercial sexual exploitation and overall account for more than half of all forms of economic exploitation. In Brazil, a country with one of the highest rates of sexual slavery in the world, the most exploited women come from the poorest sectors of society and tend to be of African descent.[88] In 2005, over 70,000 of these women and girls were working in the sex trade in foreign countries.[89] Women are often tricked into the trade with promises of well-paying jobs overseas as domestic workers, dancers or secretaries. Upon arrival, however, their documents are taken and they are forced to work as prostitutes; often they are psychologically manipulated by pimps, physically, sexually, and emotionally abused and told their families will be targeted if they try to escape.[90] While we may think that sexual exploitation is primarily a problem in the developing world, it is also a booming industry in more advanced economies. In the United States in 2005, sexual exploitation of children—including pornography, prostitution, sex tourism, and trafficking—was the third largest money maker for organized crime, behind trafficking of guns and illegal drugs.[91] Female migrants from Mexico, for example, are often held as captive prostitutes to pay off extortion bribes. All in all, extracting forced labor is a big business; profits from transnational human trafficking are estimated at $32 billion a year.[92]

Should Children Work?

Child labor is another form of labor that can be perceived as exploitative. The ILO estimates that there are 218 million child laborers.[93] Thankfully few are indentured in servitude or chained to factories. Many argue, however, that as children don't control their choice of work, schooling and leisure time, parents can make choices on their behalf that are not in the child's long run best interest. The practice of child labor is more complex: where does helping one's family end and forced labor begin? Can initiatives to end child labor tragically backfire to hurt the child?

Understanding policy solutions to child labor first requires an exploration of why children work. Think of a child as part of a short- and long-run family production function. While this is not perhaps the most idyllic way to think of childhood, in a poor country the input of children can improve the standard of a family's living either by contributing to the production of household activity or as a good to be sold in the market.[94] The economic contributions of children must be weighed against the costs of alternatives—including the direct and indirect costs of education and the valuation of play in the development of the child. As parents largely make the decision about whether the child will work and capture the immediate reward in terms of family income, children are forced to sacrifice the future value of investment in human capital against current needs.

The ILO estimates that 218 million children work in home production, the family farm or in family businesses; approximately eight million of these working kids are in horrific conditions of bonded labor, child soldiering or prostitution. There isn't a clearly internationally consistent definition of child labor. Some studies focus on wage or market determined work, although some children helping parents are not directly paid wages. The situation becomes more complicated when one considers that some work by children can be seen as culturally appropriate or developmental, for instance helping parents weave pashmina shawls or working in the fields instead of attending school. The ILO convention on child labor tries to capture work that prevents children from achieving their full physical and mental development. Age matters. The ILO defines work of more than one hour a week harmful to a child under 12, yet a child between 12 and 14 might work two hours a day so long as it is not in hazardous activities. While the literature is clear on avoiding the "worst forms of child labor," including bonded labor or child prostitution, it is more difficult to arrive at a policy answer that identifies how much work in and outside the home is appropriate. At times, this confusion can mean that initiatives to halt child labor actually end up being counterproductive. Ikea and other signatories of the fair trade weaving association Rugmark clamped down on the use of child labor among suppliers only to learn that the inability to feed the family drove child labor deeper inside less-regulated factories. Not surprisingly, child labor is also hard to estimate; companies prefer to turn a blind eye to children working rather than document it. Gender matters; boys tend to contribute more to market work while girls pick up duties of overstretched parents in the home. Geography also impacts the rate at which children work. Roughly one-third of rural children work, as opposed to one-fifth of young urban dwellers.

The globalization of communications technologies has increased attention to the worst of child labor. The possibility of a YouTube video of a child slave working for a subcontracting supplier is one of the things that keep multinational executives up at night. Google "child labor India" and see what pops up. Ikea wants imagines of its NGO MySchool circulating—not children laboring in oppressive conditions. Fear of consumer boycotts or legislative retribution has weeded out the worst cases of child labor. Empirical evidence also does not confirm the belief that children will be drawn into the export sector of countries opening to labor-intensive trade. Indeed, in contrast, Edmunds and Pavcnik find that in countries more exposed to international trade levels of child participation decrease as incomes rise.[95] This may not hold, however, in the case of cash crops such as coffee, where children can invisibly add to family earnings.

The question remains, however, about the appropriate amount of work for the remaining 200 million children whose families are delicately balancing survival strategies. A key question may be not whether children work, but the age at which children enter the workforce full time. Evidence from India and Brazil suggests a discount of between 13% and 20% of lifetime earnings with an early labor force entry, reflecting the foregone opportunities of additional schooling. Recognizing these lost earnings, some countries have tried to make it more economically viable for parents to send their children to school. In Brazil and elsewhere, social sector programs, called **conditional cash transfers,** explicitly link family welfare payments to extended school attendance from birth through the high school years. Governments and NGOs have also begun to realize the importance of creating alternatives to forced labor, rather than outright banning it. Without such alternatives to the family survival strategy, prohibiting child labor through legislation or shaming the practice through boycotts may backfire. FIFA-approved soccer balls may help college teams feel good about the product—but there is little evidence that negative branding alone helps the poor child. Instead, companies have formed partnerships with NGOs to work not only at removing children from work impeding their full development but also creating more exit strategies from poverty. Programs targeted at improving the income earning capabilities of mothers, for example, may go farther in reducing child labor than restricting the working age or hours. Programs such as Ikea's alliance with UNICEF international is an example of transforming the fundamental causes of poverty rather than punishing families trying to survive.

Social Protection and Social Inclusion

Globalization creates winners and losers. The movement of people, capital, goods, and technology is inherently a redistributive process. Those possessing the human or financial assets in global demand will benefit; others are left behind. Globalization can create growth, but its disruptive dynamic can also leave human harm in its wake. Workers who have contributed to national output under one set of rules and incentives are suddenly dislodged by job competition from labor half way across the globe. Workers are more vulnerable to unanticipated shocks. Should society consider stronger shock absorbers to minimize the negative effects on unlucky individuals and devastated communities?

Consider the plight of a line worker in a small rural town. This worker, perhaps about 45 years old, has two children and a hefty mortgage. Like most in the community, the worker started in the town's sole employer, an electronics company, upon leaving high school. The day the announcement is made to move production to Mexico, life changed dramatically. With much of the factory town unemployed, housing values plummet. Mortgages go underwater—homeowners owe more on the loan signed in a boom time than the houses are now worth. College for the two kids is put on indefinite hold. Short of foreclosure, the family can't move. And where would they move to? Mexico? That's where the jobs are for electronics workers.

This painful story of globalization is all too familiar across America. Over the past decades, the rapid shift of where and how goods are produced could not have been predicted by people making livelihoods in communities dependent on companies with global reach. As committed as a corporation might appear to a locality, it faces ruthless pressures by new global competitors. Rapid structural changes wrought by the intense velocity of changes in globalized production, trade, and financial movements raise the question of whether we need to rethink social policies to adjust to new global realities. In the United States, social policy is largely framed by unemployment insurance and welfare benefits. In a temporary downturn, unemployment insurance smooths consumption until a new job can be secured. But in an economy struck not by a cyclical pause but a structural change, unemployment insurance is unlikely to be enough. With globalization the nature of jobs has changed. That electronics assembler somehow has to be remade into a health care worker—at age 45 with a mismatched skill set and little flexibility for change. Welfare benefits might pick up when unemployment runs out, but PRWORA—as welfare is officially named—benefits are also time bound. Moreover, this dedicated employee of more than 25 years would find a life on public assistance hard to reconcile with a self-image as a contributor to family and society.

Admittedly, this story of a small-town worker is not fully representative of the options a worker in an industrialized country faces in light of globalization. Some workers hurt by global competition live in cities with more options to adjust. Others may have skills that are transferable to another sector. But the challenge remains: should societies help those who, through no fault of their own, find their lives turned upside down?

Some, despite feeling compassion for the troubles of the worker, argue no. Believing that markets work best when they are left to operate without government intervention, these market fundamentalists contend that the economic pain will create the most effective incentives for change. Others contest this view, arguing that society has a responsibility to compensate losers, especially when the costs are incurred by factors outside the individual's control. Proponents of new social policies to address costs of globalization largely focus on two policy planks: support to acquire a new skills set and underwriting mobility. Incentives to invest in one's own human capital by retraining and education are important in helping a worker in a dying industry segue to a new sector. Community colleges are playing important roles in facilitating this shift in labor market skills. Programs such as **Trade Adjustment Assistance (TAA)** are critical in smoothing the rough pathway of adult career switching.[96] Administered by the Department of Labor in collaboration with states, this program promotes adaptability in labor markets. For example, a TAA program for trade displaced shoe workers in Maine helped train workers for health professions. The reauthorization of TAA in 2013 was seen as a mark of political pragmatism—a quid pro quo for passing FTA agreements with Korea and Colombia. Labor would benefit from a degree of adjustment assistance in exchange for further trade liberalization.

But some contend that TAA isn't enough. It doesn't address the lack of geographic mobility for communities hit by global competition. One needs to prove damage, certifying that unemployment is directly related to trade. Moreover, it is reactive—a palliative after the fact. Globalization continues to transform production platforms. TAA addresses some problems created by structural change but do not help labor markets keep pace with or affect the direction of competitive advantage. More proactive policies such as those in the United Kingdom or Australia include support for intermittent work and broadened opportunities to connect people to meaningful jobs.[97] **Active labor market policies** seek to improve competitiveness in labor markets—a benefit not only for workers but also for companies.

Can Private Social Investment Help?

An obvious constraint in adopting active labor market strategies is funding. Improving efficiency in labor markets competes against other social and environmental investments in national budgets. One avenue to soften this budget constraint may be corporations themselves. Global companies have appreciate the benefits of addressing the three Ps—people, planet, and profits. Investing in people in communities in partnership with governments can deliver more-efficient outcomes at lower costs. Directing corporate social investments toward education and technical capacity building can promote a win–win in enhancing competitiveness in the markets where companies operate. Positive externalities of investments by companies in their workers and their communities include enhanced reputational value: others will be more interested in buy the products or stocks for a "good" company.

Geoffrey Heal of Columbia University writes that corporate social responsibility can be seen as a private response to the perception of unfairness in market outcomes. As inequality is accentuated by globalization, many people in the middle and upper middle classes feel they are falling further behind. Initiatives by corporations to invest in human and social capital can soften these feelings of frustration and mitigate tension. Of course, corporate engagement in the social sector is not a panacea. Social deficits cannot be addressed by the private sector alone. But strong partnerships between the state and civil societies may facilitate a smoother adjustment to the rocky road of globalization.

Summary

Globalized Production and Labor Markets

- Beyond integration in trade and finance, globalization has also changed the geography of production and distribution, transforming global labor markets. Within countries and across borders, changes in the labor market now present new opportunities and challenges to participating in the formal employment sector worldwide.

Producing Globally in the Twenty-First Century

- Companies possess different motivations for expanding production lines worldwide. Some of those motivations include natural resources, efficiency of production, access to markets, and technology.
- Horizontal FDI is motivated by access to markets within the recipient country. Vertical FDI, on the other hand, is motivated by efficient use of resources in the recipient country, like breaking up different parts of the production process across borders to minimize costs at each step.
- Transnational production is growing. The global factory encompasses this diversified production process, as companies work globally and implement both vertical and horizontal FDI to control information flows and find the lowest cost producers in a global economy.
- Many disagree as to whether horizontal and vertical FDI actually help or hurt developing countries. Modernization theorists believe the technology gains and capital investments in developing countries after receiving FDI benefits them, whereas dependency theorists see FDI as an inhibiting force in regards to organic domestic development, with a crowding out of local entrepreneurship and barriers to entry for national firms. Because of these conflicting factors, it is difficult to measure the effects of FDI on growth.

Globalization, Labor, Technology: Inequality

- By increasing the availability of workers in other countries, globalization has increased the supply of labor available to firms. The resulting effect on earnings is not a dramatic downfall, but moderated wage growth at about 1.85% annually.
- Like in trade, globalization produces winners and losers. Skilled workers benefit, whereas workers unable to invest in human capital lose out. Firms can search the global market for cheap labor, which lowers the bargaining power of workers. Technology compounds this issue as it suppresses wages of the lowest-earning employees, contributing to higher overall levels of income inequality.
- It is difficult to measure the direct correlation between increasing global interconnectedness and rising global inequality.
- As measured by the Gini coefficient, today's world is extremely unequal. Global integration through technological advancements places downward pressure on low-skilled wages, whereas greater technological literacy favors high-skilled workers.

Offshoring: Productivity Enhancer or Job Thief?

- Some see offshoring as just another form of trade, yet others see offshoring as fundamentally altering the structure of global business as labor moves beyond borders.

- Offshoring applies to both low-skilled manufacturing jobs and high-technology jobs, like the outsourcing of radiology services. Because the global workforce is more educated and easily accessible versus years past, firms now can identify not just which factories can be moved to lower-wage areas, but which specialized jobs as well.

The Movement of Labor

- The motivation to migrate is largely economic, as significant wage differentials cause people to move from low wage, high unemployment regions to high wage, low unemployment regions. The presence of these immigrants often incites anger in domestic workers, as they fear losing their jobs to foreigners.
- In the United States, foreign workers gravitate to sectors were American-born workers are scarce. The benefits of foreign workers in a domestic economy include lower priced unskilled workers and an increased efficiency of local economies.
- However, this movement of labor can contribute to issues at home. The tendency for the highly educated to emigrate from developing countries to develop countries creates burdens at home, with the most productive young minds leaving a country to find opportunities elsewhere.
- At the same time, one of the greatest gains to home countries of family members working abroad is the influx of remittance money. For many developing countries, remittances are an importance source of income, and they reduce poverty, act counter-cyclically, meet humanitarian needs during natural disasters, and provide hard currency directly to families in the developing world.

Human Trafficking

- Human trafficking encompasses the global movements of labor by force. The second largest sector of international organized crime is the trafficking of people.
- Child labor is also perceived as exploitative. While human trafficking is categorically wrong due to the use of force, understanding child labor is slightly more ambiguous: when does helping one's family end and forced labor begin?
- The ILO estimates that 218 million children work worldwide, and of this figure, eight million are in horrific conditions of bonded labor, child soldiering, or prostitution.

Notes

1. Marcus Taylor, "Who Works for Globalization? The Challenges and Possibilities for International Labour Studies." *Third World Quarterly* 30, no. 3 (2009): 435–52.

2. Theodore H. Moran, "Enhancing the Contribution of Foreign Direct Investment to Development: A New Agenda for the Corporate Social Responsibility Community, International Labor and Civil Society, Aid Donors, and Multilateral Financial Institutions" (draft, 2010).

3. Peter J. Buckley, "Internalisation Thinking—From the Multinational Enterprise to the Global Factory." *International Business Review* 18, no. 3 (2009).

4. Matthew Bishop, "A Bigger World." *The Economist*, September 18, 2008, 2.

5. Frederick Guy, *The Global Environment of Business*. New York: Oxford University Press, 2009, p. 14.

6. Peter J. Buckley, "The Impact of the Global Factory on Economic Development." *Journal of World Business*, 44, no. 2 (2009): 131–43.

7. Buckley, "Internalisation Thinking."

8. Filip De Beule and Daniël Van Den Bulcke, "Retrospective and Prospective Views about the Future of the Multinational Enterprise." *International Business Review* 18 (2009).

9. UNCTAD World Investment Report 2011.

10. Michael Porter, *The Competitive Advantage of Nations*.

11. Olivier Cattaneo, Gary Gereffi, and Cornelia Staritz, *Global Value Chains in a Post-crisis World* (World Bank Trade and Development Series) Washington, DC: World Bank, 2010.

12. UNCTAD World Investment Report 2011.

13. UN Conference on Trade and Development, *World Investment Report 2009: Transnational Corporations, Agricultural Production, and Development*. Geneva, Switzerland: UN, 2009.

14. Samuel Adams, "Foreign Direct Investment, Domestic Investment and Economic Growth in Sub-Saharan Africa," *Journal of Policy Making* 31 (2009).

15. Ibid., 941.

16. Laura Alfaro et al., "Does Foreign Direct Investment Promote Growth? Exploring the Role of Financial Markets on Linkages." *Journal of Development Economics* 91 (2010).

17. Jennifer Oetzel and Jonathan Doh, "MNEs and Development: A Review and Reconceptualization." *Journal of World Business* 44 (2009).

18. Ann Harrison and Andrés Rodriguez-Clare, "Trade, Foreign Investment, and Industrial Policy for Developing Countries," in *Handbooks in Economics: Development Economics, Volume* 5, ed. Dani Rodrick and M.R. Rosenzweig. Oxford: Elsevier, 2010.

19. Kevin Gallagher, *The Enclave Economy: Foreign Investment and Sustainable Development in Mexico's Silicon Valley*. MIT Press, 2007, and Kevin Gallaher, *Foreign direct Investment and domestic Spillovers: Hi Tech Electronics in Guadalajara, Mexico*. Presentation at CLAS Berkeley, 2005.

20. Harrison and Rodriquez-Clare, "Trade, Foreign Investment, and Industrial Policy for Developing Countries."

21. International Trade Administration, U.S. Department of Commerce: Invest in America, *FDI and the U.S. Economy Fact Sheet* [2009].

22. Oetze and Doh, "MNEs and Development."

23. Florence Jaumotte and Irina Tytell, "Globalization of Labor." *Finance and Development* 44, no. 2 (June 2007).

24. International Labor Office, *Global Wage Report 2008/09: Minimum Wages and Collective Bargaining: Towards Policy Coherence*. Geneva, Switzerland: International Labour Office, 2008, p. 59.

25. International Labor Organization Global Wage Report 2014–2015.

26. Martin Rama, "Globalization and the Labor Market," *The World Bank Research*

Observer 18, no. 2 (2003), quoted in Drusilla Brown, "A Review of the Globalization Literature: Implications for Employment, Wages, and Labor Standards," in *Globalization, Wages, and the Quality of Jobs: Five Country Studies,* ed. Raymond Robertson, Drusilla Brown, Gaelle Pierre, and Maria Laura Sanchez-Puerta. Washington, DC: The World Bank, 2009, p. 24.

27. International Labor Office, *Global Wage Report 2008/09.*

28. Ibid.

29. Robert Gavin, "Workers Do More, but Wages Fall Short: Productivity Link Broken, Study Says." *The Boston Globe*, October 10, 2006, Business Section.

30. International Labour Office, *Global Wage Report 2008/09.*

31. UN Development Program, *2009 Human Development Report: Overcoming Barriers: Human Mobility and Development.* New York: Palgrave Macmillan, 2009, pp. 206–7.

32. Branko Milanovic, *Global Inequality Recalculated: The Effect of New 2005 PPP Estimates on Global Inequality.* World Bank Policy Research Working Paper 5061, 2009.

33. Milanovic, "Global Inequality Recalculated," p. 14.

34. David A. Moss and Anna Harrington, *Inequality and Globalization.* Harvard Business Publishing, 2005.

35. ILO, *World of Work Report 2008: Income Inequalities in the Age of Financial Globalization.* Geneva, Switzerland: International Institute for Labour Studies, 2008.

36. International Labor Organization World of Work Report (2012) at http://www.ilo.org/wcmsp5/groups/public/---dgreports/---dcomm/---publ/documents/publication/wcms_179453.pdf.

37. Raymond Robertson et al., *Globalization, Wages, and the Quality of Jobs: Five Country Studies.* Washington, DC: The World Bank, 2009.

38. Elena Meschi and Marco Vivarelli, "Trade and Income Inequality in Developing Countries." *World Development* 37, no. 2 (2009).

39. IMF, *World Economic Outlook, October 2007: Globalization and Inequality.* Washington, DC: IMF, 2007.

40. Moss and Harrington, "Inequality and Globalization."

41. Brown, "A Review of the Globalization Literature," in *Globalization, Wages, and the Quality of Jobs* (see note 20), pp. 21–61.

42. Jaumotte and Tytell, "Globalization of Labor."

43. Moss and Harrington, "Inequality and Globalization."

44. Alan S. Blinder, "Offshoring: The Next Industrial Revolution?" *Foreign Affairs*, March/April 2006.

45. Gary Gereffi, "The New Offshoring of Jobs and Global Development" (paper presented at the ILO Social Policy Lectures, Jamaica, December 2005).

46. IMF, *World Economic Outlook, October 2007*; Blinder, "Offshoring: The Next Industrial Revolution?"

47. Thomas R. McLean, "The Global Market for Healthcare: Economics and Regulation," *Wisconsin International Law Journal* 26, no. 3 (2009): 611.

48. Heather Timmons, "Outsourcing to India Draws Western Lawyers," *The New York Times*, August 4, 2010.

49. Blinder, "Offshoring: The Next Industrial Revolution?"

50. Julia Hanna, "How Many U.S. Jobs Are 'Offshorable'?" Harvard Business School Working Knowledge, (December 1, 2008) at http://hbswk.hbs.edu/item/6012.html.

51. Kate O'Sullivan, "Top Five Trends in Offshoring." *CFO Magazine*, January 30, 2008.

52. Deloitte Touche Tohmatsu Global Financial Services Industry Group at http://www.deloitte.com.

53. Ajay Goel, Nazgol Moussavi, and Vats N. Srivatsan, "Time to Rethink Offshoring?" *McKinsey Quarterly*, Winter 2008; Pui-Wang Tam and Jackie Range, "Second Thoughts: Some in Silicon Valley Begin to Sour on India: A Few Bring Jobs Back as Pay of Top Engineers in Bangalore Skyrockets." *Wall Street Journal*, July 3, 2007.

54. Aaron Terrazas and Jeanne Batalova, "Frequently Requested Statistics on Immigrants and Immigration in the United States." Migration Information Source, http://www.migrationinformation.org/USfocus/display.cfm?ID=747#1a

55. "Estimates of the Unauthorized Immigrant Population Residing in the United States: January 2011." *Department of Homeland Security* (March 2012). Also see *A Nation of Immigrants*, Pew (January 29, 2013) at http://www.pewhispanic.org/2013/01/29/a-nation-of-immigrants/.

56. Jeffery S. Passel and D'Vera Chon. "US Unauthorized Immigration Flows Are Down Sharply since Mid-Decade." *Pew Hispanic Center* (September 2010).

57. Ali Mansoor and Bryce Quillin, eds., *Migration and Remittances: Eastern Europe and the Former Soviet Union*. Washington, DC: The World Bank, 2007, p. 78.

58. World Bank, "Factor Mobility and Migration," in *World Development Report 2009: Reshaping Economic Geography* (Washington, DC: The World Bank, 2009, p. 161.

59. *Educational Attainment in the United States: 2013*, U.S. Census Bureau (accessed August 4, 2014).

60. Watch the video of UFW President Arturo Rodriguez with Colbert at http://www.takeourjobs.org/.

61. Card, "Immigration and Inequality," *American Economic Review: Papers & Proceedings* 99, no. 2 (2009): 14.

62. Ibid., 14.

63. George Borjas, "Immigrants In, Wages Down: How to Do the Figuring." *National Review* (May 8, 2006).

64. Ibid.

65. Card, "Immigration and Inequality." David Card, *How Immigration Affects U.S. Cities*. CReAM Discussion Paper #11/07 (June 2007).

66. Uri Dadush and Lauren Falcao, "Migrants and the Global Financial Crisis." *Carnegie Endowment for International Peace Policy Brief* 83 (November 2009).

67. Giovanni Peri, *The Impact of Immigrants in Recession and Economic Expansion* (Washington, DC: Migration Policy Institute, 2010), 19.

68. Dadush and Falcao, "Migrants and the Global Financial Crisis," p. 2.

69. Frédéric Docquier and Hillel Rapoport, *Skilled Migration: The Perspective of Developing Countries,* Discussion Paper 2873. Bonn, Germany: Forschungsinstitut zur Zukunft der Arbeit Institute for the Study of Labor, 2007, p. 4.

70. Borjas, 2003—*The Labor Demand Curve Is Downward Sloping: Reexamining the Impact of Immigration on the Labor Market;* Mishra, 2007—*Emigration and Wages in Source Countries: Evidence from Mexico.*

71. American Civil Liberties Union, "U.S.-Mexico Border Crossing Deaths Are a Humanitarian Crisis, According to Report from the ACLU and CNDH." September 30, 2009.

72. World Bank, "Factor Mobility and Migration," in *World Development Report 2009* (see note 47), 155, 157.

73. Ibid. 157.

74. Ibid.

75. Docquier and Rapoport, *Skilled Migration*, p. 14.

76. Rapoport, "Brain Drain and Development: An Overview," p. 7.

77. The World Bank, "*Migration and Development Brief*" (April 2016) at http://pubdocs.worldbank.org/en/661301460400427908/MigrationandDevelopmentBrief26.pdf
78. Ibid., Figure 5.
79. Sanket Mohapatra, Dilip Ratha, and Ani Silwal, "Outlook for Remittance Flows 2010–2011." *The World Bank Migration and Development Brief*, No. 16.
80. Krishnan Sharma, "The Impact of Remittances on Economic Insecurity" (United Nations Department of Economic and Social Affairs Working Paper No. 78, 2009), p. 11.
81. Mohapatra, Ratha, and Silwal, "Outlook for Remittance Flows 2010–2011."
82. "United Nations Convention against Transnational Organized Crime." November 15, 2000, *General Assembly: Declarations and Conventions Contained in GA Resolutions,* Fifty-fifth Session, A/RES/55/25.
83. James Blitz, "UN Warns of Gangs' Global Muscle," *Financial Times,* June 17, 2010, http://www.ft.com/cms/s/0/75f119b8-7a3e-11df-aa69-00144feabdc0.html.
84. Johannes Koettl, *Human Trafficking, Modern Day Slavery, and Economic Exploitation,* Social Protection & Labor Discussion Paper 0911. Washington, DC: The World Bank, 2009, p. 2.
85. Koettl, *Human Trafficking, Modern Day Slavery, and Economic Exploitation,* 2.
86. U.S. Department of State, *Trafficking in Persons Report 2010*, 2010.
87. Jens Lerche, "A Global Alliance against Forced Labour? Unfree Labour, Neo-Liberal Globalization and the International Labour Organization." *Journal of Agrarian Change* 7, no. 4 (2007).
88. Sharma, "Contemporary Forms of Slavery in Brazil." *Anti-Slavery International* (2006): 9.
89. U.S. Department of State, *Trafficking in Persons Report 2005*, 2005.
90. Sharma, "Contemporary Forms of Slavery in Brazil, p. 9.
91. Alexandra Priebe and Cristen Suhr, "Hidden in Plain View: The Commercial Sexual Exploitation of Girls in Atlanta." *A Study of the Atlanta Women's Agenda* (September 2005): 5.
92. ILO, *A Global Alliance against Forced Labour.* Geneva, Switzerland: ILO, 2005.
93. Eric V. Edmonds, "Child Labor." (National Bureau of Economic Research Working Paper 12926, 2007), p. 6.
94. The following sections draw heavily from the exhaustive review of the literature on child labor by Edmonds, "Child Labor" (see note 80).
95. Eric Edmonds and Nina Pavcnik, "International Trade and Child Labor: Cross-Country Evidence," NBER Working Papers 10317. National Bureau of Economic Research, 2004.
96. http://www.doleta.gov/tradeact/factsheet.cfm and http://fas.org/sgp/crs/misc/R41922.pdf.
97. OECD Connecting People with Jobs Activation Policies in the United Kingdom, http://www.oecd-ilibrary.org/docserver/download/8114161e.pdf?expires=1414966456&id=id&accname=oid006114&checksum=A51B9E899DEEFCDBDAE189583DDBA18D.

CHAPTER SEVEN

SUSTAINABILITY

The defining challenge of the twenty-first century will be to face the reality that humanity shares a common fate on a crowded planet.

—Jeffrey Sachs, *Common Wealth*[1]

Rapidly receding ice at Briksdalsbreen Glacier in Norway.

THE REALITY AND THE PREDICAMENT

Our student from the early 1970s would have been keenly aware of the environmental debates over the planet's ecological systems, the contradictions of economic growth, population pressure, and resource constraints. During this period, national environmental policies emerged as the U.S. National Environmental Protection Act in 1969 created the Environmental Protection Agency (EPA) to protect air, water, and soil. During the early 1970s, the global community focused attention on the complexities of economic growth, population dynamics, resource and fossil-fuel energy use, and pollution levels. In 1974, the Club of Rome's controversial study *Limits to Growth* drew attention to the projected dire and unsustainable realities as populations grew, resources were depleted, and pollutants fouled the water, soil, and air.[2]

The *Limits to Growth* publication preceded the first 1973–74 OPEC oil embargo against the United States, which not only increased oil prices but also brought attention to the level of U.S. dependence on imported oil—then 44% of total domestic oil consumption. In response to this crisis, the Carter administration created the Department of Energy (DOE) in 1977 and passed the National Energy Act in 1978. This created a National Energy Plan designed to promote and develop renewable energy technologies (solar, wind, hydro, thermal, and biomass) and more efficiently utilize fossil-fuel resources. It also promoted energy conservation and efficiency measures. Then, in the context of the Iranian revolution in 1979, OPEC once again doubled oil prices from $17 per barrel to $34 per barrel. The United States found itself 46% dependent on imported oil and facing a prolonged recession as a consequence of rising inflation.[3]

The environmental, natural resource, and energy resource history from the 1980s to 2010 provides ample evidence of the global community's increased awareness of the rapid degradation of the physical environment and the economic and human costs associated with this trend. Environmental writer Bill McKibben's seminal 2004 essay reviewed the many environmental, energy, and natural resource challenges confronting humanity. He documented that we have already pushed beyond critical thresholds in our use and degradation of renewable and non-renewable resources. As the growth of the global population (particularly in developing and emerging market countries) continues, we see many symptoms of damage: early stages of global climate change, atmospheric change and ozone depletion, water scarcity, declining water quality, declining per capita grain production, soil erosion, overfishing, overgrazing, air and water pollution, and the loss of species and biodiversity. Although most of these trends were clearly identified in the 1960s and 1970s, not enough was done to change consumption habits.

McKibben continued to argue that as we use non-renewable resources (fossil fuels and mineral resources), they will not only become more scarce but also more expensive both to extract and to consume. We are challenged to replace non-renewable energy and mineral resources with sustainable alternatives (solar, wind, hydro, thermal, and biomass). Even renewable resources must be managed at rates that they can regenerate; otherwise, we will undermine the ability of these resources to replace themselves. Changing resource use patterns will all take time, scarce financial resources, and the development of new technologies. McKibben's essay raised the critical question: Are we sufficiently preparing for this global future?

Many experts believe that preventing current and future environmental degradation will require a new world view that focuses on developing environmentally *sustainable* ways to *produce, consume, distribute, and dispose of goods and services.* This argument recognizes the need for economic growth, but growth that does not fundamentally violate or degrade the physical life-support systems of the planet. Box 7.1 presents definitions of sustainability, highlighting the need for an intergenerational transfer of scarce resources. Clearly, the feverish demand for global resources will put enormous pressure on non-renewable resources and likely produce resource conflicts as a result of the decreasing ability to meet increasing needs over time in the areas of food, energy, minerals, and water.[4]

Technology allows us to know more and more about the negative effects of human-induced environmental impacts. Scientific research is providing alarming verification of the accelerated melting of the ice caps and glaciers, the warming of ocean currents, the warming of the earth, the changing of weather patterns, the frequency, severity, and location of floods and droughts, the pace of deforestation; the extinction of species; and the availability of fresh water. Yet, as environmental change unfolds over future decades, the consequences for the atmosphere to the darkest depths of the ocean are not exactly clear.

It is not surprising to find, almost every day, provocative essays in newspapers and other publications drawing our attention to these issues. For example, in a June 2011 blog from the Earth Institute Water Center at Columbia, Eve Warburton asks the question—"A Right, a Need, or an Economic Good? Debating our Relationship with Water." In another essay in *The New York Times*, "Earth-Friendly Elements, Mined Destructively," journalist Keith Bradsher tells the story of the environmentally destructive mining of elements called rare earths. Paradoxically, these environmentally destructive elements are needed for green technologies related to electric cars and wind turbines. Trace amounts are also in your cellphones. The mining of these rare earth elements in China relies on acids that wash into streams and rivers, destroying rice paddies and fish farms, and tainting water supplies. Ecological systems are undermined by this unsustainable processes associated with rapid growth. Journalist Sharon LaFraniere in her article, "Lead Poisoning in China: The Hidden Scourge," draws attention to the poisoning of workers and villagers by lead emissions from a battery factory.[5] These images from China reflect the realities of a globally integrated production system; they heighten the challenges for emerging markets like China to address environmental sustainability issues.

Even with the seemingly overwhelming challenges posed by the plethora of environmental problems, many experts believe that reversing environmental damage and preventing future damage is within our reach. For example, Worldwatch Institute's State of the World 2011: Innovations that Nourish the Planet, reveals that with respect to food and nutrition there are many viable, economical, and pragmatic innovations and solutions to promote sustainability. We have the technology to increase the availability of water for crops to help the world's poorest farmers improve crop productivity and become more food secure, improve vegetable production in Sub-Saharan Africa as a sustainable solution for a more diverse and balanced diet, guarantee the right to food, reduce food waste, feed cities, use the knowledge of farmers in research and development, improve soil fertility, safeguard local food biodiversity, cope with climate change, harness the knowledge and skills of women farmers, invest in Africa's moving eco-agriculture into the mainstream, and improve food production from livestock. It is a tall order, but within our reach.

A student today looking forty years into the future would confront all of the environmental, resource, and energy issues being considered in the 1970s, but only worse. The widespread scientific recognition that climate change and global warming is understood to be a real long-term problem has fundamentally changed the twenty-first-century human and planetary reality. Today's student must consider a set of inter-related questions having to do with the ultimate sustainability of the planet and the human race. Can we have economic growth that is sustainable? What does it mean to have sustainable growth and development? What size population can the earth support sustainably? Is capitalism as an economic system sustainable? What is the necessary role for markets in a sustainable future? What is the necessary role for government in a sustainable future? What kind of international cooperation and governance is necessary for sustainability? What has been globalization's role in shaping the character of unsustainable economic growth? What can be globalization's role in creating a sustainable international economy? It is these questions and others that we will explore in this chapter.

Globalization, the Environment, and Sustainability

We have seen that globalization as a concept is subject to diverse interpretation. The same is true for the concept of sustainability. While there are many competing definitions and interpretations (see Box 7.1), the most often quoted is the definition from the UN World Commission on Environment and Development report "Our Common Future" (the Brundtland Report)—"sustainable development is development that seeks to meet the needs and aspirations of the present without compromising the ability to meet those of the future."[6] This definition translates sustainable development as being development (growth) that requires living off nature's income, rather than consuming natural capital. Sustainable development has also come to reflect the need to alleviate global **poverty** and sustain environmental resources.

Globalization can be seen as the culprit or part of the cure for environmental sustainability. Arthur Mol in his book *Globalization and Environmental Reform* argues that globalization "is a multifaceted phenomenon with potentially devastating but also potentially beneficial consequences." Despite suggesting that globalization can be a force to improve sustainability, he points to the consensus view of its dark side:

> The common view put forward by most scholars was a rather negative one: globalization processes and trends add to environmental deterioration, to diminishing control of environmental problems by modern institutions, and to the unequal distribution of environmental consequences and risks between different groups and societies. The dominance of economic (that is, capitalist) globalization processes is often believed to be the root cause of these detrimental environmental effects.[7]

Box 7.1. Definitions of Sustainability

- A sustainable society is one which satisfies its needs without diminishing the prospects of future generations.
  Lester R. Brown, Founder and President, Worldwatch Institute
- Actions are sustainable if there is a balance between resources used and resources regenerated. Resources are as clean or cleaner at end use as at beginning. The viability, integrity, and diversity of natural systems are restored and maintained. They lead to enhanced local and regional self-reliance. They help create and maintain community and a culture of place. Each generation preserves the legacies of future generations.
  David McCloskey, Professor of Sociology, Seattle University
- Leave the world better than you found it, take no more than you need, try not to harm life or the environment, make amends if you do.
  Paul Hawken, The Ecology of Commerce
- Growth based on forms and processes of development that do not undermine the integrity of the environment on which they depend.
  Jim MacNeill, Secretary General of the World Commission on Environment and Development
- Achieving the ecological balance which allows economic prosperity and social equity to be achieved across generations.
  David Schaller
- If you get right down to it, sustainability is really the study of the interconnectedness of all things.
  Barbara J. Lither, J.D.

Source: http://yosemite.epa.gov/r10/oi.nsf/Sustainability/definitions

Another critic of globalization, the businessman, diplomat, and environmental leader Maurice Strong, who led the Stockholm Conference on the Human Environment in 1972 and the Earth Summit in Rio in 1992, also appreciates the dual nature of globalization and sustainability. Strong has argued, "Globalization is creating new wealth at an unprecedented scale while increasing the dichotomy between industrial capitalism's victors and victims." Strong lands on the negative side, suggesting that the damage outweighs the capacity for good.[8]

Economic globalization can be seen as constraining sustainability. With globally mobile capital, it is harder for governments to regulate and otherwise cope with environmental challenges. With the increase in corporate power and reach we discussed in our chapter on the global value chain, political efficacy can be weakened. The global value chain is integrated through transportation and communications technologies with largely negative environmental side effects. With population pressures, we have seen the commodification of resources such as water and the decline of traditional local control on resource use. Globalization creates a spatial separation of action of production and consumption from responsibility for their externalities.[9] This is dismal list for those interested in saving the planet.

By contrast, analysts largely from the neo-liberal and institutionalist schools, see globalization as a positive force in the quest for sustainable development and environmental quality. Their position is grounded in technological optimism—the view that technology will respond to high resource prices or government incentives to promote sustainability. These proponents believe in the potential of governments to design policy instruments to chart a course toward sustainability—usually with some suggestions for improving institutional capacity. Corporations are seen here as agents of change, transmitting best practices to new environments. As growth proceeds, they look to increasing incomes generating both more tax dollars for environmental spending and public demand for environmental amenities. Trade agreements can be seen as a mechanism to secure property rights and the returns from resource management.

International Trade and the Environment: A Pillar of Globalization

Increased trade and the deepening of the global value chain are deeply criticized by environmentalists. Their argument is straightforward. In an international market system where the prices of goods and services are not fully reflective of the environmental costs and consequences of their production and consumption, producers will tend to favor production in locations without stringent or existent (or enforceable) environmental regulations to avoid the additional transactions cost of production related to the environmental regulations (Box 7.2). To avoid strict environmental regulations and standards, producers will relocate to where these regulations are weak—dubbed the race to the bottom. Production then benefits from access to cheaper natural resources and labor that is not encumbered by environmental, health, or safety regulations. These environmental realities force a critical reexamination of traditional theories of comparative advantage and free trade.[10] The passage of the NAFTA in 1993 provides an excellent example of the environmental considerations related to free trade.

Avoiding the Cliff?

Jeffrey Sachs of the Earth Institute argues that we cannot continue on with business as usual relying on unsustainable global ecological, demographic, and economic trajectories. Sachs highlights four primary causes for the evolving crisis: (1) human pressure on the physical world, (2) population expansion, (3) extreme poverty, and (4) the paralysis of global problem solving by cynicism. To address these problems, he suggests that the global community embrace four goals in the coming decades: (1) create sustainable systems of energy, land, and resource use; (2) stabilize world population growth at eight billion people; (3) end extreme poverty by 2025; and (4) develop new strategies for solving global problems. For this to be possible, it will be necessary for the global community to engage in cooperative behavior and to create global institutions with the ability to guide and create the coming epoch of sustainability.[11] We have already discussed the shock of poverty and underdevelopment in our last chapter. Let's take a look at how global demographic changes create additional environmental pressures.

Box 7.2. The North American Free Trade Agreement (NAFTA) and the Environment

This agreement between the United States, Canada, and Mexico raised essential environmental questions associated with an expansion of trade. With the presence of hundreds of assembly manufacturing plants along the border and the prospect of hundreds more moving to Mexico, what would prevent these firms from ignoring sound environmental practices and standards (required in the United States and Canada) in their quest for lower cost production? Labor and environmental groups on both sides of the border raised these issues. In the end, for passage to be possible, there was an environmental parallel side-agreement passed that would provide for environmental accountability and dispute adjudication.

While for many reasons it is difficult to assess the impact of the trade agreement on the environment, efforts have been made to examine the experience from the vantage point of the environmental Kuznets curve (EKC) and the Pollution Haven Hypothesis. The EKC hypothesis suggests that as a country's per capita income reaches $5,000 a turning point would occur such that pollution would begin to decrease as economic growth increases. The data for Mexico suggest that growth alone will not bring with it long-term environmental improvement. The other fear was related to the Pollution Haven Hypothesis, i.e., that firms would leave the regulated realities of the more advanced countries and migrate to production locations where regulations were either non-existent or not seriously enforced. In Mexico's case, post-NAFTA the evidence suggests that very few firms decided to locate in Mexico for environmental reasons. (The primary rationale was the low labor cost.) Finally, as articulated by Kevin P. Gallagher, a research associate at the Global Development and Environment Institute at the Fletcher School of Law and Diplomacy at Tufts University, the overall conclusion is "...governments need to act to protect their environments. The costs of doing so, in terms of lost investment, are likely to be very low. The costs of inaction are likely to be very high."

Source: Kevin P. Gallagher, "Mexico, NAFTA, and Beyond," Inter-Hemispheric Resource Center, The Americas Program, September 17, 2004; see also, "Rethinking NAFTA's Environment and Labor Agreements," Gobalization 101, The Levin Institute, The State University of New York, April 22, 2008; Jeffrey Schott and Gary Hufbauer, "NAFTA Revisited," *Latin Business Chronicle*, March 4, 2008.

Demographic Projections and Megatrends: Looking toward the next 30–50 years, demographic realities will shape every facet of twenty-first-century globalization. As we saw in Chapter 5, population dynamics, particularly from developing countries, are an integral part of the environmental and natural resource dilemma. The problem is more acute than the increase in the total number of people inhabiting planet earth—it is *where* they will live that is problematic. The demographer Jack Goldstone identified four demographic megatrends that together represent a historical shift. Drawing upon U.N. Population Division projections, he predicts that human population growth will nearly halt by 2050. By that date, the world's population will have stabilized at 9.15 billion people (compared to 7.4 billion in 2015). With aging populations, the relative demographic size of the developed world will shrink nearly 25%. This will shift economic centers of growth to developing nations while also increasing flows of immigrants to work in aging economies. Population growth will be concentrated in many of the world's poorest, youngest, and predominantly Muslim countries—places that already suffer from weak education, scarce capital, and few productive job opportunities. Gladstone tells us that for the first time in human history, people will

Figure 7.1. 2050 World Population by Region

Population (billions)	2013	2050
All Africa	1.1	2.4
Sub-Saharan Africa	0.9	2.2
Latin America/ Caribbean	0.6	0.8
Asia	4.3	5.3
North America	0.4	0.4
Europe	0.7	0.7

Source: Population Reference Bureau, 2013 World Population Data Sheet.

largely live in burgeoning urban centers—again most often in cities where sustainable systems for water, sanitation, health, transportation, and policing have not kept pace with growing populations.[12] Our population challenge is less about how many inhabit the earth but in the uneven distribution of human settlements. These changing demographic shifts, also represented in Figure 7.1, map into extraordinary environmental pressure in places least able to manage sustainability.

Causes of Global Environmental Deterioration

Gustave Speth, in his highly regarded book, *Red Sky at Morning* (2004), interrogates population growth as a determinant of environmental degradation, confirming that distribution matters. In more developed countries, levels of **affluence** allow those with greater income and financial resources to consume a higher percentage of the world's resources, and to do so with higher energy intensity. For example, the United States uses around 33% of the world's resources with only 6% of the world's population. He claims that advanced industrial technology (with its tendency to be energy intensive) negatively impacts the physical environment as it extensively extracts and transforms physical resources and energy for profit without a great deal of consideration as for the environmental consequences. For Speth, the character of global poverty undermines the environment as people who are poor are forced to find ways to subsist that ultimately damage their own immediate physical environments including deforestation, water pollution, poor sanitation, poor public health, etc.[13]

Speth draws attention to the microeconomic market problem of **market failure** where the market price system does not reflect or include the **social cost of production** or, in this case, the **negative externality** of environmental degradation. In unregulated markets, firms have no incentive to consider the negative environmental externalities and change production processes to avoid them or risk having to pay fines (or face law suits) from enforced government regulations.

In Figure 7.2(a) the graph depicts a perfectly competitive firm where MC represents the marginal private costs the firm faces at different levels of output, and MSC represents the marginal social costs of production at different levels of output. MSC includes marginal private costs and marginal social costs that are external to the firm, i.e., Marginal environmental cost or MSC = MPC + MSC. In its quest to maximize profits the firm will produce at output level Qp. However, from a society's perspective at Qp, the MSC > P. For the social welfare to be maximized, it is necessary to include all of the costs of production into the price of the product. Figure 7.2(b) illustrates what happens when this is the case. The market supply curve shifts from Sp to Ss and the market price increases from Pp to Ps and the market output level decreases from Qpm to Qsm. Thus, society produces less of the product at a higher price. Speth is especially concerned about the power of large corporations that avoid paying the social costs of production with offshore operations where regulations are weakest.

Speth laments that government policy failure has matched market failure. Despite the history of international environmental policies from the 1970s to the present, these initiatives have not been very successful. Domestic and international organizations have not had the resources or power to enforce well-intentioned policies and programs, and many national governments have also been weak in their support for these programs in practice. Speth also draws attention to the **scale and rate of economic growth**, questioning if there are *physical* limits to growth. Does our globalized production and trade system run into physical limits imposed by the biological and ecological systems of the planet? This begs the question of the character of economic growth, both quantitatively and qualitatively. The distinction between the amount of growth (GDP) and the quality (composition) of the growth

Figure 7.2. Market Model of Negative Externalities and Marginal Social Cost

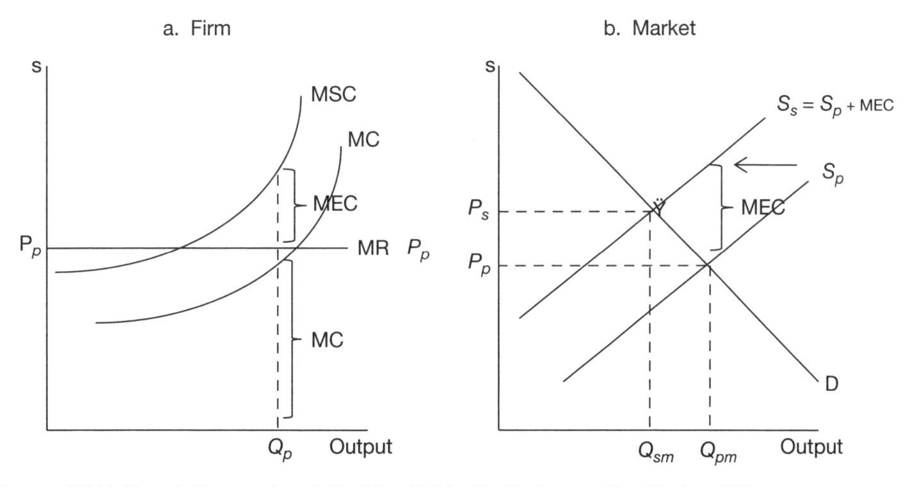

Source: Riddell et al. *Economics: A Tool for Critically Understanding Society,* 259.

matters from a sustainability and quality of life perspective. This is especially critical as we witness the rapid and projected growth rates of China and India.

Speth questions the character and nature of our economic system or capitalism. **Capitalism** as we know is an economic system based on the *private* ownership of the means of production (land, labor, and capital). At its core, capitalism relies on *markets* to allocate scarce resources efficiently according to cost criteria. Private firms engage in the production of goods and services driven by their desire to *maximize profit*. For consumers, their ability to buy goods and services is determined by their ability to sell their labor to earn income. An effective competitive market system produces consumer sovereignty as individuals pursue satisfaction or happiness. The core assumption that consumer needs and wants are *insatiable* creates the expectation that consumers always want more and different goods and services if they can afford it. The market model does not consider sufficiency—or how much is enough.

Speth argues that capitalism calls forth a **consumer culture** that drives the cultural values of materialism. This is also a market model that conceives the production process and the throughput of resources as *linear*, instead of a closed loop. A **closed loop model** would identify all externalities and feedbacks (systems model) produced along the production process, from extraction of resources, their transformation, their transportation, all energy use (including heat and wastes), all pollution (air, water, and soil), their packaging, marketing, distribution, consumption, and disposal. A full-lifecycle analysis can be demonstrated by taking the case of using coal to make electricity (Box 7.3). The coal must be extracted by mining (deep mining or strip mining) which requires the use of fossil-fuel energy and environmental consequences related to the disposal of coal waste, the transportation of coal (rail or truck), the burning of the coal (air pollution), the processing of the waste from burning the coal, the transmission of the electricity, and the use of the electricity.[14] Rather than focus attention on the carrying capacities of the earth, globalization and its associated value chain have reinforced the contradictions of the capitalist model.

Globalization and the Carrying Capacity of the Earth

The acceleration of global economic growth with increased international trade puts additional pressure on global resources and their scarcity (energy resources, agricultural resources, mineral resources, and water resources). The competitive nature of trade will encourage many countries to price their resources at levels that make it virtually impossible to maintain environmental standards and/or to manage their scarce resources in the context of sustainability. Critics point to the weakness of WTO in regulating environmental ramifications of trade.

Herman Daly, former senior economist with the World Bank, criticizes the neoclassical free-market model of trade behind our globalized economy, arguing that it ignores the *biophysical limits* of the natural system and the *distribution* questions associated with market-driven outcomes. He maintains that free trade is in conflict with the goal of sustainable development. Daly argues that the contemporary global

Box 7.3. Public Goods and the Tragedy of the Commons (Common Pool Resources)

In a 1954 paper, "The Pure Theory of Public Expenditure," Paul Samuelson defined a public good (or a collective consumption good) as "goods which all enjoy in common in the sense that each individual's consumption of such a good leads to no subtractions from any other individual's consumption of that good." This definition creates a property known as non-rivalry. Furthermore, a pure public good has another property known as non-excludability, i.e., it is not possible to exclude any persons from consuming the good. In contrast, a private good is not characterized by these properties. Non-rivalry suggests that if one person consumes an ice cream cone, it is not left for another to enjoy. A person can also be excluded from consuming the cone by requiring payment to enjoy. Another variety of good is what is called a common pool resource (examples would be timber, coal, and fish stocks). This kind of good is rivalrous but non-excludable. This kind of good (common pool resource) has a similar quality as a public good and thus is characterized by some of the problems that public goods experience. For example, it is nearly impossible to enforce restrictions on deep-sea fishing that the world's fish stocks can be seen as a non-excludable resource, but one which is finite and diminishing.

In the late 1960s, as the global environmental crisis was been focused upon, a well-known ecologist, Garrett Hardin, wrote about the tragedy of the commons. Hardin utilized the story of what happens to a pasture on common ground that is open to all for grazing their cattle. What results in time as each individual cattle owner utilizes the commons and adds more cattle to their herds is that the commons (pasture) is eventually over-grazed and ultimately destroyed. As Hardin pointed out,

Therein is the tragedy. Each man is locked into a system that Compels him to increase his herd without limit—in a world that is limited. Ruin is the destination toward which all men rush, each pursuing his own interest in a society that believes in the freedom of the commons.

His fundamental conclusion was that individual rational behavior can cause long-term harm to the environment, others, and ultimately oneself. Over the years, this tragedy of the commons experience can be seen in the areas of overgrazing, acid rain, carbon dioxide emissions, deforestation, and overfishing of the oceans.

Source: Garrett Hardin, "The Tragedy of the Commons," *Science*, 162(3859), December 1968, pp. 1243–48.

market system is in conflict with the cost of its scale in relation to the ecosystem. He believes that the economy is a sub-system within the larger ecological system. Daly characterizes the earth's biophysical and life support systems as finite; the scale (level) and character of economic growth push up against these limits, undermining and destroying the earth's natural capital that humans depend on for their existence (see Figure 7.3).

Daly maintains that market prices are incomplete signals, that markets serve *allocative efficiency* without consideration of *optimal scale* of activity, and that the market focus on growth rejects the concept of sufficiency. He challenges the notion that consumers needs and wants are insatiable and that their happiness is positively reinforced by their acquisition of goods and services. In contrast, the notion of sufficiency translates into the possibility that individuals can decide how much consumption is enough. He critiques contemporary growth theory for ignoring a direct relationship to the environment. A pure market view seems to assume a faith in

Figure 7.3. Sustainable Systems: The Economy to the Biosphere

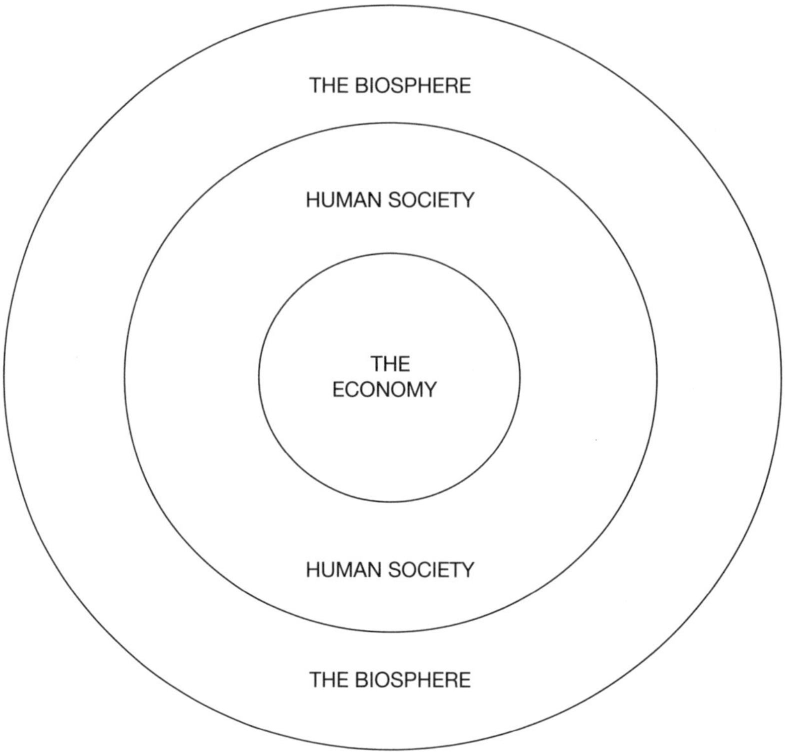

Source: Forum for the Future.

limitless resources, human ingenuity and technology to resolve environmental, energy, and long-term resource scarcity problems and challenges. This he finds naïve. While conventional environmental economics incorporates negative externalities, the internalization of social costs, command and control regulatory schemes (taxation, fines, and/or coercion), cost/benefit analysis, and risk management, Daly finds this missing the larger picture of proportionality of the economy to eco-systems.

What is the proper role and relationship of the global macro economy to the environment? How big should the sub-system be relative to the overall system? The issue is one of scale, as it relates to the *carrying capacity* of the ecosystem. Thus, the task is to keep the absolute scale of the economy from sinking the biosphere. Daly maintains that the market cannot solve the problem of optimal scale nor optimal distribution as the regenerative and absorptive capacity of the ecosystem is limited.[15]

Daly contends that we need to move beyond getting prices right for output and externalities; sustainability requires a more just distribution of resources and their use. *Community* must be fostered as a societal goal, the *scale* and size of the macro-economy should be managed and maintained within *ecological limits*. For Daly, the goal is not economic growth *per se* but sustainable development. Daly's definition of Sustainability hinges on *three* propositions: (1) Rates of renewable resource use do not exceed their rates of regeneration; (2) Rates of non-renewable resource use do not exceed the rate at which sustainable renewable resources are developed (the transition from fossil-fuel energy to renewable energy, i.e. solar, wind, etc.); and (3) Rates of pollution do not exceed the absorptive capacity of the environment. The natural service functions of the environment should be given the time and ability to absorb wastes, heat, and all forms of pollution such that they can cleanse the physical biological life-support systems of the planet.

It should be noted that Daly's analysis and critique requires a certain level of understanding of economics and environmental science—as well as thermodynamics. But even without this skill set we can appreciate the important conceptual model for understanding the relationship of the market system to the larger global macroeconomic system in the context of a finite planet. There are limits to economic growth in the context of a finite planet. It begs the question of the carrying capacity of the planet, given growing populations and a rate of economic growth that is drawing down non-renewable physical resources. Non-renewable fossil fuels are running out; their use is releasing increased amounts of carbon dioxide into the atmosphere which is contributing to the heating of the planet. As the processes and dynamics of contemporary globalization facilitate and expand these processes, it is contributing to the outcomes that are increasingly judged to be unsustainable. Thus, the challenge before us is to find ways to produce and manage sustainable economic and growth practices in a globalized world.

Energy: A Global and U.S. Perspective

Energy is the life-blood of the global economic and production system. As we reflect on the globalization experience of the past fifty years, the level and pace of global economic growth was been made possible by the availability of relatively cheap energy. This energy—most of it non-renewable fossil fuels of oil, coal, and natural gas—fuels the production, transportation consumption, and disposal of goods and services on the global value chain. The demographic explosion and geo-economic shifts of production to the Global South we discussed in Chapter 5 have pressured sustainable sources of energy. In Figure 7.4, we see that world energy consumption was at a level of almost 250 quads of energy by 2007; the rapid growth of the Global south, (largely non-OECD countries) after 2007 pivots the trajectory drastically upward. Over 90% of the projected growth in global energy is going to take place in the fast growing emerging market countries, like China and India.

Total non-OECD energy consumption will increase by 84% compared to only a 16% increase in the OECD countries. The projection assumes non-OECD average GDP growth rates of 4.4% per year and only 2% GDP growth rates for the OECD countries. As shown in Figure 7.5, total world energy use rises from 495 quadrillion BTU in 2007, to over 600 quadrillion BTU in 2020, exceeding 800 quadrillion BTU by 2040. We should keep in mind that this time frame from 2007 to 2040 captures

Figure 7.4. World Energy Consumption, 2010–40

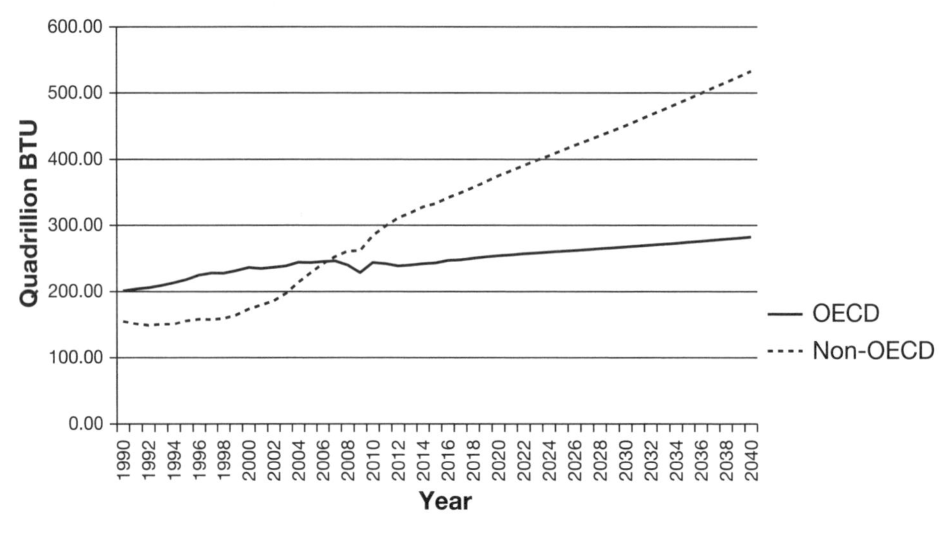

Source: U.S. Energy Information Administration, International Energy Outlook, 2016. Data post 2015 are forecasted.

Figure 7.5. World Marketed Energy Consumption, 1990–40

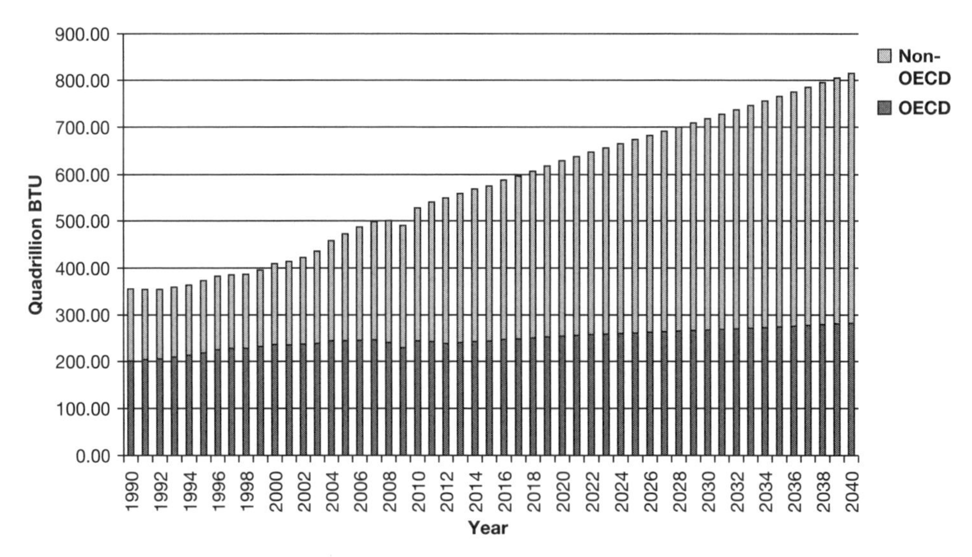

Source: U.S. Energy Information Administration, International Energy Outlook, 2016. Data post 2015 are forecasted.

the transition underway that we have explored in the book—the rapid growth of emerging markets combined with the economic slowdown of the developed world.

As we can see in Table 7.1, in 2005, the United States was the world's largest consumer of primary energy. Although thanks to increases in energy efficiency,

Table 7.1. World Primary Energy Consumption by Region, 2005–40 (Quadrillion BTU)

Region/Country	*History*				*Projections*			
	2005	*2010*	*2015*	*2020*	*2025*	*2030*	*2035*	*2040*
OECD								
OECD North America	122.5	120.2	121.3	126.1	129.7	132.9	137.2	143.6
United States	99.5	97.9	97.3	100.5	101.8	102.3	103.9	107.2
Canada	14.8	13.5	14.2	14.8	15.6	16.5	17.3	18.2
Mexico/Chile	8.2	8.8	9.9	10.9	12.3	14.1	16.0	18.2
OECD Europe	83.7	82.5	82.1	85.5	88.6	90.9	92.8	94.6
OECD Asia	38.8	39.6	40.6	43.0	44.3	45.4	46.1	46.4
Japan	23.0	22.1	21.7	22.5	23.0	23.0	22.9	22.2
South Korea	9.3	10.8	11.8	13.0	13.8	14.7	15.3	15.9
Australia/New Zealand	6.6	6.7	7.0	7.4	7.5	7.7	8.0	8.2
Total OECD	245.0	242.3	244.1	254.6	262.7	269.2	276.1	284.6
Non-OECD								
Non-OECD Europe and Eurasia	47.5	47.2	49.8	53.3	56.8	60.8	64.6	67.1
Russia	28.1	29.6	31.0	33.3	35.7	38.0	39.9	40.5
Other	19.4	17.6	18.9	20.0	21.1	22.8	24.7	26.6
Non-OECD Asia	112.8	159.0	194.3	230.3	261.6	290.4	317.2	337.5
China	68.1	101.2	132.2	159.0	180.9	198.9	213.3	219.9
India	17.5	24.4	27.5	32.1	37.2	42.6	48.7	55.0
Other Non-OECD Asia	27.2	33.4	34.6	39.2	43.5	48.9	55.2	62.6
Middle East	22.0	27.8	33.1	36.6	39.5	42.5	45.7	48.8
Africa	16.9	18.9	19.6	21.9	24.4	27.4	31.0	35.0
Central and South America	24.5	28.7	31.0	33.2	35.5	38.8	42.5	46.6
Brazil	11.2	13.7	14.9	16.5	17.8	19.9	22.3	25.4
Other Central and South America	13.2	15.0	16.1	16.7	17.6	19.0	20.2	21.3
Total Non-OECD	223.7	281.7	327.9	375.3	417.7	460.0	501.0	535.1
Total World	468.7	523.9	572.0	629.8	680.4	729.2	777.1	819.6

Source: U.S. Energy Information Administration (EIA).
Includes the 50 states and the District of Columbia.
Note: Energy totals include net imports of coal coke and electricity generated from biomass in the United States. Totals may not equal sum of components due to independent rounding. The electricity portion of the national fuel consumption values consists of generation for domestic use plus an adjustment for electricity trade based on a fuel's share of total generation in the exporting country.

Figure 7.6. World Marketed Energy Use by Fuel Type, 1990–40

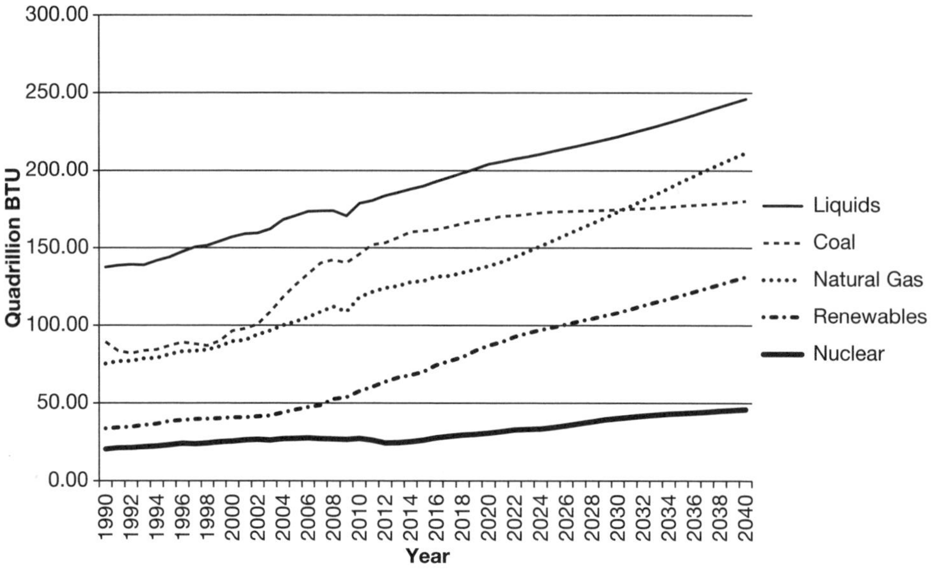

Source: U.S. Energy Information Administration, International Energy Outlook, 2016. Data post 2015 are forecasted.

U.S. energy use actually declined by 2015; in China it had roughly doubled. By 2025, it is projected to be twice the total of the United States. Yet, the average American used 4.5 times as much energy as the average Chinese person.[16] We can imagine the impact on global emissions when, with a more industrialized economy, Chinese per capita energy use reaches the United States.

The mix used to produce energy matters. As can be seen in Figure 7.6, liquids (petroleum) will reach about 225 quads of the 739 quads projected for 2040, followed by coal, natural gas, and to a lesser extent renewable and nuclear. With new suppliers of petroleum on global markets, prices plummeted in 2015; this encouraged the overuse of a temporarily cheap energy source.

Global Petroleum Demand

A central component of energy demand is petroleum. Oil has fascinated analysts since its discovery in Titusville, Pennsylvania in 1859, and the history of oil is at the center of the history of industrialization, urbanization, and globalization. Oil has transformed the way we live, where we live and work, the way that we transport goods and services, and the way we travel. The writings of Anthony Sampson, *The Seven Sisters*, Daniel Yergin, *The Prize*, and Paul Roberts, *The End of Oil*, each have documented this amazing story.[17]

Despite its centrality to our global economy, the twenty-first century represents the century of *peak oil* and quite likely *the end of the oil era.* Many analysts believe that we have already used more than half of the recoverable oil from proven reserves.

At current and projected use, the world will be facing a situation by the end of the century where the *demand for oil will far exceed the remaining supply*.[18] By 2007 (before the financial crisis and global recession), the world demand for petroleum was 86 million barrels per day (mbo/d). Of this, almost 49 mbo/d were consumed by OECD countries (with the United States consuming 20 mbo/d) and the other 37 mbo/d consumed by the non-OECD countries. The EIA projection is for world consumption in 2035 of 110 mbo/d, with the OECD consumption at almost 50 mbo/d (near the 2007 level) and the non-OECD consumption at over 60 mbo/d (slightly less than double the 2007 level).

An obvious and critical question is where the additional 25 mbo/d to fuel new global demand will come from and at what price? Most energy and oil analysts agree that the Middle East and the Persian Gulf OPEC countries will remain central suppliers. If this is true, the political situation in the Middle East will be a wildcard as Saudi Arabia, Iran, and Iraq will be three of the largest world producers (in addition to Russia, Venezuela, and Brazil) and will hold the majority of the world's proven reserves. Like petrodollar recycling discussed in Chapter 4, this will also have profound implications for the global financial system and inflation as the major oil producers will have vast oil revenues to invest and recycle in the global financial system. Oil prices by 2035 could well be around $150 per barrel or even higher. The weak oil prices of 2015 are a deceptive veil covering future constrains of this non-renewable resource.

In the next few decades, the United States will confront a series of challenges when it comes to sustainability, energy, and climate change. We remain fossil dependent with petroleum and coal accounting for 64% of energy consumption and renewables only 5%. The United States must change its energy mix, decreasing non-renewables, and developing alternatives. Some point to the benefits of nuclear energy. Even before the tsunami generated nuclear disaster in Japan, the building of new nuclear power plants had come to a halt in the United States for decades due to high costs and safety issues in building plants.[19] Nevertheless, in many parts of the world the nuclear power industry is alive and well. Indeed, China's national energy strategy is placing serious reliance on it in combination with the continued use of coal for electricity production well into the future. Many critics of climate change see the nuclear option as a necessary alternative to dirty coal. The world famous energy and climate change expert James Hansen represents this viewpoint to the chagrin of his many climate change colleagues who continue to oppose the use of nuclear power.[20]

Petroleum Markets and Prices

At the most basic level, the price of petroleum (a barrel of oil) is determined by the forces of supply and demand. The world price (North Sea Brent Crude vs. the U.S. price—West Texas Intermediate) is very much determined by the actions of OPEC (a cartel) and the price following behavior of non-OPEC independent producers. The members of OPEC meet to determine national output quotas to generate a price range (or band) that they wish to maintain—but the cartel is increasingly challenged by producers outside OPEC. In 2011, global production capacity was around 3–5 mbo/day beyond the current demand. This *excess capacity* is for the most part because of the ability of Saudi Arabia to increase its oil production by this amount, if necessary; Saudi Arabia is known to be a *swing* producer. Supply is also determined by the ability to more efficiently explore for oil, to recover secondary and tertiary oil (from previous drilled deposits), and to extract new oil. For example, new technologies are making it more cost effective to drill and produce oil from deep-water wells as well as shale oil. The United States has recently discovered huge supplies of shale oil that will significantly increase domestic production and likely reduce the U.S. demand for imported oil. This will have new geo-strategic consequences as well. In addition, new supplies are being found and discovered in Canada, Africa, the Caspian Basin, Venezuela, Norway, and Brazil. Supply is also subject to natural disasters (Katrina) and political instability (Iraq and Nigeria) and can be influenced by government policy that either makes it more attractive or more difficult to find and produce.

On the **demand** side, if global economic growth is slower and weak, the demand for oil will soften. If global economic growth strengthens, then oil demand will increase. As we have seen in recent years, the increased demand for oil by China, India, and other emerging markets has contributed to the rise in oil prices. This will likely be the long-term trend even though there will be some cyclical behavior in periods of slow growth and/or financial instability. Before the financial crisis and global recession, oil prices reached a historic high of $148 per barrel in mid-2008. When there is on-going or anticipated political conflict (war) and instability in sensitive parts of the world (the Middle East especially), there is a *risk premium* of between $10 and $15/barrel built into the price of oil driven by fear of supply interruptions. The demand for oil is also shaped by the plethora of domestic governmental and international policies including various regulations, taxes, and subsidies. For the consumer, fundamental tastes, preferences, and income will dictate their demand for oil or its byproducts (e.g. gasoline, heating oil, etc.). Finally, there is a great deal of *financial speculation* in oil markets as investors utilize oil futures options and other derivative products to trade oil.

Growing frustration with the role of the dollar as the world's key reserve currency will in time likely change its role as the world's key reserve currency and denominator for oil prices. If the United States is unable to successfully address its long-term budget deficit and public debt situation, this will more rapidly force the issue of the role of the U.S. dollar in the global financial system and the role of the dollar in the oil trading system.

The consequences of this level of energy use, geographic distribution of the resources, the inherent economic and financial costs, the environmental consequences, and the geo-strategic political and military considerations will together provide phenomenal challenges to governing the global system in the coming decades (Box 7.4). The calamity of the situation prompted the World Bank to form the Global Food Crisis Response Program in 2008 to help those suffering most from a volatile food industry.[21] Two years later, the World Bank launched the Global Agriculture and Food Security Program to move beyond emergency assistance and promote domestic agriculture to expand beyond relying on foreign aid to relieve global hunger and poverty.[22] While food prices remain volatile, countless NGOs as well as international organizations like the World Bank continue to provide aid in the hopes of eradicating the global food crisis.

Box 7.4. The Food Crisis by Becky Newman

Section one of article 25 of the Universal Declaration of Human Rights reads,

> Everyone has the right to a standard of living adequate for the health and well-being of himself and of his family, including food, clothing, housing and medical care and necessary social services, and the right to security in the event of unemployment, sickness, disability, widowhood, old age or other lack of livelihood in circumstances beyond his control.[23]

Despite this proclamation, almost one billion people worldwide are undernourished.[24] How can the human race fail so grandly in providing food to nearly a sixth of the population? The answer is complicated, with both short-term and long-term dynamics giving rise to supply and demand issues that contribute to rising food prices, increased food price volatility, and limited access to food for the world's most in need. While disasters have shocked food supply in various areas since the beginning of time (like the Irish potato famine or the Great Leap Forward in China), the dire state of providing food to all of the world's population constitutes what is known today as the global food crisis.

Understanding the global food crisis is in part a lesson in geography. Incidences of limited food access are most often found in low- and middle-income countries, and higher in rural areas versus urban ones. Low birth weights are disproportionately located in developing countries, with over 96% of the total located there.[25] Nearly 22% of children in Africa are underweight, with that figure at 22.4% for Asia. For a frame of reference, only one percent of children in the United States face the same situation.[26]

Examining the supply and demand of food globally, both long-term and short-term dynamics emerge as sources of this problem. One major source of short-term lapses in supply is weather crises like draughts or monsoons. The summer of 2012 is worsening the food crisis as the hottest temperatures ever recorded in 118 years of reporting in United States stifle food production there.[27] But some charge longer-term changes in agriculture as another source of supply problems. As many look to increase consumption of alternative forms of energy, increasingly less acreage is devoted to food and more devoted to crops like sugar and corn to produce biofuels like ethanol.[28]

On the other side of the coin, some demand-side trends are contributing to rising food prices, worsening the global food crisis. In the short-term, some blame speculative bubbles for incredible price volatility for a variety of crops, stifling small producers and their abilities to plan and save for the future. Yet others argue speculation plays a stabilizing force through investment based on market fundamentals.[29]

Furthermore, despite the many technological advancements of the past century in the field of agriculture contributing to higher caloric output per acre, many fear that the growth in population size, particularly in developing countries within the past quarter-century, presets an unsustainable increase in demand for food. Some credible evidence is the shocking growth in the world's population within the past century from about 1.6 billion people in 1900 to over seven billion today.[30]

Overall, food is misallocated around the globe. Jeremy Hobbs, International Executive Director of Oxfam, contends "there is enough food grown in the world for everyone."[31] Yet the amount of waste in countries like the United States, where one-third of adults are obese, versus the relative scarcity of food elsewhere, presents a conundrum of inefficient and ultimately unjust distribution of food resources.[32]

In 2007 and 2008, the crisis reached different kinds of peaks, as food prices soared. Many blamed speculation, but regardless of the relative weights of the factors above in contributing to the price changes, prices of staples like rice and wheat rose on the order of 16 and 77% in 2007, respectively. In the first four months of 2008, rice prices rose 141%.[33] The overall effect was devastating: many could no longer purchase basic nutrients for themselves and their families, and consequently, social uprisings took hold in as countries far as Haiti and Bangladesh during that time period.[34]

THE SCRAMBLE FOR WORLD RESOURCES AND SUSTAINABILITY

The challenge of sustainability will be further complicated by the early twenty-first-century scramble for global resources that is fast underway. The changing geo-economics distribution from North to South has spurred a global race to access and own resources. The primary focus is on agricultural commodities (food) and land, energy resources (oil, coal, and natural gas), precious metals, and minerals. China and India have established new trade relationships in all of these resource commodities with Africa, Latin America, Asia, Russia, and the countries surrounding the Caspian Basin (Iran, Turkmenistan, Kazakhstan, Russia, Dagestan, and Azerbaijan), as well as Turkey which can provide overland pipeline routes to ports.

These relationships are changing the shape and complexion of shipping centers and routes and the new geography of pipelines. All of this is taking place in the context of a post-Cold War and post-9/11 world. Michael Klare, a political economist, has written extensively about the role of natural resources in the context of global conflicts. Klare's perspective has been reinforced in a recent study, "The Age of Consequences," examining the relationship between Climate Change and U.S. National Security.[35] This global scramble for increasingly scarce resources will likely create political and military conflicts. In this sense, these global natural resource and sustainability issues become foreign policy issues as well. Indeed, food, water, and energy security translate into the core of twenty-first-century globalization national security challenges for nation-states.[36]

CLIMATE CHANGE AND GLOBAL WARMING: THE REALITY AND CONSEQUENCES

> The consequences of a delay in reducing carbon emissions are insidious and inescapable. To recap: The math of historical CO_2 accumulation gives us no choice but to slash emissions to very low levels. Earth's natural carbon sinks are becoming saturated, so our safety value is slowly closing; our planet's ecosystems face irreversible damage such as widespread extinctions; and these changes are pushing our climate system toward tipping points beyond which the domino effects could be devastating. Because many effects lag emissions, we have yet to experience the full impact of historical emissions. The longer we wait, the more drastic the cuts—and associated costs will be. If we delay action for even a decade, CO_2 emissions will likely blow past 450 ppm—and unleash the dangers of nonlinear ecological and geophysical responses. If, instead, we step up to the challenge and pass strong energy policies and invest aggressively in clean energy R&D, we have a fighting chance of containing CO_2 concentrations at 450 ppm—and averting a climate catastrophe.
>
> Hal Harvey and Sonia Aggarwal, *The Costs of Delay*[37]

With respect to the challenge of sustainability, the elephant in the room is without a doubt climate change. Indeed, some would argue that with respect to twenty-first-century globalization issues and challenges, climate change is the fundamental underlying variable that will ultimately determine what is possible and what is not possible for the global system and the human community. Indeed, the heating of the atmosphere and the planet make the issue of climate change the ultimate *public goods* challenge.

In recent years, the Fourth Assessment Report (2007) and the Fifth Assessment Report (2014) from the UN's IPCC (Intergovernmental Panel on Climate Change), as well as many other scientific experts and studies have provided substantial documentation of the contribution of fossil-fuel burning to climate change.[38] As shown in Figure 7.7, CO_2 emissions have reached historical highs.[39] Figures 7.8 and 7.9 highlight the distribution by industrial versus developing (OECD) as well by the largest polluters.

The UN's Fourth Assessment Report in 2007 concluded that "scientific evidence for warming of the climate system is unequivocal."[40] The report argues that the current warming trend is of particular significance because most of it is very likely human-induced and proceeding at a rate that is unprecedented in the past 1,300 years. For the past 650,000 years, atmospheric CO_2 has never been above 300 parts per million (ppm) until recent decades. Climate change results from the increased emissions of greenhouse gases (carbon dioxide, water vapor, methane, and nitrous oxide) in the atmosphere due to human activity largely from the burning of fossil fuel. The result is that the earth's temperature rises. The current level is approaching 400 ppm. This secular rise in CO_2 and the warming of the earth's atmosphere has been scientifically validated by the warming of the oceans, the shrinking of ice sheets, the declining Arctic sea ice, glacial retreat, and ocean acidification. The impacts from climate change are well-known and well-documented: rising ocean levels, habitat destruction, increased disease transmission, changes in agricultural productivity, changes in water availability, increased natural hazards, and changes in the chemistry of the ocean.

Figure 7.7. Climate Change Data: How Do We Know?

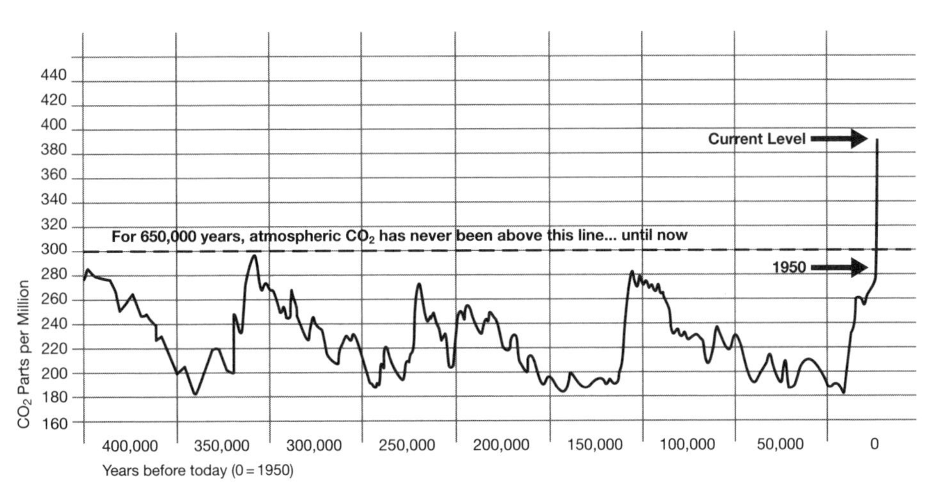

Source: NOAA; United Nations, IPCC, Fourth Assessment Review, 2007; http://climate.nasa.gov/evidence/index.cfm?Print=Ye.

Figure 7.8. World Energy-Related Carbon Dioxide Emissions, 2005–40

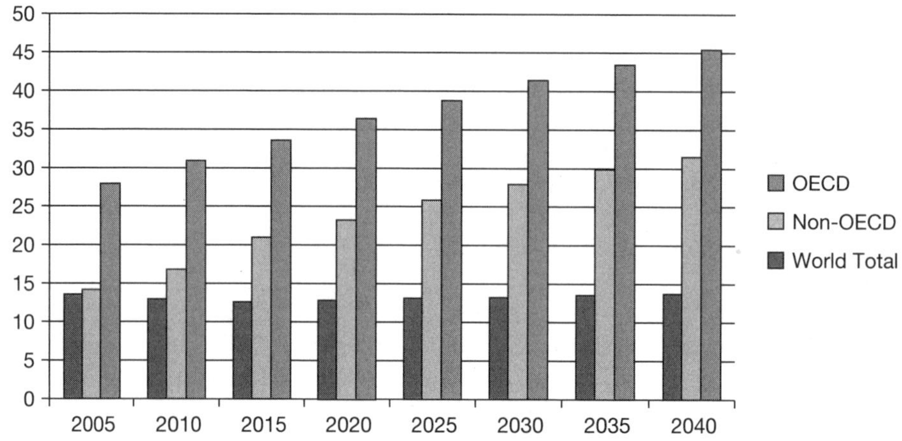

Source: U.S. EIA, International Energy Outlook, 2013.

Figure 7.9. Carbon-Dioxide Emissions, 2011

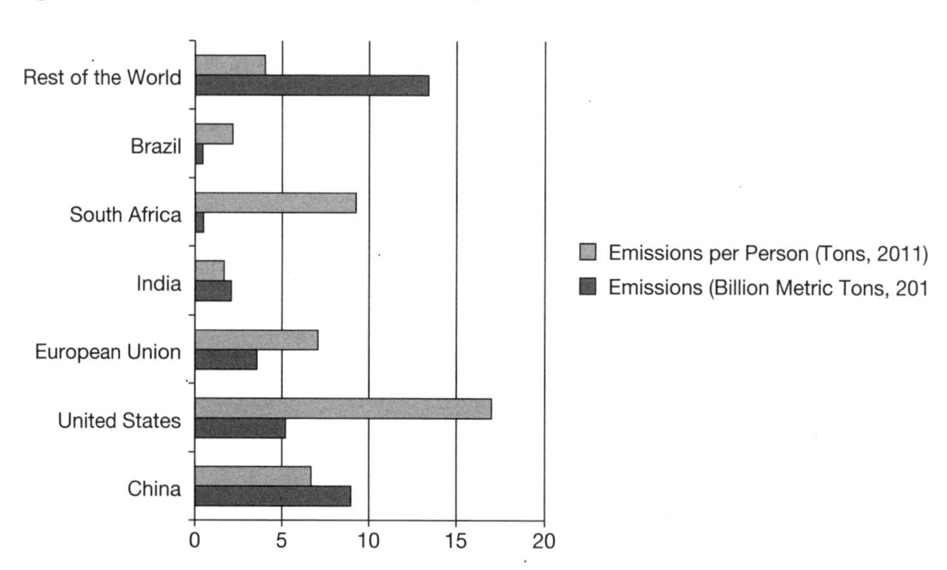

Source: World Bank Economic Indicators.

The ten-year-old Carbon Mitigation Initiative (CMI) at Princeton University (based on the scientific work of Stephen Pacala and Robert Socolow in their seminal article in *Science* magazine on *the stabilization wedge*) has promoted the idea of being able to *stabilize* CO_2 levels at 450 ppm over the next fifty years by utilizing a number of solutions now available that would eliminate the projected *business-as-usual* (not change in current policy) rise in CO_2 levels.[41] The avoided CO_2 levels vs. a level of 450 ppm represents the stabilization triangle illustrated in Figure 7.10, as the difference between business as usual and estimates of sustainable emissions (WRE).[42]

Figure 7.10. Stabilization Wedge

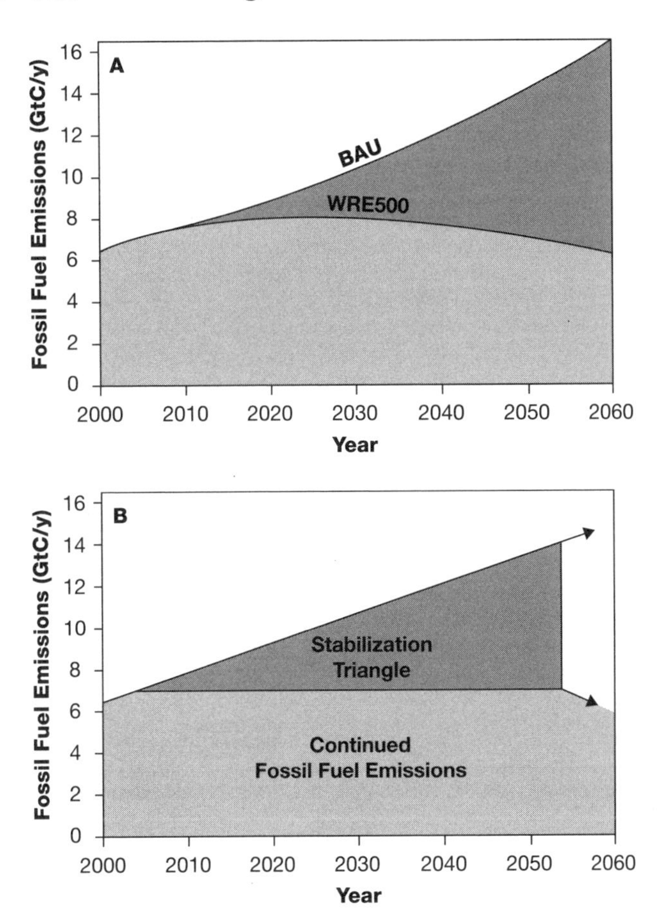

Source: Carbon Mitigation Initiative, Princeton University. http://cmi.princeton.edu/wedges/

The authors of this proposal suggest that the stabilization wedge would be made up of the following: coal to gas, carbon capture and storage (CCS), the safe expansion of nuclear energy, the increased use of renewable (wind, solar, geothermal, and biomass), efficiency gains, and an increase of natural sinks (arresting deforestation and planting more trees).

In many ways, this proposal has most of the elements detailed in other comprehensive proposals such as the one put forward by Sir Nicholas Stern, chief economist for the UN's IPPC Fourth Assessment Report, and author of *The Economics of Climate Change* and *The Global Deal: Climate Change and the Creation of a New Prosperity* (2010).[43] These are summarized in Box 7.5.

Stern argues that the global community has the opportunity not only to address the climate change challenge but also to build the technologies and institutions for sustained economic and financial prosperity, creating jobs, and improving the

Box 7.5. The Stern Review: Executive Summary

Below is a list of some of the most important conclusions from The Stern Review's Executive Summary.

- Climate change presents a unique challenge for economics. It is the greatest- and widest-ranging market failure ever seen.
- Tackling climate change is the pro-growth strategy for the longer term, and it can be done in a way that does not cap the aspirations for growth of rich or poor countries.
- The impacts of climate change are not evenly distributed—the poorest countries and people will suffer earliest and the most.
- Feasibility and costs of stabilization in the range of 450–550 ppm CO_2e peak in the next 10–20 years, then fall 1–3% per year. By 2050, global emissions would need to be around 25% below current levels.
- The annual costs of stabilization at 500–550 ppm would be round 1% of GDP by 2050—a level that is significant but manageable.
- Costs are incurred but create business opportunities as the markets for low-carbon, high-efficiency goods and services expand.
- Policy to reduce emissions should be based on three essential elements: carbon pricing, technology policy, and removal of barriers to behavioral change.
- Establishing a carbon price, through tax, trading, or regulation, is an essential foundation for climate change policy.
- An effective response to climate change will depend on creating the conditions for international collective action.
- There is still time to avoid the worst impacts of climate change if strong collective action starts now.

Source: Nicholas Stern, *The Economics of Climate Change: The Stern Review* (Cambridge University Press, 2007).

quality of life for the majority of the world's population. This of course requires a global action plan promoted by the UN Framework Convention for Climate Change (UNFCCC) with a protocol for action; the Paris agreement of 2015 is an important but insufficient step in promoting sustainability. Why is Paris so important—and why does it fall short?

Martin Wolf, an economist writing for *The Financial Times* in late 2015 argued that the Paris Agreement was a positive step forward in the prolonged process of striving to achieve global cooperation and progress toward addressing the challenges of climate change. Yet, it left a great deal to be desired as well. Targeted goals and agreements without financing and enforceable sanctions are empty. The Agreement did not provide for any mechanism to create a global carbon price. The goal of keeping global climate change from increasing beyond 2°C is actually short of what many think ought to be a goal of 1.5°C. On the positive side, there is now a process of peer review that requires updates every five years. This will provide more transparency. The real question is: What comes next?

The UNFCCC's goal is the stabilization of greenhouse gas concentrations. This would require a comprehensive global program of carbon management to prevent the atmospheric concentration of carbon dioxide from reaching unsafe levels (beyond 450 ppm). To address climate change key actions slowing or stopping deforestation, reducing emissions from coal powered electricity production and petroleum powered automobiles, cleaning up industrial processes, pursuing efficiency measures in all areas of energy use, and utilizing cogeneration whenever possible. These practices would also be a part of a more comprehensive program to develop programs and technologies that can capture and safely store carbon dioxide when fossil fuels are burned, i.e., CCS.[44]

There is a long and complicated history to the international institutional response to climate change from the passage of the initial 1997 Kyoto Protocol on climate change to the recent disappointing outcomes. The majority of developed countries *except for the United States* have been willing to set and meet carbon dioxide reduction targets as a part of a global response to this situation. The Bush administration from 2001 to 2008 essentially stonewalled the issue by refusing to acknowledge climate change as real and consequently would not engage in any meaningful policies and programs to address it. The Obama administration early on wanted to move on this issue in a positive way and have the United States join the rest of the developed countries in signing on to the original Kyoto Protocol. But the emergence of the financial crisis and the subsequent global recession delivered an economic and political environment that would not allow the Obama administration to advance its climate change agenda. The 2010 mid-term elections that produced a GOP majority in the House of Representatives shut down any prospect of moving forward in a positive way on this issue.

Climate Change and Global Warming: What to Do?

Reconciling divergent views of globalization's impact on the environment invites a conclusion that for sustainable development to be possible, globalization will need to be *managed.* This will require nothing less than the development of policies and programs at all levels of society. Given the global character of the production and growth, this will of necessity require the emergence of new global institutions and frameworks with the ability and responsibility of governing for sustainability.[45] But this is difficult as countries place different weights on the causes of climate change as well as the responsibilities for emission reductions.

The Paris agreement sets goals, leaving implementation up to each country. Most experts would argue that the logical and necessary public policy responses include conservation of energy and the development and promotion of renewable energy—wind, solar, hydro, and geothermal, a carbon tax on non-renewable fossil fuels, a cap-and-trade system to establish quotas and limits for CO_2 emissions in a market context and sustainable green/clean technologies. These initiatives along with a realistic and pragmatic approach to corporate sustainability practices could usher in a prolonged period of adjustment and growth.[46]

At the micro level, prices must be allowed to reflect the true costs of producing goods and services. This means beginning to internalize social costs and eliminating (*perverse*) subsidies that encourage fossil-fuel production and consumption. The regulatory environment would need to change to reinforce more effective and competitive prices and markets and to promote the more efficient use of capital in the form of sustainable investments and technologies. National energy and environmental policy could intelligently promote conservation and efficiency by making these options more cost competitive. Clearly, the use of a tax on carbon would make fossil fuels more expensive vis-à-vis renewable, conservation, and efficiency alternatives. A carbon tax could be collected by the government and used to promote sustainable research and development, public/private ventures, and alleviate the regressive nature of such a tax on low-income consumers.[47]

A cap-and-trade system could be implemented much like what was done in the United States to address successfully the acid rain problem years ago when utilities were dumping sulfur dioxide and nitrogen oxide into the air. Europe's experience with a cap-and-trade system provides useful information as to what such a system is, how it functions, and what is necessary to make it work more effectively. Such a system establishes a level (cap) of acceptable CO_2 emissions and allows producers of CO_2 to have a defined limit (quota). Producers would be given or buy (via auction or set price for a ton of CO_2) permits to emit. To be able to emit an amount greater than allowed, the producer would need to buy additional permits; or, if the producer had made sustainable investments to reduce their emissions, they could sell their permits to others needing to buy them. The virtues of a cap and trade are that it promoted a least cost solution to sustainability. Rather than increasing prices through a carbon tax, firms can buy reduction from the cheapest available source. Cleaning the environment becomes a profit opportunity contributing to sustainability.

Globalization creates opportunities as well as challenges for climate change mitigation. To reduce global warming it doesn't matter if CO_2 is lowered in La Paz Bolivia or Los Angeles. With less historical environmental regulation in Bolivia, there is more "low-hanging fruit" or low-cost opportunities to replace destructive production practices with sustainable options. Under a verifiable global regime of selling tradable permits, a firm in California can comply with American law by underwriting low-cost environment practices in Bolivia.

Finally, the national government could utilize its fiscal policy (taxation and spending) to promote and develop *sustainable* technologies, industries, infrastructure, education, and employment. One can imagine that it would be possible for example to implement the carbon mitigation initiative or the recommendations of the Stern Report over a period of time with proper governmental support in concert with the private sector to harness the positive powerful forces of the market with the support of the public sector in global context.[48] Evidence of extreme weather and hottest years on record are quickly raising global action on climate change to a more prominent place on the international agenda.

Summary

The World's Top Priority

- The environmental history of the past three decades includes rampant environmental degradation and increasing levels of energy use, resulting in grave human costs.

- Population growth, particularly in developing countries, pushes the limits of resource use today. Non-renewable resource use continues, and the world population consumes renewable resources at such a rate that their regeneration is at risk as well.
- Staving off future degradation requires a change in global consumption patterns now to use resources more carefully and grow economies sustainability still provide access of scarce resources to future generations. Despite the difficulties in actually achieving this change, some experts still believe reversing environmental degradation is indeed a possibility.

The Origins of the Crisis

- Economist Jeffery Sachs cites four primary causes for the current environmental crisis: human pressure on the physical world, population expansion, extreme poverty, and cynicism. To address these problems, Sachs also proposes the creation of sustainable land and energy resource use, world population stabilization at eight billion people, ending extreme poverty, and a new approach to solve global problems.
- Environmental lawyer and activist Gustave Speth proposes four primary causes of global environmental deterioration: population size and growth, affluence in more developed countries, industrial technology, global poverty, and market failure. To this last point, Speth contends that current prices fail to include the social costs of production (the negative externalities) of environmental degradation, allowing for a perpetuation of harmful activities and production processes.

Globalization and the Environment

- The UN's Commission on Environment and Development defines sustainable development as "development that seeks to meet the needs and aspirations of the present without compromising the ability to meet those of the future."
- Some scholars link globalization to environmental degradation, yielding an increased threat to the environment as the process of globalization intensifies. Although views on this contention vary, sustainable development nonetheless requires a managed globalization for all levels of national and international policy action.
- One way that globalization's harmful effects manifest themselves is in the international trade arena. Since the prices of goods and services do not fully reflect the negative externalities actually embedded in them around the globe, producers can choose to produce in areas where these costs are minimized, like in countries where environmental regulation is lax.

Promoting Growth, Reducing Energy Use: The Challenge Ahead

- More than any other factor, the global economic and production system requires energy to fuel production and consumption. Energy was cheap and dirty (in the form of mostly non-renewable fossil fuel) for advanced industrial countries during their development processes. Today, less-developed economies demand the most energy worldwide. These different stages produce a global contention between the developing and the developed. Countries within the former categorization want to use energy to promote growth without restrictions on use imposed by the latter in global policy arenas.
- Analysts estimate that at the current rate of use, oil demand will exceed supply by the end of the twenty-first century. The implications of this oil use reach beyond economic realms with severe geopolitical implications and even national security threats.
- Forces of supply and demand dictate the price of petroleum. OPEC, the largest oil cartel in the world, determines the level of output they care to export, and prices set by other global producers are influenced by OPEC's actions as well. On the demand side, slower aggregate demand suppresses global prices, while increased growth globally increases demand and the price of petroleum.
- Because oil is priced in U.S. dollars, the relationship between the values of both is extremely important to each. As the value of the U.S. dollar falls, as it generally has in the past decade, oil is priced higher to compensate for its lower value.

Climate Change: One More Hurdle

- According to the UN evidence of rising global temperatures is "unequivocal." As such, stabilizing and then reversing the debilitating effects of increased carbon dioxide levels in the atmosphere requires a tremendous and coordinated effort amongst all nations.
- One possible method to begin this healing process is implementing a cap-and-trade system to limit emissions. Another possibility is the use of taxation and government spending to promote sustainable technologies (and limited carbon dioxide use) in all industries.

Notes

1. Jeffrey D. Sachs, *Common Wealth: Economics for a Crowded Planet*. Penguin Press, 2008, p. 3.

2. Donella H. Meadows et al., *The Limits to Growth.* Signet, 1972. See also, Donella H. Meadows et al., *Limits to Growth: The Thirty-Year Update*. Chelsea Green, 2004; and, D. Meadows, D. Meadows, and J. Randers, *Beyond the Limits*. Earthscan, 1992.

3. Robert Pirog and Stephen C. Stamos, *Energy Economics: Theory and Policy.* Prentice-Hall, 1987, Ch. 1.

4. Jonathon Porritt, *Capitalism: As If the World Matters.* Earthscan, 2005; Thomas Berry, *The Dream of the Earth.* Sierra Club Books, 1988; Thomas Berry, *The Great Work: Our Way into the Future.* Bell Tower, 1999; Mary Evelyn Tucker, *Worldly Wonder: Religions Enter Their Ecological Phase.* Open Court, 2003; David Orr, *Earth in Mind.* Island Press, 2004; Thomas Homer Dixon, *The Upside of Down: Catastrophe, Creativity, and the Renewal of Civilization.* Island Press, 2006; James Gustave Speth, *The Bridge at the Edge of the World: Capitalism, the Environment and Crossing from Crisis to Sustainability.* Yale University Press, 2008.

5. Sachs, *Common Wealth.*

6. United Nations General Assembly, Report of the World Commission on Environment and Development: *Our Common Future,* 1987.

7. Arthur Mol, *Globalization and Environmental Reform.* MIT Press, 2001, p. 2.

8. Maurice Strong, *Where on Earth Are We Going?* Texere, 2001, p. 26.

9. Speth, *Red Sky at Morning.* Yale University Press, 2004, p. 145.

10. Herman Daly, *Beyond Growth.* Beacon, 1996, Ch. 10 "Free Trade and Globalization vs. Environment and Community," and Ch. 11 "From Adjustment to Sustainable Development: The Obstacle of Free Trade," pp. 143–70.

11. Sachs, *Common Wealth*, pp. 6–7.

12. Jack Goldstone, "The Population Bomb: The Four Megatrends that Will Change the World." *Foreign Affairs*, January/February 2010, pp. 31–43.

13. Speth, *Red Sky at Morning*, Ch. 7 "Globalization and the Environment," pp. 140–47.

14. Gustave Speth, *The Bridge at the Edge of the World.* Ch. 2 "Modern Capitalism: Out of Control."

15. Herman Daly, "Ecological Economics: The Concept of Scale and Its Relation to Allocation, Distribution, and Uneconomic Growth," in *Ecological Economics and Sustainable Development: Selected Essays of Herman Daly.* Edward Elgar, 2007, pp. 82–103; Daly, *Beyond Growth: The Economics of Sustainable Development.* Beacon Press, 1996, Ch. 2 "Elements of Environmental Macroeconomics".

16. "Emerging Economies to Lead Energy Growth to 2030 and Renewables to Out-Grow Oil, Says BP Analysis," January 19, 2011, http://www.bp.com//genericarticle.do?categoryId=2012968&contentId=7066696.

17. Anthony Sampson, *The Seven Sisters: The Great Oil Companies and the World They Made.* Hodder and Stoughton, 1975; Daniel Yergin, *The Prize: The Epic Quest for Oil, Money, and Power.* Simon and Schuster, 1991; Paul Roberts, *The End of Oil.* Houghton and Mifflin, 2004.

18. C. Campbell and J. Laherrere, "The End of Cheap Oil." *Science* (June 1998); C. Campbell, "The Assessment and Importance of Oil Depletion." In *The Final Energy Crisis,* ed. A. McKillop. Pluto Press, 2005; Richard Heinberg, *The Party's Over: Oil, War, and the Fate of Industrial Societies.* Clearview, 2003.

19. Mycle Schneider, Antony Froggatt, and Steve Thomas, "Nuclear Power in a Post-Fukushima World." The Worldwatch Institute, July 1, 2011. See also the writings of Amory Lovins at the Rocky Mountain Institute; Amory Lovins, "Learning from Japan's Nuclear Disaster" at http://www.pbs.org/wgbh/nova/insidenova/2011/03/nuclear-lovins.html.

20. James Hansen, *Storms of My Grandchildren*, 2011.

21. "Food Crisis: What the World Bank Is Doing." *World Bank* April 18, 2012.

22. "About GAFSP." *The Global Agriculture and Food Security Program.* Available online at http://www.gafspfund.org/gafsp/content/global-agriculture-and-food-security-program.

23. "The Universal Declaration of Human Rights." *United Nations*. Available online at http://www.un.org/en/documents/udhr/.

24. "GAFSP: Improving Food Security for the World's Poor." *World Bank* May 17, 2012.

25. "The Spectrum of Malnutrition." Food and Agriculture Organization of the United Nations (2011).

26. Ibid., 96.

27. Jason Samenow, "US Has Hottest Month on Record in July 2012 NOAA Says." *The Washington Post* August 8, 2012.

28. Bob Burgdorfer, "Drought Deepens Worries about Food Supplies, Prices." *Reuters* August 1, 2012.

29. "Price Surges in Food Markets: How Should Organized Food Markets Be Regulated?" *FAO Policy Brief* (2010).

30. "Current World Population and World Population Growth since Year One." *About.com.*

31. Jeremy Hobbs, "World Food Day: There Is Enough Food in the World for Everyone." *Oxfam International* October 16, 2009.

32. "Difference Engine: Food for Thought." *The Economist* May 19, 2012.

33. "The New Face of Hunger." *The Economist* April 17, 2008.

34. Ibid.

35. Kurt M. Campbell, Alexander T.J. Lennon, and Julianne Smith (Project Co-Directors), *The Age of Consequences: The Foreign Policy and National Security Implications of Global Climate Change*. Washington, DC, November 2007.

36. Michael Klare, *Resource Wars: The New Landscape of Global Conflict*. Holt, 2002; Michael Klare, *Blood and Oil*. Henry Holt and Company, 2004; Michael Klare, *Rising Powers, Shrinking Planet: The New Geopolitics of Energy*. Holt 2009; Michael Klare, *The Race for What's Left: The Global Scramble for the World's Last Resources*. Metropolitan, 2012.

37. Hal Harvey and Sonia Aggarwal, "The Costs of Delay" ClimateWorks Foundation, 2011.

38. "Climate Change: How Do We Know?" at http://Climate.Nasa.Gov/Evidence/Index.Cfm? July 28, 2011; See also, T.C. Peterson et al., "State of the Climate in 2008," *Special Supplement to the Bulletin of The American Meteorological Society*, 90, no. 8 (August 2009): S17–18; I. Allison et al., "The Copenhagen Diagnosis: Updating the World on the Latest Climate Science." UNSW Climate Change Research Center, Sydney, Australia, 2009, p. 11; IPCC, Climate Change 2007, The 4th Assessment Report, www.ipcc.ch (available on line in four parts).

39. Albert Gore, *The Inconvenient Truth*. Bloomsbury, 2006; Nicholas Stern, *The Economics of Climate Change: The Stern Review*. Cambridge, 2007; James Hansen, *Storms of my Grandchildren*, 2011; Mark Hertsgaard, *Hot: Living through the Next Fifty Years on Earth*. Houghton Mifflin Harcourt, 2011; Bjorn Lomborg, *Smart Solutions to Climate Change: Comparing Costs and Benefits*. Cambridge University Press, 2011; Mark Hertsgaard, "Confronting the Climate Cranks." *The Nation*, January 20, 2011; Albert Gore, "Climate of Denial: Can Science and the Truth Withstand the Merchants of Poison?" *Rolling Stone*, June 24, 2011.

40. IPCC, Fourth Assessment Report, 2007.

41. Steven Pacala and Robert Socolow, "Stabilization Wedges: Solving the Climate with Current Technologies for the Next 50 Years." *Science*, 305, no. 5686 (August 13, 2004): 968–72.

42. These estimates are provided by T.M.L. Wigley, in *The Carbon Cycle*, T.M. L. Wigley, D.S. Schimel, eds. (Cambridge: Cambridge University Press, 2000), pp. 258–76.

43. Stern, *The Economics of Climate Change*; Sir Nicholas Stern, *The Global Deal: Climate Change and the Creation of a New Prosperity.* Public Affairs, 2009.

44. Sachs, *Common Wealth*, Ch. 4, "Global Solutions to Climate Change," p. 97.

45. Joseph Stiglitz, *Globalization and Its Discontents.* Norton, 2002, p. 214; Sachs, *Common Wealth*, Part Five, Global Problem Solving, Ch 12–14.

46. Porritt, *Capitalism: As If the World Matters, Part II A Framework for Sustainable Capitalism*, Ch 6–11; see also, Ch. 14 "Business Excellence."

47. See Stern's discussion of suggested policies, *The Global Deal,* Ch. 6 "Policies to Reduce Emissions," pp. 99–124.

48. Arne Mogren and Jesse Fahnestock, *A One Ton Future: A Guide to the Low-Carbon Century*. Falth & Hassler, Varnamo, 2009.

CHAPTER EIGHT

Conclusion

We Are Bound Together

Linked highways during rush hour.

Global economic systems connect consumers in Chicago, Shanghai, and Sao Paulo with producers in Puebla, Stuttgart, and San Jose. Financialization of the global economy has expanded investment and borrowing choices from hometown banks to international lenders. Our study of these patterns in trade, production, and finance highlights the interconnected nature of these economic flows that erode national boundaries. We have grappled with the spillovers from global production to environmental sustainability and questioned the ways that international economics shape the possibilities of growth in developing nations.

One undisputable takeaway from our survey of international economic activity is that globalization has made nations more vulnerable to external shocks. Growth pathways are shaped not only by being able to take advantage of opportunities beyond a nation's shores but also by the institutional resiliency to address the darker sides of globalization. In this chapter, we pull together the key themes of our interrogation of globalization and leave you with a few provocative questions about the global economy where you will live and work.

The Changed Nature of Trade

We live in globally integrated economies. As Nayan Chanda wrote, we are bound together.[1] A visual representation of our globally connected economies is the stack of containers in port cities packed with goods arriving from China or trucks brimming with electronics crossing the border from Mexico. But even the ubiquitous "made in China" label we so often see belies that complexity of the global production process. We recall that our iPhones are designed in California and assembled in China with parts and subsystems drawing upon the global value chain. A single country rarely produces a complete good—such as a cell phone or a car; instead, our goods are assembled in a global factory.

Twenty-first-century trade has a different complexion than that formulated by the first trade economist David Ricardo: rather than goods, we exchange processes and intermediary products along the global value chain. Advances in transportation and communications systems have linked us together in a global production line that prizes specialization at the process level rather than in the final product. Commodities such as copper, oil, or soya continue to be mined or grown where they are in natural abundance, but nations less endowed with mineral or agricultural riches now pursue different strategies for trade. As the Internet makes information more accessible and transportation links open markets, competitors spring up in what Jagdish Bhagwati describes as *kaleidoscopic comparative advantage*.

Trade creates wider choices for consumers to buy a range of goods at lower prices. While displaced workers suffer the loss of local jobs to the global factory, others enjoy a consumer surplus from the cheaper clothing and toys at Walmart. Trade creates winners and losers. Consumers win as global competition drives prices lower—while those companies and workers losing to cheaper global producers struggle with displaced lives. Communities dependent on factory jobs displaced by cheaper workers thousands of miles away wither with few alternatives for meaningful work. Urban tensions mount as the old good middle-class jobs have been offshored to the growing middle class of emerging markets.

The forces of globalization have paired with labor-savings technologies to create a distributional downside for those without market-valued skills. If a good can be put in a box and shipped or codified and sent over wires, it will be produced where productivity is highest relative to wages. Workers without advanced educations find themselves out of options in a global assembly line operated by upwardly mobile Chinese who have migrated from poor rural villages to new manufacturing centers such as Guangzhou and Shenzhen. Inequality in both the United States and China is rising as globalization rewards the skilled and educated. While global competition can spur creativity, it is also disruptive of traditional patterns of production.

The global geography of trade has shifted. China and India have become leading producers *and* consumer markets. Globally, more than 2.5 billion people have become bottom-of-pyramid or middle-class consumers.[2] Two decades ago, 97% of the world's population lacked mobile phones and only the top one percent was Internet connected. Today, two-thirds of producers and consumers are linked to global markets through telephone technology, with a third communicating on the Internet.[3] By 2030, the world's population is projected to increase 18% to 8.4 billion people, with over 95% of the population growth taking place in the developing world.

These demographic shifts, reflecting the new economic power of the Global South, have thrown the governance of trade into turmoil. The Doha round, begun in 2001 with the intent of addressing trade capacities of developing countries, confronted enormous friction as the industrialized worlds was challenged by the growth of emerging markets. The WTO, having celebrating its twentieth birthday in 2015, remains relevant as an arbiter of disputes, but finds itself adrift in attempts to corral its 162 member interests toward the design of a twenty-first-century trade regime. Unable to resolve complex issues of environmental and labor standards and investment regimes through the WTO, countries have turned to negotiating regional accords. With more than 600 treaties negotiated and over 400 regionals in force, the rules of global trade are being scripted by trade negotiators. The completion of the Transatlantic Trade Partnership (TPP) in 2015 signals the use of trade agreements for geopolitical ends—a pivot of the United States toward Asia, rebalancing with Japan and other partners against China. But like other trade agreements, the TPP is facing political headwinds as the losers from globalized economies look for redress from the costs of displacement. The politics of populism is turning countries inward to protect losers against the costs of globalization.

Global Borrowing and Lending to Finance Shifting Savings and Consumption

Finance greases the wheels of production and consumption. With globally integrated capital markets, firms can raise money at lower cost either by accessing investors on an international stock exchange or by cross-border borrowing where credit is more abundant. Investors are of course looking for the highest possible return—and global capital markets expand the choice set. If economic returns are anemic in the home economy, investors are willing to take on possible exchange-rate risks for higher yields.

The technological underbelly of financial integration makes these cross-border investments as simple as a quick computer keystroke. Institutional changes in the banking industry distributed intricate financial products globally—while also creating the conditions for the perfect storms of the global financial crisis. Traditionally, banks held loans; mortgages loans to homeowners or businesses formed the basis of the bank's balance sheet. Big banks and shadow banking institutions such as hedge funds morphed this bank holding approach into a model of originate and distribute—make the loan, but repackage it in an instrument to be sold on markets. And distribute they did—globally.

The mistaken belief in the Great Moderation—the lulling sense prior to the financial crisis that central banks had tamed cycles of inflation and unemployment—led institutions to under-price the risk associated with these widely distributed but poorly understood assets. But as globalization has delicately knit capital markets together, it has also exposed foreign investors to fragilities in other economies. Unknowing Europeans invested in bad U.S. mortgages packaged neatly as collateral debt obligations; the financial crisis tripped by poorly supervised lending practices quickly spread throughout interlinked financial markets.

The global financial crisis of 2007 wasn't, however, fundamentally caused by bad mortgages in Mississippi finding their way to unsuspecting Italian pensioners. These global micro- or firm-level transactions have an aggregate or macro parallel; there was a bigger story of large global imbalances. International borrowing allows countries and companies to live beyond their means. Recall that a country's trade balance is the residual left over from national production after domestic consumption. Without global capital markets, brakes would apply to a country consuming more than it is producing. Deficit countries without the money to import would be forced into a contractionary spiral. Surplus countries such as Germany or China would also have to alter consumption preferences if they couldn't find places to place savings. Global capital markets instead allow surplus countries—those consuming less than they are producing—to channel their national savings to earn higher returns in regions of growing demand. Of course, as we observe with Chinese holdings of American debt, accrued imbalances cause international tension.

Changing Global Rules: Rebalancing Global Flows

Crisis measures to address the Great Recession—some successful, others less so—did little to address the underlying shifts in the global economy. As Martin Wolff has pointed out, the global financial crisis was born of fundamental imbalances generated by national preferences for savings rather than consumption. We recall from our national accounting equations in Chapter 3 that the mirror to being a surplus country is that demand is deficient: X - M, our trade balance, goes positive when savings is high and consumption is low. Whether by demographic changes of aging populations as in Europe, policy measures to depress wages or large national projects to suppress consumption in favor of investment, resulting surpluses on the external accounts must be placed somewhere else in the global system. Financialization allows one country's excess saving to become another nation's financial liability in the service of its overconsumption. We are financially bound together.

The creation of opaque instruments such as collateralized debt obligations were designed to slice risk and address the appetites of high-return global investors. Capital markets straining for extraordinary yields were blind to higher risks. This became especially acute in the Eurozone where investments in nations with higher returns—such as Spain, Italy, Ireland, or Greece—were falsely seen to be low risk as backed by the single European currency. Surplus countries gladly fueled booms, particularly in real estate, in this search for return. When it became apparent that the real estate boom had turned to bust, capital flight ensued. Crisis hit without a safety net. Just because Germany and Greece share the same currency doesn't mean they have equal risk valuations—but many investors, blinded by the moral hazard of the Eurozone blanket, saw it that way.

Following on the heels of the global financial crisis, the euro crisis was caused by similar underlying drivers—the incredible waves of capital flows in global markets. Resolving Eurozone imbalances has, however, been more painful than adjustment in the global arena. Two missing instruments under EU rules make for the tougher correction: the hyper-fixed exchange rate and the weak fiscal arm. A typical country in crisis will most often vent steam through an exchange-rate depreciation; this should increase exports, depress imports, and begin to redress balance. But signing on to the Euro meant foregoing this option. Eurozone countries were further constrained by the fact that they are a currency union without a parallel fiscal backbone. If Florida were to suffer a real estate crash, federal dollars would flow to the state via normal mechanisms of unemployment insurance and other social assistance channels, softening the blow. In Europe, rather than cushioning via counterbalancing flows, countries were bound by Eurozone rules to engineer painful reductions in spending to effect adjustment. There was very little political will to rally around the European flag. The 2016 exit of Great Britain from the EU—remember it never became a Eurozone single currency country—reflects the unwillingness to support weaker partners to preserve the long-term health of all economies.

Flexible exchange rates should signal adjustments to trade imbalances. The country experiencing a trade deficit should see a weakening of its currency to reflect the weak external demand for its goods. Cheaper exports should, if import and export elasticities hold, improve the trade imbalance. Those in the European monetary system are unable to use changing exchange-rate values to cushion the hard costs of adjustment; reviving domestic economies must instead come through improving competitiveness in the real economy. This sounds reasonable and even desirable—but involves very painful repression of consumption and wages to create a more efficiently produced (and cheaper) goods that global consumers will choose to buy.

But flexible exchange rates aren't a magic bullet; they can even work against you. If, as in the United States, an anemic demand for the goods a country produces is offset by strong demand for its financial products such as stocks and bonds, then the expected exchange-rate depreciation won't occur. Demand on the financial side will outweigh weakness in the "real" or goods economy, and the currency will strengthen despite a trade deficit. Capital controls—such as those employed by China—can also impede exchange-rate adjustment of the deficit country. For commodity exporters, low export price elasticities natural resource products suggest that a cheaper currency won't tempt consumers to eat much more wheat or bananas. If the grocery bill is smaller, consumers are more likely to save the difference and buy a video game or clothes for their kids than they are to eat more corn. While flexible exchange rates can cushion adjustments, they can be an imperfect tool. Furthermore, as economies are drawn into the global value chain, cheaper currencies are offset by the increased cost of imports to produce the export.

Global imbalances create vulnerability to crisis. Economies can live beyond their means only as long as international investors have confidence in future returns. When confidence is shaken, the spigots of financial flows slow or stop. Adjustment can spin out of control if institutions are too weak or constrained to cushion the shock. Where institutions have strong credibility—for example, the U.S. Fed—profound crises can be mitigated with deft policy management. Weak institutions are prone to crisis. The rapid descent of the Brazilian economy on the scandal involving its flagship national oil company or the market volatility on the Chinese stock exchange exacerbated by opaque data point to the market's need for reliable information from credible institutions. In many countries, such market institutions are still in their infancy.

Shifting Economic Geographies: Convergence or Divergence?

The integration of global production, trade, and finance offered hopes of convergence between richer and poorer countries. Michael Spence has pointed out that forty years ago the Netherlands was forty times richer than China and 24 times as wealthy as India; today that difference has compressed to eleven times India and four times China.[4] Instantaneous information flowing across borders through new electronic networks provided access to new markets, ideas, and technologies. The combination of information and technology with a better-educated global workforce and pools of capital in search of high returns was hoped to galvanize growth in less-advanced regions. Indeed we have seen global poverty fall by half, as millions of Chinese, Indians, and Brazilians have crossed poverty thresholds to enjoy opportunities of a "middle-class" life. As Steve Radelet points out, global poverty is falling faster than any time in human history. Although there is wide variation in the construction of this concept of a global middle class—and much truth to the view that what we observe is a new vulnerable working class—we see fewer people subsisting on the margins of society at less than $2.50 a day. Access to global health care is improving, and infants have a better chance of making it to their fifth birthday and later enrolling in schools. To continue this shift, however, economies must deepen the structural change from low productivity sectors—largely agriculture and informal production—to activities with increased output per worker. It is only in this context that workers can continue to be paid more, creating a new choice set for valued lives.

Measured in purchasing-power-parity dollars, China is the largest economy in the world. By 2030, India will also surpass the United States in sheer volume of GDP, followed by Indonesia, Brazil, and Mexico. These large economies will continue to attract the interest of transnational companies looking for markets for consumer products. Where transportation costs are a significant portion of the final price tag, companies such as those in the auto industry will be eager to produce in that market. Ricardo Hausmann uses the analogy of a Scrabble game to explain the convergence in wealth. Before the global value chain, countries would need the equivalent of lots of valuable letters to be able to produce point-scoring words (or technological advances); in today's global factory, countries can produce with fewer "letters." In the old, atomized production chains, to produce shoes that global consumers would covet would involve appropriating design, machine, logistics, branding, and marketing capabilities formerly outside the purview of most firms in the developing world. Today, firms in the Asian value chain can partner to cover their limited letters—or technological gaps—providing value with cheaper yet still-productive labor. Over time, firms in a value chain acquire more "letters" by virtue of learning by doing and are able to master more technological processes.

China is of course the star of the twenty-first-century globalization story. Opening the large Chinese economy to global trade and finance has caused seismic shifts in how goods are produced and traded; its focus on investment-driven growth created huge pools of capital in financial markets tied to Chinese sovereign wealth funds. China's opening was, consistent with its traditions, careful and calculated. While trade with the rest of the world exploded, financial accounts were only slowly liberalized for inward foreign direct investment. Chinese firms have, however, been aggressive in investments abroad, particularly in Africa and Latin America. Often enjoying state support, Chinese multinationals have made investments in infrastructure and mining throughout Africa and Latin America. Chinese goods follow the investment foray, displacing local artisans by cheaply made mass-produced goods from the Asian value chain. Chinese finance is beginning to trail trade and production, with the increasing use of the renminbi to settle accounts. Its recent inclusion, the IMF's SDR basket is an important symbol of China's new global power; nonetheless, the renminbi will only become a truly trusted international currency when capital controls on inward investment are lifted.

But China is likely a special case. Transformations at the bottom of the global income ladder for developing countries haven't been matched by structural changes that foster rising productivity and universally shared higher living standards. Although big emerging markets are challenging geo-economic power, few developing countries are converging to rich country standards. Rising productivity is the key to prosperity and the opportunity for citizens to choose a valued life. While adding more labor—or more capital—can increase growth, the key to making people better off is improving the way capital and labor are combined—a concept called total factor productivity (TFP). Broadly understood as technology, rising TFP will contribute to rising output per person. Development economists have long held that growth trajectories accelerate when moving labor from low-productivity rural sectors to higher-productivity modern sectors. This process of structural change moves workers from backward agriculture to higher-tech manufacturing, increasing overall national output. But few countries have made this structural leap—and the window for change might be closing.

Globalization creates opportunities and risks for countries undergoing structural change. Countries in the Asian value chain have enhanced growth by providing better-paying modern-sector jobs. But not all countries benefit equally. Taking advantage of the productivity boost requires a competitive exchange rate to price your tradable output. Commodity exporters—where the demand for minerals or agricultural product strengthens the exchange rate—have a harder time diversifying into manufactured output. Large exchange-rate swings around 2015 reflect uneven growth between leading economies in North America, Europe, and Asia—and contribute to prevailing uncertainty about the direction of the global economy. Others nations are caught in the middle-income trap. Poorer countries with cheaper labor can jump on the bottom of the global manufacturing ladder, but as national wages rise its competitive niche is squeezed out. At the top of the economic ladder, competitiveness tends to derive from combining more expensive labor with sophisticated, productivity-enhancing capital—capabilities missing in middle-income countries. For some countries such as Brazil, the commodity plus middle-income squeeze is so tight that they are experiencing deindustrialization.[5] In the rich countries themselves, the returns flow to those with capital and specialized educations—and bias against those at the bottom of the socio-economic strata.

Both middle- and high-income countries have responded to these challenges to the industrial sector by protecting domestic markets, resulting in what Ian Brenner calls guarded globalization—the use of state capitalism tools to promote local industry at the expense of global integration. State financing and ownership have created a global economy that straddles market and state direction. Those countries with sufficient fiscal space—that is, those not saddled with large external debt to GDP ratios—have newly sanctioned options to manage the impacts of global downturns without suffering the disapproval of investment rating agencies. The crisis of 2007–08 changed the rules of the global financial game. Prior to the crisis, free-market rules dominated the global arena; regulations were weak. Policy responses to address the liquidity squeeze placed government squarely in the market mix. Market intervention became accepted as necessary to tame the ferocity of the crisis, dethroning the purely neoliberal model. The market is no longer seen as automatically self-correcting.

Opportunity, Risk, Resilience, and Fragility

Globalization rewards those nations—and within countries, those individuals—who are highly skilled; but those who are poorly educated lose out. As Dani Rodrik has shown, workers displaced by globalization tend to land in less-productive sectors. It is a winner-take-all global economy. A central risk of globalization is that its losers—in absolute or relative terms—become deeply disenchanted by the unequal outcomes in the world economy. Yet nations—much less multilateral organizations—lack the capacity to promote redistributive policies responding to economic inequality. Even the IMF—formerly known as the dispenser of tough austerity medicine—is now cautioning attention to the growing polarization of societies. Its director Christine Lagarde, argues that tackling inequality is vital to restoring confidence in globalization.[6] Inequality is slowing growth. A recent IMF study shows that since 1998 the hollowing of the middle class has shaved 3.5% off consumption—the equivalent of a year of growth.

Globalization creates opportunities but also escalates risk. As Rodrik cautions, our interconnected and rapidly reacting global economy increases the benefits of getting policies right—but exacerbates the costs of policy mistakes.[7] Countries with sustained long-run growth rates are those that are able to implement mechanisms that allow for the benefits of globalization while also reinforcing systems to promote resiliency. Our global institutions are not up to the challenges brought by globalization. Nouriel Roubini characterizes Brexit—Britain's exit from the EU—as the warning from the canary in the coal mine of the fragility of our globalized economy.[8] The United Kingdom—while benefitting from financial globalization—was politically divided over the costs and benefits of immigration. Institutions to move those losing jobs into higher paying productive sectors are badly frayed; it is no surprise that those paying the costs lash out against symbols of globalization.

We also need to think about our economic systems more broadly. Coming shocks to the global system are as likely to be in the form of droughts and flooding brought on by global warming as by the proliferation of opaque financial instruments. Market failure has been compounded by policy failures to address the externalities fostered by global capitalism. As Jeffrey Sachs warns, we need a new analytical framework in economics that positions natural capital as a key variable in models of long-run growth. Investment needs to be directed not solely at assets delivering high returns in the short run but also toward long-run infusions into energy sustainability and transport architectures that promote environmentally friendly outcomes. We need to rethink our energy mix fueling globalization and work across borders to address the externalities of the global factory. The Paris Climate agreement of 2015 is an important albeit incomplete step in shifting economies from fossil-fuel dependence to more sustainable energy sources. Removing subsidies for carbon-based energy sources and redirecting resources toward a menu of sustainable energy providers would be an important pivot toward environmental sustainability.

As we put this book to press in 2016, global markets are in an unsettled, low-level equilibrium. With the exception of India, SIEMs—the systemically important emerging markets—are stalled. Commodity exporters are struggling with the slowdown of the Chinese engine. As the euphoria has gone out of the emerging-market bubble, investors are scrambling for high returns. Opaque policymaking in China heightens uncertainty. As Michael Spence notes, output gaps have emerged, where pools of underused capital—especially sovereign wealth and pension funds—are not being matched to investment needs in critical infrastructure and sustainable energy.

Increasingly the integration of capital markets demands international coordination. But the global architecture for concerted action is weak, especially in dealing with large, systemically important countries. Nations cling to the perhaps illusory notion of sovereignty. Although the IMF has the facilities to assist in the case of a single small- or medium-sized country in crisis, its resources are limited in the face of global shocks. National needs may also conflict with multilateral objectives; the drama of the Greek debt crisis is a tragic story of the European Central Bank demanding politically unpalatable and painful contraction from Greek citizens. Small changes such as admitting the Chinese Renminbi to the IMF's SDR currency basket have been made, but global governance needs to evolve to parallel the shifts in global economic power. The radical changes in the geo-economic landscape require parallel adjustments in the architecture of global governance.

These core concepts of globally integrated trade, finance, and production systems are reflected in the history of globalization; they provide our foundation to explore expectations for twenty-first-century globalization. As we saw by the late 1980s and early 1990s, globalization was entering a new era of global market liberalization fueled in part by the fall of the Berlin Wall and the rapid advances of technology. By the end of the last century, as the power of the Internet was unleashed on the world economic and production system, the prevailing world view was that globalization was likely to bring forward the widespread liberalization of markets, a rising volume and a changing composition of world trade, increased capital flows, a rise in the emerging market countries (China, India, Russia, and Brazil), a fall in world poverty, a decrease in global income and wealth inequality, an upturn in global employment, an extension of technological change, a gradual growth in the number of stable democratic governments, and an intensification in global coordination and cooperation in economic, financial, and political affairs—all contributing to a strong and dynamic period of economic growth. This was indeed a rosy picture.

By 2007, the reality of the global financial crisis and global recession changed this optimistic view of globalization. Instead, the narrative became laced with crisis and setbacks exacerbated by our tenuous global connections. Will a rosy or a chaotic view of globalization prevail? This is a subject for yet another book. Suffice it to say, that as we enter the next period of globalization, outcomes will likely be mixed. Globalization is a high-stakes game creating winners and losers. It has brought both great prosperity and enormous vulnerability. It has prompted a seismic change in economic power and fundamentally threatens environmental sustainability. As Stiglitz suggests, globalization requires skillful management to minimize the costs. Yet economic and environmental challenges will be more difficult to address as the negative outcomes of globalization promote inward-looking politics and foment military conflict throughout the world. We are bound together but we may be tearing apart.

A student of globalization might find future prospects quite dreary—a dark tale of risks and crises. A brighter tint, however, is offered by the ways in which communications technologies do link our societies together. These linkages through instant Internet communications and the accountability of cell phone videos being posted to globally accessible YouTube accounts are admittedly imperfect. Chinese citizens—and those of many other countries—live behind censored walls. But the empowerment of individuals through communications technologies is significant.

Citizens are deepening their capacities to challenge governments to act in the interest of the global commons. A rising global middle class is demanding accountability by political elites for transparency and social investment. There is no panacea for the overloaded global agenda of rising inequality, tense geopolitics, and scarcity in resources. It is, however, our hope that understanding the economic ties that bind us together through production networks, trade, financial markets—and the social and environmental costs of these deep and unpredictable global flows—will enhance your capabilities as a global citizen to help shape the global economy you would most like to live in.

Notes

1. Nayan Chanda, *Bound Together: How Traders, Preachers, Adventurers, and Warriors Shaped Globalization*. New Haven, CT: Yale University Press, 2007.

2. Over the next two decades the structure of world population and income will undergo profound changes. Global income inequality is projected to decline further in 2035, largely owing to rapid economic growth in the emerging-market economies. The potential pool of consumers worldwide will expand significantly, with the largest net gains in the developing and emerging-market economies. The number of people earning between US$1,144 and US$3,252 per year in 2013 prices in purchasing power parity terms will increase by around 500 million, with the largest gains in Sub-Saharan Africa and India; those earning between US$3,252 and US$8,874 per year in 2013 prices will increase by almost one billion, with the largest gains in India and Sub-Saharan Africa; and those earning more than US$8,874 per year will increase by 1.2 billion, with the largest gains in China and the advanced economies. (Tomas Hellebrandt and Paolo Mauro, *The Future of Worldwide Income Distribution*. Peterson Institute for International Economics, April 2015.)

3. Michael Spence, Danny Leipziger, James Manyika, and Ravi Kanbur, "Restarting the Global Economy: Three Mismatches that Need Concerted Public Action," November 4, 2015 Bellagio_2015_FINAL_web_9-29-15.

4. Michael Spence. *The Next Convergence: The Future of Economic Growth in a Multispeed World.* NY: Macmillan, 2011.

5. Margaret McMillan, Dani Rodrik, and Inico Vergallo, *Globalization, Structural Change and Productivity Growth*. World Development 2014.

6. Shawn Donnan, "Christine Lagarde Wants Softer, Kinder IMF to Face Populist anger." FT.com July 13, 2016.

7. McMillian, Rodrik, and Vergallo, *Globalization, Structural Change and Productivity Growth*.

8. Nouriel Roubini, "Globalization's Political Fault Lines." *Project Syndicate*, July 4, 2016 at https://www.project-syndicate.org/print/globalization-political-fault-lines-by-nouriel-roubini-2016-07.

Glossary

absolute advantage A country has an absolute advantage if it produces more of a product per resource unit than another country.

Active Labor Market Policy (ALMP) Any government policy aimed at getting active job seekers back to work through job training, benefit administration and job creation initiatives.

affluence According to environmental lawyer and activist Gustave Speth, affluence is one of four primary causes of environmental deterioration worldwide, as higher levels of income leads to greater consumption and production of goods and increased use of energy.

appreciation An increase in value of one currency relative to another currency.

arbitrage The practice of "buying cheap, selling dear," or exploiting price differentials to gain a return on the value of an asset after the original purchase.

asset approach One method of evaluating exchange rate determination, based on the demand for assets denominated in one currency to the demand for assets denominated in another currency.

autarky The situation in which a country is self-sufficient and does not take part in any international trade.

automatic adjustment mechanism In a pegged exchange rate system like the gold standard, a country running a balance of payments deficit should decrease its money supply via the central bank causing domestic prices to fall, incentivizing foreigners to buy more domestic goods, correcting the balance of payments deficit. Likewise, a surplus country should increase its stock of money via the central bank, increasing prices and reducing demand for domestic goods, causing the surplus to readjust back to zero. The application of this theory proved false as many countries "cheated" in pegged systems to promote expansionary monetary policy regardless of their balance of payments.

balance of merchandise trade The difference between goods exported and imported.

balance of payments approach One method of evaluating exchange rate determination, based on internal deficits or surpluses within a country. With this approach, a deficit is associated with a deprecation and a surplus should be matched by an appreciation of the currency.

balance of payments An accounting of a country's international transactions for a particular time period, including the current account, the capital account, and the financial account.

bonded labor Workers begin jobs and incur unsustainable personal debts for food, transportation, or lodging; this results in an obligation to continue working to attempt to pay off these debts.

brain drain The phenomenon of highly educated citizens in developing countries emigrating to more developed countries, leaving home countries devoid of their most productive young minds.

capital account As part of a country's balance of payments, the capital account includes capital transfers and the acquisition and disposal of non-produced, non-financial assets. These assets include debt forgiveness and migrants' transfers, the transfer of title to fixed assets, and the transfer of funds linked to the sale or acquisition of fixed assets, gift and inheritance taxes, death duties, uninsured damage to fixed assets, and legacies.

capital controls Rules implemented by a governing body within a country that prevent or place restrictions on purchases of that country's assets.

capitalism An economic system based on the private ownership of the means of production (land, labor, and capital) with resources allocated efficiently with prices based on costs and goods and services provided within a market. According to some academics, capitalism as an economic system contributes to environmental degradation because of the importance of consumption within the model.

child labor The employment of children in any way that deprives them of their childhood.

closed loop model A market model that would reflect all externalities and feedbacks incurred while producing a good in the final price of the good.

collateralized debt obligations (CDOs) Sophisticated financial instruments that package several different types of assets into one tradable package. The insurance and valuation of CDOs and their decline in value played a major role in the 2008 financial crisis.

common external tariff (CET) A uniform tariff rate. The existence of a CET defines a customs union, the stage before a common market that also allows the free movement of labor and capital among members.

comparative advantage A country has a relative comparative advantage if it produces a good or service at a lower opportunity cost than its trading partner. Countries should trade according to their relative comparative advantage, even if one country has the absolute advantage.

conditional cash transfers Social security payments received based on the completion and adherence to certain conditions outlined by the distributor of the payments, such as school attendance or pre-natal doctor's visits.

consumer culture A promotion and prioritization of buying goods and services within a group or society.

current account As a part of a country's balance of payments, the current account tallies international trade in goods and services and earnings on investments. This measure also includes merchandise trade, services, income receipts, and unilateral transfers.

dependency theorists In counterpoint to modernization theorists, dependency theorists believe that foreign direct investment hurts developing economies by stifling national growth, contributing to income inequality, crowding out local entrepreneurship, and creating barriers to entry for national firms, with little technological spillover from transnationals.

depreciation A decrease in value of one currency relative to another currency.

Doha Development Round/Doha Development Agenda (DDA) Launched at the WTO conference in Qatar, the DDA is a broad round of trade negotiations focusing on the needs and interests of developing countries. Specifically, the negotiations focus on bringing developing nations more fully into the trading arena by allowing them to exercise their own comparative advantage in areas such as food and textiles blocked by the richer world's protectionist measures.

dumping Predatory pricing in which a country exports a product at price lower than the price it normally charges on its home market or at a price below the cost of production.

economies of scale The advantage of increased efficiency in production (a lower cost per unit good) as the amount of good and services produced increases.

emerging market economies Nations in the process of rapid growth and structural change that provide new investment opportunities for global capital.

enclave economy Refers to a country receiving foreign direct investment with low linkages to the rest of the domestic economy, resulting in a limited flow of people, capital, and technology from the presence of transnational companies and little complementary growth.

exchange rate The price of one currency in terms of another.

export subsidy Low-cost loans or tax relief to companies for certain goods and services in order encourage their export and discourage selling them in the domestic market. They can be especially detrimental to small producers in poor countries.

factor price equalization A corollary to the H-O theorem that states that trade and competition among countries causes the relative prices of their respective identical factors of production to equal each other. For example, as international trade raises the price of labor in India, falling demand for labor-intensive goods produced in the United Kingdom will decrease the price of labor in the United Kingdom and draw the world price of labor together.

financial account Records transfers of financial capital and non-financial capital in the balance of payments. The financial account also encompasses U.S.-owned assets abroad, foreign-owned assets in the United States, and the acquisition and disposal of non-produced, non-financial assets (such as the rights to natural resources and the sales and purchases of intangible assets like patents and copyrights).

financial globalization Defined by the IMF as the extent to which countries are linked through cross-border financial holdings.

forward rate A reflection of future market expectations for an exchange rate between two currencies, useful when administering the asset approach to evaluate the balance of payments to understand currency demand.

free market neo-liberal One of three competing political economic schools of thought framing debates about globalization along with Institutionalist–Structuralist and Marxist. Free Market Neo-Liberals are generally supportive of large institutions, foreign investment, sound macroeconomic policies, technology, the use of markets, and global integration to reach prosperity. The IMF in this chapter is categorized as Free Market Neo-Liberal.

General Agreement on Tariffs and Trade (GATT) Established in 1947, the GATT worked to reduce tariff and non-tariff barriers to international trade through negotiations known as "rounds" with UN members until the World Trade Organization replaced it in 1995. The World Trade Organization still operates with some of the founding principles of GATT.

gini coefficient A measure of income inequality calculated as the difference between perfect income equality and a country's actual income distribution (represented by the Lorenz curve).

global factory A term coined by economist Peter Buckley referring to a worldwide production process integrating parts, suppliers, and subcontractors around the world. This global factory now consists of a network of companies delivering different services in a consolidated value chain.

globalization Although many different definitions exist and continue to evolve, the definition used in this book comes from Rennen and Martens (2003): "an intensification of cross-national cultural, economic, political, social, and technological interactions that lead to the establishment of transnational structures and the global integration of cultural, economic, environmental, political and social processes on global, supranational, national, regional, and local levels."

Heckscher–Ohlin (H-O) theorem A factor proportions model that states that a country should produce goods that use relatively intensively its most abundant factor and import goods that use relatively intensely its scarce factor(s).

horizontal foreign direct investment Foreign companies produce their goods in another country to improve access to that foreign country's domestic market and save on transportation costs.

Human Development Index (HDI) Developed by economists at the U.N., the HDI is a multidimensional measurement of development using a composite of indices. The method to calculate the HDI is a geometric mean of life expectancy, mean years of schooling, expected years of schooling, and income. While imperfect, the HDI is widely used and useful due to its blending of social and economic factors within one index.

human trafficking The recruiting, transportation, harboring or receiving persons by use of force, coercion, or deception for the purpose of exploitation, prostitution, forced labor, slavery, or servitude, as defined by the UN Palermo Protocol.

hyperglobalist One of three views of globalization along with skeptics and transformationalists, stating that a continuous history of globalization has existed for many centuries although the current form of globalization is strikingly different and unique compared to its predecessors.

import licenses A permit that allows a company to import a certain good. Domestic companies that want to purchase a certain good have to pay the government for the right to import that good.

import substitution industrialization In the 1960s, some emerging economies such as Brazil and Argentina engaged in import substitution industrialization to build up domestic industries. This process required limiting imports and forming industries to build the same goods at home, prompting consumption of domestic goods and export growth.

impossible trinity A country cannot have open capital markets, independent monetary policy, and a fixed exchange rate all at once. For example, a country must either sacrifice open capital markets or independent monetary policy to maintain a fixed exchange rate.

imputed demand Demand for a currency driven by the demand for a good priced in the same currency.

institutionalist–structuralist One of three competing political economic schools of thought framing debates about globalization along with Free Market Neo-Liberal and Marxists. Institutionalist–Structuralists are represented partly by the views of economist Joseph Stiglitz. Stiglitz encompasses the belief that institutions are necessary to complement markets and can be reformed.

International Monetary Fund (IMF) Formed after the Bretton Woods Conference in 1944 and headquartered in Washington D.C. The International Monetary Fund promotes global financial stability and growth through exchange rate and balance of payment monitoring as well as emergency lending facilities its 188 member countries.

law of one price A good should sell for the same price in all markets around the world after factoring in differences due to transportation costs.

Leontief paradox A contradiction to the H-O theorem discovered in 1954 by Professor Wassily W. Leontief. Rather than exporting good that intensely use its most abundant factor (capital) and importing good that use its scarce factor (labor), the United States exported labor-intensive commodities and imported capital-intensive commodities.

Lorenz curve A plot of the actual income distribution of a given place, shown as the percentage of the population owning a corresponding percentage of that location's income. The difference between the Lorenz curve and perfect income equality produces the Gini coefficient.

Maastricht criteria Conditions that required compliance by European Union member states before entering into the European Monetary Union, and adopting the euro as a national currency. The criteria aimed to promote macroeconomic convergence prior to launching the euro. The Growth and Stability Pact was engineered (faultily) to prevent fiscal imbalances from pressuring the euro.

market failure A price of a good or service in the market fails to reflect all costs incurred in the production of that product, i.e., the social costs of production and/or the negative externalities of environmental degradation.

marxist/dependency Marxists see underdevelopment as a consequence of capitalism, as the accumulation of capital propagates a ruling class of elites to which all other classes are dependent. These negative results of development can only be reversed by an overthrow of capitalist systems.

marxist Along with Free Market Neo-Liberal and Institutionalist–Structuralist as a type of political economic school of thought, Marxists reject the potential to reform global capitalism and view globalization as a form of imperialism protecting a ruling class in the twenty-first century.

modernization theorists Supporters of the idea that foreign direct investment helps developing countries through capital investment and superior technology transfers from transnational companies. These theorists also believe that transnational companies contribute to developing country growth by providing organizational and managerial skills, marketing know-how, and increased factor productivity.

most favored nation (MFN) A concept and national treatment that sets the standard that, with the exception of specifically negotiated trade agreements, treatment given to one member must be extended to all. MFN addresses tariffs, quotas, trade in services, and other non-tariff barriers.

negative externality A product of the production and consumption of a good that does not fall directly on either the producer or the consumer, but rather on a third party, often being the "social cost."

neo-liberal Neo-liberal thinkers believe underdevelopment to be a natural result of growth within backwards economic and political institutions. Underdevelopment is best addressed by free-market policies, according to neo-liberal theory.

net international investment position The difference between domestic investments in foreign economies and foreign investments in a domestic economy, or the measurement of one country's outstanding liabilities to the rest of the world.

net portfolio investments Listed under the financial account, the difference between domestic portfolio investments and foreign portfolio investments.

non-governmental organizations (NGOs) A legal organization formed outside of the purview of a government, ranging in scale from community-based outreach to international fixtures like the Red Cross. NGOs can take on a variety of roles from promoting social justice to environmental sustainability. The growth of NGOs towards the end of the twentieth century in response to the failures of capitalism marks a defining feature of twenty-first-century globalization.

Organization of Petroleum Exporting Countries (OPEC) Founded in 1960 and currently composed of 12 member countries (Algeria, Angola, Ecuador, Iran, Iraq, Kuwait, Libya, Nigeria, Qatar, Saudi Arabia, the United Arab Emirates, and Venezuela). OPEC works to stabilize oil prices, coordinate oil policies, and promote the individual and collective interests of members. One of its most lasting legacies was the oil embargo of 1973, which contributed to a deep recession in the United States with high rates of both unemployment and inflation.

original sin The inability to issue international debt instruments in one's own currency, rendering an economy unable to borrow internationally with its own currency and vulnerable to exchange rate effects on debt.

policy and political failure Although policy initiatives to augment environmental degradation began significantly as early as the 1970s, these efforts prove futile in practice as international organizations cannot enforce policies and many national governments fail to support international regulations as well.

policy-based selectivity The concept of giving development aid to countries based on their records of good governance. While some argue that policy-based selectivity is the most productive way to make aid actually impactful, others see policy-based selectivity as stifling since aid should be granted to underdeveloped countries regardless of previous aid endeavors.

population According to environmental lawyer and activist Gustave Speth, population growth is one of four primary causes of environmental deterioration worldwide, as a growing population yields increases demand for finite resources and limits the ability of resources to grow and expand.

poverty According to environmental lawyer and activist Gustave Speth, poverty is one of the four primary causes of environmental deterioration worldwide, as poorer populations utilize environmentally unsound methods to subsist.

preferential trading agreements (PTAs) Also called regional trade agreements (RTAs) or free-trade agreements (FTAs); provide a framework for trade opening negotiated on a limited scale among a small set of countries.

purchasing power parity (PPP) Concept used to illustrate that a good should cost the same in different countries after readjusting for price differentials caused by different currency valuations by calculating the relative prices of goods and services in one currency to another. PPP is based on the law of one price that suggests that in the absence of barriers to trade and accounting for transportation costs, a good should sell for the same price in different markets.

quota A limit on the quantity of imports. Quotas cause higher prices and hurt domestic consumers.

real exchange rate The exchange rate between two currencies adjusted for inflation, signifying the actual measure of a country's purchasing power.

remittance money A transfer of funds from a foreign worker back to family members in their home countries that plays an increasingly important role in developing countries due to their ability to reduce poverty, act counter-cyclically, meet humanitarian needs during natural disasters, and provide hard currency directly to families.

reserve currency A currency held in significant quantities by many governments and institutions as part of the international financial system. The dollar has been the global reserve currency since 1945, but recent changes in the global financial system present possible alternatives to its position in the future.

rules of origin Rules that determine in which country a good is manufactured, produced or grown. Rules of origin stipulate a percent of value added by a country. They are used in trade agreements to determine if a country qualifies for trade benefits.

scale and rate of economic growth According to environmental lawyer and activist Gustave Speth, the scale and rate of economic growth also results in environmental degradation, prompting the question: given environmental conditions and settings, are there physical limits to economic growth?

skeptic One of three views of globalization along with hyperglobalists and transformationalists. Skeptics believe that the current economy is in a similar form to years past and the sum of the developments in the international economy only change the scale and scope of globalization.

social cost of production Used interchangeably with negative externality, refers to a cost borne by society due to the production and consumption of a certain good.

spot rate The current exchange rate between two given currencies.

sterilization System printing money domestically to purchase a foreign currency to prevent contractions due to automatic decreases in the money supply with balance of payments deficits under the rules of the game in a fixed exchange rate system. Its parallel under a floating system is exchange rate manipulation.

Stolper Samuelson theorem A corollary to the H-O theorem that suggests that trade increases the wage of the factor of production used most intensely in the production of a good and decreases the wage of the scarce factors. In terms of labor, the Stolper Samuelson theorem suggests that trade in labor-abundant countries should increase the welfare of the manual laborers, often the least well-off in society.

structuralists–institutionalists Structuralists are adherents of the school of thought that underdevelopment relates to the historical context of development, particularly in terms of legacies of colonialism. To remedy this underdevelopment, structuralists believe solutions lie in state-led development policies and deepening institutions.

systemically important emerging markets Including China, India, and Brazil, refers to countries with growing international clout in international bodies like the IMF and G-20.

tariff A tax levied on exports or imports that restricts trade. Like quotas, tariff cause higher prices and hurt domestic consumers.

technology According to environmental lawyer and activist Gustave Speth, technology is one of the four primary causes of environmental deterioration worldwide, as traditionally energy-intensive technologies extract natural materials and transform physical resources with little regards to the consequences.

Trade Adjustment Assistance (TAA) A federal program set up through the Department of Labor that provides services to workers who have lost their jobs as a result of foreign trade. Services include job training, income support, and assistance with healthcare costs.

Trade-Related Aspects of Intellectual Property (TRIPS) Agreement An international agreement administered by the WTO that sets the framework for the protection of intellectual property such as copyrights, trademarks, geographical indications, industrial designs, patents, and layout designs of integrated circuits. It was negotiated in the Uruguay Round of GATT in 1994.

transformational One of three views of globalization along with hyperglobalists and skeptics. Transformationalists argue that globalization is a fundamentally new force underlying the rapid, widespread social, political, and economic changes reshaping global societies and the world order.

vertical foreign direct investment Foreign companies produce pieces of their goods in different countries to take advantage of efficient factor inputs (like low wages) in different countries.

vertical specialization Occurs when countries specialize only in particular stages of a good's production sequence. Vertical specialization does not contradict the concept of comparative advantage—it suggests that countries may have different advantages at various levels of the production process rather than the production of the good in its entirety.

voluntary export restraints Another form of protectionism. To limit the quantity imported of a certain product, a country will ask its trading partner to reduce its amount of exports for the same product.

Washington Consensus Refers to generalized principles espoused by the IMF, World Bank, and United States Treasury Department in the 1990s to promote development. Largely neo-liberal in nature, the Washington Consensus promoted sound fiscal policy, market-led forces, trade liberalization, and deregulation.

World Bank Formed at the Bretton Woods Conference in 1944, the World Bank promotes development and reduce poverty through granting low-interest loans, interest-free credits, and grants to developing countries. The World Bank itself is composed of five sub-organizations with a total of 188 member countries.

Bibliography

"About GAFSP." *The Global Agriculture and Food Security Program.* http://www.gafspfund.org/gafsp/content/global-agriculture-and-food-security-program
Adams, Samuel. "Foreign Direct Investment, Domestic Investment and Economic Growth in Sub-Saharan Africa." *Journal of Policy Making* 31 (2009): 939–949.
"African Free Trade Zone Is Agreed." *BBC News*, October 22, 2008.
Ahearn, Raymond J. "The Global Economic Downturn and Protectionism." *Congressional Research Service R40461*, 2009.
Alfaro, Laura, Areendam Chanda, Sebnem Kalemli-Ozcan, and Selin Sayek. "Does Foreign Direct Investment Promote Growth? Exploring the Role of Financial Markets on Linkages." *Journal of Development Economics* 91 (2010): 242–256.
Allison, I., et al., "The Copenhagen Diagnosis: Updating the World on the Latest Climate Science." Sydney, Australia: UNSW Climate Change Research Center, 2009, 11.
Al-Rodhan, Nayef R.F., and Gerard Stroudman. "Definitions of Globalization: A Comprehensive Overview and a Proposed Definition." *Geneva Centre for Security Policy, Program on the Geopolitical Implications of Globalization and Transnational Security*, June 19, 2006.
American Civil Liberties Union. "U.S.-Mexico Border Crossing Deaths Are a Humanitarian Crisis, According to Report from The ACLU and CNDH." September 30, 2009.
"Annex Table 8. FDI Outward Stock as a Percentage of Gross Domestic Product, 1990–2012." UNCTAD, June 26, 2013. http://www.unctad.org/Sections/dite_dir/docs/WIR2013/WIR13_webtab08.xls
Asche, Frank, and Martin D. Smith. "Trade and Fisheries: Key Issues for the World Trade Organization." *Staff Working Paper ERSD-2010-03*, 2010.
Asociación Mexicana de la Industria Automotoríz A.C. "Estadisticas." http://www.amia.com.mx/
Back, Aaron. "China Plans Additional Tariffs on U.S. Chicken." *The Wall Street Journal*, April 28, 2010.
Back, Aaron, Andrew Batson, and Bob Davis. "Early View on China's Currency Overhaul: Little Change." *The Wall Street Journal*, July 16, 2010.
Baldwin, Richard, and Simon Evenett. "Introduction and Recommendations for the G20." In *The Collapse of Global Trade, Murky Protectionism, and the Crisis: Recommendations for the G20*, ed. Richard Baldwin and Simon Evenett, 1–12. London: Center for Economic Policy Research, 2009.
Beattie, Alan. "Global Insight: Skirmishes Are Not All-Out Trade War." *The Financial Times*, March 14, 2010.
Behar, Alberto, and Anthony J. Venables. "Transport Costs and International Trade." *University of Oxford Department of Economics Discussion Paper Series* 488, 2010.
Berry, Thomas. *The Dream of the Earth.* Sierra Club Books, 1988.
Berry, Thomas. *The Great Work: Our Way Into the Future*. Bell Tower, 1999.
Bhagwati, Jagdish. "Why the World Is Not Flat." *World Affairs Blogland*, posted February 12, 2010. http://www.worldaffairsjournal.org/new/blogs/bhagwati

Birdsall, Nancy, Augusto de la Torre, and Felipe Valencia Caiocedo. Policy Research Working Paper 5316, "The Washington Consensus Assessing a Damaged Brand" *The World Bank Office of the Chief Economist, Latin America and the Caribbean Region and Center for Global Development* (2010): 23.

Bishop, Matthew. "A Bigger World." *The Economist*, September 18, 2008.

Blinder, Alan S. "Offshoring: The Next Industrial Revolution?" *Foreign Affairs*, March/April 2006.

Blitz, James. "UN Warns of Gangs' Global Muscle." *The Financial Times*, June 17, 2010. http://www.ft.com/cms/s/0/75f119b8-7a3e-11df-aa69-00144feabdc0.html

Borjas, George. "Immigrants In, Wages Down: How to Do the Figuring." *National Review*, May 2006.

Boss, Suzie. "Root Solutions." *Stanford Social Innovation Review*, 2009.

Brown, Drusilla. "A Review of the Globalization Literature: Implications for Employment, Wages, and Labor Standards." In *Globalization, Wages, and the Quality of Jobs: Five Country Studies*, ed. Raymond Robertson, Drusilla Brown, Gaelle Pierre, and Maria Laura Sanchez-Puerta. The World Bank, 2009.

Brunel, Claire, Gary Clyde Hufbauer, and Jeffery J. Schott. "What's on the Table? The Doha Round as of August 2009." *Peterson Institute for International Economics Working Paper Series 09-6*, August 2009.

Buckley, Peter J. "Internalisation Thinking—from the Multinational Enterprise to the Global Factory." *International Business Review* 18(3) (2009): 224–235.

Burgdorfer, Bob. "Drought Deepens Worries about Food Supplies, Prices." *Reuters*, August 1, 2012.

Burstein, John. *U.S.–Mexico Agricultural Trade and Rural Poverty in Mexico*. Washington, DC: Woodrow Wilson International Center for Scholars, 2007.

Business and Economics Research Advisor. "Trends in International Trade." *International Economics and Trade* 7/8 (2007).

Calvo-Pardo, Hector, Caroline Freund, and Emanuel Ornelas. "The ASEAN Free Trade Agreement: Impact on Trade Flows and External Trade Barriers Policy Research." *The World Bank Development Research Group Trade and Integration Team Working Paper 4960*, June 2009.

Cambell, Monica, and Tyche Hendricks. "Mexico's Corn Farmers See Their Livelihoods Wither Away/Cheap U.S. Produce Pushes Down Prices under Free-trade Pact." *Hearst Newspapers*, July 31, 2006.

Campbell, C. "The Assessment and Importance of Oil Depletion." *The Final Energy Crisis*. Pluto Press, 2005.

Campbell, C., and J. Laherrere. "The End of Cheap Oil." *Science*, June 1998.

Campbell, Kurt M., Alexander T.J. Lennon, and Julianne Smith. *The Age of Consequences: The Foreign Policy and National Security Implications of Global Climate Change*. Washington, DC, November 2007.

Canuto, Otaviano. "South-South Trade Is the Answer." *World Bank*, May 21, 2011. http://blogs.worldbank.org/growth/south-south-trade-answer

Card, David. "How Immigration Affects U.S. Cities." *CReAM Discussion Paper #11/07*, June 2007.

Card, David. "Immigration and Inequality." *American Economic Review: Papers & Proceedings* 99(2) (2009): 1–21.

Catholic Overseas Development Agency, ActionAid, Oxfam. "Submission to the DEFRA Consultation on Sugar Reform, January 2004." http://www.actionaid.org/docs/sugar_reform_defra.pdf

Chan, Sewall. "Rebound in World Trade Is Seen." *New York Times*, March 26, 2010.

Chanda, Nayan. *Bound Together: How Traders, Preachers, Adventurers, and Warriors Shaped Globalization*. New Haven, CT: Yale University Press, 2007.
"The Charms of Frugal Innovation." *The Economist*, April 15, 2010.
Cheen, Lim Chze. "ASEAN Economic Community and Priority Integration Sectors." Presented in Session 3a Global/Regional Integration: What Are Their Respective Roles in the Context of the Current Economic Environment? at the *Global Dialogue on Turning Crises into Opportunities through Regulatory Reforms*. Washington, DC, March 20–29, 2009.
Chen, Hogan, Matthew Kondratowicz, and Kei-mu Yi. "Vertical Specialization and Three Facts about U.S. International Trade." *North American Journal of Economics & Finance* 16(1) (2005): 35–59.
Clark, Amy. "Is NAFTA Good for Mexico's Farmers?" *CBS*, July 1, 2006.
Claudio Borio, et al., eds. "BIS Quarterly Review: International Banking and Financial Market Development." *Bank for International Settlements* (December 2006): 29.
"Climate Change: How Do We Know?" July 28, 2011. http//climate.nasa.gov/evidence/index.cfm?
Collier, Paul, Craig Burnside, and David Dollar. "Aid, Policies, and Growth." *American Economic Review,* 90(4) (September 2000): 847–868.
Cooper, William H., and Mark E. Manyin. "The Proposed South Korea–U.S. Free Trade Agreement (KORUS FTA)." *Congressional Research Service Report for Congress,* July 18, 2007.
"Crisis Triggered Historic Financial Sector Changes." *International Monetary Fund Survey Magazine*, July 14, 2010. http://www.imf.org/external/pubs/ft/survey/so/2010/new071410a.htm
Crissey, Sarah R. *Educational Attainment in the United States: 2007*. U.S. Census Bureau, January 2009.
"Current World Population and World Population Growth since Year One." About.com.
Dadush, Uri, and Lauren Falcao. "Migrants and the Global Financial Crisis." *Carnegie Endowment for International Peace Policy Brief 83*, November 2009.
Dadush, Uri, and William Shaw. *Juggernaut: How Emerging Powers Are Reshaping Globalization*. Carnegie Endowment for International Peace, 2011, 3.
Dalgaard, Carl-Johan, and Henrik Hanson. "On Aid, Growth and Good Policies." *Journal of Development Studies* 37(6) (2001): 17.
Daly, Herman. "Ecological Economics: The Concept of Scale and Its Relation to Allocation, Distribution, and Uneconomic Growth." *Ecological Economics and Sustainable Development: Selected Essays of Herman Daly*. Edward Elgar, 2007, 82–103.
Daly, Herman. "Elements of Environmental Macroeconomics." In *Beyond Growth: The Economics of Sustainable Development,* ed. R. Costanza. Boston: Beacon Press, 1996.
Daly, Herman. "Free Trade and Globalization vs. Environment and Community." In *Beyond Growth: The Economics of Sustainable Development*, ed. R. Costanza. Boston: Beacon Press, 1996.
Daly, Herman. "From Adjustment to Sustainable Development: The Obstacle of Free Trade." In *Beyond Growth: The Economics of Sustainable Development,* ed. R. Costanza. Boston: Beacon Press, 1996.
Davis, Bob. "IMF Review Called Yuan Undervalued." *The Wall Street Journal*, July 28, 2010.
De Beule, Filip, and Daniël Van Den Bulcke, "Retrospective and Prospective Views about the Future of the Multinational Enterprise," *International Business Review* 18 (2009): 215–223.
Deloitte Touche Tohmatsu Global Financial Services Industry Group. *Global Financial Services*.
"Difference Engine: Food for Thought." *The Economist*, May 19, 2012.

Di Giovanni, Julian, Glenn Gottselig, Florence Jaumotte, Luca Antonio Ricci, Stephen Tokarick, and Mary Yang. "Globalization: A Brief Overview, 2008." *International Monetary Fund*, May 2008. http://www.imf.org/external/np/exr/ib/2008/053008.htm#P32_4753

Dinmore, Guy. "Italy Denies Need for Bailout." *The Financial Times*, June 12, 2012.

Dixon, Thomas Homer. *The Upside of Down: Catastrophe, Creativity, and the Renewal of Civilization*. Island Press, 2006.

Docquier, Frédéric, and Hillel Rapoport. *Skilled Migration: The Perspective of Developing Countries*. Discussion Paper 2873. Bonn, Germany: Forschungsinstitut zur Zukunft der Arbeit Institute for the Study of Labor, 2007.

Donnan, Shawn. "Christine Lagarde Wants Softer, Kinder IMF to Face Populist Anger," FT.com, July 13, 2016.

Dugan, Ianthe Jeanne. "Crazy-Quilt Jobless Programs Help Some More than Others." *The Wall Street Journal*, April 20, 2009, A1.

Easterly, William. "The Big Push: DejaVu." *Journal of Economic Literature* 1, (2006): 44.

Edmonds, Eric V. "Child Labor." *National Bureau of Economic Research Working Paper 12926*, 2007.

Edwards, Chris. "Agricultural Regulations and Trade Barriers." CATO Institute, 2009. http://www.downsizinggovernment.org/agriculture/regulations-and-trade-barriers

"An Emerging Challenge." *The Economist*, April 17, 2010.

"Emerging Economies to Lead Energy Growth to 2030 and Renewables to Out-Grow Oil, Says BP Analysis." January 19, 2011. http://www.bp.com//genericarticle.do?categoryId=2012968&contentId=7066696.

Europa. http://europa.eu/publicprocurement/index_en.htm (accessed June 28, 2010).

"Explore. Create. Share: Development Data." *World Bank*, 2014. http://databank.worldbank.org/ddp/home.do?Step=3&id=4

Fahnestock, Jesse, and Arne Mogren. *A One Ton Future: A Guide to the Low-Carbon Century*. Varnamo: Falth & Hassler, 2009.

Faiola, Anthony, and Lori Montgomery. "Trade Wars Brewing in Economic Malaise." *The Washington Post*, May 15, 2009.

Fairclough, Gordon. "Rate Swings Sting Europe's Borrowers." *The Wall Street Journal*, July 27, 2010.

Farrell, Diana, and Susan Lund. "Why Debt Hasn't Killed Us Yet." *Newsweek*, January 2, 2008.

Farrell, Paul B. "Population Bomb: 9 Billion March to WWII." *The Wall Street Journal*, June 28, 2011.

Feils, Dorothee J., and Manzur Rahman. "Regional Economic Integration and Foreign Direct Investment: The Case of NAFTA." *Management International Review* 48 (2008).

"Food Crisis: What the World Bank Is Doing." *World Bank*, April 18, 2012.

Francois, Joseph F., and Laura M. Baughman. "Estimated Economic Effects of Proposed Import Relief Remedies for Steel." December 19, 2001. http://www.citac.info/remedy/index.htm

French, Howard W. "Kagame's Hidden War in the Congo." *The New York Review of Books*, 56(14) (September 24, 2009).

Friedman, Thomas. *The Lexus and the Olive Tree*. New York: Farrar, Straus and Giroux, 1999.

Friedman, Thomas. *The World Is Flat*. New York: Farrar, Straus and Giroux, 2004.

Froggatt, Antony, Mycle Schneider, and Steve Thomas. "Nuclear Power in a Post-Fukushima World." *The Worldwatch Institute*. July 1, 2011.

"The 4th Assessment Report." *IPCC, Climate Change*, 2007. www.ipcc.ch.

"GAFSP: Improving Food Security for the World's Poor." *World Bank*, May 17, 2012.
Gallaghar, Kevin, Enrique Dussel Peters, and Timothy Wise, eds. "The Future of North American Trade Policy: Lessons from NAFTA". *Pardee Center Task Force Report*, 2009.
Gallaghar, Kevin, and Timothy Wise. "Fixing Nafta's Flaws." *The Guardian*, January 7, 2010.
Gavin, Robert. "Workers Do More, but Wages Fall Short: Productivity Link Broken, Study Says." *The Boston Globe*, October 10, 2006, Business Section.
Gereffi, Gary. "The New Offshoring of Jobs and Global Development." Paper Presented at the ILO Social Policy Lectures, Jamaica, December 2005.
Giles, Ciaran. "Spanish, Italian Borrowing Rates Rising Again." Associated Press, July 6, 2012.
Goel, Ajay, Nazgol Moussavi, and Vats N. Srivatsan. "Time to Rethink Offshoring?" *McKinsey Quarterly*, Winter 2008.
Goghale, Ketaki. "A Global Surge in Tiny Loans Spurs Credit Bubble in a Slum." *The Wall Street Journal*, August 13, 2009.
Goldstone, Jack. "The Population Bomb: The Four Megatrends that Will Change the World." *Foreign Affairs* (January/February 2010): 31–43.
Gore, Albert. "Climate of Denial: Can Science and the Truth Withstand the Merchants of Poison?" *Rolling Stone*, June 24, 2011.
Gore, Albert. *The Inconvenient Truth*. Bloomsbury, 2006.
Goulet, Denis. *The Cruel Choice*. Atheneum, 1975.
Governments of Canada, the United States, and Mexico. "Results: North Americans Are Better off after 15 Years of NAFTA." http://www.naftanow.org/results/default_en.asp
Granitsas, Alkman, and Stelios Bouras. "Greece to Quicken Selling Off State Firms." *The Wall Street Journal*, July 6, 2012.
Guy, Frederick. *The Global Environment of Business*. New York: Oxford University Press, 2009.
Hansen, Henrik, and Finn Tarp. "Aid Effectiveness Disputed." *Journal of International Development*. 12(3) (2000): 375–398.
Hansen, James. *Storms of My Grandchildren*. 2011.
Harrison, Ann, and Andrés Rodríguez-Clare. "Trade Foreign Investment, and Industrial Policy for Developing Countries." In *Handbooks in Economics: Development Economics*, Vol. 5, ed. Dani Rodrick and M.R. Rosenzweig, 4039–4214. Oxford: Elsevier, 2010.
Harvey, Hal, and Sonia Aggarwal. *The Costs of Delay*. ClimateWorks Foundation, 2011.
Heal, Geoffrey. "Corporate Social Responsibility: An Economic and Financial Framework." National Bureau of Economic Research, 2005.
Heffernan, Shayne. "China Knowledge Report on China ASEAN Relations." Ebeling Heffernan, February 24, 2010.
Heilbroner, Robert. *The Worldly Philosophers, 7th edn*. Touchstone Press, 2004.
Heinberg, Richard. *The Party's Over: Oil, War, and the Fate of Industrial Societies*. Clearview, 2003.
Held, David and Anthony G. McGrew, David Goldblatt, and Jonathan Perraton. *Global Transformations: Politics, Economics and Culture*. Stanford, CA: Stanford University Press, 1999, Introduction, 32–86.
Hellebrandt, Tomas, and Paolo Mauro. "The Future of Worldwide Income Distribution." *Peterson Institute for International Economics*, April 2015.
"Help Quell Tire Price Sticker Shock." *Tire Business*, April 26, 2010.
Hertsgaard, Mark. "Confronting the Climate Cranks." *The Nation*, January 20, 2011.
Hertsgaard, Mark. *Hot: Living through the Next Fifty Years on Earth*. Houghton Mifflin Harcourt, 2011.

Heston, Alan, Robert Summers, and Bettina Aten. "Penn World Table Version 6.2." *Center for International Comparisons of Production, Income and Prices at the University of Pennsylvania*, September 2006.
Hobbs, Jeremy. "World Food Day: There Is Enough Food in the World for Everyone." *Oxfam International*, October 16, 2009.
Hochschild, Adam. "Rape of the Congo." *The New York Review of Books* 56(13) (August 13, 2009).
Horobin, Willian, and Gabriele Parussini. "France Set to Raise Taxes on Firms, Rich." *The Wall Street Journal*, July 4, 2012.
"How to Save Spain." *The Economist*, June 2, 2012.
Hufbauer, Gary, and Paul Grieco. "The Payoff from Globalization." *The Washington Post*, June 7, 2005.
Hummels, David. *Have International Transportation Costs Declined?* University of Chicago, 1999.
Hymer, Stephen H. "Economic Forms in Pre-Colonial Ghana." *The Journal of Economic History* 30(1) (1970).
Inter-American Dialogue. *A Second Chance: U.S. Policy in the Americas*. Washington, DC: Inter-American Dialogue, March 2009.
International Labour Office. *Global Wage Report 2008/09: Minimum Wages and Collective Bargaining: Towards Policy Coherence*. Geneva, Switzerland: International Labour Office, 2008.
International Labour Organization. *A Global Alliance against Forced Labour*. Geneva, Switzerland: ILO, 2005.
International Labour Organization. *World of Work Report 2008: Income Inequalities in the Age of Financial Globalization*. Geneva, Switzerland: International Institute for Labour Studies, 2008.
International Monetary Fund. *World Economic Outlook Database*, April 2010. http://www.imf.org/external/pubs/ft/weo/2010/01/weodata/weorept.aspx?sy=2005&ey=2009&scsm=1&ssd=1&sort=country&ds=.&br=1&c=001%2C998&s=NGDP_RPCH%2CNGDPD%2CPPPGDP%2CPPPPC%2CPPPSH&grp=1&a=1&pr.x=36&pr.y=15 (accessed June 28, 2010).
International Monetary Fund. *World Economic Outlook, October 2007: Globalization and Inequality*. Washington, DC: IMF, 2007.
"The International Role of the Euro." *European Central Bank* (July 2008): 74. http://www.ecb.int/pub/pdf/other/euro-international-role200807en.pdf
"International Telecommunication Union." United Nations. http://www.itu.int/en/about/Pages/default.aspx
International Trade Administration, U.S. Department of Commerce: Invest in America. *FDI and the U.S. Economy Fact Sheet*, 2009.
"The IMF Has a New Lease on Life." *The Financial Times*, October 1, 2009.
Isbister, John. "Imperialism," *Promises Not Kept*, 5th edn. Kumarian Press, 2001.
Jaumotte, Florence, and Irina Tytell. "Globalization of Labor," *Finance and Development* 44(2) (June 2007).
John J. Topoleski. "Extending Trade Adjustment Assistance (TAA) to Service Workers: How Many Workers Could Potentially Be Covered?" *Congressional Research Service Report for Congress*, November 23, 2007.
Johnson, Simon (app.). "Reaping the Benefits of Financial Globalization." *IMF Research Department*, June 2007. http://www.imf.org/external/np/res/docs/2007/0607.pdf
Jotanovic, Aleksandar, and Brad Gilmour. "NAFTA: Outcomes, Challenges, and Prospects." *Agricultural Policy Issues* 2(2) (2009).

Kanbur, Ravi, and Andy Summer. "Poor Countries or Poor People? Development Assistance and the New Geography of Global Poverty." *Working Paper Charles H. Dyson School of Applied Economics and Management*, Cornell University, 2011, 2.

Kandiero, Tonia, Abdul Kamara, and Leonce Ndikumana."Commodities, Export Subsidies and African Trade During the Slump." In *The Collapse of Global Trade, Murky Protectionism, and the Crisis: Recommendations for the G20*, ed. Richard Baldwin and Simon Evenett, 59–64. London: Center for Economic Policy Research, 2009.

Karlan, Dean, and Jacob Appel. *More than Good Intentions: How a New Economics Is Helping to Solve Global Poverty.* New York: Penguin, 2011.

Karlan, Dean, and Jonathan Morduch. "Access to Finance: Credit Markets, Insurance, and Saving." *Handbook of Development Economics*, 2009, 5.

Karlan, Dean, and Jonathan Zinman. "Expanding Credit Access: Using Randomized Supply Decision to Estimate the Impacts." *Center for Global Development*, 2007.

Khana, Parag. *The Second World: Empire and Influence in the New Global Order*. Random House, 2008.

Klare, Michael. *Blood and Oil*. Henry Holt and Company, 2004.

Klare, Michael. *The Race for What's Left: The Global Scramble for the World's Last Resources*. Metropolitan, 2012.

Klare, Michael. *Resource Wars: The New Landscape of Global Conflict*. Henry Holt and Company, 2002.

Klare, Michael. *Rising Powers, Shrinking Planet: The New Geopolitics of Energy*. Henry Holt and Company, 2009.

Koettl, Johannes. *Human Trafficking, Modern Day Slavery, and Economic Exploitation*. Social Protection & Labor Discussion Paper 0911. Washington, DC: The World Bank, 2009.

Kondonassis, Alexander J., A.G. Malliaris, and Chris Paraskevopoulos. "NAFTA: Past, Present and Future." *The Journal of Economic Asymmetries* 5(1) (2008): 13–24.

Koopman, Robert, Zhi Wang, and Shang-Jin Wei. "How Much of Chinese Exports Is Really Made in China?" *Assessing Domestic Value Added When Processing Trade Is Pervasive*. National Bureau of Economic Research Working Paper 14109, Cambridge, MA, 2008.

Kristof, Nicholas D. "Death by Gadget." *The New York Times*, June 27, 2010.

Kristof, Nicholas D., and Sheryl WuDunn. *Half the Sky: Turning Oppression into Opportunity for Women Worldwide*. New York: Knopf, 2009.

Lafraniere, Sharon. "Chinese Exports Increase 46% as Demand from West Rebound." *Reuters*, March 10, 2010.

Lamy, Pascal. "Comparative Advantage Is Dead? Not at All, Lamy Tells Paris Economists." *Speech Given at the Paris School of Economics,* Paris, April 19, 2010. Archived in WTO News: Speeches.

Laricella, Tom, and Dave Kansas. "Currency Trading Soars." *The Wall Street Journal*, August 31, 2010.

Larsen, Peter Thal. "Capital Flows to Developing World at Risk of Collapse." *The Financial Times*, January 27, 2009.

"The LDC Debt Crisis." *History of the Eighties—Lessons for the Future Volume I an Examination of the Banking Crises of the 1980s and Early 1990s*. Federal Deposit Insurance Corporation, 1997, 193–199.

Lerche, Jens. "A Global Alliance against Forced Labour? Unfree Labour, Neo-Liberal Globalization and the International Labour Organization." *Journal of Agrarian Change* 7(4) (2007): 424–452.

Lomborg, Bjorn. *Smart Solutions to Climate Change: Comparing Costs and Benefits*. Cambridge University Press, 2011.

Lovins, Amory. "Learning from Japan's Nuclear Disaster." http://www.pbs.org/wgbh/nova/insidenova/2011/03/nuclear-lovins.html.

Mankiw, W. Gregory. "The Trilemma of International Finance." *The New York Times*, July 9, 2010.

Mansoor, Ali, and Bryce Quillin, eds. *Migration and Remittances: Eastern Europe and the Former Soviet Union*. Washington, DC: The World Bank, 2007.

Martens, Pim, and Ward Rennen. "The Globalisation Timeline." *Integrated Assessment* 4(3) (2003): 137–144.

Mattoo, Aaditya, and Arvind Subramanian. "Beyond Doha." *World Bank Research Digest* 3(2) (Winter, 2009): 6.

Mattoo, Aaditya, and Arvind Subramanian. "From Doha to the Next Bretton Woods: A New Multilateral Trade Agenda." *Foreign Affairs*, January/February 2009.

Mauro, Paolo, and Jonathan D. Ostry. "Putting Financial Globalization to Work." *IMF Survey Magazine: IMF Research Development* (August 2007). http://www.imf.org/external/pubs/ft/survey/so/2007/res0816a.htm.

Mays, Kelsey. "The Cars.com American-Made Index." Cars.com (2016). http://www.cars.com/go/advice/.

McDonald, Joe. "China: U.S. Trade Tariffs Violate WTO Rules." *The Huffington Post*, June 10, 2010.

McGirk, Jan. "Corn Conundrums in Latin America." *ChinaDialogue*, June 17, 2010.

McLean, Thomas R. "The Global Market for Healthcare: Economics and Regulation." *Wisconsin International Law Journal* 26(3) (2009): 591–645.

Meadows, D., and J. Randers. *Beyond the Limits*. Earthscan, 1992.

Meadows, Donella H., et al. *Limits to Growth: The Thirty-Year Update*. Chelsea Green, 2004.

Meadows, Donella H., et al. *The Limits to Growth*. Signet, 1972.

Meschi, Elena, and Marco Vivarelli. "Trade and Income Inequality in Developing Countries." *World Development* 37(2) (2009): 287–302.

Milanovic, Branko. "Global Inequality Recalculated: The Effect of New 2005 PPP Estimates on Global Inequality." *World Bank Policy Research Working Paper 5061*, 2009.

Milesi-Ferretti, Gian Maria. "Fundamentals at Odds? The US Current Account Deficit and the Dollar." 2008. VOXeu.org.

Mnyanda, Lukanyo, and Roxana Zega. "German Bonds Surge as ECB Cuts Rates Without Supporting Spain." *Bloomberg*, July 7, 2012.

Mock, Vanessa. "Hollande to Submit Measures to French Parliament." *The Wall Street Journal*, June 29, 2012. http://blogs.wsj.com/eurocrisis/2012/06/29/hollande-to-submit-measures-to-french-parliament/?KEYWORDS=french+president

Mohapatra, Sanket, Dilip Ratha, and Ani Silwal. "Outlook for Remittance Flows 2011–13." *Migration and Development Brief* 16, 2011.

Mol, Arthur. *Globalization and Environmental Reform*. MIT Press, 2001, 2.

Moore, Miles. "RAW and Rising; Materials Costs Keep Going Up; Ditto for Tire Prices." *Tire Business*, April 12, 2010.

Moran, Theodore H. "Enhancing the Contribution of Foreign Direct Investment to Development: A New Agenda for the Corporate Social Responsibility Community, International Labor and Civil Society, Aid Donors, and Multilateral Financial Institutions" (draft, 2010).

Moreno, Luis Alberto. "Keeping Borders Open: Why Is It Important for Latin America and What Can the Region Do about It?" (2009).

Moss, David A., and Anna Harrington. "Inequality and Globalization." Harvard Business Publishing, 2005.

Moyo, Dambisa. *Dead Aid: Why Aid Is Not Working and How There Is a Better Way for Africa*. Farrar, Straus and Giroux, 2009.

Moyo, Dambisa. "Why Foreign Aid Is Hurting Africa." *The Wall Street Journal*, March 21, 2009.

Natsios, Andrew. "Foreign Aid in the National Interest: Promoting Freedom, Security, and Opportunity." *United States Agency for International Development*, 2002.

Nerurkar, Neelesh. "U.S. Oil Imports and Exports." *Congressional Research Service* (April 2012). http://www.fas.org/sgp/crs/misc/R42465.pdf.

Neuger, James G., and Anabela Reis. "Portugal's $111 Billion Bailout Approved as EU Prods Greece to Sell Assets." *Bloomberg*, May 17, 2011.

"The New Face of Hunger." *The Economist*, April 17, 2008.

"News Release: US International Transactions, 4th Quarter and Year 2011." *Bureau of Economic Analysis* (2012). http://www.bea.gov/newsreleases/international/transactions/2012/trans411.htm

Obama, Barak. "2008 Presidential Candidate Questionnaire." *Ohio Conference on Fair Trade,* February 28, 2008. http://www.citizenstrade.org/pdf/OCFT_%20PresPrimary-TradeQuestionnaire.

Oetzel, Jennifer, and Jonathan Doh. "MNEs and Development: A Review and Reconceptualization." *Journal of World Business* 44 (2009): 108–120.

Office of the United States Trade Representative. "Key Sanitary and Phytosanitary Barriers to American Exports" (2010). http://www.ustr.gov/about-us/press-office/fact-sheets/2010/march/key-sanitary-and-phytosanitary-barriers-american-export.

Office of the United States Trade Representative. "North American Free Trade Agreement (NAFTA)."

Offshoring Report 2007: Optimizing Offshore Operations. *A Deloitte Research Report*, 2007.

O'Neill, Jim. "Panic Measures Will Ruin the BRIC Recovery." *The Financial Times*, August 9, 2011.

O'Rourke Kevin, and Jeffery G. Williamson. "Late Nineteenth-Century Anglo-American Factor-Price Convergence: Were Heckscher and Ohlin Right?" *The Journal of Economic History* 54(4) (1994): 892–916.

Orr, David. *Earth in Mind*. Island Press, 2004.

O'Sullivan, Kate. "Top Five Trends in Offshoring." *CFO Magazine*, January 30, 2008.

Ouattaral, Alassane D. "The IMF and Developing Countries: From Myths to Realities." *The International Monetary Fund*, November 10, 1998.

Oxford Analytica. "South Korea/U.S.: FTA Jumps Major Hurdles, Faces Others." April 3, 2007.

Pacala, Steven, and Robert Socolow. "Stabilization Wedges: Solving the Climate with Current Technologies for the Next 50 Years." *Science* 5686 (August 13, 2004): 968–972.

"The Patient Capitalist." *The Economist*, May 23, 2009.

Peri, Giovanni. *The Impact of Immigrants in Recession and Economic Expansion*. Washington, DC: Migration Policy Institute, 2010.

Peterson, T.C., et al. "State of the Climate in 2008." *Special Supplement to the Bulletin of the American Meteorological Society* 90(8) (August 2009): 17–18.

Petras, James, and Henry Veltmeyer. *Globalization Unmasked: Imperialism in the 21st Century*. Macmillan Zed Books, 2001.

Pirog, Robert, and Stephen C. Stamos. *Energy Economics: Theory and Policy*. Prentice-Hall, 1987, Ch. 1.

Pitigala, Nihal. "Global Economic Crisis and Vertical Specialization in Developing Countries." *PREM Trade Notes* 133 (2009).

Pool, John C., and Stephen Stamos. *International Economic Policy: Beyond the Trade and Debt Crisis*. Lexington, MA: Lexington Books, 1989. poremp.php

Porritt Jonathon, Jonathon. *Capitalism: As If the World Matters*. Earthscan, 2005.

Porritt, Jonathon. "Part II A Framework for Sustainable Capitalism." *Capitalism: As If the World Matters*, 2012.

"Poverty at a Glance." *World Bank*, October 7, 2015. http://www.worldbank.org/en/topic/poverty/overview.

"Price Surges in Food Markets: How Should Organized Food Markets Be Regulated?" *FAO Policy Brief*, 2010.

Priebe, Alexandra, and Cristen Suhr. "Hidden in Plain View: The Commercial Sexual Exploitation of Girls in Atlanta." *A Study of the Atlanta Women's Agenda* (September 2005).

Quinn, Eamon. "Ireland Hails T-Bill Sale as Milestone." *The Wall Street Journal*, July 5, 2012.

Ramzy, Austin. "Chicken Feet: A Symbol of US-China Tension." *Time*, February 8, 2010.

Rapoport, Hillel. "Brain Drain and Development: An Overview." PowerPoint Presented at the OECD–CEPII Conference: International Migration: Trends and Challenges, Paris, France, October 23–24, 2008.

Ratha, Dilip, Sanket Mohapatra, and Ani Silwal. "Outlook for Remittance Flows 2010–2011." *Migration and Development Brief* 12 (2010): 1–18.

Reinhart, Kenneth. *Windows on the World Economy: Introduction to International Economics*. Mason, Ohio: Thomson/South-Western, 2005.

"Report of the World Commission on Environment and Development: Our Common Future." *United Nations General Assembly*, 1987.

Riddell, Tom, et al. Chapter 21. *Economics: A Tool for Understanding Society*. Boston: Addison-Wesley, 2011.

Rivoli, Pietra. *Travels of a T-shirt in the Global Economy*. New Jersey: John Wiley and Sons, 2005.

Roberts, Paul. *The End of Oil*. Houghton and Mifflin, 2004.

Robertson, Raymond, Drusilla Brown, Gaelle Pierre, and Maria Laura Sanchez-Puerta. *Globalization, Wages, and the Quality of Jobs: Five Country Studies*. Washington, DC: The World Bank, 2009.

Rodrik, Dani. "The Inescapable Trilemma of the World Economy." Blog post, June 27, 2007. http://rodrik.typepad.com/dani_rodriks_weblog/2007/06/the-inescapable.html.

Rodrik, Dani. *One Economics, Many Recipes: Globalization, Institutions, and Economic Growth*. Princeton University Press, 2008.

Rodrik, Dani, Margaret McMillan, and Inico Vergallo. *Globalization, Structural Change and Productivity Growth, World Development*, 2014.

Rosen, Howard. "Strengthening Trade Adjustment Assistance." *Peterson Institute for International Economics Policy Brief 08-2*, January 2008.

Roubini, Nouriel. "Globalization's Political Fault Lines," *Project Syndicate*, July 4, 2016. https://www.project-syndicate.org/print/globalization-political-fault-lines-by-nouriel-roubini-2016-07

Sachs, Jeffrey D. *Common Wealth: Economics for a Crowded Planet*. Penguin Press (2008): 6–7.

Sachs, Jeffrey D. *The End of Poverty*. Penguin Press, 2005.

Sachs, Jeffrey D. "Global Solutions to Climate Change." *Common Wealth: Economics for a Crowded Planet*. Penguin Press, 2008, 97.

Sachs, Jeffrey D. "Part 5: Global Problem Solving." *Common Wealth: Economics for a Crowded Planet*. Penguin Press, 2008.

Salinas, Claudia Meléndez. "Mexican Farmers Struggle to Survive." Monterey County Herald, December 2, 2007.
Samenow, Jason. "US Has Hottest Month on Record in July 2012 NOAA Says." *The Washington Post*, August 8, 2012.
Sampson, Anthony. *The Seven Sisters: The Great Oil Companies and the World They Made*. Hodder and Stoughton, 1975.
Schmuckler, S.L. "Financial Globalization: Gain and Pain for Developing Countries." *Federal Reserve Bank of Atlanta Economic Review* (2004). http://www.frbatlanta.org/filelegacydocs/erq204_schmukler.pdf.
Schott, Jeffery. "Implementing the KORUS FTA: Key Challenges and Policy Proposals." In *Understanding New Political Realities in Seoul: Working toward a Common Approach to Strengthen U.S.-Korean Relation*, ed. L. Gordon Flake and Park Ro-byug, 79–98. Washington, DC: The Maureen and Mike Mansfield Foundation, 2008.
Schott, Jeffery. "A Trade Agenda for the G-20." *Peterson Institute for International Economics Policy Brief 10–11*, May 2010.
Scott, Robert E. Pennsylvania Stagnation: Is Nafta the Culprit?" *New York Times Topics Blog*, posted April 15, 2008. http://topics.blogs.nytimes.com/2008/04/15/pennsylvania-stagnation-is-nafta-the-culprit/
Sharma, Bhavna. "Contemporary Forms of Slavery in Brazil." *Anti-Slavery International* (2006).
Sharma, Krishnan. "The Impact of Remittances on Economic Insecurity." *United Nations Department of Economic and Social Affairs Working Paper No. 78*, 2009.
"The Spectrum of Malnutrition." *Food and Agriculture Organization of the United Nations* (2011): 96.
Spence, Michael. *The Next Convergence: The Future of Economic Growth in a Multispeed World* (2011): 16.
Spence, Michael, Danny Leipziger, James Manyika, and Ravi Kanbur. "Restarting the Global Economy: Three Mismatches that Need Concerted Public Action," November 4, 2015 Bellagio_2015_FINAL_web_9-29-15.
Spencer, Strahan, and Adrian Wood. "Marking the Financial Sector Work for the Poor." *The Journal of Development Studies* 41(4) (2005): 658.
Speth, Gustave. "Globalization and the Environment." *Red Sky At Morning*. Yale University Press, 2004, 140–147.
Speth, Gustave. "Modern Capitalism: Out of Control." *The Bridge at the Edge of the World: Capitalism, the Environment, and Crossing from Crisis to Sustainability*. Yale University Press, 2008.
Speth, Gustave. *Red Sky at Morning*. Yale University Press, 2004, Ch. 7.
Speth, James Gustave. *The Bridge at the Edge of the World: Capitalism, the Environment, and Crossing from Crisis to Sustainability*. Yale University Press, 2008.
Srinivasan, T.N. "Global Economic Institutional, Intellectual and Religious Contacts: A brief History." In *Global Exchange and Poverty: Trade, Investment and Migration*, ed. Robert E.B. Lucas, Lyn Squire, and T.N. Srinivasan. Northampton, MA: Edward Elgar 2010.
Steinhauser, Gabrielle. "New Plan Sees Closer Euro-Zone Ties." *The Wall Street Journal*, June 26, 2012.
Stern, Nicholas. *The Economics of Climate Change: The Stern Review*. Cambridge, 2007.
Stern, Nicholas. *The Global Deal: Climate Change and the Creation of a New Prosperity*. Public Affairs, 2009.
Stern, Nicholas. "Policies to Reduce Emissions." *The Global Deal: Climate Change and the Creation of a New Prosperity*. Public Affairs, 2009, 99–124.

Stevis, Matina. "Doubts Emerge in Bloc's Rescue Deal." *The Wall Street Journal*, July 6, 2012.

Stiglitz, Joseph. *Globalization and Its Discontents*. Norton, 2002, 214. Story.jsp?section=top&subject=ami&story=amMade0808.

Strong, Maurice. *Where on Earth Are We Going?* Texere, 2001, 26.

Tam, Pui-Wang, and Jackie Range. "Second Thoughts: Some in Silicon Valley Begin to Sour on India: A Few Bring Jobs Back as Pay of Top Engineers in Bangalore Skyrockets." *Wall Street Journal*, July 3, 2007.

Taylor, Marcus. "Who Works for Globalization? The Challenges and Possibilities for International Labour Studies." *Third World Quarterly* 30(3) (2009): 435–452.

Terrazas, Aaron, and Jeanne Batalova. "Frequently Requested Statistics on Immigrants and Immigration in the United States." *Migration Information Source*, 2009. http://www.migrationinformation.org/USfocus/

"Transactions in Financial Derivatives." *The Bureau of Economic Analysis*. http://www.bea.gov/international/pdf/bach_concepts_methods/Transactions%20Financial%20Derivatives.pdf.

Truman, Edwin M. "Reforming the IMF for the 21st Century." *Institute for International Economics* (April 2006).

Truman, Edwin M. "The US Current Account Deficit and the Euro Area." *In speech: Frankfurt, Germany, Peterson Institute for International Economics* (2004).

Tucker, Mary Evelyn. *Worldly Wonder: Religions Enter Their Ecological Phase*. Open Court, 2003.

Tucker, Robert. "The Communist Manifesto." *The Marx-Engels Reader*. 1972, 339.

United Nations Conference on Trade and Development. *World Investment Report 2009: Transnational Corporations, Agricultural Production, and Development*. Geneva, Switzerland: UN, 2009.

"United Nations Convention against Transnational Organized Crime." *November 15, 2000, General Assembly: Declarations and Conventions Contained in GA Resolutions*. Fifty-Fifth Session. A/RES/55/25.

United Nations Development Programme. 2009 *Human Development Report: Overcoming Barriers: Human Mobility and Development*. New York: Palgrave Macmillan, 2009.

United Nations Economic and Social Commission for Asia and the Pacific ESCAP, Ten as One: Challenges and Opportunities for ASEAN Integration. Bangkok: United Nations Economic and Social Commission for Asia and the Pacific, 2007.

"United States Gross External Debt Position." *U.S. Department of the Treasury* (September 2010). http://www.treasury.gov/resource-center/data-chart-center/tic/Documents/debta910.html

"The Universal Declaration of Human Rights." *United Nations*. http:// www.un.org/ en/documents/udhr/.

U.S. Department of Labor: Bureau of Labor Statistics. Foreign-Born Workers: Labor Force Characteristics—2009. March 19, 2010.

U.S. Department of State. *Trafficking in Persons Report 2005*. 2005.

U.S. Department of State. *Trafficking in Persons Report 2010*. 2010.

"U.S. Net International Investment Position at Year End 2008." *Bureau of Economic Analysis* (2011). http://www.bea.gov/newsreleases/international/intinv/intinvnewsrelease.htm

Van Gelder, Alec. "Don't Throttle Trade." *The Australian*, July 9, 2009.

Van Harten, Gus. "Reforming the NAFTA Investment Regime." In *The Future of North American Trade Policy: Lessons from NAFTA*, ed. Kevin Gallaghar, Enrique Dussel Peters, and Timothy Wise, 43–52. *A Pardee Center Task Force Report*, 2009.

Vietnam Chamber of Commerce and Industry. "(India) Seafood Exporters Get US Duty Relief." July 21, 2009. http://chongbanphagia.vn/beta/en/news/2009-07-21/india-seafood-exporters-get-us-duty-relief

"What Can the Region Do about It?" In *The Collapse of Global Trade, Murky Protectionism, and the Crisis: Recommendations for the G20*, ed. Richard Baldwin and Simon Evenett, 21–24. London: Center for Economic Policy Research, 2009.

"Where the IMF Gets Its Money." *International Monetary Fund Factsheet*, April 30, 2010. http://www.imf.org/external/np/exr/facts/finfac.htm

Wigley, T. M. L., and D. S. Schimel, eds. *The Carbon Cycle*. Cambridge: Cambridge University Press, 2000, 258–276.

Wise, Timothy. "Reforming NAFTA's Agricultural Provisions." In *The Future of North American Trade Policy: Lessons from NAFTA*, ed. Kevin Gallaghar, Enrique Dussel Peters, and Timothy Wise, 36. *A Pardee Center Task Force Report*, 2009.

World Bank. "Factor Mobility and Migration." In *World Development Report* 2009*: Reshaping Economic Geography*, 146–169. Washington, DC: The World Bank, 2009.

World Bank. *World Development Indicators Data Set*. http://databank.worldbank.org/ddp/home.do?Step=12&id=4&CNO=2 (accessed June 22, 2010).

"World Bank World Development Indicators." *World Bank*.

"World Development Indicators Data Set." *World Bank*. http://data.worldbank.org/topic/private-sector

"World Economic Outlook." International Monetary Fund. April 2012.

"The World in 2010." *International Telecommunication Union of the United Nations*, October 20, 2010. http://www.itu.int/ITU-D/ict/material/FactsFigures2010.pdf.

World Trade Organization, *World Trade Report 2009 Trade Policy Commitments and Contingency Measures*. Geneva: World Trade Organization, 2009.

World Trade Organization, Wto.org

World Trade Organization and International Labor Organization. *Globalization and Development in Developing Countries*. Geneva: WTO Secretariat, 2009.

"The World Turned Upside Down: A Special Report on Innovations in Emerging Markets." *The Economist*, April 17, 2010.

Yergin, Daniel. *The Prize: The Epic Quest for Oil, Money, and Power*. Simon and Schuster, 1991.

Yi, Kei-Mu. "Can Vertical Specialization Explain the Growth of World Trade?" *The Journal of Political Economy* 111(1) (2003): 52–102.

Yunus, Muhammad. *Creating a World without Poverty: Social Business and the Future of Capitalism*. New York: Public Affairs, 2007.

Zahniser, Steven, and Zachary Crago. "NAFTA at 15 Building on Free Trade." *A Report from the Economic Research Service of the U.S. Department of Agriculture* (2009).

Zakaria, Fareed. *The Post-American World*. Norton, 2008.

Zhu, Min. "Emerging Challenges." *Finance and Development* (June 2011): 48.

INDEX

Note: Page references for figures and tables are italicized.

About the Authors

Patrice Franko is the Grossman Professor of Economics and Professor of Global Studies at Colby College in Waterville, Maine, where she teaches international economics, Latin American economic policy, and microeconomics. She was a Fulbright Fellow (2012) in Brazil, a Pew Faculty Fellow in International Affairs (1992–93), an American Association for the Advancement of Science Fellow in International Security Affairs (1090–91) and lectures for EMIL, the executive masters in logistics at Georgia Tech. She holds a Ph.D. from the University of Notre Dame, and her recent publications include *The Puzzle of Latin American Economic Development* 3rd edition, (Rowman & Littlefield, 2008), *The Defense Acquisition Trilemma: The Case of Brazil (INSS Strategic Forum 2014)* and "Brazil," Chapter for the *2014 Routledge Handbook To The History Of Global Economic Thought* (ed: Vincent Barnett). She lives on Great Pond in Rome, Maine.

Stephen C. Stamos Jr. is Professor Emeritus of International Relations at Bucknell University, Lewisburg, Pennsylvania. He taught at Bucknell from 1974 to 2011. He taught courses on: Latin American Economic Development, The Political Economy of Global Resources, The Challenges to Global Capitalism, Sustainability, and The Principles of Economics. He holds a Ph.D. in Political Economy from the Union Institute. While at Bucknell, he was awarded the Linback Award for Distinguished Teaching and was made a Presidential Professor. His primary book publications are as follows: *Economics: A Tool for Understanding Society, 9th edition, 2011, Addison-Wesley, with Riddell, Schneider, and Shackelford; Exploring the Global Economy, 1995, Lexington Books, with John C. Pool; The ABCs of International Finance, 2nd edition, Lexington Books, 1991, with Franko and Pool; International Economics, 1990, Lexington Books, with John C. Pool; International Economic Policy: Beyond the Trade and Debt Crisis, 1989, Lexington Books, with John C. Pool; Energy Economics, 1987, Prentice-Hall,* with Robert Pirog. He continues to reside in Lewisburg, Pennsylvania.